FAITH
AND
OPINION

The Bible Study Textbook Series

NEW TESTAMENT

New Testament & History By W. Wartick & W. Fields Vol. I - The Intertestament Period and The Gospels	The Gospel of Matthew In Four Volumes By Harold Fowler	The Gospel of Mark By B. W. Johnson and Don DeWelt
The Gospel of Luke By T. R. Applebury	The Gospel of John By Paul T. Butler	Acts Made Actual By Don DeWelt
Romans Realized By Don DeWelt	Studies in Corinthians By T. R. Applebury	Guidance From Galatians By Don Earl Boatman
The Glorious Church (Ephesians) By Wilbur Fields	Philippians - Colossians Philemon By Wilbur Fields	Thinking Through Thessalonians By Wilbur Fields
Paul's Letters To Timothy & Titus By Don DeWelt	Helps From Hebrews By Don Earl Boatman	James & Jude By Don Fream
Letters From Peter By Bruce Oberst	Hereby We Know (I-II-III John) By Clinton Gill	The Seer, The Saviour, and The Saved (Revelation) By James Strauss

OLD TESTAMENT

O.T. & History By William Smith and Wilbur Fields	Genesis In Four Volumes By C. C. Crawford	Exploring Exodus By Wilbur Fields	Leviticus By Don DeWelt
Numbers By Brant Lee Doty	Deuteronomy By Bruce Oberst	Joshua - Judges Ruth By W. W. Winter	I & II Samuel By W. W. Winter
I & II Kings By James E. Smith	I & II Chronicles By Robert E. Black	Ezra, Nehemiah & Esther By Ruben Ratzlaff & Paul T. Butler	The Shattering of Silence (Job) By James Strauss
Psalms In Two Volumes By J. B. Rotherham	Proverbs By Donald Hunt		Ecclesiastes and Song of Solomon — By R. J. Kidwell and Don DeWelt
Isaiah In Three Volumes By Paul T. Butler	Jeremiah and Lamentations By James E. Smith		Ezekiel By James E. Smith
Daniel By Paul T. Butler	Hosea - Joel - Amos Obadiah - Jonah By Paul T. Butler		Micah - Nahum - Habakkuk Zephaniah - Haggai - Zechariah Malachi — By Clinton Gill

DOCTRINE

The Church In The Bible By Don DeWelt	The Eternal Spirit Two Volumes By C. C. Crawford	New Testament Evidences By Wallace Wartick	Survey Course In Christian Doctrine Two Bks. of Four Vols. By C. C. Crawford
New Testament History — Acts By Gareth Reese	Learning From Jesus By Seth Wilson		You Can Understand The Bible By Grayson H. Ensign

WHAT THE BIBLE SAYS SERIES

WHAT THE BIBLE SAYS ABOUT

FAITH AND OPINION

By

W. Robert Palmer

*From The Library of
Greg Cheatham*

College Press Publishing Company, Joplin, Missouri

Copyright © 1980
College Press Publishing Company

Printed and bound in the
United States of America
All Rights Reserved

Library of Congress Catalog Card Number: 79-57088
International Standard Book Number: 0-89900-076-2

Scripture quotations are from the New American Standard Bible. © The Lockman Foundation 1960, 1962, 1963, 1968, 1971, 1973, 1975.
Topical Index from *Topical Index and Digest of The Bible* edited by Harold E. Monser. Reprinted 1960 by Baker Book House and used by permission.

DEDICATION

I would like to dedicate this book to my wife, Margery, who, with patient encouragement and careful transcribing, helped make it possible for me to stay with this extended study until its completion.

Table of Contents

Dedication		v
Preface		ix
Chapter		*Page*
One	Introduction	1

Part I — PRECEPT

Two	Authority	17
Three	Precept Defined	56
Four	Saved by Grace	79
Five	God's Norm for Salvation and the Church	89
Six	Christian Fellowship—Precept	96

Part II — PRECEDENT

Seven	Precedent Defined	142
Eight	Purposes and Dangers	154

Part III — OPINION

Nine	Opinion Defined	163
Ten	Law of Opinion	194
Eleven	Christian Fellowship—Opinion	229
Twelve	Sources and Attitudes	256
Thirteen	Opportunities and Dangers	277
Fourteen	Conclusion	301
Topical Index		315
List of Other Topics		352
Bibliography		355

Preface

The subject of faith and opinion touches *every* thought regarding Christian belief and practice. It includes every person. It covers all ages. It reaches all places. Yes, anything we can think of is included.

During my preparation to preach the gospel I continually found myself asking, "Is this idea from the mind of God or from the mind of man? Is it a matter of faith or opinion?" I wanted to know the answer to this question in order to be faithful to the Lord and honest with my hearers and with myself. I devoted a large amount of time and energy to pursue this matter. Since serving out on the field in the preaching ministry my interest in the subject has never diminished. Real life situations have increased my concern and study in this area. This book is the result of my study thus far. I hope to excite you to see the importance and the vital need to resolve the issue of distinguishing between matters of faith and matters of opinion.

I have sought to identify and use every Scripture I could find that related to the subject. If I have omitted any relevant passage it is due to oversight, not manipulation. Over the years I have never ceased to "search the Scriptures" in this matter.

I have quoted extensively from a number of our pioneer thinkers in the Restoration Movement. They continually came to grips with this problem and included a number of excellent observations and studies sprinkled thoughout much of their writing. Their thinking provides us with more than just a rich heritage—they give us insights which can help us resolve the matter in our time. However, I have never found a major work written on this subject. Thus I felt motivated to offer this book. To my knowledge there is one exception which appeared in 1958, that of *We Be Brethren*

WHAT THE BIBLE SAYS ABOUT FAITH AND OPINION

by J. D. Thomas. It was directed mostly to the "non-instrument" brethren of the Church of Christ. If any reader knows of such a work, the writer would be most interested in being informed as he continues his study.

At times I have called into question the interpretation, practice or logic of some of the writers whom I have quoted. Whenever this occurs I ask the reader not to read into my work any hostility, arrogance or a contentious spirit on my part. And certainly it is not a personality conflict. This subject demands intellectual honesty and the candid confrontation of thinking in the name of truth. A polemic approach does not necessarily indicate a lack of spirituality. When my views are challenged I am driven back to the reassessment of my own thinking. My efforts are motivated by a faith in God and His Son, a love for lost souls and love for the brethren. My approach is to attempt to follow Paul's admonition, "And the Lord's bond-servant must not be quarrelsome, but be kind to all, able to teach, patient when wronged, with gentleness correcting those who are in opposition; if perhaps God may grant them repentance leading to the knowledge of the truth" (II Timothy 2:24, 25). Also, "I, therefore, the prisoner of the Lord, entreat you to walk in a manner worthy of the calling with which you have been called, with all humility and gentleness, with patience, showing forbearance to one another in love, being diligent to preserve the unity of the Spirit in the bond of peace" (Ephesians 4:1-3).

This work is not intended to be the final word on the subject. I am constantly trying to grow and hope that this book will excite the reader to enlarge on it or change it wherever the truth demands it. In the closing word of the Apostle Peter, "Grow in the grace and knowledge of our Lord and Savior Jesus Christ. To Him be the glory, both now and to the day of eternity. Amen" (II Peter 3:18).

Chapter One
Introduction
THE PROBLEM

In the Christian system of life we are constantly being entangled in a web of "thou shalts" and "thou shalt nots"; in "you may do this" and "you may not do this." At times the whole issue appears to be a dilemma from which a Christian will never escape.

What power or principle should govern the behavior pattern of the Christian? What issues are to be labeled faith and what opinion? Or is it possible to so label them?

According to the record of the Bible this problem arose "in the beginning," when the devil said to the woman,

> Now the serpent was more crafty than any beast of the field which the Lord God had made. And he said to the woman, "Indeed, has God said, 'You shall not eat from any tree of the garden'?" And the woman said to the serpent, "From the fruit of the trees of the garden we may eat; but from the fruit of the tree which is in the middle of the garden, God has said, 'You shall not eat from it or touch it, lest you die.'" And the serpent said to the woman, "You surely shall not die!" (Genesis 3:1-4).

The first weapon the arch-enemy of God used against God's creation was this problem. He sowed a doubt in Eve's mind about God by straightway convincing her that a matter of faith (law) was, after all, a matter of opinion. The result: sin, alienation, death!

Then the devil wasted no time in reversing the plan: by subtlety and insinuation he put a matter of opinion (conjecture) into the realm of faith by saying, "For God knows that in the day you eat from it your eyes will be opened, and you will be like God, knowing good and evil" (Genesis 3:5). In other words she *ought* to eat it in order to have the mind of God in matters of right and wrong.

WHAT THE BIBLE SAYS ABOUT FAITH AND OPINION

THE PURPOSE

The purpose of this book is to teach what the Bible says about the subject of faith and opinion. This will involve the consideration of definition, distinction, and result.

As with the study of nearly any problem the first concern is with *definition*. With terms such as faith, precept, precedent, opinion, and their attendant terms clearly defined, the problem is well on the way to solution. Too much confusion and haziness in identifying these words results in disobedience, division, bigotry, weakness, error, and failure on the part of the children of God.

Then, and only then, can one *measure the relative weight* of each area and draw any definite line of demarcation between them. Bible scholars have always acknowledged the realms of precept (divine) and opinion (human), but they have never agreed where the line of separation should be drawn. Can this matter be categorically settled? Must man forever debate one of the most pertinent and vital issues of the Christian system? To this arbitrary division precept and opinion, we add a third, precedent. Its justification will be seen later. And in these three areas of study will also appear other related terms, dealt with in due turn.

The third purpose will be a study of the *various problems* which arise from the failure of Christendom to accomplish the two preceding purposes. These problems are of no small consequence. They have never ceased to plague those who seek the Lord. No subject in Christianity escapes this issue of faith and opinion. Every element of thought must either come from the mind of God or from the mind of His creatures.

THE PLAN

In a careful study of a topic one should state his purpose and then list his basic assumptions. He should set forth his

INTRODUCTION

starting point by listing each basic principle or fact in logical order with a brief explanation of its relationship to the theme. From these fixed premises he should develop a reasonable study by using simple logic and understanding. He will reach into the field of revelation (Bible) and research (wisdom of qualified men). The author hopes that as this book follows this plan it will result in a logical, Scriptural, orderly, and well-catalogued study of one of the most important themes of the Christian system—faith and opinion.

The discussion in this book will build upon a basic foundation. It is not the purpose of this book to prove the following points but these basic principles are stated here so the reader will understand the foundation upon which the author is basing his discussion.

THE PREMISE

God has spoken directly to man. From all the observations of reason and the nature of the universe this immediately becomes axiomatic. "In the beginning God created the heavens and the earth. . . then God said, . . . then God said, . . . then God said" (Genesis 1:1ff.).

That this revelation is the Bible. This excludes all apocryphal writings and is the Bible canon as we know it today. This is God's purposed message to man. He had to use some medium for transmitting the content of His mind to the mind of man. The Bible is His means of communicating with man.

It is not a *product* of man reaching for a god, but the *tool* of God reaching down to man (I Corinthians 1:21).

Some modern scholarship denies that the Biblical writers received direct revelation from God. One writer says:

WHAT THE BIBLE SAYS ABOUT FAITH AND OPINION

The Bible is a revelation of God to man; in other words, the discoveries which a devout and conscientious people have made concerning God. In so far as the writers caught the Spirit of God their works have been termed inspired.[1]

Alexander Campbell in one of his lectures on the Bible sums it up this way:

> The Bible is the book of God. God is not only its author, but its subject. It is also the book of man. He, too, is the subject and the object of the volume . . .
> It spans the arch of time, which leans upon an eternity past and an eternity to come. It came to us through the ministry of angels, prophets and apostles, and is to be transmitted by us, in all languages, to nations and generations yet unborn. It contains treasures of wisdom and knowledge beyond all the learning of earth and all the philosophy of man. It not only unveils to us the future of time, but lifts the curtain that separates the seen from the unseen, earth from heaven, time from eternity, and presents to the eye of faith and hope the ineffable glories of a blissful immortality. It is to us, indeed, the book of life; the charter of an "inheritance incorruptible, and undefiled, and that fadeth not away." It has already measurably civilized many nations and empires. It has enlightened, moralized, sanctified and saved untold millions of our fallen and degraded race, and will continue to enlighten, sanctify, and bless the world, until the last sentence of the eventful volume of human history shall have been stereotyped forever. But alas for the unfaithful stewards, the inconsiderate and presumptuous sentinels of Zion, who, instead of guarding the ark of the covenant, set about allegorizing, mystifying, and nullifying its sacred contents![2]

---

1. Maurice S. White, *Bible Facts*, Booklet No. 212 (Washington, D.C.: The Washington Information Bureau, 1942), p. 4.
2. Alexander Campbell, *Popular Lectures and Addresses*, (Cincinnati: Standard Publishing Company, 1863), pp. 600-601. See Hebrews 1:1-4.

INTRODUCTION

The Bible of our translations today is substantially identical to the original records.

Floyd Hamilton observed:

> The text of the Greek New Testament used today, . . . is so accurate that in the opinion of eminent scholars it is the same as when it came from the hands of the original writers in 999 words out of every thousand, and the one word out of every thousand about which there is still doubt in no instance affects the meaning of any vital doctrine of the church.[3]

However, it is imperative that we pursue the next step — putting it accurately into our language of today. As Dr. Lewis Foster writes, "The Bible was written in the living language of the people to whom God had originally directed this inspired Word. Did it not stand to reason that, when it was translated into another language, it should be translated in the living language of that people also?"[4]

Let no one mistake the importance of this issue. Unless we have reliable translations of the ancient manuscripts into modern tongues, the message of God, no matter how clearly revealed, will be inaccurate. Inferior translations may be produced by deceitful, prejudiced, skeptical, opinionated, dated, or ignorant translators. The bias which enshrouds oneself as a result of his own local environment is altogether too common and never completely overcome.

To show how this one factor affects the theme we might select the perennial problem of baptism. The refusal of most translators to translate this word, but rather transliterate it, bears directly on the issue of faith and opinion. How many questions of unity, Christian fellowship, and evangelism

---

3. Floyd Hamilton, *The Basis of Christian Faith*, 4th ed. (New York: Harper & Row, Publishers, 1964), p. 207, 208.

4. Lewis Foster, *Selecting a Translation*. (Cincinnati, Ohio: Standard Publishing, 1978), p. 5.

would have been eliminated in the very beginning had this word been merely translated, and the translation followed by all the churches?

The original thought content *must* be reproduced in modern tongue, lest we entangle ourselves in a maze of problems before we hardly begin to exegete so important a document.

> It follows, therefore, that its faithful preservation and transmission from age to age, and from nation to nation, is and ought to be, the paramount duty and concern of every one who believes its Divine authenticity and realizes its transcendent value.[5]

Let every translator respect the sound warning of the apostle John:

> I testify to everyone who hears the words of the prophecy of this book: if anyone adds to them, God shall add to him the plagues which are written in this book; and if anyone takes away from the words of the book of this prophecy, God shall take away his part from the tree of life and from the holy city, which are written in this book (Revelation 22:18, 19).

We shall assume from now on, the trustworthiness of the text in our possession today. Our translations, as they are, are sufficient to solve our thesis problem:

> Emphasizing infinitesimal blemishes in translation, variations in manuscripts, and discrepancies of numbers, etc., when all competent authorities tell us that in no case do they affect any article of faith or obscure any duty, is idle.[6]

---

5. Campbell, *op. cit.*, pp. 569, 570.
6. B.C. Deweese, "Revelation a Development; its Transient and Permanent Phases," *The Missouri Christian Lectures*, (St. Louis: Christian Publishing Co., 1892), p. 142.

INTRODUCTION

The Bible is infallible as God's record to man. The Bible will thus be accepted as the Word of God—not merely a word of God, or containing the word of God. This is what the Bible claims for itself.

> For no prophecy was ever made by an act of human will, but men moved by the Holy Spirit spoke from God (II Peter 1:21).

> All Scripture is inspired by God and profitable for teaching, for reproof, for correction, for training in righteousness; that the man of God may be adequate, equipped for every good work (II Timothy 3:16, 17).

> The law of the LORD is perfect, restoring the soul; The testimony of the LORD is sure, making wise the simple. The precepts of the LORD are right, rejoicing the heart; The commandment of the LORD is pure, enlightening the eyes (Psalm 19:7, 8).

Without this conviction we have no solid basis for discussion. In a recent oral discussion between two preachers there continually arose a decided difference on nearly every Christian issue. There was no agreement at all in deciding issues of precept and opinion. The one preacher quoted the Bible authoritatively. The other followed reason alone, each time dismissing the issue with the terse charge, "Well, you believe the Bible is infallible." With this difference there can be no ground of discussion, let alone agreement. Little wonder why John gave such a blunt warning:

> Any one who goes too far and does not abide in the teaching of Christ, does not have God; the one who abides in the teaching, he has both the Father and the Son. If any one comes to you and does not bring this teaching, do not receive him into your house, and do not give him a greeting; for the one who gives him a greeting participates in his evil deeds (II John 9-11).

WHAT THE BIBLE SAYS ABOUT FAITH AND OPINION

We can rely on the Bible as genuine — exactly what God claims it to be.

The Bible is complete and final. Any record, though it would be true, inspired, and infallible, it if were incomplete, would not be *perfect*. Man must have the complete story, the whole truth, (as God intended for man) lest he be imperfectly led.

> Many mere human productions show excellent unity of design and execution, but swiftly pass from the stage of human attention to make way for some better book which has not only unity, but later and more valuable information and content. It is axiomatic that for anything to be final, it must be perfect.[7]
>
> God, after He spoke long ago to the fathers in the prophets in many portions and in many ways, in these last days has spoken to us in His Son, whom He appointed heir of all things, through whom also He made the world. And He is the radiance of His glory and the exact representation of His nature, and upholds all things by the word of His power. When He had made purification of sins, He sat down at the right hand of the Majesty on high; having become as much better than the angels, as He has inherited a more excellent name than they (Hebrews 1:1-4).
>
> Beloved, while I was making every effort to write you about our common salvation, I felt the necessity to write to you appealing that you contend earnestly for the faith which was once for all delivered to the saints (Jude 3).

In Jesus, His word and deed, there is finality; in the progressive revelation of truth to man there is finality; in

---

7. R.C. Foster, *Christian Standard* (August 5, 1944), p. 5.

INTRODUCTION

the pattern for holy belief and life there is finality; in the program of salvation by grace there is finality; in the system of faith in Jesus Christ as the perfect sacrifice for sin there is finality. (See Part II.) Where could we advance from here? Nowhere! We have *the* faith.

Therefore, let us not use the Bible as an elementary key to the truth, later to be discarded or made secondary, because one has "grown up" in Christian life and now is gifted with some "higher" revelation, or spiritual insight, or "new pentecostal" experience. The Bible is the truth, not a mere key to the truth.

The Bible is an intelligible and understandable message. It is not some kind of charm which, the mere possession of it, the wearing of it, or the casual reading of it, guarantees some magical blessing. It is first, last, and always, a *message*. And of what use would a revealed message be to man, no matter how holy and wonderful, if it were not understandable? This was one of the pleas of Alexander Campbell which made his debating tactics so powerful:

> The Whole Christian religion, in its facts, its precepts, its promises, its doctrine, its institutions, is presented to the world in a *written* record. The *writings* of Prophets and Apostles contain all the divine and supernatural knowledge in the world. Now, unless these sacred *writings* can be certainly interpreted the Christian religion never can be certainly understood. Every argument that demonstrates the necessity of such a written document as the Bible, equally demonstrates the necessity of fixed and certain principles or rules of interpretation: for without the latter, the former is of no value whatever to the world.[8]

---

8. Alexander Campbell, *Campbell on Baptism*, (Bethany, Va.: Printed and published by Alexander Campbell, 1853), p. 49.

WHAT THE BIBLE SAYS ABOUT FAITH AND OPINION

If we have a *revelation* from God in human language, the words of that volume must be intelligible by the common usage of language; they must be precise and determinate in signification, and that signification must be philologically ascertained — that is, as the words and sentences of other books are ascertained by the use of the dictionary and grammar. Were it otherwise, and did men require a new dictionary and grammar to understand the Book of God, — then, without that divine dictionary and grammar, we could have no *revelation* from God; for a revelation that needs to be revealed is no revelation at all.

Again, if any *special rules* are to be sought for the interpretation of the sacred writings, unless these rules have been given in the volume, as a part of the revelation, and are of divine authority; — without such rules, the Book is sealed; and I know of no greater abuse of language than to call a *sealed book* a revelation.[9]

Scripture reminds us we are expected to understand its message:

For whatever was written in earlier times was written for our instruction, that through perseverance and the encouragement of the Scriptures we might have hope (Romans 15:4).

and that from childhood you have known the sacred writings which are able to give you the wisdom that leads to salvation through faith which is in Christ Jesus. All Scripture is inspired by God and profitable for teaching, for reproof, for correction, for training in righteousness; that the man of God may be adequate, equipped for every good work (II Timothy 3:15-17).

God, in this message, has something to say to man — not to Himself. "*God has spoken by men, to men, for men.*

---

9. *Ibid.*, p. 54.

INTRODUCTION

The language of the Bible is, then, *human* language."[10] Thus we have anthropomorphism — God speaking in man's language to convey his thought to human mind. As Paul said, "I am speaking in human terms because of the weakness of your flesh" (Romans 6:19).

A word must have a thought. And man must attach grave concern and logic to every word, and to every arrangement of words. Let us not be guilty of what Z.T. Sweeny called "articulation without cerebration." Mr. Campbell accused some theologians of doing this with God's message in the name of interpretation:

> They will only submit to be tried by their own standards; that is, in other words, by their own opinions, as if the word had no certain, fixed or express meaning of its own, but just what they are pleased to give it.[11]

The Bible can be understood by man. Man is a free moral agent capable and obligated to reason and thus accept the Bible for what it is intended.

Man is more than animal. He has within him the image of God. He has character, the right to reason and decide, the power of moral choice. Therefore, since the Bible is intelligible man is able to accept by faith and knowledge the message of the Bible.

It has been said of two of the world's greatest reformers, that Martin Luther gave man the privilege to *read* the Bible, but Alexander Campbell convinced man he could *comprehend* it.

---

10. Alexander Campbell, *Christianity Restored* (Rosemead, CA: Old Paths Book Club, n.d.), p. 22.

11. Robert Richardson, *Memoirs of Alexander Campbell*, Vol. I (Nashville, Tenn.: Gospel Advocate, 1956 reprint of 1897 ed.), p. 338.

See chapters 2 and 5 following.

WHAT THE BIBLE SAYS ABOUT FAITH AND OPINION

Now, as God is infinitely wise and benevolent, in his oral communications to men, he proceeded upon the principle that they were, by this native art competent interpreters of his expressions; for otherwise, his addresses could be of no value. He could not even begin to teach them a new art of interpretation, as respected his communications, but by using their own words in the stipulated sense, unless we imagine a miracle in every case, and suppose that all his words were to be understood by a miraculous interposition. And this idea, if carried out, would make a verbal revelation of no value whatever to the children of men.[12]

We, therefore, conclude that God never would have spoken to man if man could not hear him; and that man never would have heard his word if he could not believe what God said to him. The fact, then, that God has given to the world a revelation, is, with me, a demonstration that man has the power to believe it—provided only, his heart and attention are devoted to it. It is an intelligible, veritable, and credible document, worthy of God as its author, and of man as its object.

Both oral and written testimony are addressed to our reason; for, although the written testimony is designed for the eye, and the oral testimony for the ear, both are addressed to our reason—to our power of discriminating the characters of truth from those of falsehood. There is in this also a sort of tacit agreement or understanding between the parties—as much as there is between two persons speaking the same vernacular, in the use and meaning of the words and phrases, of the tones and gestures employed in their intercommunications with one another.[13]

Man is able to find this truth by using the Bible as his *workshop*, and reason and wisdom as his *tool*. He needs no

---

12. Alexander Campbell, *Campbell on Baptism*, p. 51.
13. *Ibid.*, p. 64.

INTRODUCTION

mystical operation of the Holy Spirit, miraculous intervention, apostolic succession, authoritative key, nor exclusive ability of a recognized clergy. Truth is available for the wholesome desire, healthy logic, and the earnest effort of man.

One of the lesser known but most revealing demonstrations of this fact, can be found in the example of the Island of Iona, just off the coast of Scotland. This small island became a center of Christian learning and pure religion:

> Amidst the darkness and idolatry that then brooded over Great Britain, when an imperfect and Popish Christianity, mingling itself with the barbarous superstitions of Scandanavian mythology . . .[14]

formed the religious attitude and theology of the day. This condition was due to the efforts of one named Columban, who in the 6th century set up a school of instruction for the inhabitants. Though he kept monastic orders, he encouraged individual freedom in the use of the Scriptures.

> After all the controversies that have been waged in reference to the history of these Culdees of Iona, it is generally admitted that their doctrines and their lives were pure and simple; that they rejected the Romish ceremonies, doctrines, and traditions; that, as even Bede admits, though himself indignant at their repudiation of the authority of the Bishop of Rome, "they preached only such works of charity and piety as they could learn from the prophetical, evangelical, and apostolic writings"; that they boldly asserted the exclusive authority of the Scriptures, and that their modes of worship and their forms of church government were primitive and simple.[15]

Thus many of the important things that have distinguished the Lutheran and other great religious reformations were

---

14. Robert Richardson, *Memoirs of Alexander Campbell*, I, p. 119.
15. *Ibid.*, p. 120.

WHAT THE BIBLE SAYS ABOUT FAITH AND OPINION

taught and practiced in this lonely isle, under the influence of that Divine light which, at sundry times and in various modes, and in different places, have strangely and unexpectedly shone forth amidst the darkness of the nations. This light, however, has long since departed from Iona.[16]

Thus, the truth is available for those who seek it. How well Jesus taught this principle in His parable on the sower (Matthew 13:1-9, 18-23), and in the intervening sermon:

> You will keep on hearing, but will not understand;
> And you will keep on seeing, but will not perceive,
> For the heart of this people has become dull,
> And with their ears they scarcely hear,
> And they have closed their eyes;
> Lest they should see with their eyes,
> And hear with their ears,
> And understand with their heart and turn again,
> And I should heal them (Matthew 13:14, 15).

He who desires to know the Word, to understand it, to believe it, and to obey it—will be blessed for his attitude (I Corinthians 2:9-16). When man sinned in Eden, God punished him with the curse: "by the sweat of your face you shall eat bread" (Genesis 3:19). Does not this same principle hold true with the spiritual "bread of life"? Truth known is the result of truth sought with all of the strength and resources of man. "He who abandons the personal search for truth, under whatever pretext, abandons truth."[17]

However, there is some truth not intended for man's knowledge. Man has always speculated where God has not revealed. This danger, with all of its attendant ramifications, should be apparent at the very outset of this discussion.

---

16. *Ibid.*, p. 124.
17. Drummond

INTRODUCTION

If any one advocates a different doctrine, and does not agree with sound words, those of our Lord Jesus Christ, and with the doctrine conforming to godliness, he is conceited and understands nothing; but he has a morbid interest in controversial questions and disputes about words, out of which arise envy, strife, abusive language, evil suspicions, and constant friction between men of depraved mind and deprived of the truth, who suppose that godliness is a means of gain (I Timothy 6:3-5).

But refuse foolish and ignorant speculations, knowing that they produce quarrels (II Timothy 2:23).

If God has expressed His power in His ultimate creation — a man, and his ultimate revelation — a written record, then we must logically deduce that man is responsible to the record for what it is.

The Gospel addresses itself to men as if they were capable of believing it, receiving it, and obeying it, and thereby enjoying it, and the responsibility for not doing so need not be laid upon God for withholding the enabling act of his omnipotence, but upon man who refuses to accept the divine testimony, and to yield obedience to the divine requirements.[18]

Man must, therefore, get to the revealed truth. There is a high premium in being a possessor of the truth. Man must be right — as well as sincere. As Henry Clay once said, "I would rather be right than president." Man needs to uncover the truth at *any* cost to his own ideas, habits, or feelings — for ultimately, it is for his own good (II Timothy 3:15-17). "May it never be! Rather, let God be found true, though every man be found a liar," (Romans 3:4). There never can be unity between God's truth and man's error.

---

18. J.H. Garrison, *The Story of a Century* (St. Louis: Christian Publishing Co., 1909), p. 206.

WHAT THE BIBLE SAYS ABOUT FAITH AND OPINION

How God blessed a broken, weak, and fallen nation when she paused "at the square," and gave an attentive ear to Ezra as he restored "the law" and "read from the book . . . so that they understood the reading" (Nehemiah 8:8, cf. 8:1-8). "He who will not reason is a bigot; he who cannot is a fool, and he who dare not is a slave."[19]

Let us now get to the business of this study—which is purely a matter of exegesis, not apologetics. *What does God say about matters of precept, precedent, and opinion?*

---

19. Sir William Drummond

Part I — Precept

Chapter Two

AUTHORITY

Our beginning point is authority. By its very nature it becomes primary. For out of it come *all* the issues of every Christian problem—especially those of our theme. Lay a poor foundation in this regard and we will ever be confused. Now that we are established as having the "Book of God," what is our authority?

Authority is the "ultimate power or control," the "right to command and act." Where is this authority? Identify it! Without its law and order, there can only be anarchy and chaos. There must be that "ultimate" to which every religious appeal must be made.

The Bible, by its very nature and in view of what we have accepted it to be, points to God as *the* authority. It does not seek to prove God, it rather declares Him to be—and straightway seeks to reveal what He thinks and does. Thus, God by His very nature is the ultimate authority for His entire creation.

Now two things are essential to the exercise of authority: (1) one party is commanded to speak or write a message, and (2) the second party is commanded to receive that message. This has been done in the form of our Scripture; and we notice by its form that God has used many persons, styles, methods, and means to bring this about. However, a survey of the complete record overwhelmingly points to One who was the final, complete, and perfect expression of all revelation—one called Jesus Christ, the only begotten Son of God.

> God, after He spoke long ago to the fathers in the prophets in many portions and in many ways, in these last days has spoken to us in His Son, whom He appointed heir of all

WHAT THE BIBLE SAYS ABOUT FAITH AND OPINION

things, through whom also He made the world. And He is the radiance of His glory and the exact representation of His nature, and upholds all things by the word of His power. When He had made purification of sins, He sat down at the right hand of the Majesty on high; having become as much better than the angels, as He has inherited a more excellent name than they (Hebrews 1:1-4).

The New Covenant, and final Covenent, God made with man, in all of its meaning, is pin-pointed in *Christ*. He is *the* one, *the* hope, *the* message, *the* teacher, *the* priest — *the* authority.

And when they saw Him, they worshipped Him; but some were doubtful. And Jesus came up and spoke to them, saying, "All authority has been given to Me in heaven and on earth (Matthew 28:17, 18).

For no man can lay a foundation other than the one which is laid, which is Jesus Christ (I Corinthians 3:11).

. . . which He brought about in Christ, when He raised Him from the dead, and seated Him at His right hand in the heavenly places, far above all rule and authority and power and dominion, and every name that is named, not only in this age, but also in the one to come. And He put all things in subjection under His feet, and gave Him as head over all things to the church, which is His body, the fulness of Him who fills all in all (Ephesians 1:20-23).

I charge you in the presence of God, who gives life to all things, and of Christ Jesus, who testified the good confession before Pontius Pilate; that you keep the commandment without stain or reproach, until the appearing of our Lord Jesus Christ, which He will bring about at the proper time — He who is the blessed and only Sovereign, the King of kings and Lord of lords (I Timothy 6:13-15).

Jesus was unique. In Him only dwells the fullness of God and the fullness of the Holy Spirit. Thus, Jesus spoke

PRECEPT: AUTHORITY

with authority and not *by* authority. This indeed was a shock to the first disciples, for immediately they noticed that "he was teaching them as one having authority, and not as the scribes" (Mark 1:22). The scribes, like any man before, had to refer to an authoritative command or commission. Jesus merely spake—that in itself was authoritative.

In every institution we must have system, law, order, and authority. This is government. Even the home, the first institution of man, must have government. So with God's institution between Himself and man—the spiritual house —the church as it was created of the new and last covenant God made with man! And Jesus is King—by inheritance, by blood, by power.

However, throughout the history of the church human authorities have often usurped the divine. Various types of government have been innovated in the name of Him who gave no system other than that carefully prescribed in Scripture.

Categorically there have been and still are, three types of government:

1. The first is that *divine* system—conceived by God in Heaven, made a reality by Christ, commanded by the Holy Spirit through His word, delivered by the apostles, and adopted by the primitive church. Many of its factors will be unfolded as our study progresses. For now—let us establish Christ as king—the authority.

2. The second type, for want of a better term, will be called *private*. How did it come into being? It was born in the mind and heart of a strong, yet narrow, dishonest, or ignorant person. This party creedalizes his own thought and thus rules himself, and often those about him. By sheer power of personality this person becomes *the* government.

WHAT THE BIBLE SAYS ABOUT FAITH AND OPINION

One common seat of authority in a private government is man's own *conscience*. What a power it can exert!

> Conscience! War-cry of the hero and shibboleth of the petty partisan! The sectary's boast and the Martyr's consolation! Refuge of ignorance, conceit, and passion! Vantage-ground of godlike self sacrifice! Home by turns of deity and demagog — what deeds of splendor and ignominy bear thy name!
>
> Men, as conscience impelled them, have bathed nations in the blood of innocents. Other men, impelled by conscience, have braved the terrors of the battlefield, carrying succor to the wounded.
>
> Men of conscience have revolved the thumbscrew, driven the wedge in the iron boot, and turned the rack to the last point of agony. Other men of conscience have broken down their dungeons, freed their white-haired captives and ground to powder the instruments of their inquisition.
>
> Men of conscience — women of conscience — have tossed their brothers over precipices, bound them to stakes in the midst of advancing tide, heaped firebrands against their blackening flesh. Other conscientious men have taught and endured, endured and taught, till Martyr's Memorials arose in the scenes of their sufferings.
>
> This inner voice that we call conscience we always assume to be the voice of God. History and observation alike should convince us that it is often the voice of quite other than God.[1]

How undependable man's feelings, intuition, "inner voice" can be in the things of this world, let alone the spiritual and eternal issues of life.

Another voice of private authority which seems to be much louder is that of *reason*. God gave man this precious

---

1. Amos R. Wells, *That They May All Be One* (New York: Funk and Wagnalls Co., 1905), pp. 43, 44.

gift. But not to create a religion—only to find and know the one He has already given! And yet man will continue to worship the tool rather than the Creator. What unholy systems have been devised in the name of scholarship. Can not man learn the limitation and the use of his own mind?

> And this is one direction in which the rationalistic theory is at fault. It does not take sufficiently into account the disabilities of reason. It assumes reason to be in a normal condition, whereas its eye may be dim through the influence of an abnormal moral condition.[2]

Here we see the liberal leader and his satellites, the "creator" of a new church, the persuasive orator, the presiding "official," the "preacher at large," the theological professor, the appointed "secretary," the convincing writer, the cantankerous elder, the influential deacon, the ruling preacher, the selfish benefactor, the "policy" man, and the church "boss." All these tend to become or definitely are governments all of their own.

The scholar may reap the harvest of all heathen philosophers and sages, all the voices of poets, men of genius, and noble learning—he will yet rise no higher than his own reason.

> Where is the wise man? Where is the scribe? Where is the debater of this age? Has not God made foolish the wisdom of the world? For since in the wisdom of God the world through its wisdom did not come to know God, God was well pleased through the foolishness of the message preached to save those who believe. For indeed Jews ask for signs, and Greeks search for wisdom; but we preach Christ crucified, to Jews a stumbling block, and to Gentiles

---

2. A.B. Bruce, *Apologetics* (Edinburgh: T. & T. Clark, 1892), p. 498.

foolishness, but to those who are called, both Jews and Greeks, Christ the power of God and the wisdom of God. Because the foolishness of God is wiser than men, and the weakness of God is stronger than men (I Corinthians 1:20-25).

3. The third category of authoritative governments we shall term *ecclesiastic*. It too is human; however, its birth has been more organized and commonly sanctioned. It may begin as the preceding system did, and then develop into a more permanent and organized form. It is often orderly, scholarly, attractive, respectable, and even Christ-like in a number of ways—however, it remains a usurped government. It is human. Some, or all, authority has been taken from Christ, leaving but a mausoleum holding a dead Jesus rather than a house of the living Lord.

This system appears in several ways. The most complete and elaborate type is the autocracy (totalitarian)—the Roman Catholic Church. It has all authority placed in a "vicar" of Christ. Because this system employs so sweeping a change to human authority in one head its uniformity has often been mistaken for unity.

This whole idea rests on the theory of an "apostolic succession." Here we have authority being handed down—when Christ never surrendered it. The only thing to be handed down is the *Word* of authority. There is the power of God. True "apostolic succession" is not in a continuous lineage, but in saying what the apostles said and doing what they did.

The church is but the assembly of the saved. Each one received that salvation by individual faith and obedience to the Gospel, and that Gospel came by revelation, that is, the Word. Thus the church can not create religion. It can only preserve what has been revealed. The church has no

PRECEPT: AUTHORITY

business to supplant, change, over-rule, or rival the Word—only to guard and preach "the faith which was once for all delivered to the saints" (Jude 3).

Rome advocates an infallible interpretation by an infallible Church of an infallible revelation—that is, the Bible and other authenticated tradition. Protestantism holds that the Bible is the sole, infallible rule of faith and life, and that private judgment is responsible for its right application.[3]

However, Protestantism has violated this premise and, in many forms and degrees, has itself become a giant *ecclesiastic* system. It has rebelled against *calling* any man father (Matthew 23:9), yet it has ever *made* man father in a thousand instances. Bureaucratic, republican, and democratic forms of government have robbed Christ of authority in many ways and by many degrees.

The work and plea of Alexander Campbell is the logical outcome of the work of Martin Luther. What did Campbell do but apply in this country and in this century the selfsame principles which Luther applied in Europe in the sixteenth century? Refer to the principles of the Lutheran reformations. Its first and fundamental principle is the priesthood of all believers, from which come as corollaries the doctrines of private judgment and justification by faith. Campbell's starting point also was the priesthood of all believers. His first grievance against the church of his time was the arrogance and intolerance of the Clergy. They had, in his belief, largely appropriated to themselves the privileges and prerogatives which belong alike to all the followers of Christ. On the other hand private Christians had surrendered in great part their obligations and responsibilities to the ministers and

---

3. B.C. Deweese, *The Missouri Christian Lectures* (St. Louis: Christian Publishing Co., 1892), p. 137.

were too content to follow whithersoever their spiritual lords might lead them. Thus, the church had become, in the opinion of Alexander Campbell, a veritable kingdom of the clergy, whose divine call and right no presumptuous layman might question.[4]

This is exactly what Mr. Richardson pointed out. Protestant ecclesiasticism had reached its ultimate in the Presbyterian Church of Scotland in the days of the Campbells.

> Each member of the congregatrion is subject, in conversation and doctrine, to the Session; the decisions of the Session to the Presbytery; those of the Presbytery to the Synod, and those of the Synod to the general assembly. Thus, with them, the Church consists of congregations, with all the required church-courts, comprising a complete system of absolute clerical domination.
>
> Among these courts, it is the general assembly which is the true exponent of the nature and animus of the entire system. This supreme court is the eye and ear and efficient head of the whole body. For to use the vision of Assyria's king, if the Session be the legs of iron, emblem of popular strength, mixed at the feet with the miry clay of the unofficial laity, if the Presbytery be the belly and thighs of brass, and the Synod the breast and arms of silver, it is the General Assembly that constitutes the golden head, which is the crowning glory of the Presbyterian image.[5]

Is it any wonder why Alexander Campbell, in the process of numerous Bible studies, should ask,

> Who has authority? Who gave the Presbytery authority to license men? Who gave the Presbytery authority to make laws for the Church? Who gave the Presbytery authority to

---

[4]. J.M. Trible, "Reformation in The Church," *The Old Faith Restated,* J.H. Garrison, ed. (Joplin: College Press, reprint of 1891 ed.), p. 304.

[5]. Robert Richardson, *Memoirs of Alexander Carnpbell,* I (Nashville, Tenn.: Gospel Advocate, 1956 reprint of 1897 ed.), pp. 66, 67.

PRECEPT: AUTHORITY

decide religious matter by vote? Who gave the Presbytery authority to choose ministers?[6]

The ecclesiastic method with all of its methods and machinery has but one logical ending:

> As respects Civil authorities, there ought to be inferior and superior courts. But with us, we have the same Judge always upon the bench. We do not commence our suits in the cellar, and then ascend to the middle story, and then to the upper story of Christ's house. Few men see the absurdities of carrying up doctrinal points in controversy and cases of conscience, as they try civil or criminal pleas, because the whole matter of ecclesiastical politics is hid in the mists and fogs of theological maxims, causes and precedents. There is no end of the appeal system, if once you transcend a single committee of umpires. When you commence in the *court* system, you must ascend, step by step, till you find a pope, a vicegerent, a demi-god.[7]

The other extreme of ecclesiasticism is the democratic method. It follows the old Latin proverb, "The voice of the people is the voice of God." All issues of faith and practice are to be decided by a consensus of opinion, compromise, the level of greatest agreement. Authority thus rests in mere common opinion.

Mr. Robert Hopkins in a letter regarding baptism stated, "There is no higher authority among us than the local congregation."[8]

Out of this maze of ecclesiasticism has come the curse of human creeds.

Phillip Brooks, an Episcopalian, stated in his day,

---

6. *Ibid.*, p. 387.
7. Alexander Campbell, *A Debate between Rev. A. Campbell and Rev. N.L. Rice* (Nashville, Tenn.: Gospel Advocate, reprint of 1844 ed.), pp. 836, 837.
8. Robert M. Hopkins, *Christian Standard* (July 13, 1946), p. 2.

25

WHAT THE BIBLE SAYS ABOUT FAITH AND OPINION

If there has been one change, which above all others has altered our modern Christianity from what was the Christian religion in apostolic times, I think beyond all doubt it must be this, the substitution of a belief in doctrines for loyalty to a Person as the essence and test of Christian life![9]

We must get back to Christ—He is Christianity. Let man enthrone Him and not a creed about Him. The weakness of a creed is not mainly in its errors, nor its complexity, but in its being substituted as the supreme authority (see Part III). We must go back beyond the creed to Jesus Christ Himself. Man is not saved by his creeds, but God may save him in spite of them.

This idea became the genius of the Restoration Movement of the 19th century. Its leaders learned a lesson which was long since forgotten or diluted by the ages. This movement,

> ... led to a re-discovery of Christ. A new and independent study of the Scriptures took Christ out of the circumference, where the theology had placed him and put him in the center, as the sole object of saving faith, the only authority in Christianity and the only basis of Christian union.[10]

When will men ever learn the full import of being a bondservant of Christ (slave) (I Corinthians 7:21-23; Ephesians 6:5-8)? The New Testament concept is that one who accepts Christ as Lord becomes His slave with all of its meaning of ownership, dependence, and obedience. Our authority IS Christ; it is in "Christ, not other religious Masters, not the individual reason, not the Church, not even the Bible."[11]

---

9. George Plattenburg, "The Unity of The Church," in *The Old Faith Restated*, ed. by J.H. Garrison (Joplin, Mo.: College Press, reprint of 1891 ed.), p. 341.

10. J.H. Garrison, *The Story of a Century* (St. Louis: Christian Publishing Co., 1909), p. 34.

11. A.B. Bruce, *Apologetics*, p. 493.

PRECEPT: AUTHORITY

However, how is this Christ appropriated today? How may one gain access to Him in this time? By what method or instrument may we implement His Lordship over us?

Since our access to God is not direct, but indirect, through Christ as His Son, whom He has clothed with authority, and since His authority is ultimate and final, we are very definitely concerned that we learn all that is knowable about that. We want to know where the depository of His truth is located; how and by whom it is to be interpreted; how we should administer the authority, if any, that has been delegated to us. These are the essential and practical phases of the authority of Christ in which our interest centers just now.[12]

There are three critical issues, two of which have been assumed in our introduction. First, the Bible is that "depository of His truth." It is not *the* authority but it is *the source* of authority. It is the channel (intelligent and tangible) through which the authority reaches the mind and heart of man. This leads to the second issue, that man is to be the interpreter. It was intended for man who by faith, intelligence, and industry can ascertain the body of truth about this authority (II Timothy 3:14-17; John 20:30, 31; Ephesians 3:3, 4). As Z.T. Sweeney once asked,

> Would you know God? Know Jesus Christ whom He hath sent. Would you know Christ? Know the apostles whom He hath sent. God in Christ, Christ in the apostles and the apostles in the world is the source of authority in Christianity, or there is none.[13]

---

12. W.R. Walker, *Christian Unity Quarterly* (April 1943), p. 4.
13. Z.T. Sweeney, *New Testament Christianity*, Vol III (Joplin: College Press, reprint of 1930 ed.), p. 517.

WHAT THE BIBLE SAYS ABOUT FAITH AND OPINION

To do this is not a matter of believing in the apostles, or their doctrines, or the doctrines of Christ, but believing *in Christ*.

The real problem then is how should this "depository" be handled so as to clearly understand every trace of this authority. This is the field of exegesis—the aim of this study.

The tendency of many believers and unbelievers alike has been to belittle the value of the written Word through word, practice, or innuendo.

Here is a believer who refers frequently to the operation of the Holy Spirit on the heart of a man in conversion and Christian living. He begins with the sound premise that today we are living, under the "age of the Spirit." He straightway sidesteps the Scripture, the very instrument of the Spirit, to promise the Spirit's direct and miraculous operation on the heart of man, in spite of the Scripture. Why should the Spirit deliver *the Word*, and then throw it aside and act directly on a man's heart?

The Scriptures say that "faith comes from hearing, and hearing by the word of Christ" (Romans 10:17). This does not make the process of conversion and teaching mechanical. It only puts the written word of God in its proper place. To do otherwise results in confusion, speculation, and contradiction. Alexander Campbell fought long to restore the Bible to its rightful place as the disciplinary force on man. He never entered into the discussion of the *nature* of the influence which came of the gospel—only that it could not come without the Word.

> I do teach that the Holy Spirit renovates the human mind by the instrumentality of his Word; while you and many others seem to me to contend that the Holy Spirit personally descends from heaven, enters the human heart, and, without his Word, miraculously creates a man anew. . . . I pretend

PRECEPT: AUTHORITY

not to separate the Word and the Spirit of God. I do not say the Word alone nor the Spirit alone enlightens, sanctifies or saves. With the Lord Jesus I would pray to thy Father, "Sanctify them through thy truth; thy word is the truth." I would not say with you; Sanctify them by thy Spirit alone.[14]

The human heart must be changed and renovated by some cause; for unless the heart be reconciled to God, purified, cleansed, *no man can be admitted into the society of heaven.* These views I have always presented to the public, but the question is, *How is this moral change to be effected? By the gospel facts alone? By the Word alone?* I do not affirm any one of these propositions. *I never did affirm any one of them.*

How the Spirit operates in the Word, through the Word, by the Word, or with the Word, I do not affirm. I only oppose the idea that anyone is changed in heart or renewed in the Spirit of his mind by the Spirit without the Word.[15]

The liberal theologian by exalting his own reason reduces the written scriptures to a book of moral treatises. It is truth, they contend, but rather than truth as a God-given discipline it is truth as a record of human experiences in the field of religion. Professor Smith testified, "We are being accustomed to the use of the Bible as a book of religious experience, rather than a supernaturally produced literature."[16]

Thus, according to this view, the Bible is not static, but alive with the growing eternal word of God. It can now hold, with the help of twentieth century higher criticism something that originally was not put there by God. Are we able to know more about God today than did Christ? Or more

---

14. Robert Richardson, *Memoirs of Alexander Campbell,* II, p. 404.
15. *Ibid.,* p. 405.
16. Gerald Birney Smith, *Christian Standard* (March 13, 1948), p. 11.

WHAT THE BIBLE SAYS ABOUT FAITH AND OPINION

about the church today than did Paul? Are we to use the Bible today as a "primary ladder" — use it as our first book in the school of religion, only to outgrow it by reason and experience, and reach heights never dreamed of by the inspired writers?

The Scripture record is the clearest record of God's will that man has. No human sequel, condensation, elaboration, creed can add any new knowledge from God.

> When God speaks, exact conformity to his words should be the law of life. Who, it was asked, was empowered to say that any matter purely and distinctly of revelation might be in any wise different from its precise presentation in the Scriptures themselves? Who can place himself in an attitude to see the great problems of redemption in other lights than those revealed in the words which "the Holy Ghost teacheth."?[17]

Paul affirms:

> All Scripture is inspired by God and profitable for teaching, for reproof, for correction, for training in righteousness; that the man of God may be adequate, equipped for every good work (II Timothy 3:16, 17).

What more can man do that God has not already done? What improvement can be made on one who is being "equipped for every good work."?

Let no one dismiss the power of revealed instruction with the shallow excuse, "But we all have our different interpretations." Do we have unlimited liberty in interpretation? This would make reason, or feeling, or local circumstance

---

17. George Plattenburg, *The Old Faith Restated*, ed. by J.H. Garrison, pp. 314, 15.

PRECEPT: AUTHORITY

our final seat of authority. And the Scriptures would be reduced to a weather vane pointing any way the wind happens to be blowing.

Let the Bible student know from the beginning that he is limited by the factor of inspiration. When God said something through the medium of language, He had a definite thought in mind. As Paul enjoined a young student, "Retain the standard of sound words which you have heard from me, in the faith and love which are in Christ Jesus" (II Timothy 1:13). Notice, there is a "pattern" (form, system, order, prescribed area and design) of words. Thus, we have no liberty other than to *uncover* the thought God originally intended. We must treat the written pattern of words, which was God's chosen medium of revelation, with all the fair laws of common sense and intelligible understanding.

The liberal thinker would fix upon each word an elusive fluid or manifold connotation — depending on certain factors today. Words change their meaning for different minds.

Alexander Campbell, quoting a certain professor, said:

"All men, in their daily conversation and writings, attach but one sense to a word at the same time and in the same passage, unless they design to speak in enigmas. Of course, it would be in opposition to the universal custom of language, if more than one meaning should be attached to any word in Scripture, in such a case" — that is, in the same passage, and at the same time.[18]

Even one of the great creeds of church history testifies to the singular thought content of Scripture. The Westminster Confession (Section IX) reads,

---

18. Alexander Campbell, *Campbell on Baptism* (Bethany, Va.: Printed and published by A. Campbell, 1853), p. 56.

WHAT THE BIBLE SAYS ABOUT FAITH AND OPINION

> The infallible rule of interpretation of Scripture is the Scripture itself; and therefore, when there is a question about the true and full sense of any Scripture (which is not manifold, but one), it must be searched and known by other places that speak more clearly.[19]

And Mr. Campbell, in his opening remarks in his McCalla debate, pointed out this fact with his following comment,

> The sense of every passage of Scripture is ONE, not two or three or manifold. How many thousands of volumes of sermons and interpretations of Scripture would it send to the flames or to the moths if it were duly recognized and acted upon? There is but ONE meaning in every passage of Scripture, and that *one meaning* must be always found from its context.[20]

The ultimate hope of the liberal has always been the *relativity* of truth. If this be absolutely true that we have no absolute truth — this in itself is one grand contradiction — then any hope of a tangible stream of thought (for man or God) is totally impossible — and man is found in an overwhelming predicament.

But we are beginning with Scripture, and its testimony is different. Its teaching and its very existence emphasizes the *absolute* nature of truth. And the Scripture, not only *contains* the truth, it *is* truth. "Sanctify them in the truth; Thy word is truth" (John 17:17).

Paul, a bond-servant of God, and an apostle of Jesus Christ, for the faith of those chosen of God and the knowledge

---

19. Phillip Schaff, *Creeds of Christendom*, III, 6th ed. (Grand Rapids: Wm. B. Eerdmans Co., reprint of 1890 ed.), p. 56.
20. Robert Richardson, *Memoirs of Alexander Campbell*, II, p. 76.

PRECEPT: AUTHORITY

of the truth which is according to godliness, in the hope of eternal life, which God, who cannot lie, promised long ages ago, but at the proper time manifested, even His word, in the proclamation with which I was entrusted according to the commandment of God our Savior (Titus 1:1-3).

If any one advocates a different doctrine, and does not agree with sound words, those of our Lord Jesus Christ, and with the doctrine conforming to godliness, he is conceited and understands nothing; but he has a morbid interest in controversial questions and disputes about words, out of which arise envy, strife, abusive language, evil suspicions (I Timothy 6:3, 4).

As the philosopher John Locke said of the Bible, "It has God for its author, salvation for its end, and truth without any mixture of error, for its matter."[21]

There is but *one* truth—it is singular. If however, it is relative, then there is no basic foundation for the study of the subject of faith and opinion.

As Professor Foster points out:

> Now this will seem fantastic to one who has a conception that truth is relative and that therefore no man can claim that he has perfect truth, and that all of his system must be true. McGarvey made just such a claim concerning his system. His truth came from God and, therefore, must be perfect. One who rejected it, rejected God, and in this respect was beyond defense! The proposition that there is no such a thing as absolute truth, that truth itself is merely relative, immediately wrests everything in the realm of faith and moves it all into the field of opinion, leaving nothing indispensable, nothing authoritative, nothing certain.

---

21. John Locke as quoted by Alexander Campbell, *Popular Lectures and Addresses* (Cincinnati: Standard Publishing, 1861), p. 600.

WHAT THE BIBLE SAYS ABOUT FAITH AND OPINION

The proposition that truth is relative is, of course, a throwback to the system of philosophy of the German scholar Ritschl and his "value judgements."[22]

A case in point is the advice given by a liberal professor to a young student preacher. This young man was confronted by a woman, who asked him about Lazarus' resurrection — if Christ really restored him to life or not. The student wondered how he would give an honest answer without betraying his true unbelief. He was advised to agree with her in view of this instruction:

Do not feel that this is a dishonest procedure. You well know that today there is no *absolute* truth. All is relative. What is sin for one is not sin for another. No one moral code can be superimposed upon all men. It is likewise with religious truth, all is relative. For the old-fashioned and uneducated, the literal statements of Scripture convey much "religious value" to their hearts, and it does them much good. We should never be so ruthless as to crudely rob them of the comfort they have thereby received. It does this elderly woman much good to realize that by the simple word, Lazarus had been raised from the dead. Therefore, when I reply, "I believe the same thing," I mean it with all my heart. I see that her believing the miracle does her good. Since truth produces good, I am obliged to confess that the story is true so far as she is concerned. But mind you, this truth is relative and not absolute. For should another person ask the same question, whose outlook is more skeptical and modern, and who therefore discounts the miraculous elements of the story, you can quickly detect that it has no "religious value" to him, and with peace of conscience say that so far as he is concerned you do not

---

22. R.C. Foster, *Christian Standard* (February 15, 1941), p. 8.

PRECEPT: AUTHORITY

believe that Christ raised Lazarus. We must perform the function of ministers by continually seeking to conserve all things of a "religious value" in the people of our congregations. We are not to proclaim absolutes, for there are none to proclaim. Because human nature varies, all "religious values" vary. What is truth for one is sheer superstition for another.[23]

Truth is not relative, however it is *progressive*. God did not reveal the full truth in a single communication; but carefully and methodically dispensed the elements of truth, each at its opportune time, relative to the condition of man —the object of all revelation. "God, after He spoke long ago to the fathers in the prophets in many portions and in many ways, in these last days has spoken to us in His Son" (Hebrews 1:1, 2).

Thus to be honest and accurate the Bible student must seek to know, collect together, and relate all of the elements of truth in order to learn the total truth. Each passage of revelation is truth, but consists only in one portion of the total truth. All passages assembled together on a given subject constitute the totality of truth for that subject. Professor J.W. McGarvey, in commenting on a seeming contradiction in the records Matthew, Mark, and Luke gave concerning fasting, made this observation:

> Each tells the truth, but each tells only a part of what was true, and we get at the whole truth by putting both of their statements together as one. This circumstance furnishes a key to the reconciliation of the different writers in many other places where there is an appearance of discrepancy, and we have used it freely. We should always, in such cases,

---

23. As quoted in the *Christian Standard* (December 2, 1944), p. 5, citing the *Christian Beacon* (August 31, 1944).

WHAT THE BIBLE SAYS ABOUT FAITH AND OPINION

suppose both statements to be true, and regard each as a part of the whole truth.[24]

Therefore, one must be ever active in the search for all of the truth. No one can relinquish his search — lest he become hopelessly opinionated in a rut of creedal forms and dogmas. One of our "restoration forefathers," Barton W. Stone once said,

> We do not believe that all the seals of the Book are yet opened, therefore we do not wish to bind our hands nor the hands of our brethren with the fatal cords of authoritative creeds and confessions of faith. We wish ever to be open to truth and to follow it whenever it appears beaming from the Book of God.[25]

So let every Bible lover search the record with all industry so that he may truly assimilate that "faith which was once for all delivered unto the saints" (Jude 3).

The New Testament is pre-eminently the book of authority and guidance under the Christian dispensation, because it contains the constitution and revelation of the New Age. It contains the last will and testament of our Lord Jesus Christ on the question of human redemption, the history of the incarnation, the record of the atonement, the proofs of the resurrection, the ministrations of the Holy Spirit, and the work of the Apostles in building the Christian Church and providing for instruction in all things that pertain unto life and godliness, and is hence the source of religious knowledge, and infallible, spiritual directory, and the only rule of faith and practice for all men from Christ to the millennium. When the peculiar functions of the Testaments in their

---

24. J.W. McGarvey, *New Testament Commentary*, I, *Matthew and Mark* (Nashville, TN: Gospel Advocate, reprint of 1875 ed.), p. 276.
25. Barton W. Stone, *Christian Standard* (October 28, 1944), pp. 1, 2.

PRECEPT: AUTHORITY

relations to each other, and to the Christian world, are thoroughly understood, the Judaizing errors indicated will pass away and both the science of Biblical interpretation and the way of salvation will become so plain that a wayfaring man though he be a simpleton need not err therein.[26]

Having obtained that truth and ready to disseminate it, one ought to then remember his sacred trust. As Hight C. Moore commented on the Scriptural injunction, "and the things which you have heard from me in the presence of many witnesses, these entrust to faithful men, who will be able to teach others also" (II Timothy 2:2):

> The same commit thou. The same; nothing more; nothing less; nothing other. The same in substance; the same in emphasis; the same in presentation; the same in power.
> You are dealing with the Water of life. Don't sweeten it. Don't poison it. Don't dilute it. Don't divert it. Don't stop it. Don't try to purify it. Don't try to analyze it. Pour it out and pass it on! The denizens of our desert earth are thirsty for it unto death.
> You are sharing the Bread of life. You can not make it. You can not bake it. You must not break it. Simply take it from the Master's hand and heed His word, "Give ye them to eat!" Then the famishing multitude will be fed.[27]

In this discourse on the subject of "authority," we now arrive at two necessary conclusions:

1. The Bible is *the only rule of faith and practice* in the Christian system of life. This is dogmatic and exclusive. But it is necessary, lest the Bible lose its intended purpose and power. The Bible is the solitary truth of God revealed to

---

26. J.J. Haley, "The Progress of Revelation," *The Old Faith Restated*, J.H. Garrison, ed., pp. 147-8.
27. Hight C. Moore, *United Evangelical Action* (July 1, 1949), p. 9.

WHAT THE BIBLE SAYS ABOUT FAITH AND OPINION

man and thus comprises the only divine norm for the individual and for the church.

Let one of the chief defenders of this principle, Alexander Campbell, state it:

> The Bible alone must always decide every question involving the nature, the character or the designs of the Christian institution. Outside of the Apostolic Canon, there is not, as it appears to me, one solid foot of terra firma on which to raise the superstructure ecclesiastic. The foundation of apostles and prophets is that projected and ordained by the Lawgiver of the universe. On this, and on this only, can we safely found the Church of Jesus Christ, whether we contemplate its doctrine, its discipline or its government. Nothing less authoritative and divine can fully satisfy the conscientious of all parties, or withstand the assaults of the adversaries of our most holy faith. Whenever we close the apostolic records and open the volumes of the "primitive Fathers," the converts and successors of the apostles, as they are reverentially designated, we find ourselves on a sea of uncertainties, without a single haven in our horizon or in our chart.[28]

One small word can make a great difference. In this case it is the word "a" and the word "the." To say that the Bible is "*a* rule of faith and practice" in Christianity leaves the door open for most anything. It is so wide that the Scriptures can be changed, diluted, nullified, and even eliminated in favor of some "superior" rule.

To change this principle and have it read: the Bible is "the rule of faith and practice" means everything. In the Scriptures we have the mind of Chirst, our authority—as

---

28. Robert Richardson, *Memoirs of Alexander Campbell*, II, p. 495.

PRECEPT: AUTHORITY

contrasted with every other mind in the world. Therefore, as Mr. Cowden points out:

> Through his words, deeds and character, as revealed in the Christian Scriptures, he has expressed his mind on every essential matter that has to do with the church; and this should be final with all that accept his mind as the Christian standard of authority. No difference can be settled without a common standard of authority. Without a common standard of weights and measures business differences could not be settled; but with it differences in business can be settled. Just so religious differences can be removed by submitting them to the mind of Christ for settlement. But the trouble is, we are not always willing for Christ to break down our differences; we want to be heard ourselves, and are not always willing for Christ who is our peace, to break them down.[29]

But what has been the record of Church history? Many "rules" have been added: the voice of "speaking in tongues," of religious experience, of post-Scriptural prophecy, of the conscience of councils, of tradition, of authoritarian prelates, yes, and even the "voice of the people." And now today, there rises up the popular manifestations of subjectivism — feelings, special Holy Spirit revelations, added enlightenment, existentialism, etc. The great protestant reformation made a forward advance in the right direction; however, it was partial.

The early reformers, and in fact the later as well, did but imperfectly apprehend by what rule the church was to be reformed. It is part of the glory of John Wickliffe that he

---

29. John B. Cowden, *Saint Paul on Christian Duty* (New York: Fleming H. Revell Co., 1923), p. 71.

WHAT THE BIBLE SAYS ABOUT FAITH AND OPINION

discerned with singular clearness of mind that the word of God must bear an important part in the reformation of the church. But even he did not realize how important; he does not clearly apprehend as yet that it is the sole source of authority in the church, and itself at once an all-sufficient warrant and an all-sufficient rule for the task of reforming the church of its errors and its sins. Other reformers of his time, notably Savanarola, scarcely perceived any connection between the reformation of the church and the restoration of the authority of Scripture. The Florentine reformer looked to princes and civil magistrates and general councils for the Church's reformation. Even Luther adopted the word of God as the rule of reformation timidly and only partially at last. The Lutheran Establishment was in fact constructed according to two rules: the rule of Scriptures and the rule of tradition. Its polity and liturgy, not a little of its doctrine, hold hard to the forms and traditions of the medieval church. The cost of a radical and sweeping reform was greater than even Luther's intrepid spirit could consent to pay. Such reform seemed even to the wisest of his time, nothing short of revolution.[30]

Yes, many denominationalists have said, "the Scriptures of the Old and New Testaments having been given by inspiration of God, are the all-sufficient and only rule of faith and practice and judge of all controversies."[31] But for man to acclaim the principle and to live by it can be two different things. The statement of this rule has been an age-old dogma. It has been declared and defended in nearly every era of reformation of the Roman Catholic system.

Examine all the creeds of Evangelical and modern Protestantism. Notice the place that this principle holds in nearly

---

30. J. M. Trible, "The Reformation in The Church," *The Old Faith Restated*, J.H. Garrison, ed., pp. 298-9.
31. Charles Hodge, as quoted in the *Christian Standard*, (March 13, 1948), p. 11.

PRECEPT: AUTHORITY

every one of them. For example, we cite from one of the greatest, the Westminster Confession of Faith. In the early portion of this creed we find this introductory law, "All which are given by inspiration of God to be the rule of faith and life."[32] This is elaborated and qualified by article VI:

> The whole counsel of God, concerning all things necessary for his own glory, man's salvation, faith, and life, is either expressly set down in Scripture, or by good and necessary consequence may be deduced from Scripture: unto which nothing at any time is to be added, whether by new revelations of the spirit, or traditions of men. Nevertheless, we acknowledge the inward illumination of the Spirit of God to be necessary for the saving understanding of such things as are revealed in the Word; and that there are some circumstances concerning the worship of God, and government of the Church, common to human actions and society, which are to be ordered by the light of nature and Christian prudence, according to the general rules of the Word, which are always to be observed.[33]

Here our principle is stated clearly, with the injection of one "loose end" — the latter part declaring an "inner light" rule. This has caused much confusion and can be the downfall of the entire rule.

However, the former part has been declared by other great creeds (some with even greater clarity), e.g., Formula Concordial (Lutheran),[34] French Confession of Faith,[35] The Belgic Confession,[36] Scotch Confession of Faith,[37] Thirty-nine Articles of Religion of the Church of England,[38]

---
32. Philip Schaff, *Creeds of Christendom*, III, p. 602.
33. *Ibid.*, pp. 603-4.
34. *Ibid.*, pp. 93-94.
35. *Ibid.*, pp. 357-62.
36. *Ibid.*, pp. 387-89.
37. *Ibid.*, p. 464.
38. *Ibid.*, pp. 489-500.

WHAT THE BIBLE SAYS ABOUT FAITH AND OPINION

Irish Articles of Religion,[39] Five Armenian Articles (vague),[40] Declaration of the Congregational Union of England and Wales,[41] Declaration of Faith of the National Council of Congregational Churches,[42] The Oberlin Declaration of the National Congregation Council,[43] The Baptist Confession (Philadelphia Confession — slight modification of Westminster Confession),[44] The New Hampshire Baptist Confession,[44] The Confession of the Waldenses,[46] and the Methodist Articles of Religion.[47] In view of this overwhelming testimony there looms up a strange contradiction between Protestant *claims* and Protestant *history*. It appears that all of the major reforms began on the same platform, but their courses of practice have been varied and contradictory. It follows that the very creed written to declare and follow our principle has been the tool for its destruction.

J. S. Lamar drew this conclusion about Isaac Errett:

> There is no question, for example, that the Bible and especially the N.T., is the only rule of faith and practice — the only one which is truly authoritative — which it is legitimate to enforce, or which it is sinful to disobey. This was the original Protestant doctrine, and that which alone justified the Protestant cause. Now the disciples, with whom Mr. Errett was identified, had come into being in consequence of the fact, which they clearly perceived, that the various sects of Protestantism had abandoned their own fundamental and justifying principle. They had adopted other standards of faith and other rules of conduct; and while each party claimed that *its* system was *according* to the word, though

---

39. *Ibid.*, p. 526.
40. *Ibid.*, p. 549.
41. *Ibid.*, pp. 730, 31, 33.
42. *Ibid.*, p. 734.
43. *Ibid.*, p. 737.
44. *Ibid.*, p. 738.
45. *Ibid.*, p. 742.
46. *Ibid.*, p. 758.
47. *Ibid.*, p. 808.

PRECEPT: AUTHORITY

not the word itself, it was manifest that this was but the substitution of human *inferences* for divine *authority;* and that if *logic* was to rule, the Romanist could argue as plausibly as the Presbyterian, and make out as strong a case as the Methodist. Moreover, the logic of the Presbyterian locked horns with that of the Methodist, while the Baptist had something to say for his side and against every other; and so with the Episcopalian and dozens of other different sects and sectaries. The whole religious world was in confusion; and to the great mass of men everything seemed unsettled, and nothing could be known and accepted as *certain truth.* And all this fearful evil had resulted from one and the same cause — the practical departure from that great principle which had given birth and legitimacy to the Protestant Movement.

Now what the Disciples designed and attempted to do was simply go back to this abandoned principle, and to carry it out in all the details of individual and church life. The purpose was most noble and unselfish and manifestly in harmony with the very spirit of the Lord Jesus; and it is amazing to reflect how bitterly they were opposed! and how persistently they were misrepresented and traduced![48]

The whole issue goes back to our starting point—the authority of Christ in every issue of faith and life. But where has authority actually rested? The *Claim* is "in Christ" and none other. The *practice* has been "in Christ" and some other.

A civil case relative to this point is that of a certain city government. Here we find corruption, vice, and lawlessness had plagued the city. Why? Not because of any inferior nature within the system of government itself. But because:

---

48. J.S. Lamar, *Memoirs of Isaac Errett,* I, (Cincinnati: Standard Publishing, 1893), pp. 66-67.

WHAT THE BIBLE SAYS ABOUT FAITH AND OPINION

> The city has two governments. One consists of the duly elected and appointed officials, headed by the mayor. The other is an invisible government made up of private persons who control certain phases of the administration—particularly law enforcement in respect to rackets—for personal or partisan gain. No new law is needed to end this double government.[49]

This has been identical to the situation in the past two thousand years of church history. The church (colloquial sense) has been plagued with hidden and "invisible" governments. In addition to the divinely ordained system, it has been intentionally or unintentionally cumbered with all types and variations of *private* and *ecclesiastic* systems (see pp. 19-24). Thus, with more than one system in operation at one time the result has been strife, division, weakness, secularism, contradiction—and a world pretty well lost to Christ.

Therefore, the plea of "restoration" was to go back beyond every human system of government ever devised, to the simple New Testament norm. One of the tap-roots of this movement, the *Declaration and Address* by Thomas Campbell, declared in its very first words, "and to take all our measures directly and immediately from the Divine Standard; to this alone we feel ourselves divinely bound to be conformed; as by this alone we must be judged."[50]

The aim of this movement is singular—we must go to the Bible to *obtain* our beliefs, not to *sustain* them. When P.S. Fall heard Alexander Campbell preach he suddenly was aware of a new method, approach, and attitude in using the Bible.

---

49. Editorial in *Youngstown Vindicator*, January 2, 1947.
50. Thomas Campbell, *Declaration and Address* (Lincoln, IL: Lincoln Christian College, 1971 reprint of 1809 ed.), p. 1.

PRECEPT: AUTHORITY

It was seen at once that it was the duty of the speaker and the privilege of the hearer to ascertain simply *what the divine Word says, and why it is said.* We had been accustomed to make the Scriptures a book of text-proofs of our doctrines. We now saw that we had everything to learn but *nothing to prove* in using God's word. On the former plan we knew as much when we came to the Bible as when we left it. We might have been more fully confirmed in what we had accepted as scientific religious truth, but this was all. For the connection in which every proof-text stood we had not much use, and thus a great portion of God's word was not only neutralized, but rendered absolutely worthless. Upon the new plan we had use for every word the Holy Spirit had spoken. We supposed ourselves to know nothing when we approached the sacred books, and were to be mere listeners and thereby learners. We had no proof-texts before us, implying a preoccupied mind, but accepted simply the *statements* of divine truth in the connection in which the Holy Spirit had placed the words and sentences he had uttered.[51]

Sometime later, another great "Bible restorer" said,

In saying that we receive this book as the only rule of faith, we mean, first, that we receive all of its utterances as true in the sense which properly belongs to them, and therefore as objects of belief; and second, that nothing else, as a matter of religious belief, is to be required of us. Of course, this does not bind us to any book now printed in the Bible which may prove to have been improperly inserted, or to any passage in any book which may prove to be an uninspired interpolation. In receiving it as the only rule of practice, we bind ourselves in conscience to observe all that

---

51. P.S. Fall, as quoted by Robert Richardson, *Memoirs of Alexander Campbell*, II, pp. 121-22.

it appoints for us to do, distinguishing what it appoints for us from what it appointed for others in former dispensations; and we refuse to be bound by anything which it does not thus appoint.[52]

This explanation immediately calls for our second conclusion:

2. The Bible *must be properly exegeted.* Our divine record of authority must be carefully and accurately understood lest we make it null and void as the only rule of faith and practice. We do not wish to be guilty of misplacing, misrepresenting, or misusing our only holy instruction book. Thus, with mental precision we seek to examine the content of the Biblical record by following all the laws of common sense.

The method of the liberal is just the reverse. Rather than use the Bible as the supreme authority and reason the tool, he begins with reason as authoritative, and the Bible as his toy. He proceeds to cut out, eliminate, enhance, alter, glorify, to suit the experience and play of his reason. Rather than exegesis, there is "exit-Jesus," according to D. R. Dungan.[53] There is no real problem of exegesis, no such problem as involved in this book. "Exegesis" (drawing out of) is replaced by "eisegesis" (reading into). Issues of faith, precedent, and opinion all precipitate into one general attitude—these are matters of "one's own viewpoint."

Thus, all areas of Bible thought dwindle down to mere opinion. And mental exercise is the only good that can ever come from such discussion.

---

52. J. W. McGarvey, "Grounds on Which We Receive the Bible as the Word of God," *The Old Faith Restated,* J.H. Garrison, ed., p. 11.
53. D. R. Dungan, *Hermeneutics* (Delight, Ark.: Gospel Light, reprint of 1888 ed.), p. 68.

PRECEPT: AUTHORITY

Contrary to this is the authoritative direction of Scripture. When each Christian dutifully attains an understanding of this message he will truly "grow in the grace and knowledge of our Lord and Savior Jesus Christ" (II Peter 3:18).

But one caution! Let not a man, even with honest purpose, violate the word of Peter: "But know this first of all, that no prophecy of Scripture is a matter of one's own interpretation, for no prophecy was ever made by an act of human will, but men moved by the Holy Spirit spoke from God" (II Peter 1:20, 21).

This truth is of primary importance. *Never* is the Scripture a matter of reading in one's own interpretation — whether it be writer or reader. We must not come to the study of the Bible with our minds already made up on what it means, rather we must read the Bible with a willingness to learn the thoughts God expressed therein by inspiration.

How many inspired writers ever fully comprehended the significance of what they wrote down for the Lord? Thus, as readers we must never inject *our word* or *our will* into God's.

One of the very first statements of a great freedom charter by Thomas Campbell naturally began thus:

> We are also persuaded that as no man can be *judged* for his brother, so no man can *judge* for his brother: but that every man must be allowed to judge for himself, as every man must bear his own judgment: must give an account of himself to God . . . that as the divine word is equally binding upon all, so all lie under equal obligation to be bound by it, and it alone; and not by any human interpretation of it.[54]

His son, Alexander, in turn elaborated on the issue by answering:

---

54. Thomas Campbell, *Declaration and Address*, p. 1.

WHAT THE BIBLE SAYS ABOUT FAITH AND OPINION

Of what use, then, is the Bible to the bulk of mankind, if you are not to presume to examine it for yourselves, or to think yourselves capable of judging of it? This is to make you the dupes of haughty leaders, who will cause you to err. To attempt, directly or indirectly, to dissuade you from thinking and examining for yourselves, by putting creeds already framed into your hands, or the works of men instead of a pure Word, is, in my opinion, so far depriving you of the key of knowledge.[55]

All men can and must know the Scriptures. Is it asking too much to expect man to rise above the "laity" philosophy — and eat heartily of the "bread of life" rather than nibble patiently at the crumbs cast down by the "Clergy"? Where in Scripture has the Lord sanctioned the dole system? And yet, this pitiful system has colored all post-apostolic church history. This has been the curse of the dark ages, and the plight of the reformation.

J. M. Trible points out that Protestanism fell into the same folly that characterized the Roman system:

> In Luther's time the pope and the councils had usurped for themselves the common right of all Christians to interpret the Scriptures. But no sooner had Protestantism wrested this right of interpretation from the pope, than it began to transfer it to the creeds and to the clergy. And so, two centuries later, we find the Bible again chained and sealed, no man daring to go contrary to the creed in his interpretation, except at the peril of excommunication.[56]

In view of this, Alexander Campbell again asked:

---

55. Robert Richardson, *Memoirs of Alexander Campbell*, Vol. II, p. 27.
56. J. M. Trible, "Reformation in the Church," *The Old Faith Restated*, J.H. Garrison, ed., p. 305.

PRECEPT: AUTHORITY

> What is the great difference between withholding the Scriptures from the laity, as the Romanists do, and rendering them unintelligible by arbitrary interpretation, forced criticisms and fanciful explanations, as many Protestants do, or making the people believe that they are nearly unintelligible by urging the necessity of what is called a learned clergy to explain them? If a translation can only be understood through the originals, might it not as well have been withheld? If the labors of a learned clergy be still necessary to render a translation intelligible, upon whose skill and fidelity as translators and upon whose judgment as expositors the people must still rely, and to whom they must still look up as their religious guides and dictators, of what use is a translation?[57]

Thus, Mr. Campbell liked the freedom of Bible interpretation shown in his early days by the Independent Movement in Scotland, for here a man had a right to judge for himself the meaning of Scripture. This was not allowed in the Presbyterian Church or the Church of England—as well as the great Roman Church. A plea for tolerance was made to the Presbyterian Church—in regard to all Protestant doctrine. To this, one Presbyterian cried:

> Toleration will make the kingdom a chaos, a Babel, another Amsterdam, a Sodom, an Egypt, a Babylon: toleration is the grand work of the devil, his masterpiece and chief engine to uphold his tottering kingdom: it is the most compendious, sure way to destroy all religion, lay all waste, and bring in all evil. As original sin is the fundamental sin, having the seed and spawn of all sin it it, so toleration hath all errors in it and all evils.[58]

---

57. Robert Richardson, *Memoirs of Alexander Campbell*, Vol. II, p. 41.
58. *Craik's History of England*, Book VII, Chap. II.

WHAT THE BIBLE SAYS ABOUT FAITH AND OPINION

This movement of "restorationism" (cf. Chapter 5) was an attitude against this unholy fallacy of a "holy interpreter." Truth is not a clergy's exclusive right to know or impart. And the great reformer contrasted the futile efforts of his father, Thomas, to introduce various reforms, especially in regard to the Lord's Supper, only to be rejected by the Presbytery and Synod (who had no desire to change), with the glorious freedom of the Independents.

What unholy things have been born in the name of interpretation. As an old veteran once remarked: "Interpretation is making the Bible mean a lot of things it doesn't say." Too many have violated the injunction of the Apostle Paul (I Timothy 1:8), that we never use the Law unlawfully. This same rule applies to the gospel as well as the Law. But each must strictly seek to "be diligent to present yourself approved to God as a workman who does not need to be ashamed, handling accurately the word of truth" (II Timothy 2:15).

The scholar, Albert Barnes, warned, possibly with a little too much agnosticism:

> It is not to be assumed, then, by the Christian or the infidel, that we have in fact, in our creeds and in our interpretation of the Bible, *precisely* the system which was revealed. That we have the true *record* in the Bible we are to believe, and the infidel may hold us to that; but we have the proper *interpretation* of that record is not to be assumed as certain.[59]

The obvious premise that underlies this whole issue, as stated by Z. T. Sweeney, is that "authority *precedes* the

---

59. Albert Barnes, *The Evidences of Christianity in the 19th Century*, (New York: Harper and Brothers, 1870), p. 354.

PRECEPT: AUTHORITY

giving of a message; interpretation *follows* the giving of the message."[60]
Thus cautioned A. B. Bruce:

> Recognizing Him as an authority in his general attitude of reverence for the Scriptures, we must further recognize Him as an authority in His discriminating use of the Scriptures. Nay, in the very fact of that discriminating use we must recognize Christ setting Himself as an authority above the Scriptures. He judges them, teaches the right, reasonable, profitable method of using them, as opposed to the wrong. Loyalty to Him as the supreme authority requires that we should accept His verdict, and use the sacred writings in His spirit; *and above all, that we should be careful not so to use them that He shall be eclipsed and His own teaching made void.*[61]

This whole matter may be likened unto the three legal branches of the government of the United States. First, is Congress with its authority and responsibility to make law. Secondly, the President is authorized to enforce the law. And, lastly, the Supreme Court, as the judicial body, must sanction or disapprove the law according to a standard, the Constitution. What destruction can be wrought on law, as great as it might be, by this third body!

So in Christianity, man has at times deliberately, and often unknowingly, reverently stepped aside as God made and enforced His holy law — only to flagrantly destroy its total effect by "unconstitutionalizing" it out the window through "his interpretation." Many would raise their voices

---

60. Z. T. Sweeney, *New Testament Christianity*, III, p. 505.
61. A. B. Bruce, *Apologetics*, p. 508.

in horror and protest at such an accusation—however, the record of church history stands.

Alexander Campbell's simple rule was this:

> Let us simply promulgate them [glad tidings—Scripture] in all their simplicity and force, unmixed with theory, uncorrupted with philosophy, uncomplicated with speculation and unfettered by system, and mark the issue.[52]

Man must cease using the Bible as a charm, and start using it as a message. Has not man made it just another Jewish "phylactery"—wearing it about his person as an ornament? To know it, quote it, possess it, or to wear it, is not necessarily sufficient. It must be treated as a message. Its thought content must be taken as the *only* rule of faith and practice or the whole matter is in vain.

Now, the Bible is God's word. But what is meant by this? One vital and final ramification of this issue is now noted. J. W. McGarvey touches it off with this observation:

> In saying that we receive the Bible as the word of God, we distinguish between the word of God and the words of God. We do not mean that all of its words are words of God; for some of them are recorded as the words of angels, some as the words of men, some as those of demons, and some as those of Satan. We mean that it is God's word in the sense that God, by the inspiration of its writers, caused to be written this record of things that were said and done by himself and certain of his creatures.[63]

In view of this, the following problem is immediately noted:

---

62. Robert Richardson, *Memoirs of Alexander Campbell*, Vol. II, p. 155.
63. J. W. McGarvey, "Ground on Which We Receive the Bible as the Word of God," *The Old Faith Restated*, J.H. Garrison, ed., p. 11.

PRECEPT: AUTHORITY

All who receive the Bible as the word of God agree that it is a divinely appointed rule of faith and conduct. They agree that if a man denies any part of the Bible, interpolated passages excepted, he is to that extent unsound in the faith; if he refuses to obey any precept among those now binding, he is to that extent sinful; and that in both cases he is to be dealt with accordingly by the church and by individual disciples.[64]

What of this problem? What is the intensity of authority in the various portions as the whole is divided? Does it not make a vast difference who is speaking to whom, when, or under what condition and time?

It is definitely true that *all* the Bible is divine, no matter who spoke, etc. There is a vast difference between saying, "The Bible contains the word of God," and "The Bible is the Word of God." Some claim there is a distinction between the Bible and the word of God. They view the word as a precious metal, and must be separated from the foreign (human) elements with which it is intermingled. Some claim the work of the Holy Spirit is to come into the individual heart, and separate the human from the divine. This leads to the conclusion that one man's opinion of what God ought to have said is what God actually has said. This is little better than the Roman idea—human conscience being the authority.

Let no one deny, as B. C. Deweese declares, that:

> The word spoken by angels was just as divine as the Sermon on the Mount, and this is not denying that the letter manifests a higher type of thought and duty. We who have heard all our lives sermons on rightly dividing the Word should appreciate this position. The failure to discriminate between dispensations is fruitful of error.[65]

---

64. *Ibid.*, pp. 44-45.
65. B. C. Deweese, *Missouri Christian Lectures* (St. Louis: Christian Publishing Co., 1892), p. 141.

WHAT THE BIBLE SAYS ABOUT FAITH AND OPINION

However, these factors mentioned above do make a difference in Christian faith and duty. There is an authoritative difference for man today. As Deweese continues:

> The Bible is what it is, with its history, its human sayings, its prophetic visions, its law, its poetry, its biographies, because God made it so. Here we must face alleged difficulties about inspiration. In the Bible are long speeches filled with bad advice and unsound argument, historical narratives, and some words from the devil himself. Are all these elements inspired? Let us not confuse our minds by false issues. Because these things find place in the Bible, nobody claims that bad arguments, or the devil's views, must be adopted. Inspiration is responsible for a correct report of what man thought and said, and of Satan's efforts to ruin him; but it does not stand responsible for the soundness of the reasoning of Job's friends, for example. The Bible records these things to show us that in manifesting himself as man's Redeemer, God understood the case—that he met the real issues before man. We could not see the full significance of God's speech in the closing chapters of Job, were it not that we have such fine groundwork in the speeches that precede it. It corrects their faulty teaching, and shows the way out of darkness.[66]

It does make a difference in the weight of authority, whether one is reading Paul's word to Christians, Peter's words to the unsaved at Pentecost, Jesus' words to the Jews, Gamaliel's advice to the council, or James' words to the church at Antioch. Only that which God intended should be binding on a particular man today—should be left binding, no more or no less. This is the problem of precept, precedent, and opinion under the last covenant given man through Jesus Christ.

---

66. *Ibid.*, pp. 142-43.

PRECEPT: AUTHORITY

As J. W. McGarvey concludes the issue by saying,

Because the Old Testament was the God-given law of the old dispensation, and is still binding on the faith of Christians, many have concluded that it is still binding as our rule of conduct; but the New Testament makes it clear that this conclusion is erroneous. The voice of God in the scene of the transfiguration, proclaiming, in the presence of Moses the lawgiver and of Elijah the prophet, "this is my beloved Son: hear ye him," made Jesus not only the supreme, but the only lawgiver in the new dispensation. In compliance with this proclamation, we are taught by the Apostle Paul that while the law was our tutor to bring us to Christ, now that faith is come we are no longer under the tutor; that Christ has abolished, in his flesh, the law of commandments contained in ordinances; that the first Covenant, having been found defective, has vanished away and given place to the second. In this change from the old to the new, much of the old has been re-enacted, including all that was originally intended to be perpetual and universal. This part is binding now, not because it was in the old, but because it is re-enacted in the new. The New Testament is, then, the divine rule of discipline under Christ; and our final question is, whether it is the only rule, whether it excludes all rules devised by the wisdom of men.[67]

In closing, there is no more noble endeavor than that of fully restoring the authority of Jesus Christ, the Son of God.

---

67. J. W. McGarvey, *op. cit.*, p. 45.

Chapter Three
PRECEPT DEFINED

Although man wants liberty, he needs law. In the words of Heraclitus of Ephesus, twenty-five hundred years ago, "The major problem of human society is to combine that degree of liberty without which law is tyranny with that degree of law without which liberty becomes license."

Without a sound and equitable system of law there can be no liberty; few of the precious freedoms would survive.

The bill of rights found in the Constitution of the United States is cherished by every grateful citizen. But the bill of rights *must* be preceded by a bill of law. This principle is as basic as the everyday system of chastisement and reward exercised on every new child brought into the world.

That old trite political cry, "You can't legislate virtue," is heard again and again. In other words it is futile to try and make people better than they really are by simply passing a law.

At times and under certain conditions, this maxim may seem to have logical substance. Nevertheless, in regard to the Man-God relationship, law is God's implement for accomplishing His holy purpose.

Man has always had the tendency toward tyranny. This was shown in the Eden record at the very beginning. Man did not have to be such. He just chose such. Law is God's right and God's answer to this condition. Law, or precept, is good for man; it was conceived, designed, and produced for man. It really is more natural than tyranny itself.

> The law of the LORD is perfect, restoring the soul;
> The testimony of the LORD is sure, making wise the simple.
> The precepts of the LORD are right, rejoicing the heart;
> The commandment of the LORD is pure, enlightening the eyes
> (Psalm 19:7, 8).

PRECEPT: PRECEPT DEFINED

To the good man, law is fitting and appropriate to secure decency and happiness. And in addition it assures him that the vile indecency of others shall not destroy his rights. To the wicked it aims to be corrective, pointing him toward the system of life God intended when he made man in the very beginning.

All Scripture is inspired by God and profitable for teaching, for reproof, for correction, for training in righteousness; that the man of God may be adequate, equipped for every good work (II Timothy 3:16, 17).

The end of the matter is simply: we need law because God said so. Now, what is the substance of law or precept? What form does it actually take—in the written record called the Bible? Law is "a rule of conduct, or action prescribed by the supreme governing authority and enforced by a sanction, as any edict, decree, order, ordinance, statute, judicial decision, etc."[1] A precept is "any commandment, instruction, or order intended as a rule of action or conduct; esp., a practical rule guiding behavior, technique, etc."[2] Now that the attempt has been made to delineate clearly the authority over us today (Chapter 2), we must ask what is the exact area of precept emanating from this authoritative source—the Scripture? Can it be exactly defined?

With precept being authoritative man has but two responsibilities. He must understand the scope of precept (not always the reason and motive behind it) and obey it. It is not his to decide on its validity by compromise, debate, concensus of opinion (popular vote), judicial decision, delegate decision or council decision. Man must not continually debate feasibility of precept—he must only dig for

---

1. "Law," *Webster's New Collegiate Dictionary* (Springfield, Mass.: G. & C. Meriam Co., 1956), p. 476.
2. "Precept," *Ibid.*, p. 664.

a perfect understanding of its holy content. "Cease striving and know that I am God" (Psalm 46:10). It would be well for man today to avoid the folly of Saul by heeding the prophet Samuel, when he warned, "Has the LORD as much delight in burnt offerings and sacrifices as in obeying the voice of the LORD? Behold, to obey is better than sacrifice, and to heed than the fat of rams" (I Samuel 15:22).

As it is recorded in the episode of the Jerusalem Council (Acts 15), the "necessary things" were those things which seemed good to the Holy Spirit. The whole church was thus brought to one judgment. And they abided by this judgment.

Man today had better go back and be refreshed by God's instruction to His prophets (Ezekiel 11). They were to say repeatedly to the people, "Thus says the Lord." That was sufficient. That settled the matter once and for all. Every precept of the Lord handled accurately must be taken at its face value.

Christianity (as well as all former covenant relationships of God with man) is a revealed "religion" — God has spoken His mind and has had it recorded. This is the Bible. So, when God speaks we have no right to project our thoughts, conjectures and judgments in the areas where God has already revealed His mind. Man has no right to argue with, ignore or "toy with" a "thus says the Lord." When God speaks and delivers His law (precept) man should respond in but one way — believe it, have confidence in it, trust it, conjoined with obedience to it — all of which manifests the meaning of the Greek word, *pistis,* faith or belief. The word in New Testament usage has different shades of meaning (knowledge of revelation, mental assent to its meaning, confidence or trust in it and obedience), depending on the particular context of the passage under consideration.[3] This

---

3. For further study I refer the reader to Gareth L. Reese, *New Testament History — Acts* (Joplin, Mo.: College Press, 1976), pp. 598-610.

PRECEPT: PRECEPT DEFINED

is why this area is often called "matters of faith." The liberal evades this issue with the apology that, after all, Jesus did not give petty laws and precepts, but that He merely laid down general principles and attitudes. Possibly the liberal has overlooked the great commission (an exact phrasing of a precept if there ever was one); or again, the word of Jesus, Himself, "If you love Me, you will keep my commandments" (John 14:15).

Was the great sermon on the mount such a lesson on "attitudes"? Then notice the conclusion of the sermon (Matthew 7:24-27). The wise man is the man who hears Christ's words and obeys them. J. S. Lamar's comment on the early "restoration" leaders reveals the soundness of this kind of obedience today:

> Their faith, their rule of faith, their confession of faith, their conditions of salvation, their bond and test of fellowship, were not inferences from the New Testament, and which might or might not have been accurately drawn, but were presented in the exact language of that book—were indeed a careful and scrupulous reproduction of apostolic teaching and precedent.[4]

R. C. Foster has pointed out that this practice does not make man guilty of being either a Bibliolator, a book worshipper, nor a legalist.[5]

Man has attempted to ignore or toy with the precepts of the Lord again and again. But, he should never allow any "seeming truth"—no matter how it has been tried and tested by experience—to surpass in weight a simple and direct precept of the Lord. This whole scope of Christian truth—whether precept appears as a positive commandment, prohibition, or categorical statement—becomes the

---

4. J. S. Lamar, *Memoirs of Isaac Errett*, Vol. I (Cincinnati: Standard Publishing, 1893), p. 225.
5. R. C. Foster, *Christian Standard* (November 30, 1946), p. 3.

WHAT THE BIBLE SAYS ABOUT FAITH AND OPINION

essentials of the Christian system. And essentials are not debatable, equivocal, nor indifferent. Alexander Campbell declared that:

> The Christian institution has its facts, its precepts, its promises, its ordinances, and their meaning or doctrine. These are not matters of policy, of arrangement, of expediency, but of divine and immutable ordination and continuance. Hence the faith, the worship, and the righteousness; or the doctrine, the piety, and the morality of the gospel institution are not legitimate subjects of human legislation, alteration, or arrangement. No man nor community can touch these and be innocent. These rest upon the wisdom and authority of Jehovah; and he that meddles with these presumes to do that which the cherubim and seraphim dare not. Whatever, then, is a part of the Christian faith or the Christian hope — whatever constitutes ordinances or precepts of worship, or statutes of moral right and wrong, like the ark of the covenant, is not to be touched with uninspired and uncommissioned hands.[6]

The old story is told of a son who remarked to his father, "Father, how soon will I be old enough to do as I please?" To which the father replied, "I don't know. No one has ever lived that long yet." No man has the right to do as he pleases unless he pleases to do right. When God speaks, man keeps still. When God's will is evident, man's will must be silent. The restoration fathers preached the simple dictum, "Where the Bible speaks, we speak; where the Bible is silent; we are silent."

How can precept have any value at all if it becomes arbitrary? Precept from the Lord ceases to be such if it allows man the right to decide on its validity. As John B. Cowden said:

---

6. Alexander Campbell, *The Christian System* (Nashville, Tenn.: Gospel Advocate Co., 1974 reprint of 1939 ed.), p. 74.

PRECEPT: PRECEPT DEFINED

There is, therefore, no liberty to do or not to do the things prescribed by the Spirit of the Lord. Paul was the spokesman of the Spirit on matters pertaining to Christian liberty; but he never granted the liberty to do or not to do what Christ commanded. He insisted on the liberty of doing or not doing what Moses commanded, as, for instance, circumcision and all other requirements of the Jewish law, saying, "for freedom did Christ set us free; stand fast, therefore, and be not entangled again in a yoke of bondage," but what the Lord Jesus Christ prescribed through the Spirit must be obeyed; and only by obedience thereunto is freedom secured. "His commands are not grievous," but "reasonable," and insure liberty the highest type. They constitute the essentials of Christian unity, and define the requirements of Christian loyalty, which consists of strict obedience and faithful conformity to what Christ requires. Through such loyalty liberty is gained, and unity is secured, because Christian loyalty requires the same things of all; and the two are thereby connected and harmonized.[7]

It is much easier to preach this rule, than to practice it. To apply it to life means a progression of Christian life, a development of character, an advancement in faith and obedience. The "restoration fathers" soon were aware of the revolutionary consequences of practicing this principle. For example, the issue of "infant baptism" began to appear in meeting after meeting, following the public pronouncement of the rule. Finally, after it had been repeatedly cast aside as being a matter of indifference, it was squarely faced by Alexander Campbell. He was forced by all that was logical and honest, to either abandon the principle or answer the particular problem which it raised. From time to time theologians have made this point clear. The late Karl Barth wrote

---

7. John B. Cowden, *St. Paul on Christian Unity* (New York: Fleming H. Revell Co., 1923), p. 191.

about it in his study of baptism in the New Testament: "From the standpoint of a doctrine of baptism, infant baptism can hardly be preserved without exegetical and practical artifices and sophisms — the proof to the contrary has yet to be supplied! One wants to preserve it only if one is resolved to do so on grounds which lie outside the Biblical passages on baptism and outside the thing in itself."[8]

The liberal has cried out for local autonomy (personal or congregational) when often the issue is one of divine precept. This has been one of the pleas for the practice of "open-membership." Has the church, or any segment, or any association of churches, any right to make a regulation — where God has already done so? Let man heed this rule: local autonomy is *always* limited by sovereign autonomy.

No matter how often nor how flagrantly divine precept is violated, it gives no freedom for another to violate it to any degree. The apostle Paul was aware of this as he gave a much-needed rebuke to one whom he had no right to rebuke (Acts 23). Others, in their treatment of the apostle, had continually over-looked the law of God. However, this gave him no "speck of freedom" to be disobedient to the Lord.

Law has a concrete form. It can not, it must not, be twisted, diluted, nor evaded to satisfy personal desires. This practice is the curse of civil law. Earl L. Douglass relates the following incident:

> No Parking From Here to Corner!
> He can read as well as anyone else, and furthermore, he can see that the front wheels of his car are already abreast of that sign. There is no more parking space left.

---

8. Karl Barth, *The Teaching of The Church Regarding Baptism* (London: SCM Press, 1948), p. 49.

PRECEPT: PRECEPT DEFINED

But what's he doing? He's parking right in front of that other car. . . . Well of all things! He's moving that parking sign up to the front of his own car. And there he goes down the street whistling and stopping now and again to look into a store window. He hasn't broken the law; he has stretched a city ordinance to meet his convenience.

Some people treat all laws that way, especially the Ten Commandments. When these interfere with convenience, they stretch them out a bit. When high heaven itself sets a limit in matters of conduct beyond which they cannot go without breaking the moral law and violating their conscience, they should worry; they move the No-Parking sign. Their slogan is, "If you don't like the way a law operates, make it operate the way you like."

It's amazing how far some people can stretch the thou-shalt-nots of the Decalogue without actually breaking them.[9]

There is hardly a law made that can not be stretched or circumvented. Divine precept is no exception. If the desire and reason are strong enough, one can rationalize a portion of it away.

But the exact pattern and substance of precept must be religiously preserved by every one professing guidance by the word of the Lord as recorded in Scripture. Alexander Campbell warned that:

Positive ordinances are belittled by most parties who have substituted human institution for divine enactments. They enthrone their *beau-ideal* of the Christian virtues under the name of "Christian Charity," and desecrate divine ordinances under the name of "Rites and Ceremonies." But let me say it once and for all, and most emphatically, that Divine ordinances are the very marrow and fatness of the

---

9. Earl L. Douglass, *Youngstown Vindicator*, August 11, 1949.

Christian institution — the embodiment of its spiritual promises, joys and consolations. They are like the sun, moon and stars, those Divine ordinances of nature in which and through which God communicates light and life and health to the world. They are as the dew, and the sunshine, and the early and the later rain, to our hills and valleys, that make them verdant and fruitful, and vocal with the praise of the Lord.[10]

What rules might one well know if he has good intention of knowing the patterns and substance of precept? 1. First, precept need not always be fully understood in order for it to be accepted (and obeyed, if a command). Failing to comprehend fully does not preclude faith and obedience. But the lack of knowledge is the very opportunity of faith and obedience. Robert Richardson illustrates it this way:

> As the child who refuses to obey his father until the latter first explains to him the particular reasons for his commands, shows that he acts not from love and trust, but that he disbelieves and doubts, and prefers the conclusions of his own feeble understanding to reliance upon superior wisdom, so the individual who must know the philosophy of God's commandments, and satisfy himself as to their propriety before he will obey them believes not in God, but in himself . . . it is not permitted that reason should take the place of Faith, or that human views of expediency should usurp the province of Divine wisdom.[11]

Many so-called higher critics seek to probe the mind and heart of Jesus for every motive, reason, and feeling behind precept. Inference is thus pushed so high in importance that clear precept loses all, or nearly all, of its power. Is man ever so intelligent that he can reason behind each precept,

---

10. Alexander Campbell, *Popular Lectures and Addresses* (Cincinnati, OH: Standard Publishing, 1863), p. 627.
11. Robert Richardson, *Memoirs of Alexander Campbell*, I, pp. 406-7.

PRECEPT: PRECEPT DEFINED

see its holy design, and thus use or not use it according to his own discretion?

2. There is the positive and the negative aspect of precept. Both are essential. One complements the other. For instance, we have the positive injunction of Jude, "contend earnestly for the faith which was once for all delivered to the saints" (Jude 3). Mr. Campbell comments on this:

> He [Jude] saw the efforts to introduce new things by the converted Jews and pagans, incorporated in the Christian family, and in the midst of these efforts wrote this epistle. Such a precept, emanating from such circumstances, is equivalent to a positive prohibition of every thing but *the faith*, the truth, the identical words commended by apostles and prophets, as the foundation of the Christian temple, and the constitution of the Christian church.[12]

3. There is often an over-lapping of different precepts within the scope of a single problem. Precepts are often such that two or more of them have certain ramifications in one single problem. Such a case is the problem of the Christian view of war. Does war have both good and evil in it? What then shall be done with the word of Paul, "Abhor what is evil; cleave to what is good"? (Romans 12:9). Must not the Christian honestly and intelligently weigh every precept relative to the problem, and then, as does the physician, make a decision based on the "totality of symptoms"? God has a will in the matter, and man must find it and abide by it, to the best of his ability.

4. One precept may limit, define, or qualify another. In reading the Christian injunction that saints are not to be

---

[12]. Alexander Campbell, *A Debate Between Rev. A. Campbell and Rev. N. L. Rice* (Nashville, Tenn.: Gospel Advocate, reprint of 1844 ed.), p. 819.

"bound together with unbelievers" (II Corinthians 6:14-18), we would immediately take it as a blanket prohibition. And yet, in reading the law (I Corinthians 7:12-17) governing this condition when found in the home (between those already married), we see that the prohibition is reversed. This latter precept merely qualifies the first in a given situation.

5. A precedent may limit, define, or qualify a precept. (See Chapter 8, pp. 154-162.)

6. Precepts complement one another. Precepts are not mere isolated regulations—but parts of a system of life and truth. Man must therefore, seek to know them relatively as well as singly. He must associate parts of truth to ascertain the whole truth. The more a man knows about all precepts the more he ought to know about them separately. A good case in point is the important subject of "What must a person do to be saved?"

7. Precepts must be properly divided. Whether or not a precept was addressed to a believer or an unbeliever can make all the difference in the world. (See Chapter 5.) Who is the writer? When was it written? What is the place or circumstance of the writing? These are all vital issues. The local situation of a precept is a vital point. If this issue is neglected, then man violates the very things which an inspired man commanded of an uninspired man, "But we know that the law is good, if one uses it lawfully" (I Timothy 1:8).

Do different precepts carry different measures of weight? Surely precept is absolute. But, for instance—what about the qualifications for Elders (I Timothy 3:1-7; Titus 1:5-9) and Deacons (I Timothy 3:8-13) as indicated in Scripture? In what sense are these absolute? Are they to be rigid rules, and man may never elect any one to this work unless the candidate is qualified to fulfill every detail? Or is it absolute

PRECEPT: PRECEPT DEFINED

in that it is the only divine guide that man should use in selecting others to do this work? Or is it absolute only in the sense that it is the ideal goal, and only those men who are attempting to reach this goal and who are the nearest to the goal, of the men available, should be selected?

Without entering into an exhaustive study of the principles of good Bible exegesis, we conclude this portion of discussion on precept with a grave warning. Let each one, in his study of the meaning of precepts, be guided by the scientific principles of good exegesis, so that there will be imparted to his mind the identical meanings intended by the inspired writers.

Now in regard to precept there is a strange paradox. It has already been stated that when God declares or legislates, man has no liberty to speak nor command. However, there is a type of liberty within the scope of precept. (See Chapter 9.) As we sing over and over again:

> America! America!
> God mend thine every flaw,
> Confirm thy soul in self-control
> Thy liberty in law.[13]

Some one has said that all men are slaves, but with the one choice of choosing his own master. Such it is morally. Man can serve God or the devil. If he chooses God as Master —then He will return a certain type and measure of liberty to the bond servant. This liberty is both a command and a promise of the Lord. In accepting Christ as the supreme authority of life there are two areas to be recognized, as W. R. Walker puts it:

---

13. Katherine Lee Bates

The first embraces all His teachings, personally, and also that of His inspired followers. This, for want of a better term, I shall call the "vocal area." But there is another area, one not so clearly defined, but discernible nevertheless, which I shall call, "the area of silence." This distinction has been recognized by Christian reformers and leaders through the centuries. An aphorism, "where the scriptures speak, we speak; where the scriptures are silent we are silent"; coined long ago, expresses the same thought.[14]

This second area, the liberty of private opinion, must be respected. That is law in itself. Remember, there is "a time to be silent, and a time to speak" (Ecclesiastes 3:7). When God authoritatively designated a certain area of life to be governed by man's own will, or by a consensus of wills, then man must recognize it. This is the authority for the field of opinion. (See Part III.)

The question arises at this point: What kind of freedom does man want? Politically, if a man desires freedom from ownership, responsibility of private achievement, venture of private enterprise, let him choose the tyranny of materialistic communism. However, if he desires freedom from fear, mental slavery, despotic regimentation, let him choose genuine democracy.

So it is in religion. What kind of freedom does the religionist want? The type of freedom must correspond to its benefactor. As the late Frederick Gielow, Jr. said, "Every element of freedom has its corresponding element of bondage or necessity. The question is, 'What type of bondage shall we choose to correlate with our liberty?' "[15] Thus, if man would hold the freedom he desires he must remember the

---

14. W. R. Walker, *Christian Unity Quarterly* (April, 1943), p. 7.
15. Frederick J. Gielow, *Christian Standard* (January 18, 1941), p. 5.

word of Thomas Jefferson, "Eternal vigilance is the price of liberty." The record of church history is proof that man has seldom been willing to pay the price. Man is a creature to be *influenced*. And as soon as the holy oversight of the apostles was lost to the church, she began to waver, with increasing intensity as the years passed, under the great influences of her day: Greek culture, oriental cults, paganism, and Roman politics. The latter exerted great influence, emanating primarily from Rome, and was seen to blossom in the Roman Catholic Church in the centuries to follow.

Frederick Kershner wrote:

> The genius of Roman politics was essentially monarchial and imperialistic. Everything centered in the imperial city of the Caesar. There was a glamour about the very name of Rome which attracted universal attention. The idea of individual freedom was gradually swallowed up in the idea of ordered autocracy.[16]

Nathaniel Taylor once said, "In order to be free, a man must be able to do not only as he pleases, but to do as he doesn't please." The freedom of Christ is complete submission to His will. It is being led by God's Spirit. And the Word is the word of the Spirit.

One cannot "love God, and do what you please," as Augustine said. Freedom is not license. It is not a freedom to do evil. "For you were called to freedom, brethren; only do not turn your freedom into an opportunity for the flesh, but through love serve one another" (Galatians 5:13).

In Paul's two great letters (Romans and Galatians) on justification by faith in Christ, rather than works of law (See Chapter 4), he gives the solemn warning that this principle does not allow license, but requires obedience.

---

16. Frederick Kershner, *The Restoration Handbook*, IV, pp. 22-23.

WHAT THE BIBLE SAYS ABOUT FAITH AND OPINION

Liberty must have limits. Adam and Eve were given all fruit of the garden to eat, but one. That was one restriction within a host of liberties. Disobedience to the said law deprived them of some of those liberties. This story has been repeated in the life of every sinner. Therefore: "It was for freedom that Christ set us free; therefore keep standing firm and do not be subject again to a yoke of slavery" (Galatians 5:1).

Now, one important distinction in precept that must be made is that between its *moral* and its *ceremonial* aspects. Both come from the same God and are found in the same Book. However, they each operate in different spheres and carry different kinds of weight.

First, a moral law, or as it is often better called, a moral principle, is inherently right—right by its very nature. It is right because of the nature of God, its Author. For instance, consider the matter of "truth." Speaking the truth and not a lie is a moral law. With God as authority it could never be otherwise. Thus moral laws stand as irrevocable monuments on the pages of Scripture.

Secondly, what is ceremonial law—or positive divine law? It is not intrinsically or naturally right. It is right, not by reason, morality, observation, nor by necessity—but only because God said it was. That is necessity in itself. A thing is right when God declares it so. The first commandment given was such, "You shall not eat from it [tree of knowledge] or touch it, lest you die" (Genesis 3:3). What moral harm was here? As Voltaire asked, "What harm is there in eating an apple?" The harm is merely in the disobedience of a precept. It was a trial of faith. Whereas a moral law is a test of morality, ceremonial law is more of a test of faith.

PRECEPT: PRECEPT DEFINED

Benjamin Franklin said that there were three degrees in this test:
1. To obey when we can not see that the thing commanded can do any good in itself.
2. To obey when we can see pretty clearly that the thing commanded can *not* do any good in itself.
3. To obey when we can see that the thing commanded is clearly *wrong* in itself, morally speaking.[17]

Is there really this sharp distinction between moral and ceremonial law? Take one portion of Scripture for example, and examine the precepts. J. J. Haley writes:

> One can not read without some degree of astonishment the prohibitions that are indiscriminately mingled of the grossest sensual crimes and offenses that have in them no element of moral evil whatsoever. The yoking of an ox and an ass together, and the mixing of linen and woolen in the same garment are forbidden on the same page and in the same terms as the worst offense against morality. The distinction between moral and ceremonial law, and the classification of offenses accordingly, is the product of a later age and a higher religion.[18]

But the Bible is the progressive revelation of God to man, not the progressive discovery of God by man. Furthermore, in the New Testament what seems relatively trivial, such as not being "a troublesome meddler" is connected most intimately with warnings against murder and robbery (I Peter 4:15). This is in no sense an evidence of "a lower religion" or "an earlier age," but is only a common sense effort to deflate the latest egotism of the reader.

---

17. Benjamin Franklin, *New Testament Christianity*, II, ed. by Z. Sweeney, (Joplin, Mo.: College Press, reprint of 1926 ed.), pp. 126-27.
18. J. J. Haley, *Missouri Christian Lectures* (St. Louis: Christian Publishing Co., 1892), p. 173.

WHAT THE BIBLE SAYS ABOUT FAITH AND OPINION

Man is continually confusing these two issues. Sometimes he looks for a ceremonial (detailed) law when God may have only given a moral law. Or again, he may want the moral law to contain more specific details than God intended it to have. In regard to many modern questionable issues of amusement the Lord left a principle, not a list of specific regulations, e.g., "Abstain from every form of evil" (I Thessalonians 5:22). But what are the "forms"? Man must take this principle, along with other pertinent laws, and "work out your salvation with fear and trembling" (Philippians 2:12). Let us follow the example of the apostle as "Paul settles the humblest difficulties by appealing to the loftiest principles."[19]

But which is greater, or which carries the more weight— moral or ceremonial law? How shall they be related? Has man too often reverenced moral law at the expense of ceremonial law? Down through the ages, has he not been afflicted with the spirit of counting ceremonial law a matter of little consequence? What does the Bible say? And show?

J. V. Coombs says, "Just as sure as a man suffers when he violates physical or moral law, he will suffer when he transgresses positive law."[20] But suppose the two types of law clash in a single instance, what is man to do? Benjamin Franklin asks,

> What would you do if you should come to a positive commandment that would come in direct collision with moral law? Do you say that such a thing can never occur? But such a thing did occur. The question is not whether it

---

19. J. W. McGarvey, P. Y. Pendelton, *Thessalonians, Corinthians, Galatians, Romans* (Cincinnati, Ohio: Standard Publishing, 1916), p. 109.
20. J. V. Coombs, *The Christ of the Church* (Cincinnati, Ohio: Standard Publishing Co., 1916), p. 70.

occurred, or can occur, but what would you do in a case of this kind? Do you say that you would obey the moral law, and let the positive go? But you say, "Where did a case of that kind occur?" It occurred when God commanded Abraham to offer Isaac. It was wrong to kill, and worse to kill a child, and worst to kill an only child. The Lord called "Abraham!" the venerable patriarch and servant of God, never ashamed, but always ready, responded, "Here am I." The Lord proceeded, "Take thy son," and, as if to give it force and penetrate into the depths of his soul, he added: "Thine only son Isaac, whom thou lovest, and get thee into the land of Moriah; and offer him there for a burnt-offering upon one of the mountains which I will tell thee of."[21]

What was Abraham to do? How he could have rationalized out of this whole predicament. But he did not. He obeyed to the letter, until God stepped in and altered the case. Abraham, however, met the test of faith. The epistle to the Hebrews explains how Abraham was able to accomplish this supreme test of obedience: he believed that God "is able to raise men even from the dead" (Hebrews 11:19). The command of God was essential because God declared it such. And, when there is such a clash, the specific, definite command to an individual rose above the moral law. Man has no right to argue the issue—it is in itself a moral principle. Let man learn the lesson, and henceforth, never fall into the plight of Uzzah (II Samuel 6:6, 7). Here was a man (not a Levite) who was given a positive commandment not to touch the ark of the covenant. And yet, in the name of a great principle, he reached out his hand to save a toppling ark, only to suffer the punishment for disobedience. The law of good intentions never surpasses a positive divine law.

---

21. Benjamin Franklin, *New Testament Christianity*, II, p. 136.

WHAT THE BIBLE SAYS ABOUT FAITH AND OPINION

Now, what about the durability or stability of precept? Is law transient or permanent; changing or changeless? Unless this matter is understood man will either make the law of God so wide that it loses its authority, or else so narrow that it becomes contradictory. The whole issue revolves around the distinction which has just been made. Mr. Campbell marked the difference, thus:

> Moral laws, properly so called, are, indeed, immutable; because the principle of every moral law is *love,* and that never can cease to be not only a way and means, but the *only way* and *means,* to rational, to human happiness. Positive precepts, however, prescribing the *forms* of religious and moral action, emanating from God himself, have been changed, and may again be changed, while all the elements of piety and morality are immutable.[22]

A moral principle is immutable while positive (ceremonial) divine law is variable. As our fathers used to quote, "Methods are many, principles are few; methods may vary; principles never do." How can a moral principle, by its very nature, be anything but permanent? How can God abrogate His moral law? As I. B. Grubbs has written:

> From the very nature of the Divine law and its relation to the character of God, as the mirror of his changeless attributes, we see that in form alone, in essence never, is it subject to alteration. As an authoritative principle of moral obligation it can never pass away. The reign of law, so clearly observable in the physical world, is, with all its varying uniformity, but faintly indicative and illustrative of the still more imperative force of law in the moral universe. The laws of crystallization or of chemical combination, for example,

---

22. Alexander Campbell, *The Christian System,* p. 90.

though permanently fixed under the present order of things, may, without absurdity, be regarded as liable to infinite modification and final abrogation by the will of him who built up this beauteous temple of Nature. A different sort of world, with different adjustments and adaptations, is altogether conceivable. But the eternal harmony in the higher world of God is but the efflux of his own moral beauty, and in the depths of his being among his glorious perfections we find at once the source and explanations of the constitution of the moral universe. Above God, indeed, or beyond him, there is no law to which he is subject. But he is a law unto himself. In harmony with his own nature, his will must ever be; and it is on the former, rather than on the latter, that the foundations of morality immovably remain.[23]

The Apostle illustrates, by a single instance, the nature and perpetuity of ethical obligation, when he affirms that "it is impossible for God to lie." This means that he can never revoke the law, which says: "Thou shalt not bear false testimony against thy neighbor." But this again is equivalent to saying that God's moral law is binding, not because of its presence in either Testament, but because it is the reflection of his own unchangeable character and attributes.[24]

For instance, it is a moral principle that man is to live by faith—under any dispensation. By faith a man pleases the Lord (Hebrews 11:6). This is the immutable approach. And yet God may use a host of methods and systems at different times to implement and test that faith.

When Jesus was asked what was the first commandment, He answered, "You shall love the LORD your God with all your heart, and with all your soul, and with all your mind.

---

23. I. B. Grubbs, *Commentary on Paul's Epistle to the Romans* (Nashville, Tenn.: Gospel Advocate, reprint of 1913 ed.), pp. 62-63.
24. Ibid., p. 65.

WHAT THE BIBLE SAYS ABOUT FAITH AND OPINION

This is the great and foremost commandment. And a second is like it, You shall love your neighbor as yourself" (Matthew 22:37-39). This is basic and absolute, no matter where we read it in Scripture. It includes all righteousness and excludes all sin. It applied to Adam, to Moses, to David, to Paul, and now, it applies to man today. The Mosaic law was soon to be superseded by a new system, as soon as Jesus could sign it with his own blood. It even had provisions within itself for its own termination. That is why Jesus said, "Do not think that I came to abolish the Law or the Prophets; I did not come to abolish, but to fulfill" (Matthew 5:17). And when a new ceremonial law was ratified and written in a new covenant, and in a new era (Christian) it was superior and final for this life. But, throughout this change, moral law remained changeless. That is why Jesus had to remind the strict Pharisees of moral principles. They buried moral law in heaping human traditions over ceremonial law.

This was no doubt His purpose in preaching the "Sermon on the Mount." And also, when He warned, "Woe to you, scribes and Pharisees, hypocrites! For you tithe mint and dill and cummin, and have neglected the weightier provisions of the law: justice and mercy and faithfulness; but these are the things you should have done without neglecting the others" (Matthew 23:23). Notice, "these are the things" (ceremonial) that still should have been done, as the Jew forgot not the moral principle. We quote J. J. Haley:

> In God's revelation to man there is nothing transient but method and form; in *substance* it is eternal, for truth in its essence is as imperishable as its Author. *Inspiration* was transient because it was the *method* of *revelation*, miracles were transient because it was the *method* of *authentication*

PRECEPT: PRECEPT DEFINED

of the truth revealed; all *symbolism* has in it an element of transiency because the truth symbolized may, and sometimes *must*, exist apart from its symbol. All forms are necessarily symbolical and constitute no *essential* part of the truth of which they are but the outward representation. When the truth has been communicated by inspiration, authenticated and certified by miracles, and its earlier forms of manifestation and preservation outgrown by expanding life and new conditions of growth, the old forms and methods drop away and perish, except as historic testimonials of the truth and development of spiritual life.[25]

This is typified in the matter of sacrifice in the two great covenants. In the Mosaic Law, the sacrifice (animal) was transient—awaiting the perfect sacrifice of Christ. In the Christian, the Lord's Supper is transient—only in the sense of the end of all time, remembering that perfect sacrifice—until it is passed away as the Christian sits down with the Lord once for all in heaven.

And yet, let every one be cautioned by the word of B. C. Deweese:

> Revelation can not be transient. There were transient ordinances and elementary instruction, but no transient revelation. Everything revealed remains forever a part of the knowledge imparted form on high, and will forever continue to produce its intended effects. Under the first covenant were "carnal ordinances, imposed until a time of reformation." The law led men to Christ. When He came we were no longer under the law. We go to Christ, not to Moses, for ordinances; but we go to both for God's revelation.[26]

---

25. J. J. Haley, *Missouri Christian Lectures*, pp. 186-87.
26. B. C. Deweese, *Missouri Christian Lectures*, p. 153.

WHAT THE BIBLE SAYS ABOUT FAITH AND OPINION

In conclusion, this whole matter of precept to the Christian, thus becomes a matter of absolute necessity. It is plainly a matter of faith. We say with Hall L. Calhoun:

> ... whenever God enjoins anything upon us it must be done, and whatever He prohibits must not be done. If domestic authorities interfere, we must obey God, for Jesus said, "He that loveth father or mother more than me is not worthy of me, and he that loveth son or daughter more than me is not worthy of me" (Matt. 10:37), and in Luke 14:26 Jesus says: "If any man come to me and hate not his father and mother and wife and children and brethren and sisters, yea, and his own life also, he cannot be my disciple." In John 14:21, 23, Jesus says, "He that hath my commandments and keepeth them, he it is that loveth me"; and, "If a man love me, he will keep my words." If Jesus be the Judge, then, no man loves Jesus who refuses to obey Him, no matter who interferes. If civil authorities interfere, we must obey God. Like Daniel of old when the king's decree conflicted with his duty to God, we must obey God regardless of consequences. (See Dan. 6:1-28.) Jesus says in Matt. 22:21, "Render unto Caesar (the civil authority) the things which are Caesar's and unto God the things that are God's."
>
> If religious authority interferes, we must obey God. When the highest religious authorities among the Jews had commanded the apostles not to teach in Jesus' name, Peter and the other apostles answered: "We ought to obey God rather than men" (Acts 5:29). In matters of necessity God speaks and we must always obey Him.[27]

If we usurp divine authority by innovating private opinion in the place of divine precept—can we expect to reap divine results?

---

27. Hall L. Calhoun, quoted by J. B. Cowden, *St. Paul on Christian Unity,* pp. 194-95.

Chapter Four
SAVED BY GRACE

By the works of the Law no flesh will be justified in His sight; for through the Law comes the knowledge of sin. . . . for all have sinned and fall short of the glory of God, being justified as a gift by His grace through the redemption which is in Christ Jesus; . . . For we maintain that a man is justified by faith apart from works of the Law. For the wages of sin is death, but the free gift of God is eternal life in Christ Jesus our Lord (Romans 3:20, 23, 24, 28; 6:23).

Under God's last covenant with man the system adopted is grace. Man is saved by grace, not merit. The Roman letter is Paul's grand sermon on this theme. No man by any work of goodness can ever merit God's justifying approval. "But if it is by grace, it is no longer on the basis of works, otherwise grace is no longer grace" (Romans 11:6). Justification is not a matter of earning any title, or office, or relationship. It is simply the act of declaring one righteous and acceptable by a token which God, the Justifier, has set in operation. The token itself can never earn the promise. For justification is a declaration, made by the holy decision of our Judge. The Scripture makes it clear that man can do no work of righteousness by which he can save himself. Only Christ can save!

Christ alone is the Saviour (the "saver") as appointed by God. He is the One who made our justification possible. He controls it and makes it effective. By His life and death (His sacrifice became our propitiation, the covering of our sins) God was able to "be just and the justifier of the one who has faith in Jesus" (Romans 3:26). We quote Alexander Campbell:

> It is highly important that this great proposition be somewhat elaborated and demonstrated; — that *salvation is not in*

WHAT THE BIBLE SAYS ABOUT FAITH AND OPINION

the act of believing, but *in the object or proposition that is believed.* It is the object or proposition that is believed. It is the object of faith, and not faith itself, that has the power to save. If we examine our physical, intellectual, and moral constitution, in all their organs, faculties, and capacities, one by one, we shall find that it is neither the possession of them nor the employment of them that affords us health, safety or happiness; but the objects on which they are employed. It is not the eye, nor the act of seeing, that affords us pleasure or pain. It is the thing seen. It is not the ear, nor the act of hearing, but the thing heard, that soothes or irritates. So of the organs of tasting, smelling, feeling. The pleasures of sense, derived from tastes, odours, and contacts, are not in the senses or organs themselves, nor in the operations of the organs, but in the object on which these senses act.

. . . .

But the power and efficacy of faith depend not so much upon the act or manner of believing, nor upon the certainty of the evidence, nor even upon our assurance of its truth, as upon the nature and value of the thing that is believed. THE POWER OF FAITH IS IN THE TRUTH BELIEVED. The power of faith is in the power of truth. It is not eating that sustains or destroys human life. *It is what is eaten.* Some eat and live—others eat and die. Some believe and are saved—others believe and are damned. Both characters truly and sincerely believe. But the former believe the truth and are saved—the latter believe a lie and are damned. So true it is, that it is not the *manner* of believing that saves or destroys; nor the sincerity of believing; but the meaning or nature of that which is believed.[1]

---

1. Alexander Campbell, *Campbell on Baptism* (Bethany, Va.: Printed and published by Alexander Campbell, 1853), pp. 71-72.

PRECEPT: SAVED BY GRACE

How does faith in and obedience to the law of Christ carry any weight? How does precept fit into a system of grace? Why seek to answer the question "What must I do to be saved?" if salvation is a free gift from God? We have here a confusing paradox unless we allow the Scriptures to enlighten us.

The main weakness has been in a misunderstanding of the system of grace, and how it is to be appropriated. To begin with, grace uses faith and obedience, and depends on them. These issues are not antagonistic, they are complementary. They fit together to make one intelligible whole.

For instance, consider the issue of faith. Where can there be any exercise of God's grace without faith in the object through which God said He would implement that grace? Mr. Campbell now adds:

> Hence, by a figure of speech which puts the instrument for the agent, salvation is ascribed to faith, while it virtually belongs to the sacrifice and intercession of the Messiah. The gospel, then, as ministered now by the Holy Spirit, is "the power of God for salvation to every one that believes it." Faith indeed, is but the hand that apprehends and appropriates Christ as revealed to us by the Holy Spirit sent down from heaven. Salvation, then, is of faith, that it might be by grace. For as the hand that plucks the fruit is not the fruit, is not that which either creates or sustains life, but only that which ministers to its development and preservation—so faith's sublime efficacy is not in itself, but in that which it receives and appropriates to the soul of man, in which alone is the spring and fountain of eternal life.[2]

"For this reason it is by faith, that it might be in accordance with grace, in order that the promise may be certain to all the descendants" (Romans 4:16a).

---

2. *Ibid.*, pp. 72, 73.

WHAT THE BIBLE SAYS ABOUT FAITH AND OPINION

This is a good place to pause and note the distinction between a system of merit and one of grace. I. B. Grubbs asked the question, "What is the true import of the contrast between legalistic doing and evangelistic believing?"

Is it that there is merit in the latter and none in the former? Or may we conclude that the Apostle intends to teach us that there is a peculiar virtue in faith as an inner state of the soul apart from all outward manifestations of it in religious activity? Upon either hypothesis we would come back in principle to the ground of the legalist. We would lay in man himself the foundation of his hope. The ground of his justification would not be objective, as "in Christ," but merely subjective, as in himself. There is no more merit or peculiar efficiency in the act of believing than in any other act of the believer whether internal or external. There is nothing meritorious about man, or salvation would not flow from the grace of God as its only source. On the other hand, the spiritual value of faith itself, be this whatever it may, attaches of necessity to all action springing from faith. The stream is, in quality, as the fountain whence it issues; the branches, leaves and fruit, as the tree on which they grow. Paul was never so unwise as to suppose any incompatibility between faith and what he calls "the obedience of faith" (1:5 and 16:26). For, in every act produced by faith in Christ, the believer is really looking to him and reposing upon him as the ground of all hope and the source of all life. It is in this and this only that either faith or "the obedience of faith," has any real worth, as constantly fixing the eye of the soul upon Jesus.

But he who relies on legalistic morality for his justification looks not toward Calvary, but in another direction, and thus practically repudiates Christ himself, and, of course, all personal need of faith and of grace. Hence the Apostle says: "If they who are of the law be heirs, faith is made void and the promise of none effect." Not so, however, does he reason

PRECEPT: SAVED BY GRACE

respecting obedience to Christ as springing from faith in him. He who, "in obeying the truth" is leaning on Jesus for blessing, does not declare faith needless nor turn away from its great object, but rather turns away from every system of self-righteousness and delusive reliance on human goodness. So thought Paul, or he would not have represented in this argument (4:12), righteousness as imputed to those who not only inwardly believe, but "who walk in the steps of that faith which Abraham had in uncircumcision." For Abraham himself constantly walked in obedience to God by a living, trusting faith from the very time that on being called out of Chaldea "he obeyed and went out, not knowing whither he went." While, therefore, neither faith nor deeds of faith can constitute the ground of justification, any more than legal works, yet, the blessing of God may be conditioned as much on obedient acts produced by faith as on the act of believing itself without any detriment whatsoever to the remedial system. The public confession of Christ's name (Matt. 10:32), and "the baptism of repentance for the remission of sins" (Mark 1:4; Acts 2:38 and 22:16), are not legalistic pretentions of merit, but simple elements of the economy of grace divinely approved. Surely the need of forgiveness is the need of grace, and he who seeks it by being "baptized into Christ" (Rom. 6:3; Gal. 3:27), is not looking to himself, but to Jesus; he is not "going about to establish his own righteousness" by seeking justification on the imaginary ground of sinless perfection, but is looking for salvation on the feasible condition of trust in his Redeemer.[3]

This distinction is further marked by the chart on justification tabulated by Mr. Grubbs.[4] (See Figure 1, page 84.)

---

3. I.B. Grubbs, *Commentary on Paul's Epistle to the Romans*, 6th ed., edited by George Klingman (Nashville, Tn.: Gospel Advocate, reprint of 1913 ed.), pp. 69, 70.

4. *Ibid.*, p. 80.

With this in mind, faith and obedience to the law of the Gospel is not only compatible in a system of grace, but essential. The Lord has every right to condition His grace.

A COMPARISON OF SALVATION BY FAITH VERSUS SALVATION BY WORKS

JUSTIFICATION		
By Works of the Law is	versus	By Faith in Christ is
Meritorious (4:4)	versus	Gratuitous (3:24)
As of the Sinless (Gal. 3:10)	versus	As of the Sinful (4:5)
HENCE IS:		
1. Without Pardon (3:20)	versus	1. Through Pardon (4:6-8)
2. Without Grace (4:4)	versus	2. By Grace (3:24)
3. Without Christ (Gal. 2:21)	versus	3. Through Christ (3:24)
4. Without Faith (4:14)	versus	4. By Faith (3:28)
5. Without the Obedience of Faith (4:14)	versus	5. Through the Obedience of Faith (4:12)
RESULTING IN		
1. Occasion of Boasting (4:2) and	versus	1. Exclusion of Boasting (3:27) and
2. Reward as a Debt (4:4)	versus	2. Reward as a Gift (Eph. 2:8)

Figure 1

PRECEPT: SAVED BY GRACE

He stipulates a holy means by which His creatures may put themselves in a position to receive that grace. Three questions are readily answered by Scripture: (1) Does grace eliminate the act of faith?

> But now apart from the Law the righteousness of God has been manifested, being witnessed by the Law and the Prophets; even the righteousness of God through faith in Jesus Christ for all those who believe; for there is no distinction; . . . being justified as a gift by His grace through the redemption which is in Christ Jesus; whom God displayed publicly as a propitiation in His blood through faith. This was to demonstrate His righteousness, because in the forbearance of God He passed over the sins previously committed; . . . For we maintain that a man is justified by faith apart from works of the Law" (Romans 3:21, 22, 24, 25, 28, also Ephesians 2:8, 9).

(2) Does this faith in turn eliminate works of obedience? "Do we then nullify the Law through faith? May it never be! On the contrary, we establish the Law" (Romans 3:31; Case of Abraham—Romans 4:12).

"Even so faith, if it has no works, is dead, being by itself" (James 2:17). "You see that a man is justified by works, and not by faith alone. . . . For just as the body without the spirit is dead, so also faith without works is dead" (James 2:24, 26). Our Lord asked, "And why do you call Me, 'Lord, Lord,' and do not do what I say?" (Luke 6:46). Paul in discussing becoming all things to all men said that he became "to those who are without law, as without law, though not being without the law of God but under the law of Christ, that I might win those who are without law" (I Corinthians 9:21).

(3) The question "Does grace eliminate obedience?" is thus answered: Obedience is not eliminated because when

Jesus comes again His judgment will fall on "those who do not know God and to those who do not obey the gospel of our Lord Jesus" (II Thessalonians 1:8). The Holy Spirit is given "to those who obey Him" (Acts 5:32). In the early days of the church "a great many of the priests were becoming obedient to the faith" (Acts 6:7). Through whom Paul "received grace and apostleship to bring about the obedience of faith among all the Gentiles, for His name's sake" (Romans 1:5). The necessity of obedience is underscored by Peter's somber rhetorical question about judgment, "What will be the outcome for those who do not obey the gospel of God?" (I Peter 4:17).

It is important that we notice the different uses of the word "works" as found in the New Testament. Sometimes God refers to "works" of the *Law* (Romans 3:21-28; Galatians 2:16). Then there are those references to "works" of *merit* (Ephesians 2:8, 9) — these are works of human merit. In addition to works of law and works of man there is the work of *God.* When He commands faith (John 6:29) and obedience (Acts 10:34, 35) these are works which man is responsible to render but which in no way contradict being saved by grace. This is what James is trying to tell us (James 2). So Paul and James do not contradict one another. When Paul writes, "For by grace you have been saved through faith; and that not of yourselves, it is the gift of God; not as a result of works, that no one should boast" (Ephesians 2:8, 9) and James said "You see that a man is justified by works, and not by faith alone" (James 2:24), they are referring to two different kinds of works.

Grace does not allow license. One of the most destructive notions of grace, as stated by John C. Miller, is that:

PRECEPT: SAVED BY GRACE

... Grace is opposed to all law, and that a Christian is wholly released from all law of every kind; that he must be entirely controlled by spirit impulses, which he is to woo for himself by means of prayer alone; that, if he does anything else, he is in danger of legalism.[5]

Under grace man has no right to live and do as he pleases —but as his Benefactor pleases. Faithful obedience does not invalidate grace—nor necessitate legalism. Only when man glories in his own works, and not in the cross and the saving blood of Jesus, does the whole matter become vain and legalistic.

When Paul condemned the Galatians for returning to circumcision (after becoming Christians) it was on the basis of their reaching for merit (Galatians 3:1-6). He does not condemn the act of going back to some law of the Old Covenant, for he did this himself in the sense of studying the Old Testament, or citing it for illustration of God's final revelation. But it was their practice of going back to the spirit of merit by obedience (which oftentimes led men of the Old Testament). The Galatians had found the new (which had been manifested in the case of Abraham's faith—Romans 4), the perfect; why then, go back to the imperfect? Meet the demands of the law of grace—what better or holier thing can man do?

Today, man may find himself in one of two abominable conditions. He who lives by works of merit, and not grace— "For as many as are of the works of the Law are under a curse; for it is written, 'Cursed is every one who does not abide by all things written in the book of the Law, to perform them' " (Galatians 3:10). "For whoever keeps the whole law

---

5. John C. Miller, *New Testament Christianity*, III, ed. by Z.T. Sweeney (Joplin, Mo.: College Press, reprint of 1930 ed.), pp. 551, 552.

and yet stumbles in one point, he has become guilty of all" (James 2:10). His only hope is Christian conversion—so that he can say with Paul,

> "I have been crucified with Christ; and it is no longer I who live, but Christ lives in me; and the life which I now live in the flesh I live by faith in the Son of God, who loved me, and delivered Himself up for me. "I do not nullify the grace of God; for if righteousness comes through the Law, then Christ died needlessly" (Galatians 2:20, 21).

Or, secondly, he who lives by faith in the grace of God, but omits the works of faith—"Even so faith, if it has no works, is dead, being by itself" (James 2:17). (See also II Thessalonians 3:11-15.) He immediately destroys his professed faith.

A Christian need not be found guilty of either, when he truly understands what it means to be "saved by grace." Whenever the Lord speaks by precept the Christian will faithfully obey to the letter—and yet, never once forgetting that in lieu of all his faithful doing, it is God's wondrous grace that has declared him acceptable. Grace covers man's *inability,* faith and obedience covers man's *ability.* "For the wages of sin is death, but the free gift of God is eternal life in Christ Jesus our Lord" (Romans 6:23). Thanks be to God for a grace that takes man on to the crown when he has done his miserable best. Grace includes a thousand holy thoughts and motives in the mind of God—faith and obedience include a human walk in the way God has chosen to reveal. In return for man's best, God is more than willing to provide His grace.

> "Amazing grace, how sweet the sound,
> That saved a wretch like me!" —*John Newton*

Chapter Five
GOD'S NORM FOR SALVATION AND THE CHURCH

The source of all precept and teaching has now been traced and identified. God's Word, the Bible, is the authority for all faith and practice. God has expressed His truth in precepts. The purpose and object of God's revealed truth is that man may come to know the truth of God. What does God want a man to do today? What precepts apply to him now? Which Scriptural precepts are essential for man to understand and obey in order to be saved?

One need not read far in the New Covenant without learning that there are two categories of humanity—the saved and the lost, the sinner and the redeemed, the damned and the justified, the Christian and the non-Christian. The distinction is vital. Jesus continually preached on this. For each of these two conditions or relationships is allotted a different set of divine precepts. The unsaved person must ask, "What must I do to be saved, redeemed, justified,— to be 'in Christ'?" "How can I definitely get into the divinely sanctioned relationship with God?" Is there not a norm, a pattern, a model for this? Or has the Lord been vague and indefinite about the most important thing in the world? Or if He has been definite, is not the Scripture capable of expressing it? Let a man begin at the right point in Scripture for his answer and he will find a norm—*the* one, singular, positive norm of salvation. When the Lord ratified His glorious New Covenant He charged His followers with His concise commission (Matthew 28:18-20; Mark 16:16; Luke 24:45-49). In the book of Acts one can see how His inspired apostles (and in turn, the disciples) fulfilled this charge. The answer is a clear, definite, and singular pattern. The pattern or norm had no deviation. When one studies carefully the New Testament epistles (Romans through Jude), he will grow in his understanding of the essentials in God's norm, His plan of salvation. Simply stated, in word outline the norm was and is today: hearing, believing, repenting, confessing, and being baptized (Acts 2:38; 16:31; 17:30; 22:16; Galatians 3:27; Romans 10:10). This thought and action pattern, called conversion, brings one into a holy relationship to God through Christ.

If a man has found salvation in Christ, then his question is, "What must I do to remain saved, redeemed, justified — to remain 'in Christ'?" This question leads one to a new area of precept — the norm of Christian life and growth. Its pattern is defined by precept and by precedent. The standards of spiritual growth find their basis in the life and teachings of Jesus and their explanation and application in the epistles.

When persons have followed the first norm (the plan of salvation) and are following the second (the standards of Christian growth) they are the church. The assembly of those in Christ make up the body of Christ as defined in the New Testament. Fellowship is the partnership and togetherness of Christians. Now if the Lord has a norm for the Christian individual, does He not have a norm for the Christians as a group? If the individual asks, "What must I do to be a Christian — 'in Christ'?" then should not a group ask, "What must we do to be a church 'of Christ'?" And should not the answer be as singular and definite?

W. N. Briney quotes a young author: "Nobody knows what the apostolic church was. Besides, if we could restore the apostolic church, none of us would stand for it for ten minutes. It is not up with the times."[1]

---

1. W. N. Briney, *The Watchword of the Restoration Vindicated* (Cincinnati, Ohio: Standard Publishing, n.d.), p. 38.

PRECEPT: GOD'S NORM FOR SALVATION AND THE CHURCH

This is the liberal theologian's concept. It is far too common today. This means that any attempt to find and understand and follow a New Testament norm is entirely futile—and even undesirable. The existentialist would say, "I'll determine what the norm is for myself." Some advocates of form criticism would say that first of all they would have to use their own methods to "demythologize" the New Testament in order to determine what they would declare to be "the norm."

Herbert Willett's attack on the Campbells for their work in restoring this norm for the church (cf. Chapter 4) is shown in the statement:

> But perhaps the most interesting modification made in the thinking and practice of the fathers and their successors related to their conception of the apostolic church as a static and invariable institution, set up once for all in the world, and not to be modified by any human device.[2]

The writer's reason for coming to this conclusion is revealed in his premise—with no norm, there is nothing to restore:

> The fact that neither the Savior nor the apostles had any fixed norm of church organization, and the significant appeal of every type of church administration to the New Testament as if it were a source-book upon the subject, did not at the time disturb these earnest seekers after a way of peace.[3]

Nevertheless there is a norm both for the individual and for the community of believers. Let the Scriptures illustrate this principle. Apollos was a man "mighty in the Scriptures. This man had been instructed in the way of the Lord; and

---

2. Herbert Willett, *Progress*, (Chicago: The Christian Century Press, 1917), p. 27.
3. *Ibid.*, pp. 23, 27.

WHAT THE BIBLE SAYS ABOUT FAITH AND OPINION

being fervent in spirit, he was speaking and teaching accurately the things concerning Jesus, being acquainted only with the baptism of John" (Acts 18:24-28). Here is a man with sincere faith and accuracy of knowledge in what he knew. There still remained a definite area of vital truth which he possessed not. Thus, it was necessary for Priscilla and Aquila to take him aside, and they "explained to him the way of God more accurately" (Acts 18:26). This was to satisfy the requirements of a norm, a pattern of truth to be believed and followed.

Then there was the case of the Ephesians who found themselves in a similar plight (Acts 19:1-7). They had found themselves short of the conversion norm. It was a deficiency in the matter of baptism — which today is often ruled out of the pattern of conversion into the vast field called, "It does not make any difference." They were taught by an inspired apostle that it did make a difference. There was a norm and they obeyed what they learned.

Saul himself was a good example when he called out for a definite answer, "What shall I do, Lord?" And by the time he reached the preacher, what he had yet to do, in order to fulfill all the requirements of the conversion norm, he was definitely commanded: "And now why do you delay? Arise, and be baptized, and wash away your sins, calling on His name" (Acts 22:16).

Is there not also a form and pattern in regard to the church? It is positively the *only* divine institution mentioned in the New Covenant — the last and final covenant for man today. Cannot that church which Jesus promised (Matthew 16:18) be singled out of Scripture — no matter in what city it was established — and its pattern traced? Can not the vital questions of composition, identity, purpose, message, and

PRECEPT: GOD'S NORM FOR SALVATION AND THE CHURCH

function, all be answered in Scripture? If not, what then did the author of Hebrews mean when, in contrasting and comparing the two covenants, he said, "See," He says, "that you make all things according to the pattern which was shown you on the mountain" (Hebrews 8:5)? What bearing does that have on the new covenant? — and on the only divine institution promised and given in the new covenant? This church, this "spiritual house," this "people for his own possession," this "body of Christ," — has it no form, no pattern? "Whence the church, by evolution or revelation?" Revelation is the only alternative.

What did the inspired apostle mean when he instructed Titus in his ministry with the Church at Crete? "For this reason I left you in Crete, that you might set in order what remains, and appoint elders in every city as I directed you" (Titus 1:5). What was Titus' guide? How was he to know what was lacking? Was there not a definite revealed pattern that he was commanded to follow faithfully?

Man must sit at the same school-desk as did Timothy, when the great teacher said, "Retain the standard of sound words which you have heard from me, in the faith and love which are in Christ Jesus" (II Timothy 1:13). The word "standard" means a "model" or "pattern" that has definite size and shape for the purpose of seeing something definite and maintaining a sameness in meaning. As Paul expected Timothy to listen so must man today translate and read. And in so doing he must, with all fidelity, put into that word "pattern" all that God intended.

That pattern is available today. It is not something fluid, elusive, or undiscernable. As Charles M. Sharpe said in the typical liberal manner:

WHAT THE BIBLE SAYS ABOUT FAITH AND OPINION

> Should we regard the restoration of New Testament Christianity as the main purpose and end of our being we would still be without a measure of progress, since scholarship was never less able than now to tell us just what New Testament Christianity was in essence.[4]

This attitude undermines the whole Christian system. It is utterly a false premise. And it leads man to believe that Christianity is reduced to a heterogenous collection of moral adages — and man is forever resigned to a fate of disunity and confusion. H. W. Everest says:

> These objections may all be fairly summed up in the one statement that the Protestant denominations cannot agree in respect to what the apostolic church was. It must be admitted that to whatever degree this statement can be made good, to that degree will Christian unity be difficult of achievement. Let us not shut our eyes to this difficulty, but carefully consider how much it means.
>
> The logician can not be asked to prove all his premises, for this would require an infinite regression of proofs. He must begin with undemonstrable, admitted, axiomatic truth. You must grant the mathematician his definitions, postulates and axioms, or he cannot take a single step. So in religious matters, we must have a beginning place. The Catholic begins with an infallible pope and church. The Protestant begins with the Bible as the Word of God. The Protestant assumes that the New Testament is an inspired volume, that it is not ambiguous nor self-contradictory, and therefore that it can be, and ought to be understood. Now, I stand by this assumption, and maintain that all Evangelical Protestants *can agree* in regard to this basis of union, and that *there is,*

---

4. Charles M. Sharpe, *Progress* (Chicago: The Christian Century Press, 1917), p. 78.

substantially, an agreement. I cannot consent that essential Bible truth cannot be reached, that the Scriptures are but a musical staff on which any tune can be written.

This agreement is possible, if we shall endeavor to arrive at the sense of Scripture through the application of the same rules. The Bible facts are the same for all; and if the same rules are applied, the same results will follow. The more intelligently and scientifically the Bible is studied the more perfect the agreement.[5]

In closing, allow Thomas Campbell to ask:

> Why should we deem it a thing incredible that the church of Christ, in this highly favored country, should resume that original unity, peace, and purity, which belongs to its constitution, and constitutes its glory? Or, is there any thing that can be justly deemed necessary for this desirable purpose, but to conform to the model, and adopt the practice of the primitive church, expressly exhibited in the New Testament? Whatever alterations this might produce in any or all of the churches, should, we think, neither be deemed inadmissible nor ineligible. Surely such alteration would be every way for the better, and not for the worse, unless we should suppose the divinely inspired rule to be faulty, or defective. Were we, then, in our church constitution and managements, to exhibit a complete conformity to the apostolic church, would we not be, in that respect, as perfect as Christ intended we should be? And should not this suffice us?[6]

---

5. H. W. Everest, *Missouri Christian Lectures* (St. Louis: Christian Publishing Co., 1892), pp. 28, 29.

6. Thomas Campbell, *Declaration and Address* (Lincoln, IL: Lincoln Christian College Press, 1971 reprint of 1809 ed.), pp. 12, 13. See Conclusion, pages 301-314.

Chapter Six
CHRISTIAN FELLOWSHIP

Now that a definite norm for salvation and the church has been established, what about the Christian's relationship with other Christians?

The proper starting point is with the New Testament term that denotes the joint-operation of Christians resulting from the holy relationship which God has established between them. There is a word that ties one Christian to another in all Scriptural, communal activities. This is the word "fellowship." It was born with the church. For on the day of Pentecost, they [church] were continually devoting themselves . . . to fellowship . . . " (Acts 2:42). It continued on as an integral part of the New Testament church, not only in name but in reality. What a power it was again and again in the first century. The gospel was the "dynamo" of God, and fellowship united its impulses together into one world-shaking system.

How Paul must have gloried in Christian fellowship on his mission tours! It was experienced by actual physical presence, by letter, and by oral report. For instance, as Paul was ending his third great tour, how rich must have been the fellowship which was his as he entered Tyre, and Christians received a very tired warrior of the cross (Acts 21:4-6).

But what is fellowship? What is the New Testament concept? The twentieth century concept frequently goes no deeper than feeling and emotion, as manifested in some form of socializing. Fellowship and good will too often have been accepted as synonymous. A shallow treatment of the word has robbed God-fearing people of one of our richest blessings the Lord ever offered by way of His Son. Fellowship is like a precious diamond, many facets of which have never even been seen, let alone appreciated.

PRECEPT: CHRISTIAN FELLOWSHIP

To have the blessings of Christian fellowship some requirements are necessary. It is a give and take matter. It produces a gracious blessing resulting from faithful, individual industry. The word itself, in its generic sense, means only a communion, or a "togetherness," or a companionship. Now with the Christian prefix added its meaning is qualified by a certain Scriptural pattern. Fellowship alone means little, but "in Christ" it means much.

The Greek word is "koinonia" and means: (1) the share which one has in anything, participation; (2) intercourse, fellowship, intimacy; (3) a benefaction jointly contributed, a collection, a contribution.[1]

Vincent defines the word as "a relation between individuals which involves a common interest and a mutual, active participation in that interest and in each other."[2] Now let Christ enter the matter. And let this kind of fellowship be exhibited in the Scripture and a clear pattern of its meaning will be seen. The requirements are three.

1. *A Common Relationship* is primary. Unless this issue is clearly settled, fellowship becomes impossible, partial, or a sham. There is a holy chain-reaction that must be set in operation. When certain factors are laid hold of and united together in a certain order and pattern, then a fellowship will and must result. When man has learned how to fellowship with God (I John 1:3), and in turn with the Holy Spirit (II Corinthians 13:14), and in turn with the Son (I Corinthians 1:9), he then in turn will be ready to fellowship with other Christians of like condition (I John 1:7; Ephesians 3:4-6;

---

1. J. H. Thayer, *Thayer's Greek-English Lexicon of the New Testament* (New York: American Book, 1886), p. 352.
2. Marvin R. Vincent, *Word Studies in the New Testament,* Vol. I (Grand Rapids: Wm. B. Eerdmans, reprint of 1887 ed.), p. 456.

Galatians 3:28) — and not before. The relationship factor is vital because God said so.

2. *A Common Purpose* necessarily follows. The aim and direction must be singular. If there is no common purpose or interest there can be no grounds of fellowship. In Paul's instruction to Christians concerning non-Christians he asks,

> Do not be bound together with unbelievers; for what partnership ["metoche" — partnership] have righteousness and lawlessness, or what fellowship has light with darkness? Or what harmony has Christ with Belial, or what has a believer in common with an unbeliever? Or what agreement has the temple of God with idols? (II Corinthians 6:14-16).

When individuals are properly related they will naturally have common aims and purposes. They cannot help but have them. Two men who are molded by the one master pattern will begin to have the same loves and labors. Paul said,

> Now I exhort you, brethren, by the name of our Lord Jesus Christ, that you all agree, and there be no divisions among you, but you be made complete in the same mind and in the same judgment (I Corinthians 1:10).

This answers Amos' question, "Do two men walk together unless they have made an appointment?" (Amos 3:3).

And this oneness of purpose and aim may be obtained in this generation by submitting to the same pattern that marked New Testament fellowship. And, as said before, that body of truth is available and understandable today. Listen to the apostle John when he says, "What we have seen and heard we proclaim to you also, that you also may have fellowship with us; and indeed our fellowship is with the Father, and with His Son Jesus Christ" (I John 1:3).

PRECEPT: CHRISTIAN FELLOWSHIP

3. *A Common Operation* is the outcome. Fellowship thus becomes a vehicle by which these common purposes may be jointly implemented. The word "fellowship" can not stand alone—there must be a fellowship in something. This is the substance of fellowship—the actual joint participation in those common aims. And its companion factor will be a joint partaking of accompanying blessings. As J. W. McGarvey said, "The fellowship in which they [Acts 2:42] continued was their joint participation in religious privileges."[3] Thus, in the act of fellowshipping there are many expressions. Such expressions as: the Lord's Supper; public prayer; hymn singing; stewardship of time, talent, and possessions; preaching and teaching of the Word; suffering and rejoicing; benevolence; and a ministry of comfort, all become mutual in operation. Some of these, by their very nature, must be mutual. For instance, there can be no teaching of the Word without students. Thus, we find an imperative expression of Christian fellowship.

The New Testament often uses the word "fellowship" in one of these specific senses. This is due to the concept of "contribution" or "mutuality" which the word conveys. And the word is then used to point to that particular expression of fellowship which is in point. Otherwise, the word is more comprehensive—pointing to all of the ways fellowship is expressed through joint participating and partaking. Claud F. Witty sums it up:

> We may say that Christian fellowship means that two or more Christians that have joint participation, joint interest, or partnership in the work and worship of the church are in fellowship with each other.[4]

---

3. J. W. McGarvey, *New Commentary on Acts of Apostles* (Cincinnati: Ohio: Standard Publishing, 1892), p. 46.
4. Claud F. Witty, *Christian Unity Quarterly* (May, 1943), p. 41.

Unless fellowship has this foundation, then what man calls fellowship is something short of Christian fellowship. It may have good within it, good aims, good results—however, when New Testament fellowship is reproduced then we shall have New Testament results. Professor R. C. Foster declares:

> Fellowship is far more than a mere friendliness or comradeship. It is all that and more. It is a community of feeling, of activity, or interest, of nature. It is a community of life growing out of a community of faith, and love and loyalty to a common Lord. It is not membership in an institution or organization that makes fellowship. Rather, one has fellowship and therefore finds himself joining in membership in an institution of men of like faith and life. Fellowship is not the *forgetting* of differences but it is the *having* of a unity in faith and feeling. The fellowship in the community of material possessions is simply the outward expression of the inward community of faith and ideals.[5]

Now the supreme question—can Christian fellowship be *tested?* Is there some qualifying standard for fellowship; some measure by which the practice of fellowship may either be acceptable or objectionable in the eyes of the individual? There are two radical answers to this question. The liberal or "misinformed" will emphatically cry out, "No." There never was a test, there never can be a test, and any test would be futile. There is absolutely no way of testing fellowship, for the whole matter, after all, is arbitrary. The rules of testing are myriad—as many and varied as the opinions and mind of men. So, for the sake of feeling, goodwill, and "brotherhood" let all men freely and fully fellowship together

---

5. R. C. Foster, *Bible Teacher and Leader,* Vol. 49, No. 4, (Cincinnati, Ohio: Standard Publishing, 1947), p. 68.

(so called "Christian") regardless of any differences. This answer leads to a poor and dangerous substitute for Christian fellowship. It reduces it to a mere unholy alliance, with unholy trends, crowned with unholy results—and yet supposedly, it is a holy thing.

The opposing radical answer is just as emphatic a "yes." But the test is carefully and minutely submitted by one claiming to be "the" faithful expositor of God's law. Unless this test is rigidly accepted by man, then let him be anathema. He has studied the Scripture and demands that others accept, to the letter, his detailed catalogue of all necessary laws—this is the code of fellowship and all must subscribe to it. This is the curse of "creeds." The last two thousand years of church history is enough testimony to show how futile, divisive, and evil this practice is. But are not creeds mere "dead letters" today? Some which are resurrected in the mind of man today as unwritten creeds become as binding and narrow as any written creed ever was. There are the new creeds of "ecumenicity," "federationalism," "fundamentalism," "councilism," "charismatic declarations" and "cultic pronouncements" of this day. The coercion of the bigot and sectarian mind is ever present—only in new clothes.

What is the Scriptural answer to this question? Fellowship was tested, and can be tested today. The same rules as issued and practiced by the inspired apostles must be used now. Let man lay aside "how he feels" about the matter. Too many have opened their hearts so wide that their minds have fallen through. And too, the tendency to reason out and speculate has its dangerous trends toward the wrong answer. As Isaac Errett once wrote:

> Seeing how many needless and ruinous strifes have been kindled among sincere believers by attempts to define the

WHAT THE BIBLE SAYS ABOUT FAITH AND OPINION

indefinable, and to make tests of fellowship of human forms of speech, which lack divine authority, we have determined to eschew all such mischievous speculations and arbitrary terms of fellowship, and to insist only on the "form of sound words" given to us in the Scriptures concerning the Father, the Son, and the Holy Spirit.[6]

So let man simply return to the days of Christ and His apostles and see what they did to test fellowship. The answer is clear — for we can know definitely what one had to know, believe, and do in order to enter into such Christian fellowship. The Word is our guide. It was the only vehicle by which Israel found its peculiar fellowship. So it is with the church today. The Word is the only substance of the test — as the wood, figures, glass, and mercury when intelligently assembled make the instrument which conveys the test of air temperature. One can not rely on his "feelings," nor even on intelligent speculative conclusions. But he can rely on an inerrant instrument that can be seen and read. We quote John Locke on this issue:

> But since men are solicitous about the true church, I would only ask them, here by the way, if it be not more agreeable to the church of Christ to make the conditions of her communion to consist in such things, and such things only, as the Holy Spirit has in the Holy Scriptures declared, in express words, to be necessary for salvation? I ask, I say, whether this be not more agreeable to the church of Christ, than for men to impose their own inventions and interpretations upon others, as if they were of divine authority; and to establish by ecclesiastical laws, as absolutely necessary to the profession of Christianity, such things as the Holy

---

6. Isaac Errett, *Our Position* (Cincinnati, Ohio: Standard Publishing, n.d.), p. 7.

PRECEPT: CHRISTIAN FELLOWSHIP

Scriptures do either not mention, or at least not expressly command?

Whosoever requires those things in order to ecclesiastical communion, which Christ does not require in order to life eternal, he may perhaps indeed constitute a society accommodated to his own opinions and his own advantage; but how that can be called the church of Christ, which is established upon laws that are not his and which excludes such persons from its communion as he will one day receive into the kingdom of heaven, I understand not. But this being not a proper place to inquire into the mark of the true church I will only mind those that contend so earnestly for the decrees of their own society, and that cry out continually, the Church! the Church! with as much noise, and perhaps upon the same principle, as the Ephesian silversmiths did for their Diana, this, I say, I desire to mind them of, that the gospel frequently declares that the true disciples of Christ must suffer persecution; but that the church of Christ should persecute others, and force others by fire and sword and embrace her faith and doctrine, I could never yet find in any of the books of the New Testament.[7]

Men cry out today that when they submit their creeds and and practices as a test—it is only a test for entering their own denomination. They are not saying that men of other denominations are not Christians. According to Scripture, sectarianism, no matter now solicitous and gracious it may become, is wrong.

Let men heed the confession of Alexander Campbell:

> I commenced my career in this country under the conviction that nothing that was not as old as the New Testament

---

7. John Locke, quoted by Alexander Campbell, *A Debate Between Rev. A. Campbell and Rev. N. L. Rice* (Nashville, Tenn.: Gospel Advocate, reprint of 1844 ed.), p. 795.

should be made an article of faith, a rule of practice, or a term of communion amongst Christians.[8]

Distinction should be made between "matters of faith" and "tests of fellowship." We should understand that a matter of faith in the Lord's revelation of truth does not always function as a test of fellowship in His body, the church. Any statement of truth in God's word is a matter for us to believe. What the Scripture expressly teaches calls for but one response from man—his faith and obedience. The believer is never given any right to use his powers of reason to change, nullify, add to, nor discount a "thus saith the Lord."

However, a person may believe Jesus Christ is Lord and accept the truth in Jesus before he recognizes all particular items of truth in the Biblical revelation. We can still have Christian fellowship with this person. The New Testament makes it clear that certain things are essential for one to be saved and to remain a Christian. If a person is not a Christian or has ceased to be a Christian, then believers can not enter into full fellowship with him.

1. Christian fellowship is the joint operation resulting from common purposes and issuing from a common relationship. This definition is progressive. Each factor is present, and in its proper order. As the words unroll in order the thought progresses from a source to a result, like a chain reaction. Now, the nearer we get to the source, the severer will be the test of fellowship. Thus, relationship is basic. It is the primary issue. If this first phase of the test is deficient, then fellowship is seriously impaired or destroyed at the very outset.

---

8. Alexander Campbell, from the *Christian Baptist*, cited by A. W. Fortune, *Adventuring With Disciple Pioneers*, p. 27.

PRECEPT: CHRISTIAN FELLOWSHIP

Now, at the very outset, the absolute negative test of Christian fellowship is that of the Christian's relationship to the unbeliever. Here there is *no* Christian fellowship (II Corinthians 6:14-18). For the basic factor—relationship to God, Christ, Holy Spirit, and eventually each other—is entirely without substance. Now, of course, there may be associations: that which is political, fraternal, geographical, economic, etc. And even in this matter of association the Christian must be cautious lest he mislead or hurt other Christians (I Corinthians 8), or himself. Nevertheless, there is no Christian fellowship. How can there be? Association and fellowship are not to be confused.

But, in turn, can the unbeliever be tested as to his unbelief? Can he be clearly identified without violating our preceding issue of "creed making"? The answer is to go back to the passage in point and see what Paul identified as an unbeliever. This can be done today.

What is the standard relationship? Herein lies one of the greatest issues to face all "Christendom." But it should not be. If men will approach the Scripture in the right place (Acts, and the attending Epistles—of the New Covenant) with the right question (What must the lost do to get in the proper relationship with God, Christ, and Holy Spirit?) they can not help but come out with a singular answer. This, and this alone, is the one relation standard basic to the beginning of Christian fellowship. Any other demand, no matter how honest and well intentioned, is a violation of the sovereignty of the Lord. The entrance into the fullness of this relationship means the beginning of the fullness of Christian fellowship. As Isaac Errett once said:

> We demand no other faith, in order to baptism and church membership, than the faith of the heart in Jesus as the Christ,

the Son of the living God; nor have we any term or bond of fellowship but faith in this Divine Redeemer, and obedience to Him. All who trust in the Son of God, and obey Him are our brethren, however wrong they may be about any thing else; and those who do not trust in this divine Saviour for salvation, and obey His commandments, are not our brethren, however intelligent and excellent they may be in all beside.[9]

When two persons submit to the one perfect pattern of conversion in order to get "into Christ" (does not mean a perfect person) they make the initial step which is the coming into a common relationship, a Scriptural relationship of one with another. This, in turn, is the one legitimate step for now reaching a set of common purposes and having common accord in the things the Lord deems essential. While this does not always follow, it should do so. By making this kind of beginning there is thus laid the widest grounds for *full* fellowship. And this full fellowship was, and should be now, the complete acceptance of each other in all the workings and activities of the church. (Unless some anti-Scriptural practice mar this fullness. See p. 122.) All rights and privileges pertaining to the church (this "called out" fellowship of God's people) are to be fully given and received — nothing withheld. If there are any reservations, then man is guilty of making something the test of fellowship which the apostles never made.[10] This is the sin of Diotrephes (III John 8-10).

Now, is this first step, a common relationship, so definite that it can be made a positive test of fellowship? To this many reply, "There is the rub, for we are not to judge man."

---

9. Isaac Errett, *Our Position*, p. 8.
10. See chapter 11.

PRECEPT: CHRISTIAN FELLOWSHIP

Let us probe this matter a little further. What will one do with the injunction: "You will know them by their fruits" (Matthew 7:16)?

Is this not a definite judgment of some kind? Wherein is the difference? It must be remembered that there are several areas of fellowship, each with its attendant responsibilities. Here is fellowship of man with God, Christ, the Holy Spirit, and with another man. Each has its own respective catalogue of responsibilities for the parties involved. The last one mentioned, fellowship of man to man, is our concern. Therefore, man must have some kind of test which he is capable of applying. When we come to the actual steps of conversion as definitely leading to the relationship necessary for Christian fellowship, what can we test? There was hearing, believing, repenting, confessing, and being baptized.

Is there a positive judgment here? For instance, what about the matter of repentance? If one comes forward to accept the fellowship of a body of those claiming to be the church, how can his repentance be tested for validity? Can his heart be read? Can his sincerity be measured? Can the reality of repentance be tested by cataloguing a series of deeds that must be done over a certain period of time?

Returning to our former point, we might ask, what responsibility rests with which party? Is it man's responsibility to judge motives, feelings, attitude, sincerity—or God's? "For man looks at the outward appearance, but the LORD looks at the heart" (I Samuel 16:7). As for all of this matter let God be the judge over that which He alone can examine. What *can* man judge? Only that which God gave him the power and right to judge! Consider the steps again and observe man's area of responsibility.

WHAT THE BIBLE SAYS ABOUT FAITH AND OPINION

Hearing (the responsibility of those in Christ is to teach and preach) should never allow a single opportunity to slip away. Believing is the responsibility for that which is preached, a faithful exposition of the revealed gospel of salvation. Repenting provides the lost with every opportunity and inducement to *will* to repent. Confessing provides the lost with the ways and means to appear before witnesses to confess that Jesus is Lord and Saviour. Being baptized requires the opportunity and instrument necessary for an accurate fulfillment of this commandment, even as it requires an obedient hearer.

Here the responsibility ends in regard to *this test*. Here is something positive and tangible well within the capability of man. Anything else, anything deeper or more hidden, belongs to God. If man does his part in a particular case wherein the candidate has successfully deceived "the elect," then God, and He alone, will judge that heart. "Therefore do not go on passing judgment before the time, but wait until the Lord comes who will both bring to light the things hidden in the darkness and disclose the motives of men's hearts; and then each man's praise will come to him from God (I Corinthians 4:5). Man has done his part in this initial step, although future days may open up new responsibilities on the part of the Christians toward this party.[11]

Man's sole right is to judge only that area of faith and obedience alloted to him. No more and no less! As Thomas Campbell warned:

> The Divine word is equally binding upon all, so all lie under an equal obligation to be bound by it alone, and not by any human interpretation of it; and that, therefore, no

---

11. See page 133.

PRECEPT: CHRISTIAN FELLOWSHIP

man has a right to judge his brother except in so far as he manifestly violates the express letter of the law. That every such judgment is an express violation of the law of Christ, a daring usurpation of his throne, and a gross intrusion upon the rights and liberties of his subjects.[12]

This introduces the issue commonly called "open membership." This is the practice of accepting one into the full fellowship of the church who has not been baptized. Although, if the church lowers any of the bars of the conversion norm it is guilty of this practice. It is the sin of putting a matter of precept in the field of opinion. It cries for tolerance in regard to the "mode of baptism" (which in itself is a contradictory phrase). They who practice such "will fellowship the unimmersed on exactly the same grounds that they will fellowship those who have obeyed the word of God."[13] There is simply Christian baptism in the New Testament— no interpretations, "modes," or types to be discussed. So when a candidate comes to the point of baptism in conversion there is only one thing for the church to do and that is become the Scriptural baptizer. No matter what kind of life may have been lived or what kind of substitute for baptism may have been practiced. The trite phrase "but it does not matter" can not enter the picture.

In a letter written by Robert Hopkins on this issue in the church, the writer says, "Each congregation decides for itself what its practice shall be in recognizing the status of Christian people of varying fellowships."[14] Does a church have this authority? Remember, personal autonomy and

---

12. Thomas Campbell, *Declaration and Address* (Lincoln, IL: Lincoln Christian College Press, 1971 reprint of 1809 ed.), p. 1.
13. Claud F. Witty, *Christian Unity Quarterly* (July 1943), p. 34.
14. Robert M. Hopkins, *Christian Standard* (June 22, 1940), p. 2.

communal autonomy are *always* limited by sovereign autonomy. The church has a right and a responsibility to settle a thousand questions, but not this one. Since that baptismal pattern has been clearly revealed, it is already settled. Therefore, if any man approaches the church for membership with the statement that he has conformed to the original pattern of New Testament conversion, with one minute exception — that sprinkling was substituted for the "small detail" of immersion (or something similar) — he shall rightfully be rejected. Is this narrow? We answer by asking, "Were Jesus and His apostles narrow?" However, if that man obeys Christ in baptism, regardless of who he is, he should then, without despising his past record of prolonged disobedience, be immediately accepted into full fellowship. It is not in man's realm to test where, why, who aided in conversion; it is only his to test that which is rightfully his.

"But," objects the "open-membership" advocate, "we must not judge." Examine the facts and see who really is doing the judging. He accepts a man (unimmersed) into full fellowship because he feels he is good enough. Good enough for what? for salvation? for acceptance by God? Is this not judging — substituting character for baptism? The Lord never gave us the right to pass such sentence. He only gave us the right to preach His commandments, which when obeyed, leads to salvation. Therefore, to demand of others strict adherence to those commandments is merely accepting the authority and pattern inaugurated by the Lord. To do this, and strictly, is *not* judging a man's salvation. That part is the Lord's. Man has a right and is obligated to test fellowship; God will test salvation. Open membership is either the result of ignorant inconsistency, outright rebellion, or dishonesty.

PRECEPT: CHRISTIAN FELLOWSHIP

These "open-membership" advocates go further by asserting that their position is the only logical conclusion to the restoration genius; that the Campbells, with their unsectarian and considerate spirit, would have taken this position had they been able to advance to our progressive stage today. Just what attitude did the Campbells hold?

It is true that Alexander Campbell at first ascribed this whole issue of baptism to the field of opinion. For a time he passed it by, ignored it, placed it in the area of forebearance. He said, "As I am sure it is unscriptural to make this matter [baptism] a term of communion, I let it *slip*. I wish to think and let think on these matters."[15] Even with his effort to make all "musts" a product of "thus saith the Lord," he continued to delay this issue.

Then, along came Mr. Campbell's first child. What about infant baptism? He now could no longer delay the issue; it faced him in the form of his own flesh and blood. Thus, he began his unbiased and scholarly search for the scriptures for the Lord's answer. And before long he had it. In throwing aside the thought and practice of infant baptism as completely unscriptural, he, in turn overcame his own deficiency in this matter, with the result that he and his wife, and five others were Scripturally baptized. And the price his father had to pay, being a Paedo-Baptist for twenty-five years, was finally and eagerly paid, too. This was the only logical end to the restoration plea.

Suppose, one who has not fully submitted to this conversion pattern, insists on joining into the various services held by the church. Is he not fellowshipping in the preaching, offering, the Lord's Supper, etc.? He is to a certain

---

15. As quoted in Robert Richardson, *Memoirs of Alexander Campbell*, I (Nashville, Tenn.: Gospel Advocate, 1956 reprint of 1897 ed.), p. 392.

extent, and no more. He is always considered as one "from without," no matter how noble and righteous he may be. And the church had better use every chance to instruct him and challenge him to do the thing he ought to do. This should be done in the spirit of love, patience and compassion. Treat him as a "brother in prospect." If he wishes to persist in this, he will usually drop out or one day "enter in." He remains in that suspended state under his own judgment by the Lord. This persistence has usually been born and kept alive because he holds some common purpose or purposes with the church. May he persist long enough to learn of the common relationship he may have through Scriptural conversion. The church should never compromise this matter, only preach in hope and love. Zeal and compassion must never eclipse its faithfulness to the Lord.

What about "open" and "closed" communion? This often follows in the wake of the "open membership" question. However, the cases are not comparable. If the communion bread and cup are passed to the unimmersed person present in a worship service, is the church fellowshipping with him? And this question can thus be extended to all the factors of communal worship. Alexander Campbell often thought on this problem in his day, and noticed the inconsistencies practiced among professed believers in Christ:

> There is a certain place, called *The Family Altar*. Baptists and Paedo-Baptists of different name often meet at this "family altar," and there unite all in one communion. In their monthly concerts for prayer, etc., there is another "altar," and at which all sects sometimes meet, and all have full communion in prayer and praise. But if, on the next day, the Lord's table was furnished, they would rather be caught in company with publicans and sinners than sit at the

PRECEPT: CHRISTIAN FELLOWSHIP

side of those with whom they had full communion in prayer and praise a few hours before. Their consciences would shudder at the idea of breaking bread in full communion with these with whom, yesterday or last night, they had full communion in adoring, venerating, invoking and praising the same God and Redeemer.[16]

And some carry this even further as in the case of John Walker, an independent preacher from Dublin, Ireland. Robert Richardson writes:

> He was Calvinistic in doctrine, but carried separatism so far that it was a special point with him strictly to prohibit the performance of any religious act without removing to a distance (if in the same room) from every person who refused to obey a precept that could be generally applied; insisting that true worship could be rendered only by those who receive and obey the same truths in common.[17]

It is not strange that communion has become the debating ground of this issue? Prayer, preaching, etc., are all types of communion in worship. Why make the Lord's Supper so distinctive? As Isaac Errett pointed out:

> Men will sing together, pray together, preach together, work together in every possible way, until it comes to the observance of the Lord's Supper—and then there is trouble about *communion!* just as if they had not been *communing* all the while! It is the absurd notion that this ordinance was meant to be a touchstone of orthodoxy or of sanctity.[18]

What is the answer? It has been partially answered in the preceding discussions. In addition, we note in the New

---

16. *Ibid.*, II, pp. 137, 138.
17. Robert Richardson, *Op. Cit.*, I, p. 61.
18. J. S. Lamer, *Memoirs of Isaac Errett,* II (Cincinnati, Ohio: Standard Publishing, 1893), p. 156.

Testament, that the issue of so called "open-membership" has been positively answered. This is a matter of entrance into the relationship with Christ — the body of Christ. Whereas, in the "open" or "closed" communion case, the Lord has not spoken. This is a different kind of factor altogether. The Lord's Supper is an expression of one's own faith in the Lord and the covenant which He made. So let a man "prove himself" and then decide personally whether or not he will partake.

As P. H. Welshimer says:

> The right of an individual to commune with his Lord is not to be interfered with by another individual any more than is his right to pray to the Lord or to sing His praises or to testify in His behalf. In communion we are not communing one with another, but each individual is directly communing with his Lord. In communion we are not ratifying matters of belief or opinion. Communion is an individual matter. We are not commanded to administer communion to anyone, nor to withhold it from anyone. Christ said to the disciples: "This do in remembrance of me," and "As oft as ye do this, ye do show forth the Lord's death until he come." Paul taught the Corinthians that a man should examine himself; that in communing one should discern the body and blood of the Lord. It is ours to spread the table, as did the early disciples, upon the first day of every week, thereby giving opportunity to every man who believes in Jesus Christ to exercise his own privilege and desire in appropriating this means of grace which Christ has given, by which the spirit may be renewed and his mind stirred up by way of remembrance. In this we are not appropriating unto ourselves authority, we are not changing laws nor tampering with ordinances. We are simply practicing the Scriptural plan.[19]

---

19. P. H. Welshimer, "Open Membership Question," *Christian Standard*, (May 31, 1919), pp. 22, 23.

PRECEPT: CHRISTIAN FELLOWSHIP

In view of all this it would be well for the church to constantly teach the purpose and responsibilities concerning the Lord's Supper.

We quote D. R. Dungan:

> The church at the city of Corinth had members in it that were very far from being children of God according to the teaching of the Savior and the apostles, and yet there was no objection raised to them respecting the communion. If the Master and the apostles would now do with those who have been unfortunate enough to be misled respecting baptism as they did with those who entertained errors for which they were more responsible, there would be no bars to prevent them from coming to the table of the Lord. I think they would plainly teach them the duty which they have not yet performed, but having done that, they would not prevent any devotion which might be prompted by their love for the Savior.
>
> The language, "Let a man so examine himself and so let him eat and drink," has been taken out of its meaning. It does not mean to decide if he is worthy to eat and drink. It related to the manner of his eating and drinking. On the other point there was no question: that they had a right to commune was not under discussion. It was the manner of their partaking that was being censured. They had turned the breaking of bread into a kind of Sunday Club-Dinner, and to eat and drink thus unworthily was to eat and drink damnation.[20]

2. Now when the matter of relationship is settled there should build up from it an ever progressing common ground of purposes and desires. The more genuine the foundation

---

20. D. R. Dungan, "The Lord's Supper," *The Old Faith Restated*, J. H. Garrison, compiler (Joplin, Mo.: College Press, reprint of 1891 ed.), pp. 243, 244.

of fellowship, the more in common will be the superstructure. If conversion has been valid then the new convert "in Christ" will launch out (along with others of like condition) on the supreme task of forming within himself:

> . . . the Mind of Christ, which is one and indivisible, the ultimate and only conscience of His people; that Mind whose will is our authority, whose command is our program, and whose longing it is, and, through the sad, waiting centuries ever has been, that they all may be one.[21]

And to accomplish this the Christian will never cease to learn to love, to hate, to say, to do, the same things which Christ loved, and hated, and said, and did. In this way man can know the mind of Christ to the extent he was intended to. As Paul said, "Have this attitude in yourselves which was also in Christ Jesus" (Philippians 2:5). Jesus is "the truth," and the more men walk in Him the more able they will be to walk together in the things pertaining to Him.

Now in this field, (of common purposes) fellowship is often relative. Fellowship, not being able to stand alone, must have certain practices which are the expressions of those common purposes. What happens then when purposes, aims, or goals are *not* held in common? not held in common by a people of a common relationship? Can two work together on a common project being of adverse mind on that matter involved? Can there be a withdrawing of one "working" of fellowship without the destruction of all fellowship? Much depends on the nature and intensity of agreement.

---

21. Amos R. Wells, *That They All May Be One* (New York: Funk & Wagnalls Co., 1905), p. 52.

PRECEPT: CHRISTIAN FELLOWSHIP

First, consider a point of difference which is simply a matter of opinion[22] not "thus saith the Lord." This kind of difference is as common as the myriad of opinions of men. One member of a congregation may not agree that a certain special offering is the best thing to do. He may, as it is his right to do, withdraw from fellowshipping in this matter. This is the relative operation of fellowship—for a particular aim or purpose is uncommon. This does not sever his relationship with the group, for he will continue in the fellowship of worship, etc. However, if such a practice be such that it hurts one's conscience too severely to remain with that group, he has the full right once again of withdrawing *all* fellowship from that group and accepting the fellowship of another group sympathetic to his view. This matter must always be one of private volition—and never coercion or restraint on behalf of a church or any part of it. If this is done without hate, or sectarianism, or ascribing unfaithfulness to the first group, it is legitimate.

Such are the "non-instrument" brethren, some of which have fellowshipped together in the activities of worship without the aid of musical instruments (because they honestly feel it is more suited to New Testament worship) without denying brotherhood to those who do. To withdraw a particular "working" of fellowship does not *necessarily* mean an acknowledgement of sinfulness nor unchristian behavior or status on the part of all those who differ. It may and it may not, depending on the nature of the difference. In the field of opinion, when men have a common relationship, the law of love will overlook, tolerate (and often finally correct) the host of differences that reach into every congregation. The more harmony in the purposes and aims of a

---

22. See chapters 9 and 11.

congregation the more rich and intense will be the activity and spirit of fellowship. The closer the views the closer the fellowship.

There occur differences, however, in purposes and aims that often reflect doubt on the validity of the relationship factor. What is the nature of these differences? To begin with, if fellowship is an inclusion, it is also an exclusion. The *only* standard of inclusion into Christian fellowship and exclusion from Christian fellowship is the instruction which the Bible gives on this matter. Where there is a test of fellowship there follows a test of disfellowship. As Mr. Alexander Campbell once said:

> Every church that has a door into it, has also one out of it. We let them in by the BOOK, and put them out by the BOOK. God has given us instruction in our CREED BOOK how to manage these matters. . . . Is the Bible so defective as to give no laws for the reception and exclusion of members?[23]

There is a definite Bible basis for withdrawing fellowship. This is a severe matter and ought to be pursued with all humble caution. And yet, when it is totally neglected and overlooked one wonders what the Lord thinks. Has not God allowed His people to suffer much strife and weakness because they have not faithfully executed this "in and out" policy with all Scriptural precision? Here are the words of Jesus:

> And if your brother sins, go and reprove him in private; if he listens to you, you have won your brother. But if he does not listen to you, take one or two more with you, so that by the mouth of two or three witnesses every fact may be

---

23. Alexander Campbell, *A Debate Between Rev. A. Campbell and Rev. N. L. Rice*, p. 810.

PRECEPT: CHRISTIAN FELLOWSHIP

confirmed. And if he refuses to listen to them, tell it to the church; and if he refuses to listen even to the church, let him be to you as a Gentile and a tax-gatherer. Truly I say to you, whatever you shall bind on earth shall have been bound in heaven; and whatever you loose on earth shall have been loosed in heaven. Again I say to you, that if two of you agree on earth about anything that they may ask, it shall be done for them by My Father who is in heaven. For where two or three have gathered together in My name, there I am in their midst" (Matthew 18:15-20).

J. W. McGarvey expresses the gravity of the matter by pointing out that:

> Binding is the infliction of the penalty of non-fellowship, while loosing is withholding it or removing it in cases of penitence. The promise is that whatsoever the apostles should thus bind or loose would be bound or loosed in heaven; and it follows, that whatsoever the church now binds and looses in accordance with apostolic precept and precedent is also bound and loosed in heaven. It is from this promise that the act of excommunication derives its peculiar solemnity and its fearful effects.[24]

Now where there is one test of full fellowship—Alexander Campbell says there are three tests of full disfellowship:

> There are none excluded from our communities but those who deny the faith, those immoral or unrighteous, and those who are schismatics. These three classes are by divine authority to be severed from the faithful. The schismatic is excluded, not for his opinion, but for the unrighteous use he makes of it.[25]

---

24. J. W. McGarvey, *New Testament Commentary — Matthew and Mark*, pp. 159, 160.
25. Campbell, *op. cit.*, pp. 798, 799.

119

WHAT THE BIBLE SAYS ABOUT FAITH AND OPINION

When a so-called brother insists on denying the faith, manifesting outright disbelief in the gospel of Christ (and this is defined in Scripture) then the faithful must "withdraw" from such. Notice in the following passage of Scripture different stages of disfellowship — all the way from "avoiding them" to "handing them over to Satan."

> Now we command you, brethren, in the name of our Lord Jesus Christ, that you keep aloof from every brother who leads an unruly life and not according to the tradition which you received from us (II Thessalonians 3:6).
>
> Now I urge you, brethren, keep your eye on those who cause dissensions and hindrances contrary to the teaching which you learned, and turn away from them. For such men are slaves not of our Lord Christ but of their own appetites; and by their smooth and flattering speech they deceive the hearts of the unsuspecting (Romans 16:17, 18).
>
> For many deceivers have gone out into the world, those who do not acknowledge Jesus Christ as coming in the flesh. This is the deceiver and the antichrist. Watch yourselves, that you may receive a full reward. Any one who goes too far and does not abide in the teaching of Christ, does not have God; the one who abides in the teaching, he has both the Father and the Son. If any one comes to you and does not bring this teaching, do not receive him into your house or give him a greeting; for the one who gives him a greeting participates in his evil deeds (II John 7-11).

And when one persists in walking in outright sin, with no indication of repentance, then again shall the faithful "put away the wicked man" from among themselves (I Corinthians 5; II Thessalonians 3:6). This course must be pursued with all caution.

This is not judging a man's motives nor his heart, but only the outward deed which is purposely and flagrantly

PRECEPT: CHRISTIAN FELLOWSHIP

continued. Man is capable of passing this kind of judgment. Paul said of such, "They profess to know God, but by their deeds they deny Him, being detestable and disobedient, and worthless for any good deed" (Titus 1:16).

And, thirdly, when one becomes schismatic and factious the church should "turn away" from him (Romans 16:17-18; Titus 3:9-11). This is the person who persists in dividing the household of faith, the "church wrecker," the instigator of unnecessary divisions within the body of Christ. Lest we misuse this right of disfellowship every one ought to carefully and patiently take stock of his attitude and behavior. For one can easily, in a zealous moment, unlawfully use the law of God. This action of disfellowship is the exception, and not the common practice. Notice in Scripture when men sinned, as in the case of Simon the Sorcerer, there was an effort to admonish, to forgive, to help, to encourage, to warn — not to withdraw fellowship (Acts 8:9-13, 18-24). Disfellowship is always the last resort to preserve the church. We do not want to share in the sinful folly of Diotrephes who tyrannically withheld and withdrew fellowship which was not his right to do (III John 9, 10). The attitude of the church toward a wayward brother should not be indifference nor scorn but genuine concern as taught by Paul:

> And if anyone does not obey our instruction in this letter, take special note of that man and do not associate with him, so that he may be put to shame. And yet do not regard him as an enemy, but admonish him as a brother (II Thessalonians 3:14, 15).

3. This now has led us to the third phase of fellowship: the activity of cooperation in these common purposes. What is cooperation? It is a truly important problem.

To begin with, "cooperation" is not synonymous with "fellowship." It is but a part, a function of fellowship—the external common activity which has been prompted by common relationships and common purposes. It is but the practical and working phase of fellowship. It concerns Christians doing things together.

The validity of cooperation rests on the two above mentioned premises, but the actual implementation of it falls within the area of expediency. The how, the when, the what of cooperation is to be settled by the spiritual effort of Christians. As Alexander Campbell said, "But cooperation itself is one thing, and the manner of cooperation another."[26] This "manner" business is to be determined by such elements as efficiency, convenience, workableness, and economy—rather than a blanket necessity. Charles H. Phillips has written that, "Cooperation consists not in the uniform activity of all the brethren in many tasks, but the diverse performance of a common undertaking."[27] Remember the case where Paul and Barnabas decided not to work together (Acts 15:36-40). But some cry for cooperation as a complete must. It is imperative that one be cooperative in any cause that has any spark of good in it, they say. It does not matter so much what the cause is, or how done—everyone must enter into this cooperation. They even go so far at times as to declare any kind of cooperation as being a good and holy thing. This is taking cooperation to mean the same as fellowship, when after all, it is only a part or a function of it.

If cooperation, which certainly is essential to fellowship (for fellowship must be outwardly expressed), is but the expedient implementing of common purposes, then the

---

26. Alexander Campbell, *Christian System* (Nashville, Tenn.: Gospel Advocate Co., 1974 reprint of 1939 ed.), p. 75.
27. Charles H. Phillips, *Christian Standard* (February 9, 1946).

PRECEPT: CHRISTIAN FELLOWSHIP

act of cooperating *must* be controlled and conditioned by those purposes involved. Precept (faith) is always greater than expediency. The purpose in precept must be the common denominator of fellowship. This oneness of purpose gives birth to cooperation, and without it there can be no life in cooperation. It is reduced to a mere piece of machinery which is very often useless and even harmful. In the case of the collections taken for the poor saints in Judaea it was the natural, free flowing expression of cooperative giving, prompted by a common faith and purpose, and not by a mere urge to do something together, nor by a piece of church machinery that solicited support. (See Acts 24:17; Romans 15:25; I Corinthians 16:1-4; II Corinthians 8 and 9.) Those who make all cooperative efforts mandatory are removing it from its legitimate place. It sounds something like the accusation made by John when he said to Jesus,

> "Teacher, we saw someone casting out demons in Your name, and we tried to hinder him because he was not following us." But Jesus said, "Do not hinder him, for there is no one who shall perform a miracle in My name, and be able soon afterward to speak evil of Me" (Mark 9:38-40).

When the grounds of fellowship grow more deficient or varied (relationship and purpose) then the workings of fellowship (cooperation) will become less and less. This is between one party (private or communal) and another. This is the logical result of our progressive definition of fellowship. And the closer the deficiency gets to the source of this "chain reaction" the lesser will be the grounds for any cooperation. That is why the workings and nature of fellowship need to be carefully understood, and that persons, "churches," and organizations should be constantly analyzed by every earnest Christian so that this holy grace of Christian fellowship may be gloriously appropriated in our day.

WHAT THE BIBLE SAYS ABOUT FAITH AND OPINION

Thus, every Christian and every church, being on guard in this matter will often be judged narrow, and even divisive. Mr. Campbell was severely criticized for taking a critical attitude toward some of the "clergy" and some of the Sunday School, missionary, and educational societies of his day — to which he replied:

> My opponents do represent me as opposing the means of converting the world, not wishing to discriminate, in my case at least, between a person opposing the abuses of a good cause and the cause itself.[28]

This Scripture makes every Christian responsible to judge his own working of fellowship, to discriminate between holy and unholy purposes, aims, and methods. Thus, to refuse cooperation in certain matters is not only within a Christian's right, but also within his responsibility. As we note again the words of Paul:

> And if anyone does not obey our instruction in this letter, take special note of that man and do not associate with him, so that he may be put to shame. And yet do not regard him as an enemy, but admonish him as a brother (II Thessalonians 3:14, 15).

We should remember that there is a relative operation of fellowship. That faithful person, and church, will find itself expressing true Christian fellowship in a constant flow of cooperative and non-cooperative efforts. Both are essential to fellowship. Z. T. Sweeney one time wrote this:

---

28. Alexander Campbell, from *Christian Baptist*, Vol. I, p. 208, quoted in *Memoirs of Alexander Campbell*, II, p. 57.

PRECEPT: CHRISTIAN FELLOWSHIP

> We all recognize the spiritual character and worth of our brethren of other communions, likewise their practical zeal and devotion. We fellowship all this in them, and do so gladly, because we can do so in faith. But where we are called upon to fellowship a form that is not only unscriptural, but robs the "mould of the doctrine" of Christ of all meaning, we can not do it, because we can not do it in faith. We fellowship them in all things wherein we believe them to be right, and only withhold fellowship in those things wherein we believe them to be wrong.[29]

There are many today, who scream for the *cooperative spirit* of the Campbells. Just look at what they did to heal wounds, sweeten the bitterness, and dissolve the barriers of their day. The same pleaders, however, will refuse to follow the *spirit* of *faithfulness* to precept which gave their cooperative activities a refreshing validity quite rare in that day. Let men imitate their faithful ideals and they will not sacrifice any element of faith for mere cooperative expediency.

The writer was once in an area where there were several cooperative organizations each determined by the amount and nature of the grounds of fellowship. Some were very narrow, some very wide. First, there was the Niles ministerium, limited to the "clergy" on but two general grounds: geography and "non-Catholic" basis. The cooperative efforts had to be on general purposes and often limited severely by diverse opinions. Then there was the Tri-State Evangelistic Rally, a fellowship of persons freely persuaded to come together (with common relationship) to cooperate in

---

29. Z. T. Sweeney, *Should Churches of Christ Receive Unimmersed Into Formal Fellowship* (Cincinnati, Ohio: Standard Publishing, 1942), p. 1.

the sole aim of preaching the gospel and edifying the people as to the primitive New Testament Church, both locally and in new untouched areas. This fellowship was rich and full. Again, there was the Fundamental Ministers fellowship of Warren and Trumbull County. This fellowship was determined by a "clergy" which would submit, without reservation, to the plea of "fundamentalism"—the Trinitarian doctrine and the verbal inspiration of the Scripture, etc. This group was also determined by geography. Thus, fellowship here was limited by the creedal formula of the "fundamentalists." Many New Testament patterns were omitted—and fellowship became so limited. Then, there was the Youngstown (and vicinity) Council of Churches. This was a geographical organization of many non-Catholic churches, with the threefold platform: "We resolve to love: agree to differ: unite to serve!" Therefore, any agency or person advocating this purpose was presented as worthy of all cooperative effort. This fellowship practically was reduced to mere "association." Its policy was so wide open for contradiction and unchristian factors that the word fellowship was hardly fitting anywhere.

Finally, we mention the District Convention of Disciples of Christ. This fellowship was based on geography, the "hangover" of some tradition, and the cooperative plea of agency and method. This basis was narrow and often exclusive of some of the genuine purposes of the New Testament. It declared all who refused to share this activity to be "the non-cooperative" brethren, charging such with making inconsequential things a test of fellowship. Thus, when purposes and aims are at variance, then the grounds for cooperation are very thin, and the occasions of cooperation are very rare. Cooperation is a serious matter and has

PRECEPT: CHRISTIAN FELLOWSHIP

potential dangers that can become real—and must not easily be brushed aside with a feeling of good will.

1. One must first guard against the temptation to *compromise* precepts of the Lord in the name of cooperation. Opinion yes, but precept—no! In a complicated society this becomes an acute problem, which Christians face again and again. There are so many pleas for cooperative efforts between Christians and churches that assail God-fearing people today that the course of least resistance is all too tempting. One might as well give in to any such effort, "for all are working toward the same end," is the current attitude.

To compromise is to make mutual concessions. Does man have a right to concede *any* point merely on the basis that there is a difference? Our fathers used to say "to condone a thing is to commit that thing." No one, who is truly a steward of the truth of the Lord, has any right to concede property not his. And such is a precept of the Lord! And yet, man today, will compromise at different costs. It has been said that every man has a price at which he will "sell out" his honor, or his conviction. Is this absolute? And yet some do follow this pattern when different sets of pressures come to bear on them. The noble cry for a world church and the sympathetic pleading of well-intentioned peoples are used by some to rationalize their compromise.

We often hear the plea today, that the divisive problems can be, not so much solved, as dismissed on the basis of a "higher unity." What is a "higher unity"? When honestly and critically examined this goal is proven rather ethereal and without substance. It sounds good, but it lacks the holy fiber necessary for Christian fellowship.

But what about cooperation on a "common denominator" of faith? Can not the ground of cooperation be established on a body of precept which groups hold in common? This is the plea of some conservative groups. Stephen W. Paine defends this position with an answer to the question, "How can groups fellowship together which have different doctrines?":

> The answer is that we have not for one moment consented to the proposition that our distinctive doctrines are unimportant nor a matter for indifference. We frankly do have doctrinal differences about which, to use Paul's words, we are fully persuaded in our own minds. But we have found that our area of agreement embraces those truths which we all hold to be essential to salvation. We have come to realize that despite areas of doctrinal disagreement, we are dealing with people who give evidence of being New Testament Christians, and who have a theological platform consistent therewith.
>
> We therefore base our cooperation fully and solely upon the common faith of us all, allowing each other complete freedom in our distinctives.[30]

This is a compromise to agree to evade all issues, right or wrong, precept or opinion, which are not held in common. This position avoids problems which man must answer. And yet it has done some good in spite of evil things it has at times led to. Here is a vital issue: Where does such a policy or program lead?

Man has sacrificed two important things in the name of cooperation. One is loyalty to creeds and traditions. Here is a good result. J. H. Garrison says:

> Christian people, who are consciously at one in their attitude to Christ and in their sense of obligation to Him, see that they are kept in different communions, and incapacitated from cooperation in work and worship, because they

---

30. Stephen W. Paine, *United Evangelical Action* (May 1, 1949), p. 12.

have inherited different theological traditions to which they are assumed to be bound. Without entering into any discussion of what these theological traditions — call them creeds, confessions, testimonies, or whatever else — are worth, they feel in their souls that they are not bound to them, and ought not to be, with the same kind of bond which secures their allegiance to Christ. For the sake of getting nearer to those who share this allegiance, and cooperating with them in the service of the Lord who holds their hearts, they contemplate with more equanimity the slackening or dissolution of the bonds which attach them to the theology, or, if we prefer to call it so, the Christian thought of the past.[31]

The second item sacrificed, which is not good, is loyalty to Christ. The same attitude that works against the one, too often works against the other. There are some precepts of the Lord that discourage, limit, qualify, and even prevent cooperation. Since loyalty to Christ is pre-eminent, cooperation must issue from it, or not issue at all. There is no compromise in precept. That is why much of fellowship is relative. There are certain things in which one can not loyally fellowship.

And yet in view of this strict policy the Christian must be careful that his attitude of no-compromise does not negate the very stand of loyalty which he has taken. A good example of the right attitude was expressed in the relation between Alexander Campbell and Robert Owen, an infidel, in their famous debate of 1829. Mrs. Trollope reports:

> At the conclusion of the debate (which lasted for fifteen sittings), Mr. Campbell desired the whole assembly to sit down. They obeyed. He then requested all who wished well

---

31. J. H. Garrison, *The Story of a Century* (St. Louis: Christian Publishing Co., 1909), p. 272.

to Christianity to rise, and a very large majority were in an instant on their legs. He then requested them to be seated, and then desired those who believed not in its doctrine to rise, and a few gentlemen and one lady obeyed.

This was a result that might have been perhaps anticipated, but what was much less to have been expected, neither of the disputants ever appeared to lose his temper. I was told they were much in each other's company, constantly dining together, and on all occasions expressed most cordially their mutual esteem.[32]

Responding to her surprise at their friendliness, Professor Foster asks: "Does she mean that men discussing such life-and-death matters as the very existence of God — Christian and atheist boldly arguing their cases — should not then pause and engage in social conversation as they eat a meal together?"[33] Foster then recounts this incident:

The pointed and frank discussion of the hope for a life after death which arose when Owen visited Campbell at Bethany before the debate has become famous. When they met together again in private, personal farewell conference after the debate, Alexander Campbell urged Owen so earnestly to abandon his atheism and come back to God that Owen was moved to tears, although he did not change his adherence to atheism.[34]

Though there was friendship, courtesy, and charity, Mr. Campbell never compromised one factor of precept. One need never compromise — nor ever seek a substitute for the genuine. And yet man, through weakness of faith or the flesh, has repeatedly done so.

---

32. Mrs. Trollope, quoted by R. C. Foster, *Christian Standard* (January 4, 1941), p. 8.
33. Foster, *Ibid.*, p. 9.
34. *Ibid.*, p. 9.

PRECEPT: CHRISTIAN FELLOWSHIP

2. Another danger apparent in cooperation is that tendency to become *ensnared in some entangling alliance.* Commitments involved in such transactions often become embarrassing, or lead to a ground of compromise or outright disloyalty to the Lord. Again, there is the caution: Where does such a danger lead?

The weighty consequences of this issue are set forth in the remarks made on a passage (II Corinthians 6:14-16) in the McGarvey-Pendleton commentary:

> In the first epistle to the Corinthians the apostle had reasoned with the Church, giving it instruction as to marriage ties between pagans and believers, and as to the social and other fellowships which tempted the Corinthians to take part in idol feasts. In all this his language had been careful and guarded, and he had recognized to the full every principle of Christian liberty involved in these questions. He now lays aside the argumentative reserve which characterized his first letter and tells them plainly that by thus going to the extreme limits of their liberty they are liable to make the grace of God in vain as to them. That life is a brief day of probation wherein they should not hazard their salvation. Then, by a series of short, terse questions he shows the utter folly, the inconsistency and incongruity of every form of alliance which entangles the children of God with the children of the devil. The world has not so improved, and Satan has not so repented, as to in any way nullify, or even weaken, the weight and applicability of this apostolic warning.[35]

Every Christian and every church must weigh this matter carefully. For the issues of this danger are many and often complicated. It is not always easy to give a categorical answer

---

35. J. W. McGarvey, P. Y. Pendleton, *Thessalonians, Corinthians, Galatians, and Romans* (Cincinnati, Ohio: Standard Publishing, 1916), p. 203.

to one's own convenience, but no one is excused from not putting forth an honest effort. There is an integrity and personal loyalty surrounding every cooperative decision which each one *must* preserve.

Alexander Campbell gives an account of how he answered this problem:

> When I unite in prayer with a society of disciples, I have full communion with them in certain petitions, confessions and thanksgivings; but requests may be presented, confessions made and thanksgiving offered in which I have not full communion. The same may be said of any other social act of worship. All that I intend by the phrase is, that I will unite with any Baptist society in the U.S. in any act of social worship, such as prayer, praise or breaking bread in commemoration of the Lord's death, if they confess the one Lord, the one faith, the one hope, and the one baptism; provided always that, as far as I can judge, they piously and morally conform to their profession. . . . I consider every act as only expressing approbation of the thing represented, and of them in so far as they conform to it. Therefore, I frankly and boldly declare to them as Paul did to the Corinthians, the things in which I praise them, and the things in which I praise them not. And I know of no way, of no course that any Christian can pursue consistently with the New Testament, consistently with his serving God and his own generation, but this one. Therefore, I advocate it and practice it.[36]

Thus, Mr. Campbell entered into cooperative activities of the Baptist society of his day (it being the nearest community to that of the New Testament pattern) with the reservation that his alliance went only as far as New Testament

---

36. Robert Richardson, *Memoirs of Alexander Campbell*, II, pp. 136, 137.

PRECEPT: CHRISTIAN FELLOWSHIP

precept, and no further. He always made his position clear when the issue was one of faith, and withdrew himself completely from every anti-scriptural practice.

3. A third danger in exercising the right of cooperation is that of the possibility of the *wrong influence* emanating from one's action to the detriment of the weaker Christian. The Christian is ever on guard against any of his deeds becoming "a stumbling block in his brother's way," of wounding his conscience (Romans 14:13, 21; I Corinthians 8:9-13). This is no little matter, and cooperative endeavors are constantly being limited by this danger.[37]

The culmination of this entire first section should point to one thing at least, i.e., the first step toward Christian unity. What a noble aim! Some have cried out today that "unity is in the air." But what is it? Let man bring it down to earth, re-examine it, and then practice it according to the dictate of the Lord.

To begin with, unity in itself is not the supreme goal; it is not the most important thing for Christians to consider. It must be held in its proper perspective lest it flood out all the Scriptural grounds on which it is to be erected. One can not allow the end to justify the means, the result to belittle the method, a dream to cloud out the pattern. As C. V. Dunn says:

> If unity is more important than loyalty to Christ, then all sincere non-Catholic believers should unite with the Roman Catholic Church. If unity is more important than loyalty, then Huss, Wycliffe, Luther, Calvin and all the rest of the reformers were mistaken in leaving the Roman Catholic Church. If unity is more important than loyalty, then the

---

37. See chapter 10.

Campbells, Stone, Scott and others were mistaken when they left denominational bodies to stand upon the inspired Word of God. If the great reformers had taken the stand some take today, we would be still under the domination of the church of Rome.[38]

Any unity that is an answer to Christ's prayer must be *"in Him"* (John 17). Unity means little standing alone; however, with the prefix "Christian" added it is limited and qualified to be a certain brand.

Too many unity programs want to begin at the wrong place to accomplish its task, when it should begin with the method of the pattern. Unity is a gracious blessing bestowed on a people who have faithfully qualified themselves before the Lord. But man thinks he can begin with the result—by building an organization, by designing cooperation, by manipulating a federation of bodies, and thus work back to the source. Whereas unity is the crowning glory of Christian fellowship. And this fellowship is progressive, working from source, to purpose, to cooperative efforts.

Cooperation is too often confused with unity when it is but a segment of fellowship which in turn is but a part of the working toward unity. Cooperation should demand unity, but unity does not necessarily demand cooperation. Unity is a more basic and deeper issue than cooperation in all of its forms. Cooperation is the mere doing together; unity is the result of believing, thinking, purposing, obeying together.

Therefore, union has been confused with unity. But union is not the answer. Nor does union tend to lead to unity. Robert Richardson one time wrote:

> Denominational union is not, and never can be, Christian union. It rests not on that Christian unity, which can be the

---

38. C. V. Dunn, *Christian Standard* (December 30, 1944), p. 3.

PRECEPT: CHRISTIAN FELLOWSHIP

the only true basis of Christian union, but on the miserable and varying formulas of human opinion, and the narrow *knife-edged* support of an ignorant and intolerant dogmatism. The true children of God, who are *in* these denominations, but not *of* them, are united to each other by far higher and holier ties, than those which bind together the masses of these communities, and, were it not that they are entangled by the artful policies and selfish interests of the parties in which they find themselves arrayed, they could not long remain separated from each other.[39]

Unity begins with the person — what he believes, thinks, how he obeys. It is a personal matter, as seen in the working of fellowship. It involves the relationship of persons, depending on the faithful initiative of such. Thus, it falls the lot of *each* person to begin to practice Christian unity. And this is accomplished by a personal devotion to the Lord of unity. It is often much easier to fight for something than to live for it. Any other way is not good enough. The fusing of two or more church bodies is trying to attain unity in reverse. J. H. Garrison says:

> As a substitute for that impracticable dream is the gradual approximation of all Christian bodies to the mind of Christ, as revealed in the New Testament, "until we all come to the unity of the faith and of the knowledge of the Son of God."[40]

"Even as Thou, Father, art in Me, and I in Thee, that they also may be in Us; that the world may believe that Thou didst send Me (John 17:21).

Thus, this whole issue comes back to precept. When individuals return to the law of Christ — and faithfully learn

---

39. Robert Richardson, *Millennial Harbinger* (1859), p. 64.
40. J. H. Garrison, *The Story of a Century*, p. 219.

how to "enter into Him" and "grow in Him," they will have laid the first foundation stone for unity. A unity in precept is primary. We quote from the *Christian Standard* of 1866:

> We seek to unite those only who acknowledge the one divine standard—the Word of God. Roman Catholics, with their co-equal authority of Church and Pope; rationalists, to whom the Bible has no authority, only as it bows to the reason which they worship; Quakers, to whom the "inner light" is authoritative; Mormons, with a Bible of their own—none of these are embraced in this plea, because they do not accept the authority of the Holy Scriptures, which evangelical Protestants acknowledge. We plead for the union of all who hold to the supreme authority of the Lord Jesus, and, therefore, lift up the Christian standard, which they all declare to be alone authoritative. We present it in opposition to all human standards as the rallying point for looking "unto Jesus, the author and finisher of the faith"; they may gather about Him as the center of faith, love and unity, and, with one mind, "may strive together for the faith of the gospel." Then will theology give place to religion; the pride of party, to glorying in the cross; the strife of rival sects, to a glorious warfare against the world, the flesh and the devil, and the weakness of our present distracted state to a strength and beauty worthy of the sacramental host of God's elect. Believers will be one in Christ, as He is one with the Father, and the world will bow to the eloquence of love and the beauty of holiness as they have never bowed to the potency of logic or the dogmatisms of theology. May the Lord hasten it in His time.[41]

But, cried out the modernist, there is no pattern. "Unity is not found in conformity to a Divine Pattern, but in surrender

---

41. Editorial in *Christian Standard*, first issue, quoted in *Christian Standard* (April 1, 1944), p. 5.

to a Divine Person," says O. T. Foster.[42] What a contradiction!

At an assembly of the Congregational churches in Oberlin, Ohio, in 1948 Dr. Albert W. Palmer presented the slogan: "In things where we agree, unity; in things where we differ, liberty; in all things the will to be one."[43] This is the old concept of unity which holds that the only tenable common denominator for unity is the concensus of opinion — points of agreement, rather than divine precept. It makes "the inner conscience" instead of the Word of God the basis of unity. To this slogan is added a comment by the *Christian Evangelist* that it is a "rendition of a famous slogan of the Disciples."[44] No doubt the implication was pointed to the plea stated and defended by Restoration leaders, and originated by Rupertus Mildenius, i.e., "On essentials, unity; in non-essentials, liberty; in all things, love." This is an old saying, and saturated with Scriptural teaching. However, it is certainly not comparable to that "rendition" given by Mr. Palmer. They are poles apart in meaning. Unity must not begin with mere human agreement but with divine agreement.

This teaching of unity on precept is common Scriptural teaching (John 17; Ephesians 4) and apostolic precedent. As C. F. Witty points out:

> In faith unity. In the churches of the first century under the direct oversight of the inspired apostles, there was a known and fully understood formula that was accepted and followed by every person that had any part in setting in order and governing the fully established local congregation of the church of God, and by every person that had any part

---
42. O. T. Foster, *Christian Evangelist*.
43. Albert W. Palmer, *Christian Evangelist* (October 25, 1950), p. 1044.
44. *Ibid*.

in conducting the public worship in the assembled congregation of God.

If this is a true statement then every person that came into the fellowship of the churches of the first century came in exactly like every other person that came in, and every person that set order or had any part in governing any local congregation of the church set it in order and governed it by exactly the same formula as was used in setting in order and governing every other church, and every person that conducted the public worship in the assembled congregations followed the same formula as was used in the public worship in every other assembled congregation.

Results: unity and fellowship among all the churches of that age.[45]

Now the very thought of unity in precept is limiting and confining, and there comes into play the law of "antithesis." If there is a rightful ground for unity, then there is a rightful ground for division. All division is not wrong. There is a time to unite and there is a time to divide. Unity is not the whole Bible story. However, people must be cautioned to examine and know the ground for each — as found in Scripture. The trouble is that we get these two confused.

When any one takes it upon himself to be a reformer, or better still, a restorer of Bible precept, the result will almost invariably be divisive. For instance, for nearly 1000 years the Roman Catholic Church had a type of external unity (uniformity) and singular influence over the known western world. But when men arose to reform evil and restore some primitive New Testament precepts there rightfully was division. This was the right condition and time to produce

---

45. Claud F. Witty, *Christian Unity Quarterly* (August, 1946), pp. 23, 24.

PRECEPT: CHRISTIAN FELLOWSHIP

such results. However, with this break—there would then have been the time for unity. But this reformation was not severe enough and denominationalism, a chain reaction of other division, ensued.

Today when men will fight to restore New Testament precept they will be accused of being divisive. One who works for Bible unity, and nothing less, is labeled narrow. A number of followers of Thomas Campbell found this stand "too rich for their blood" when they foresaw where the principle, "Where the Scriptures speak, we speak; and where the Scriptures are silent, we are silent," would eventually lead them. So they broke away as was regretfully expected.

To plead for division at the right time does not necessarily mark one as a separatist, a partisan, nor a non-cooperative isolationist. Nor to plead for unity at the right time does not necessarily mark another guilty of compromise.

When people do not care what they believe, *union* will often be the result. But when people do care what they believe, then *unity* or *division* will be the result, depending on the object of their belief. Is it tradition, conjecture, or the precepts of the Lord? These factors determine which of the two alternatives it will be, and the severity of each.

The classic example of this twofold principle working in the Restoration Movement is the oft-repeated case of the censure of Thomas Campbell for taking the Lord's Supper to a people who seldom enjoyed this privilege. It happened in an area near Pittsburgh, Pennsylvania. Another member of his Presbytery "spied out his liberty" and reported that Mr. Campbell had served the Lord's Supper to those other than members of his own Seceder branch of the Presbyterian Church. He was thus called to defend himself before his Synod. And this was his appeal on the basis of the Scripture:

WHAT THE BIBLE SAYS ABOUT FAITH AND OPINION

So far am I from this, that I dare not venture to trust my own understanding so far as to take upon me to teach anything as a matter of faith or duty but what is already expressly taught and enjoined by Divine authority; and I hope it is no presumption to believe that saying and doing the very same things that are said and done before our eyes on the sacred page, is infallibly right, as well as all-sufficient for the edification of the Church, whose duty and perfection it is to be in all things conformed to the original standard. It is, therefore because I have no confidence, either in my own infallibility or in that of others, that I absolutely refuse, as inadmissible and schismatic, the introduction of human opinions and human inventions into the faith and worship of the Church. It is, therefore, because I plead the cause of the Scriptural and apostolic worship of the Chruch, in opposition to the various errors and schisms which have so awfully corrupted and divided it, that the brethren of the Union should feel it difficult to admit me as their fellow-laborer in that blessed work.[46]

From this time on, his Presbytery took every opportunity to watch him, spy out on his preaching with bitter and unrelenting spirit. Sectarianism had overruled a Bible defense and was making sure there would be no repeated offense against "the church." When Mr. Campbell expected an air of freedom in his new country, he found an air of bigotry, corruption, apostasy, and tyranny in his own church. There was only one inevitable result — he withdrew. There was no other course.

This was the first such test-case, in regard to precept and opinion. And it had to come when a man determined to be a restorer of divine precept. And from then on it had to come

---

46. Robert Richardson, *Memoirs of Alexander Campbell*, I, pp. 226, 227.

PRECEPT: CHRISTIAN FELLOWSHIP

a thousand times—times of importance, times of unimportance; times of eminence; times of obscurity; times involving many; times involving but two parties. This is the old story, oft repeated in history.

Division and unity are always mingled in the same stories. But where men are determined to "be one" on the precepts of the Lord, there will begin Christian unity. It is the inevitable and inescapable foundation of Christian faithfulness. And, thus to some degree, more or less, there has been the kind of unity the Lord wanted in some place in every age in church history. As Robert Richardson wrote in the *Millennial Harbinger:*

> In this view (of John 17), it will be apparent that the usual interpretation of this prayer is incorrect, which mistakes unity for union, and supposes it to relate to some future fusion of all religious parties into one, or to the creation of some grand overshadowing community whose members shall be united upon some simple formula of Christian truth, and thus induce the world to acknowledge the Messiahship of Jesus. The truth is, that this prayer of Christ *has been already answered,* for the Father heareth Him always, and has certainly, in every period of the church, granted to all true believers, that spirit which establishes unity with Christ, and enables its possessors to manifest to men the life and character of Christ and to "shine as lights in the world." Just in proportion as this spiritual unity has been established, and, as the proper fruits of the Spirit have been manifested in the lives and character of Christians, so has the world believed in the Divine mission of Jesus. Thus, has the prayer been fulfilled in every age of the church, and thus it will continue to be fulfilled to the end of the world.[47]

---

47. Robert Richardson, *Millennial Harbinger* (1859), p. 64.

Part II — Precedent
Chapter Seven
PRECEDENT DEFINED

In the early pages of this book space was allotted to the supreme and primary issue of divine authority. We first discussed the expression of this authority in precept. Another aspect of authority which demands attention is precedent.

In former chapters we could not help touching on it. But now it must be clearly labeled and its force accurately measured. It is closely related to precept. They both have much in common. When authority is discussed precept and precedent are repeatedly linked together as the companion and complementary implementation of God's will. The third article in Thomas Campbell's *Declaration and Address,* is stated:

> Nothing ought to be inculcated upon Christians as articles of faith; nor required of them as terms of communion; but what is expressly taught and enjoined upon them, in the Word of God. Nor ought anything be admitted, as of divine obligation, in their church constitution and managements, but what is expressly enjoined by the authority of our Lord Jesus Christ and his Apostles upon the New Testament church either in expressed terms, or by approved precedent.[1]

In view of all this, precedent has a meaning and operation all of its own. Though it emanates from the same authority as does precept, its nature and working is distinctive. All too often it has been neglected.

Webster's New Collegiate Dictionary defines precedent: "Something done or said that may serve as an example to authorize or justify a subsequent act of the same or an analogous kind."[2]

---

1. Thomas Campbell, *Declaration and Address* (Lincoln, Il.: Lincoln Christian College Press, 1971 reprint of 1809 ed.), p. 23.
2. *Webster's New Collegiate Dictionary* (Springfield, Mass.: G & C Merriam Company, 1956), p. 664.

PRECEDENT: PRECEDENT DEFINED

God has more than one way of inducing His creatures to submit to His will. He may state a truth or command categorically, or He may show it through providential incidents. Truth may be shown as well as told. Both are effective expressions of revelation. And that which is shown must be given its rightful authoritative force.

This is what Paul meant when he used Israel as a lesson for the Corinthian Church (I Corinthians 10). In unfolding Israel's story of disobedience he said,

> Now these things happened as examples for us, that we should not crave evil things, as they also craved. . . . Now these things happened to them as an example, and they were written for our instruction, upon whom the ends of the ages have come" (I Corinthians 10:6, 11).

Paul wrote to the Philippians: "The things you have learned and received and heard and seen in me, practice these things; and the God of peace shall be with you" (Philippians 4:9).

John B. Cowden quotes M. C. Kurfees, a chief opponent of musical instruments in worship, as saying:

> "A thus did the Lord and His apostles" is just as important and binding as "a thus said the Lord and His apostles." Let it be cheerfully admitted, if we have Apostolic example for the practice, then all opposition to it should cease; for if we are not to follow the leadership of inspired Apostles in our efforts to worship and praise God, then we are in a hopeless confusion, and it is needless to look elsewhere for guidance.[3]

---

3. M. C. Kurfees as quoted by John B. Cowden, *Christian Worship* (Cincinnati, O.: The Standard Press, 1920), pp. 324, 325.

WHAT THE BIBLE SAYS ABOUT FAITH AND OPINION

This is to say then, that precedent is precept in action, and in turn is passed on to a third party. That would point to us today. Thus, the force and weight of precedent is divinely authoritative. Not that it carries more or less weight than precept, but only a different kind of weight. It is the same authority, but a different medium of transmission. When men speak of the will of God they should then give equal attention to both precept and precedent. They both complement each other and round out revelation.

For example of the power of precedent we note the case of James Haldane and John Aikman, two pious and Scripture loving men of Scotland. The "clergy" of their day, as well as civil powers, became hostile toward all "lay" preaching. Thus, these two men faced great opposition to their desire to preach the gospel. In the year 1797 they made this defense on the basis of Bible precedent. They claimed the right to preach:

> Upon the indispensable duty of every Christian to warn sinners to flee from the wrath to come, and to point out Jesus as the way, the truth, and the life. Whether a man declare these important truths to two or two hundred, he is, in our opinion a preacher of the gospel, or one who declares the glad tidings of salvation, which is the precise meaning of the word preach. In harmony with this view, we find that, in the beginning when the members of the Church at Jerusalem numbering then eight to ten thousand, were all scattered abroad except the apostles, they went everywhere preaching the word.[4]

Were they right? Did they have authority to preach? Is there any precept to negate this stand?

---

4. Robert Richardson, *Memoirs of Alexander Campbell*, I (Nashville, Tenn.: Gospel Advocate, 1956 reprint of 1897 ed.), pp. 160-161.

PRECEDENT: PRECEDENT DEFINED

If ever the "Restoration Movement" has made a contribution to the Christian world it has been in the area of restoring the divine authority as manifested through "precedent." J. D. Thomas writes,

> Before we attempt the solution of the problem of when and how examples teach, we should first demonstrate that they do teach, inasmuch as some who have been involved in the present controversy have come to the conclusion that examples by and of themselves teach nothing! Those who reject the teaching of examples feel that examples have value for New Testament interpretation only in that they illustrate optional matters; and that there is no such thing as a required or binding teaching unless there be a command somewhere in the New Testament covering the point. These people have arrived at this view and hold it in spite of the fact that all our brethren have always, up to now, believed that examples—approved precedents—do teach us concerning required things. . . . Unquestionably examples do teach required matters; and therefore do establish pattern authority![5]

Now the important question: Is every incident divine precedent? Every thing that Jesus did, that the apostles did, that early Christians did, that the apostolic church did—are all of these precedents for us today? If so, we would soon be entangled in a maze of inconsistencies. It reminds one of the hackneyed joke in which the following Scripture passages are misused: "And Judas went and hanged himself." "Go and do thou likewise." "And what thou doest, do quickly."

---

5. J. D. Thomas, *We Be Brethren* (Abilene, TX: Biblical Research Press, 1958), p. 50.

Mr. Cowden comments, "What was intended as authoritative precedent in the New Testament, and what as historical example, is difficult to tell. . . ."[6] Not every example nor every incident is precedent. Every revealed fact has a purpose, but the purpose may not necessarily be that of authorizing a subsequent act similar to that recorded. Therefore, we say that it must be an "approved precedent" before it carries the weight God intended it to carry. What is an "approved precedent" and how is it recognized?

W. R. Walker writes:

> We sometimes hear of an "approved precedent" cited as having apostolic origin and authority. There is such a thing. But it is to be found in the example or procedure of the apostles' work in executing Jesus' commands, not in their personal conduct, in which human weakness may be detected occasionally.[7]

(1) Every thing the apostles did certainly was not inspired. Look at Paul's censure of Peter's behavior (Galatians 2:11-21). It is admitted that the apostles spoke and wrote under divine direction, but they did not live under such direction. They had to will to obey the Lord as did any one else. Therefore, how far can the example of the apostles be accepted as inspired? It can be accepted only as far as it was approved by the Holy Spirit. Notice the case of the ordination of Saul and Barnabas (Acts 13:2-4). It is distinctly stated that the Holy Spirit directed this whole procedure. Here is a clear-cut case of "approved precedent" and is easily adaptable to like situations today. Whenever the record states that a particular case was directed by God, Christ, or the Holy Spirit, then one can be sure it was "approved."

---

6. John B. Cowden, *Christian Worship*, p. 174.
7. W. R. Walker, *A Ministering Ministry* (Cincinnati, O.: Standard Publishing, 1938), p. 101.

(2) Another test of approval is the sanction given by the apostles. They were inspired and given power to identify certain examples as precedents to be followed. Note how Paul challenged the Corinthian Church to use the example set by the Churches of Macedonia as their guide. In lauding the stewardship of the Macedonians he says to the Corinthians,

> But just as you abound in everything, in faith and utterance and knowledge and in all earnestness and in the love we inspired in you, see that you abound in this gracious work also. I am not speaking this as a command, but as proving through the earnestness of others the sincerity of your love also (II Corinthians 8:7, 8).

This whole picture is one of a Church manifesting Christian stewardship in action, the principle of which, and the working thereof, is to be emulated by churches today (II Corinthians 8:1-15). This is precedential authority.

This is the subjective side of "approval." Now look at its objective side—its play on man to whom it is directed. It is imperative that one must "handle accurately" precedent as well as precept. Are some precedents provincial, some conditional, and some specific? Should we not ask the same exegetical questions of precedent that we ask of precept? "To whom is it directed, under what condition, at what time, and for what purpose?" Is it pointed to sinner or saint? Is it conditioned by certain circumstances?

Notice the case of the stewardship in the Jerusalem church (Acts 2:44-45). Here was an extreme type of having all things in common, and yet there is no indication according to the record that it was practiced by other apostolic churches. Is this not a conditional precedent?—a precedent to be heeded only when conditions of extreme poverty and totalitarianism prevail like that experienced by the Judean Church?

Or was this merely a recorded fact of extreme sacrificial living which God never intended to be a precedential? The Holy Spirit led the Jerusalem church in this extreme sacrifice so that when the church was scattered to the four winds their assets were liquid, the financial means were afforded for journeying to far countries with the gospel, and no loot was available to the persecutors.

Look at a few of the practices which some one or some group held in the Apostolic era as recorded in Scripture. There was fasting, the holy kiss, foot washing, the working of inspiration, the functioning of miraculous powers, the inducting into the Apostolic office, the imparting of the Holy Spirit through the laying on of hands, circumcision, communion at the Lord's table, the love feast.

Moreover, in pursuing this further what about such instances as the disciples singing a hymn when they left the Lord's supper (Matthew 26:30)? The new church continuing steadfastly in the apostles' teaching and fellowship, in the breaking of bread and the prayers (Acts 2:42)? Philip's preaching "Jesus" and immediately baptizing the listener in water (Acts 8:35-38)? Paul's joining himself ("placing his membership") with the Jerusalem congregation (Acts 9:26, 27)? The early disciples being called "Christian" (Acts 11:26)? Paul preaching in the synagogues (Acts 13; 14:1; 17:1, 2)? Paul's going by boat to preach the Gospel (Acts 16:11; 21:1)? Paul and Silas baptizing the jailor the "same hour of the night" (Acts 16:33)? Paul baptizing the Ephesians into Christ after learning they had only known "John's baptism" (Acts 19:3-6)? Paul speaking 3 months in the synagogue (Acts 19:8)? Paul teaching in the school of Tyrannus (Acts 19:9)? The Church at Troas breaking bread on the "first day of the week" (Acts 20:7)? The church meeting in an upper room (Acts 20:8)? Paul appealing to the civil government to protect his rights (Acts 22:23; 23:17; 25:11)? We could go on and on with recorded incidents.

Does consistency call for the blanket acceptance of all of these as practices to be kept intact by the church today? If so, there will be some very embarrassing and inconsistent results.

Should not these issues be "handled accurately" as any other portion of Scripture should? When not done there arises great differences of attitudes and thus these things become part of the walls of division separating the sects of today.

Each case must be considered separately. And when each is properly weighed, its purpose uncovered, its object and field of working identified, and its circumstantial conditions outlined, then its precedential value will truly be known. One might catalogue all historical incidents recorded under apostolic oversight, and each, when properly examined, will fall into one of three classes:

(1) It may be a mere incident recorded to teach some particular truth, thus having no authoritative value of actual precedent except belief in and adherence to the truth which is taught. Illustrations of this would be foot washing and the holy kiss.

(2) Or it may be precedential in a restricted or conditioned sense, conditioned to a specific time, place, person, or purpose. This is the case of the impartation of the Holy Spirit by the laying on of hands. This was done by the apostles only, and all such activity was precedent for them only. When the last of the apostles died, then this precedent lost its field of operation. It was precedent, but was qualified by conditions which are no longer present. "Pentecostal" people ask the

question, "can't the Holy Spirit work miracles today?" That's not the question to ask. It is not "can He" but does He choose to do so today? One must be careful then not to apply precedent in a field where it was not intended.

(3) Or lastly, an incident may have general precedential value — reaching out to all Christians (or to all non-Christians, whichever the case may be) in all times, and in all places, and in all conditions. Such is the Lord's Supper. This rich Christian experience is taught to us by means of precept and precedent. Thus, all precedential material found in the New Testament ought to be carefully weighed by Christians today. In this way we will duplicate this wondrous ordinance as nearly like the original practice as is humanly possible. Once again, as it was in precept, we see the important place which exegesis holds in solving the main problem of this book.

How then does one differentiate between an historical incident and an event that has precedental authority for us today? Dr. Lewis A. Foster (Cincinnati Christian Seminary) and Professor Lynn Gardner (Ozark Bible College) have done some excellent work in this area. Here we suggest 6 tests for each occurrence needing such a decision:

1. How does it fit into the context of the verses before and after it, the context of the whole book, the context of the whole Bible? Remember the simple truth that there is harmony and consistency within the total revelation of God.
2. What was the original meaning as the writer intended? This is a valid rule of exegesis.
3. Was it rooted in an ordinary custom of that time when it occurred? The "holy kiss" is an excellent case in point, when we understand the function of this social custom of that day.

PRECEDENT: PRECEDENT DEFINED

4. Did it meet a cultural need at that time? Foot washing was a needful service which a host was expected to provide for all guests and usually performed by one of the lowest servants of the household. In the upper room no such service was provided so Jesus performed it to teach the apostles a great lesson (John 13:3-17).
5. Examine the outcome and ask, did it continue on as a practice in personal or church life? The Lord's Supper is a good case in point.

We like J. D. Thomas' conclusion: "The contextual situation should be exactly parallel to our situation today, before we can decide that it is a principle for all ages and binding on us today, rather than merely a local and temporal matter with application only for its own day and its own contextual situation."[8]

6. If it does not literally carry over into today's practice, what then is the general principle or lesson to follow?

Those of the "restoration plea" are often criticized for over-emphasizing certain Bible things or for emphasizing the wrong things to the detriment of other things. Here the critics point out that we over-play the issue of "applying water" in administering baptism. And, that in turn, we have failed to question and test the candidate on the "greater factors" in conversion. Such an accusation reveals a cardinal failing in denominational exegesis—that of either misusing precedent, or else denying its presence and function entirely in believing and obeying the will of the Lord. It has truly been a sad story, in which God-fearing people, down through the ages, have not earnestly sought to detect every divine

---

8. J. D. Thomas, *We Be Brethren*, p. 59.

WHAT THE BIBLE SAYS ABOUT FAITH AND OPINION

precept, while at the same time they have so flagrantly discounted divine precedent.

When it comes to testing fellowship, precedent must play an important part in determining the nature and severity of the test. This was indicated in Chapter 4. Let the denominationalist examine the Holy record and see what the Lord emphasized as important. There is the power of precedent. One will soon learn that precedent answers many questions which precept does not always attempt to answer.

Consider the problem of "conversion." Notice the consistent place of baptism in actual case histories, and in turn, the utter lack of quizzes, probations, personal confessions and testimonials, and catechetical tests. Does not this mean something for today? Does not this reveal the things God wants emphasized and de-emphasized? Look at Pentecost when three thousand persons of every variety of sinful color, all did the same simple things in order to receive the promise of salvation and the complete fellowship of the church. There was a singular test of faith, both demanded and precedented on that day. Isaac Errett once wrote:

> We submit *no other tests* but faith and repentance, in admitting persons to baptism and church membership. We present to them no Articles of Faith other than the one article concerning the Divinity and Christhood of Jesus; we demand no narration of a religious experience other than is expressed in a voluntary confession of faith in Jesus; we demand no probation to determine their fitness to come into the church; but instantly, on their voluntary confession of the Christ, and avowed desire to leave their sins and serve the Lord Christ, unless there are good reasons to doubt their sincerity, they are accepted and baptized, in the name of the

PRECEDENT: PRECEDENT DEFINED

Lord Jesus, and *into* the name of the Father, the Son, and the Holy Spirit.[9]

Thus, Christians must be ever cautious in determining the scope of both precept and precedent. Both are vital. Both have a function in rounding out the divine pattern for the private and communal life of a Christian. It was indeed fitting for Mr. Campbell to append the following warning into his *Declaration and Address:*

> We dare therefore neither do, nor receive anything, as of divine obligation, for which there cannot be expressly produced a "thus saith the Lord" either in express terms, or by approved precedent.[10]

---

9. Isaac Errett, *Our Position* (Cincinnati, O.: Standard Publishing, n.d.), pp. 9-10.

10. Thomas Campbell, *Declaration and Address,* pp. 41-42.

Chapter Eight
PURPOSES AND DANGERS

Henry Clay once said, "Precedents deliberately established by wise men are entitled to great weight."[1] How much more is the weight when God is the author, and man the object? What noble and holy purposes generate God's creation? "Divine precedent" rises much higher than mere good taste, antiquated example, or suggestive material. God has a pattern. God is incorporating into life something essential, something which man can not afford to live without.

Thus, the purpose and function of divine precedent is distinctive. It has a mission to fulfill. And God-loving people ought to be almost insatiable in detecting, analyzing and following precedents engineered by the Lord.

(1) One of the first purposes of precedent, already hinted, is that of revealing a divine pattern for the faith and life of both individual and the church. God, with all care and design, providentially lifts the curtain of time and reveals legitimate "actors" portraying life. They are God's people living God's pattern of life in a particular instance. The "drama" is practical and impressive — for precept is being lived by man. It is descriptive and revealing. It is life.

J. D. Thomas stated the matter as a major premise in the syllogism of Bible interpretations:

> Any New Testament example that implies an underlying command, which requires specific action or attitudes of its exemplary characters, establishes a pattern, which requires the same specific action or attitude of people today. And conversely, any New Testament example that does not imply an underlying command which would require specific action or attitudes of the exemplary characters, establishes

---

1. Henry Clay, *Familiar Quotations*, John Bartlett, ed., p. 329.

PRECEDENT: PURPOSES AND DANGERS

no pattern whatever, and serves only to illustrate matters that are purely optional for people today.[2]

Samuel Johnson wrote that, "Example is always more efficacious than precept."[3] It may not always be "more," but it certainly does have an efficacy all of its own.

Twenty centuries of man's tampering with the precedential pattern of the church ought to be sufficient to silence man into embarrassment forever. He has added to and subtracted from the pattern a thousand times. He has assumed the attitude of God's "efficiency expert" with power to innovate scientific improvements in the simple church-pattern so that it will always be "up with the times." And what has been the result? After taking inventory of the record of history let man hang his head in shame for his folly. For this "improved" church *never* has been able to accomplish the holy task as well as did the simple church of the first century under apostolic oversight (Matthew 16:16-18; 18:18-20; John 17:20-23).

When man follows precedent he will have its blessings. This is simple arithmetic. Thomas Campbell wrote:

> For, if the first Christian Churches, walking in the fear of the Lord, in holy unity and unanimity, enjoyed the comforts of the Holy Spirit, and were increased and edified, we have reason to believe, that walking in their footsteps will every where, and at all times, ensure the same blessed privileges. And it is an exact conformity to their recorded and approved example, that we through grace, would be desirous to promote the erection of Churches; and this we believe to be quite practicable, if the legible and authentic records of *their* faith and practice be handed down to *us* upon the page of New Testament Scripture; but if otherwise, we cannot

---

2. J. D. Thomas, *We Be Brethren* (Abilene, TX.: Biblical Research Press, 1958), p. 91.

3. Samuel Johnson, *Familiar Quotations*, John Bartlett, ed., p. 232.

help it. Yet, even in this case, might we not humbly presume, that the Lord would take the will for the deed; for if there be first a willing mind, we are told, "it is accepted, according to what a man hath, and not according to what he hath not." It would appear, then, that sincerely and humbly adopting this model with an entire reliance upon promised grace, we cannot, we shall not, be disappointed.[4]

Does man know better than God? Can he improve on a pattern which God approved? Is man so audacious that he can afford to ignore a holy pattern? Does he presume to devise something better than that which he feels is hardly suggestive of precedential action? What man has often conceived as an improvement, is but a confession of his inability to see the ways of the Lord, or of his outright rebellion.

Oh the depth of the riches both of the wisdom and knowledge of God! How unsearchable are His judgments and unfathomable His ways! For who has known the mind of the Lord, or who became His counselor? Or who has first given to Him that it might be paid back to him again? For from Him and through Him and to Him are all things. To Him be the glory forever. Amen (Romans 11:33-36).

Precedent is efficiency at its best as the Lord knows what is to be the standard precedure for His own work.

(2) The value of precedent as a teacher is not to be overlooked. Precedent has a way of teaching which precept finds well nigh impossible to do. Precedent has a warm way of unfolding truth whereas precept often appears cold and stiff. So together they complement one another.

Disraeli once spoke the line, "A precedent embalms a principle."[5] It has a way of preserving intact the wondrous

---

4. Thomas Campbell, *Declaration and Address* (Lincoln Il.: Lincoln Christian College Press, 1971 reprint of 1809 ed.), pp. 41, 42.
5. Disraeli, *Familiar Quotations*, John Bartlett, ed., p. 419.

PRECEDENT: PURPOSES AND DANGERS

facts of the Lord for our present day observation. Thus, to know fully the truth, one must become a student of precedent. Thus, no man today can confess to have an accurate knowledge of the church of Christ until he has allowed the weight of precedent to teach him. Isaac Errett said:

> Every careful reader of the New Testament must be impressed with the fact that, instead of positive laws describing the officials to be recognized in the church, defining their duties and marking the limitations of their authority, there is simply *an historical development* of church life, arrangements being made and officials being appointed to meet contingencies as they rise. Instead, therefore, of looking for a *thus saith the Lord* respecting church ministers and church work, we must reach our conclusions respecting the officers and work of the primitive churches from an induction of the historical facts in which their church life is set forth.[6]

Here we inject a worthy lesson to be learned by every Bible reader. Frequently a precept is *conditioned,* or an opinion *overruled,* by the presence of a precedent. We shall consider the classic example of the frequency of observing the Lord's Supper. It was definitely the Lord's wish that every follower of His, through this simple ordinance, remember His death until He comes again (Matthew 26:26-29; I Corinthians 11:23-25). In challenging Christians in this matter the apostle Paul said, "For as often as you eat this bread and drink this cup, you proclaim the Lord's death until He comes" (I Corinthians 11:26). This is the oft-quoted verse which many have used to prove that there is absolutely no instruction as to when the supper is to be observed. If

---

6. J. S. Lamar, *Memoirs of Isaac Errett,* II (Cincinnati, O.: Standard Publishing, 1893), p. 150.

there is no qualifying precedent or precept, then this is a proper judgment in exegesis. However, this is not the case. Precedent does qualify the issue. For Luke said, "And on the first day of the week, when we were gathered together to break bread, Paul began talking to them . . ." (Acts 20:7). The Greek language conveys the idea that it was a custom on the Lord's Day—and it was under apostolic oversight. Therefore, the phrase "for as often" (I Corinthans 11:26) is not intended to declare the *frequency* of the observance, (it leaves it completely open), but what is to be the *significance* when it is observed—a proclamation of the death of Christ until He comes again. The faithful weekly observance of the Lord's Supper is the teaching of precedent added to precept.

In his chapter on "Excursus: When Observe the Lord's Supper?" J. D. Thomas uses the sound exegetical "pattern principle" by carefully examining and comparing the four related passages of Scripture, Hebrew 10:25; I Corinthians 16:1, 2; I Corinthians 11:20-26 and Acts 20:7; to show that the qualifying factor of the frequency of the Lord's Supper found in the Acts 20:7 passage, has a definite teaching thrust and throws further light on the meaning of the precepts regarding the assembly of Christians for observing the Lord's Supper in worship.[7]

If precept does not answer a question then let man listen to the voice of precedent. If neither speaks out, then, and only then, dare he let opinion reign. (See Part III.)

(3) It has now been declared that precedent has value in pictorially revealing divine will and teaching divine truth. In view of this, a third purpose is that of affording a generous amount of freedom to man in his submission to precedent

---

7. J. D. Thomas, *We Be Brethren*, pp. 93-106.

PRECEDENT: PURPOSES AND DANGERS

as such. Too often man has foolishly desired of God, a rigid code of laws, carefully catalogued and filed for every condition of life. Why has God not done this? The answer lies in the consideration of any hypothetical case had He done so. Would there have been room in man for any ingenuity, freedom, initiative, aspiration if God would have used this method? No! Man would have become a docile automaton. But with the minimum of precept carefully portrayed in precedent look what man can do. He has a pattern for life, the essentials of which are told and shown, yet leaving the widest area for the fullest expansion of personal character possible. There is rigidity—yet with a full measure of freedom.

Look at the case of church government. As long as man allowed precedent to rule his behavior, as well as precept, he has had ample freedom in church life. For those factors outside the area of theocracy God has allowed wide spaces of democracy. Much of the church is democratic with all of its attendant freedoms and opportunities. That God so designed His church is the lesson of precedent.

However, ecclesiasticism in all of its forms has either been afraid, ignorant of, or rebellious toward the teaching of precedent. It has entered the field, originally held as democratic, to legislate and regulate a myriad of church forms and thoughts. Where precedent has allowed variation ecclesiasticism has created tradition and ritualism.

Now the dangers in departing from precedent ought to be very apparent. There are some occasions when man can "learn by experience." This is one.

(1) One obvious danger is that departure from precedent, is a departure from the Holy pattern of God—in which He has certain intentions, purposes, and plans, even though man may not comprehend them. No detail of precedent

must be overlooked in the name of "incidental." What man calls "detail" may be what God designed as indispensable. And a casual departure from details often leads to an imperceptible departure from Holy pattern.

In the case of the Lord's Supper it is safe and sane to accurately duplicate each item precedented in Scripture and directed toward us. Lest we violate divine pattern we ought to do that much, which certainly is far from difficult. Though we may not agree with the extent of D. R. Dungan's statement, it is well to carefully assess his warning:

> A beautiful lesson can be seen in the use of the roll of unleavened bread. I have seen this lesson covered from the from the sight of all worshipers by having two or three rolls or loaves; by the use of light bread which could not represent the body of the Savior with any propriety; sometimes there are plates with several hundred pieces or small cubes of light bread. This may not be regarded as a desecration of the Lord's Supper, and yet it approximates it so nearly that anyone taught in the Word of God must hesitate respecting the propriety of participating. In the whole affair there has been such a reckless disregard for what the Savior did and required us to do till he come again, that it hardly amounts to more than a fairly well-executed caricature on the institution. While we may bear with it for the time, such ignorance or indifference, or both, should not go long uncorrected. There may be those who can discern the Lord's body in such a mutilated service, but it is of a piece with the whole line of human substitutions for divine teaching.[8]

Let no church or individual ever allow itself to be coerced away from precedent in the name of *any* cause. Precedent is authoritative pattern and that is that.

---

8. D. R. Dungan, "The Lord's Supper," *The Old Faith Restated*, ed. by J. H. Garrison (Joplin, Mo.: College Press reprint of 1891 ed.), p. 234.

(2) For another danger, look at the tendency in human behavior to be influenced. Let one Christian relax a single item of Christian behavior, and there is always a score of others behooved to follow. There is a certain contagion about life that can not be ignored. That is why every follower of the Lord must be most careful never to allow his action to "put an obstacle or stumbling block in a brother's way" (Romans 14:13). It is little wonder then, why Paul admonished Christians to be most careful how they ". . . walk, not as unwise men, but as wise, making the most of your time" (Ephesians 5:15-16).

Let the church, or any part of its leadership, grow lax in the faithful weekly communion at the Lord's Table, and there will immediately arise a throng who will dismiss its importance and practice at "the drop of a hat." A specific violation of precedent often leads to a general violation of the same. Its companion result is a frequent violation of precept.

(3) A third danger is that tendecy to inaugurate new precedents. Rather than protecting divine precedents from the past it is easy to project human precedent into the future. Thus, it should be the desire of Christians today to conform to divine precedents, not to set up new ones of their own.

Such was the case of the Church at Corinth, which Paul rebuked with the words, "Was it from you that the word of God first went forth? Or has it come to you only?" (I Corinthians 14:36). On this J. W. McGarvey and P. Y. Pendleton provide the commentary:

> Becoming puffed up by the fullness of their spiritual gifts, the Corinthians were acting as if they were the parent church and only church. They were assuming the right to set precedent and dictate customs, when it was their duty to conform

to the precedents and customs established before they came into existence. Their pretensions needed this indignant rebuke.[9]

The only precedent they had a right to set were those occasions of obedience to revelation given them and which God saw fit to transmit to others. Their opinions are not to be our law. Neither should any subsequent tradition be our law nor our opinion today be precedential law for any people yet to come.

---

9. J. W. McGarvey, P. Y. Pendleton, *Thessalonians, Corinthians, Galatians, and Romans* (Cincinnati: Standard Publishing, 1916), pp. 143-144.

Part III — Opinion

Chapter Nine

OPINION DEFINED

Every single word and deed of the Christian must be done under the lordship of Christ. Thus far we have sought to analyze how and where "God *speaks*" His will through precept and precedent. Now it is time to enter the vast area of *silence*. This is the field of opinion.

"Where the Scriptures speak, we speak; where the Scriptures are silent, we are silent." This was declared, and defended, and practiced by Mr. Campbell. Of this J. H. Garrison once wrote:

> It will be seen from the foregoing that this saying of Thomas Campbell was a two-edged sword, one edge cutting off the pretended liberty to ignore or slight what God has commanded, and the other edge cutting away the pretended authority that attempts to bind men where God has left them free.[1]

As quoted before, W. R. Walker points out that the authority of Christ is extended toward man in two ways.[2] One is the "vocal area," which has already been treated. Now the second, "the area of silence," must be respected as well as the first area. This is our field of opinion. When God authoritatively requisitions a certain area of our lives to be governed by our personal wills, or a consensus of wills, then we *must* recognize it. It is imperative for man to do his own thinking when God so ordains it.

It is unthinkable to even imagine that God is going to do *all* of man's thinking for him. Alexander Campbell commented on this:

---

1. J. H. Garrison, *The Story of a Century* (St. Louis: Christian Publishing Co., 1909), pp. 40-41.
2. See p. 68.

WHAT THE BIBLE SAYS ABOUT FAITH AND OPINION

To ask for a *positive* precept for everything in the details of duties growing out of the various exigencies of the Christian church and the world would be quite as irrational and unscriptural as to ask for an immutable wardrobe or a uniform standard of apparel for all persons and ages in the Christian church.[3]

Differences of opinion are natural in every walk of life. They are the wholesome fruit of the process of human thinking. Unless God reduces man to a mere automaton, the same will apply to his Christian duties. This was another keen observation of Thomas Campbell as he penned the *Declaration and Address:*

> Every sincere and upright Christian, will understand and do the will of God, in every instance, to the best of his skill and judgment; but in the application of the general rule to particular cases, there may, and doubtless will, be some variety of opinion and practice. This we see was actually the case in the apostolic churches, without any breach of Christian unity. And if this was the case, at the erection of the Christian church from amongst Jews and Gentiles, may we not reasonably expect, that it will be the same at her restoration, from under her long anti-Christian and sectarian desolations?[4]

Now the wise proverb stated and emphasized by Mr. Campbell[5] is also an old saying. It has been phrased in different ways. For instance: "In doubtful questions, liberty; in essentials, unity; in all things, charity."[6] "In things essential

---

3. As quoted by Garrison, *op. cit.*, p. 165.
4. Thomas Campbell, *Declaration and Address* (Lincoln, Il.: Lincoln Christian College Press, 1971 reprint of 1809 ed.), p. 42.
5. Quoted on p. 163.
6. St. Augustine.

unity; in things not essential liberty; in all things charity."[7] "In necessary things unity, in doubtful things liberty, in all things charity."[8]

But to understand it exactly or apply it has been another matter. Essentials and non-essentials! Oh, what battles have been fought on this ground! And the two chief issues of the contest have ever been alive. We now consider them.

Before proceeding with this distinction let us pause long enough to make a definition. Dr. James B. North writes: "What are we talking about when we say 'essential'? The dictionaries define the word 'essential' as meaning something absolutely necessary—the bare minimum requirement for something. . . . Another clarification we need to make concerns the question, 'Essential to what?'. . . May I say that we need to consider what is essential and what is non-essential in three different areas: (1) What is essential to salvation? (2) What is essential to fellowship? and (3) What is essential to leadership?"[9]

(1) First of all, is there a distinctive difference between essentials and non-essentials? Between faith and opinion? Between the law of the Lord and the conjecture of man?

The answer, as already given, is a decided "yes." There is a positive line of demarcation between the two fields. They are separate and distinguishable. Alexander Campbell said, "Our faith, then, and our opinions, do not clash, for *we never have both faith and opinion on the same subject.*"[10]

At one of the tap roots of the "restoration movement" young Alexander saw his father face this old problem. Within

---

7. Rupertus Augustine.
8. Latin. Also attributed to Melanchthon.
9. James B. North, *Christian Standard* (July 29, 1979), p. 5.
10. Alexander Campbell, *A Debate Between Rev. A. Campbell and Rev. N. L. Rice* (Nashville, Tenn.: Gospel Advocate reprint of 1844 ed.), p. 836.

the Presbyterian denomination there were several parties warring against one another. Mr. Campbell, himself, was an anti-Burgher of the Seceder branch. "But the disposition to confound matters of opinion and questions of expediency with the things of faith and conscience still continued to display its power . . . ," so commented Mr. Richardson.[11] And how Mr. Campbell hated these trivial fightings in which he was engulfed!

The more accurately persons mark the true distinction between faith and opinion, the more will genuine unity become a reality. This truth is the philosophical basis behind the "obvious unity" (though it be coerced — and better labeled "union") of the Roman Catholic Church. She has the good sense to draw a definite line between faith and opinion on every issue thinkable — by vote of council or decree of pope. This is a rigid and dogmatic rule. The Catholic has a positive categorical answer to his every question down to the last detail. But which is better: For man to sell out his right of conscience and God-given liberty to interpret the Scriptures and have Roman Union? Or for him to cherish and retain his liberty to labor hard in study (of Scripture) to ascertain the true difference between faith and opinion without ever perfectly reaching the ideal of Christian Unity? The answer ought to be obvious. More on this later.

(2) But, where is the line of distinction to be drawn? This second question is the immediate issue coming out of the first question. Is the answer to be found in the oft-repeated cry of today: "We ought to magnify our agreements and minimize our differences"? Nor is the problem easily solved by merely pleading for people to lay aside the trivialities and

---

11. Robert Richardson, *Memoirs of Alexander Campbell,* I (Nashville, Tenn.: Gospel Advocate, 1956 reprint of 1897 ed.), p. 55.

incidentals for the "great things" of the faith. This is begging the question. There has already been too much vagueness and too many generalities on this subject. It is about time that these "non-essentials" be identified for what they are.

What is a Christian opinion? Where is it recognized in Scripture? What are its prescribed boundaries? Let us cite in full the answers given by several truly great scholars.

> ... That there is a manifest distinction between an express Scripture declaration, and the conclusion or inference which may be deduced from it; and that the former may be clearly understood, even where the latter is but imperfectly, if at all perceived; and that we are at least as certain of the declaration, as we can be of the conclusion we draw from it; and that, after all, the conclusion ought not to be exalted above the premises, so as to make void the declaration for the sake of establishing our own conclusion; and that, therefore, the express commands to preserve and maintain inviolate Christian unity and love ought not to be set aside to make way for exalting our inferences above the express authority of God.[12]

Here Thomas Campbell marks the positive difference that exists between an express Scriptural declaration and the conclusions springing from it and the superior force of the former. There are so many examples of violation of this rule. Take the case of baptism. All the inferences and conclusions drawn from Scripture which tend to soften the command itself must not negate the simple and plain fact that it is essential: a direct command of God.

Now we turn to the great Campbell-Rice debate. First, Alexander Campbell said:

> We long since learned the lesson, that to draw a well-defined boundary between *faith* and *opinion*, and, while we

---

12. Thomas Campbell, *Declaration and Address*, p. 38.

earnestly contend for *the faith* to allow perfect freedom of *opinion,* and of the expression of opinion, is the true philosophy of church union, and the sovereign antidote against heresy.[13]

Mr. Rice appropriately answers with the challenge:

The gentleman appears to attach great importance to a distinction he makes between *faith* and *opinion.* I DESIRE TO KNOW WHERE FAITH ENDS, AND OPINION BEGINS. I wish information on this subject particularly; because unless I greatly err, Mr. Campbell's church are constantly acting in violation of their own principles in relation to it.[14]

And then followed Mr. Campbell's clear defense:

With us, then faith is *testimony believed;* knowledge is our own *experience;* and opinion is *probable inference.* Whenever we have clear, well authenticated testimony, we have faith, and this faith is always in the ratio of the testimony we have, or in our apprehension of its truth and certainty. Our personal acquaintance with men and things constitutes our knowledge; of which different individuals, according to their discrimination and capacity, have various proportions. But, in the absence of our own personal acquaintance, observation and experience, and in the absence of good and well authenticated testimony, we have mere *opinion.* So I define and use these terms. Some of our dictionaries are not clear, in marking their respective boundaries. But all men have a right to define in what sense they use leading and important terms, as signs of their own ideas. If I may explain by a single example, I will say, I *believe* that Julius Caesar was assassinated in the Roman senate-house, at the statue of Pompey; I *know* that the sun is the source of

---

13. Alexander Campbell, *A Debate Between Rev. A. Campbell and Rev. N. L. Rice,* p. 797.

14. N. L. Rice, *Ibid.,* p. 801.

our light and heat; and I am *of opinion,* that Saturn is inhabited.

Now, as diverse in religion as in nature, are these terms and their associations. In religion, we have one Lord, one faith, one baptism, one body, one Spirit, one hope, and one God and Father. But we have many opinions. The church, then, may have opinions by thousands while her faith is limited to the inspired testimony of apostles and prophets: where that testimony begins and ends, faith begins and ends. In faith, then, all Christians may be one, though of diverse knowledge and of numerous opinions. In faith we must be one, for there is but one Christian faith; while, in opinions we may differ. Hence we are commanded to receive one another, without regard to differences of opinion. Rom. XV. 1,2.

The grand error in Presbyterianism is, that it seems never to recognize where faith ends, and where opinion begins; nay, it very often confounds faith and opinion, and lays full as much emphasis upon right opinions, as upon right faith; and, in some instances, places opinion above faith. Our faith, then, and our opinions, do not clash, for *we never have both faith and opinion on the same subject.*[15]

Robert Richardson explains it thus:

> With us everything in religion must have a Scripture warrant; human authority is regarded as wholly incompetent to the decision of any question which may legitimately arise in regard to the great matters of faith and duty. Whatever rests upon a divine warrant is a matter of faith. Whatever subordinate and collateral questions may exist, which have not this warrant, are matters of opinion which each one is at liberty to entertain according to his own pleasure and to which no one, from the very nature of the case, can attach any importance.[16]

---

15. Alexander Campbell, *Ibid.,* pp. 835-836.
16. Robert Richardson, quoted by S. S. Lappin, *Christian Unity Quarterly* (May, 1946), p. 10.

WHAT THE BIBLE SAYS ABOUT FAITH AND OPINION

Hall L. Calhoun calls opinion a matter of indifference. He defines it in these words and proposes three categories:

All scriptural things are divided into three classes, viz.: *Necessary* things, *expedient* things, and *indifferent* things. Necessary things are things *right, advantageous and commanded;* expedient things are things right and advantageous, but *not commanded;* indifferent things are things right, but *neither advantageous nor commanded.*[17]

Now he elaborates on these matters which are "indifferent":

In I Cor. 8:8 Paul, speaking of meat, said: "But food will not commend us to God; we are neither the worse if we do not eat, nor the better if we do eat." A thing the doing of which makes one neither better nor worse must be a matter of indifference. At what particular hour on the Lord's day shall the Lord's Supper be observed? At 11 A.M. or at 8 P.M. or at some other hour? Certainly it may be said of this that the exact hour of the observance of the Lord's Supper is a matter of indifference. If a man eat at 11 A.M., he is neither better nor worse than if he ate it at any other convenient hour of the Lord's day.

Likewise the position of the BODY in prayer must be a matter of indifference, since men "ought always to pray" and to "pray without ceasing." This, of course, can be done only by prayer being acceptable in all different positions of the body.

Matters of indifference are matters of mere personal privilege, which may or may not be done without sin, so far as the things themselves are concerned.

This class of things is as clearly recognized and defined in the Bible as necessary things are.

Nothing can belong to this class of things which is either enjoined or prohibited in the Scriptures. If it is enjoined in

---

17. Hall L. Calhoun, as quoted by John B. Cowden, *St. Paul on Christian Unity,* p. 194.

OPINION: OPINION DEFINED

the Scriptures, it is a necessary thing, and must be done; if it is prohibited in the Scriptures, it is a sin and it must not be done.[18]

Thus *faith* is a reliance on God's thoughts, *precedent* is an imitation of God's thought in action, and *opinion* is a sanctified experiment with man's own thought. This distinction must be religiously kept. Does this not answer the question, How can we find a basis for Christian solidarity without violating Christian individuality? The working of faith and opinion as separate, yet complementary, functions is the answer. Think of what the field of opinion offers the inventive genius in human nature. What a generous area it includes. As "Raccoon" John Smith once said, "While there is but one faith, there may be ten thousand opinions; and hence if Christians are ever to be one, they must be one in faith and not in opinion."[19]

Let every Christian observe how each Christian deed must be broken down into the threefold pattern of the exegetical weight of this book on faith and opinion. Consider the grace of the stewardship of possessions. As a precept it is clearly commanded of Christians (I Corinthians 16:1-2). In the area of precedent again we find definite teaching as to the motive and condition of giving as found in the Macedonian example (II Corinthians 8:1-15). Then, the working of stewardship finds a multitude of expressions and methods allowed in the name of personal opinion. Here there are a myriad of ramifications.

NOW FOR THE NUMBER ONE PROBLEM OF THIS BOOK: THE CONFUSION OF THESE THREE FIELDS — PRECEPT, PRECEDENT, AND OPINION! **Nearly every Bible student will admit that**

---

18. *Ibid.*, p. 195.
19. "Raccoon" John Smith as quoted by P. H. Welshimer, *Concerning the Disciples* (Cincinnati: Standard Publishing, 1935), p. 84.

there is a line separating the three—precept, precedent, and opinion. Or at least, they acknowledge the twofold principle of faith and opinion. However, the supreme question is, *where shall we draw the line?* Where does precept end and opinion begin? It is not so much a question of the existence of a line as it is the position of it.

It is true that some would declare the "line" to be very arbitrary in its position; that it really does not matter after all where it is, for the very placing of the line is a matter of opinion. This evades the question and does not answer it. It really ascribes supreme authority to man's own power to reason. And it does not belong there; supreme authority belongs to Jesus Christ. See Figure 2, page 173.

Again, some one declares the line to be relative or hazy. Rather than there being a sharp division there is a blending together—one with another (as illustrated by Figure 3, p. 173). And therefore, the Bible interpreter must never be too dogmatic unless he is sure that he has entered deep enough into one or the other field.

In Figure 4, page 173, we depict another concept. Here the line of demarcation, under certain conditions, has a shifting effect. Here there is some overlapping. The difference appears to be somewhat elusive. And with this arises a host of problems, the answers of which will always provide a perpetual ground for religious bantering and hopeless debate.

To this discussion we add the following five conclusive remarks regarding this "line" of difference. (1) It is definitely there. (2) It is not fluid, nor elusive, nor arbitrary. See Figure 5, page 173. (3) It will be seen only by growth in the wisdom of God. (4) It is the prize of only those who by implicit faith and obedience to revealed truth seek it honestly, diligently,

OPINION: OPINION DEFINED

intelligently, and charitably. Thus some men, whether scholarly or uneducated, will see it far more clearly than others. Its existence is not relative, but, its apprehension will be relative. (5) Therefore, it is an ideal goal toward which all men must work, but which, like any other Christian goal, is never perfectly attainable because of human limitations.

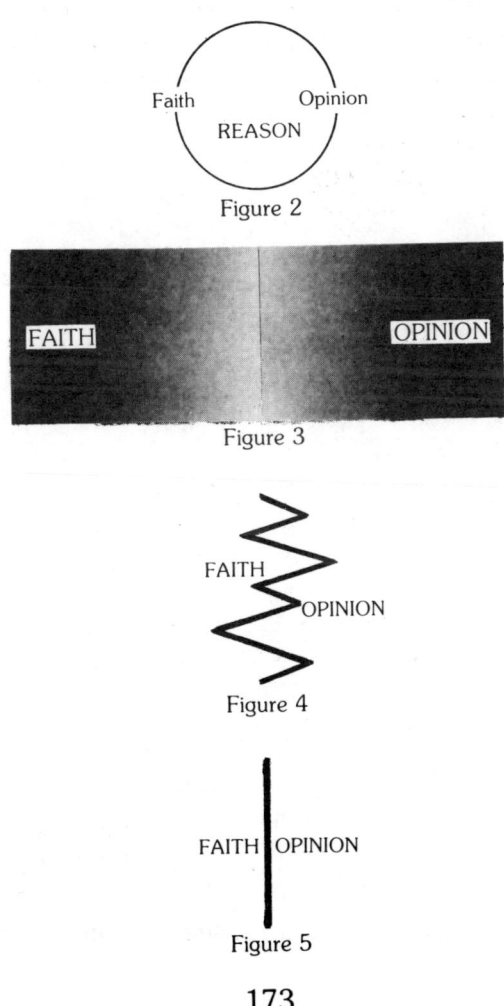

Figure 2

Figure 3

Figure 4

Figure 5

WHAT THE BIBLE SAYS ABOUT FAITH AND OPINION

This problem of differentiating between faith and opinion strikes at the heart of the baptism question. Most denominational bodies ascribe its necessity, as an act to be done, to the field of precept. And then straightway, they defeat the whole issue by placing several of its prescribed factors, e.g. when observed, "mode," or who can be a candidate, etc., in the field of opinion, with the trite rebuttal: "After all, it does not matter. The important thing is the spirit of the thing."

Let us consider a classic example of how vital this matter is. In the case of the Lord's Supper we are listing some questions which at various times have been asked concerning the practice. In the form of a questionnaire we list them:

QUESTIONS
commonly asked about the Lord's Supper

Question	No	Yes	Doesn't Matter
1. Is the frequency of the Lord's Supper important			
2. Is the hour of observance important?			
3. May it be observed more than once on a given day?			
4. May it be observed on a week day?			
5. Is the place of observance important?			
6. Is a "sanctuary" necessary?			
7. Is the choice of emblems to be consumed important?			
8. Should the bread be unleavened?			
9. Should the bread be in one piece?			
10. Should the "fruit of the vine" be fermented?			
11. May it be diluted with water?			
12. Should it be in one vessel?			
13. Must any particular kind of vessel be used?			
14. How should remnants of emblems be discarded?			
15. Must there be two prayers at the table?			
16. Must it be an Elder who offers the prayer?			
17. May a woman offer the prayer at the table?			

OPINION: OPINION DEFINED

18. May an "unordained" person offer prayer at the table?			
19. Should a person come to the table to partake?			
20. Is the posture of a participant important?			
21. Should the participants remain seated?			
22. Should the participants kneel?			
23. Is it important who serves the emblems?			
24. May women serve the emblems?			
25. Should the two emblems be passed separately?			
26. Should the people eat and drink simultaneously?			
27. Should the preacher have part in serving the supper?			
28. Should the preacher be one to offer a prayer?			
29. Should the preacher read Scripture, give instructions?			
30. Is music an important item during the supper?			
31. May choral music be used?			
32. May instrumental music be used?			
33. Should a participant pray during the supper?			
34. Is the purpose of the prayer important?			
35. Is the length of the prayer important?			
36. Should immersed believers be only ones to partake?			
37. May the pious unimmersed partake?			
38. May the backslider partake?			
39. May the reprobate partake?			
40. Should both "laity" and "clergy" partake?			
41. May those who are unworthy partake?			
42. Is there a Scriptural name for this ordinance?			
43. Is there a definite purpose behind this ordinance?			
44. Is there a definite meaning in this ordinance?			
45. Is there a definite physical and mental action necessary for the participant to perform?			
46. May there be a dramatics or pageantry incorporated into the observance?			

Would anyone in his right mind presume that all of these questions are of equal importance? Certainly not! Some would be automatically dismissed from one's mind as being non-essential. Some would be answered "yes," and some "no." Why? What makes the difference? Is it entirely because of expediency or taste? No! The correct answer lies in the Scriptures. Some of these questions are categorically answered by divine precept; some by divine precedent; and some, by the very silence of Scripture, are left open to the careful and wise discretion of man. In this final area man must use all of the good common sense, love, decorum, and taste that he can muster together. On this D. R. Dungan gives the following instruction:

> The importance of the institution indicates the necessity of observing it just as it was delivered. But in deciding this question, we must not mistake incidents for essentials. There are, too, matters of propriety that we can hardly say are either right or wrong in themselves. And yet this liberality may extend too far, and the whole institution be given away by an impropriety that, at its beginning, could have been borne with, but which may be carried to the extent of disloyalty to Christ.
> Certainly the Savior did not direct every possible thing that might occur, as to the hour and minute of the day, the place where it should be observed, whether one or more than one should assist in distributing the bread and wine, what kind of a cup and plate should be used, the posture of the body at the time of participation. These and a hundred others like them have been left largely to the consecrated common sense of those who are engaged in the service. Christ met the disciples in a large upper room, and the brethren at Troas met also in an upper room, but nothing may be pleaded from these facts that the ordinance demands such surroundings. But while the place of partaking of the supper is left to the disciples, and while we regard it as a question of propriety, still such indifference to the purity of the communion might be exhibited in the selection of place

that the institution itself would be invalidated. "Decency and order" should be preserved, and while some irregularities and improprieties may be tolerated, yet the line of decorum must be drawn somewhere, beyond which the ordinance is not observed. A careful reading of I Cor. 11:17-34 will reveal the fact that the Church had gone beyond the lines of propriety so far that they were no longer eating the Lord's Supper.[20]

It is most difficult, to appropriate the proper balance (between faith and opinion) assigned to each Christian work by the Scripture. The natural trend seems to be two-pronged. If man seeks to be particular, unyielding, uncompromising on matters of faith—the tendency in turn is often to do the same in matters of opinion. This psychological factor must be acknowledged. This was one of the great problems which the forefathers of the restoration plea had to encounter. Men, in their zeal for Bible loyalty, had passed this spirit on into the field of opinion. Here they remained firm and unyielding on many issues. Thus their attitude in one respect was to be admired; in another, to be condemned. The work of the Campbells was thus pretty well defined by this general violation of the law of opinion. Now the converse!

The opposing to be yielding, compromising, generous toward opinion often leads men to do the same in matters of faith. If the lessons of history and observation mean anything it would teach us that this alternative appears to be the dominating curse today. The pendulum has swung to the opposite side since the Campbells, and preaching today must aim its sights in the opposite direction in order to restore

---

20. D. R. Dungan, "The Lord's Supper," *The Old Faith Restated*, ed. J. H. Garrison, p. 233.

the normal balance as measured in Scripture. Listen to the cry today: what is most common? "It does not make any difference what you believe." So union, compromise, and the ignoring of all differences is the trend. Mass denominational movements "steam-roller" right over the great fundamental issues of faith. The irony of the whole thing is the picture of a church which decides to become so charitable and yielding on these issues of faith, only to be torn and divided within over issues of pure opinion.

What is needed? That which we shall call: *The law of equilibrium.* This is the advanced Christian grace to be unyielding on all matters of faith, but yielding on all matters of opinion. Narrow in faith, liberal in opinion! Firm and loyal on every issue of precept and precedent, but generous on every issue of mere opinion! This is difficult to attain. It is one significant mark of genuine Christian growth. But, the growing Christian will always have an open mind, willing to continue to learn more accurately how to discriminate between faith and opinion.

There will always be the Sadducees and the Pharisees who violate this law. The Sadducees will ever fall short of precept. They will put many matters of precept and precedent in the field of opinion. They will be liberal with things which are not theirs to manipulate. And there will be the Pharisees who persist in going beyond precept and precedent. They will legislate, demand, ordain, and even coerce, where they have no right. For such should remain in the field of opinion. But by their traditions they add human precept to the divine and thereby invade the free ground of opinion. See Figure 6, page 179.

As advocates of the "Restoration Plea" we thus have a meaingful dichotomy of practice within our singular appeal

OPINION: OPINION DEFINED

to fully restore the authority of Christ—on one hand we speak to the liberal world (in all its degrees of liberality—falling short of precept) and urge firmness, faithfulness, uncompromising steadfastness; while on the other hand we preach to the fundamentalist world (in all its degrees of going beyond precept and precedent) and appeal to them to be more yielding, tolerant and compromising. This paradox is often misunderstood by those around us.

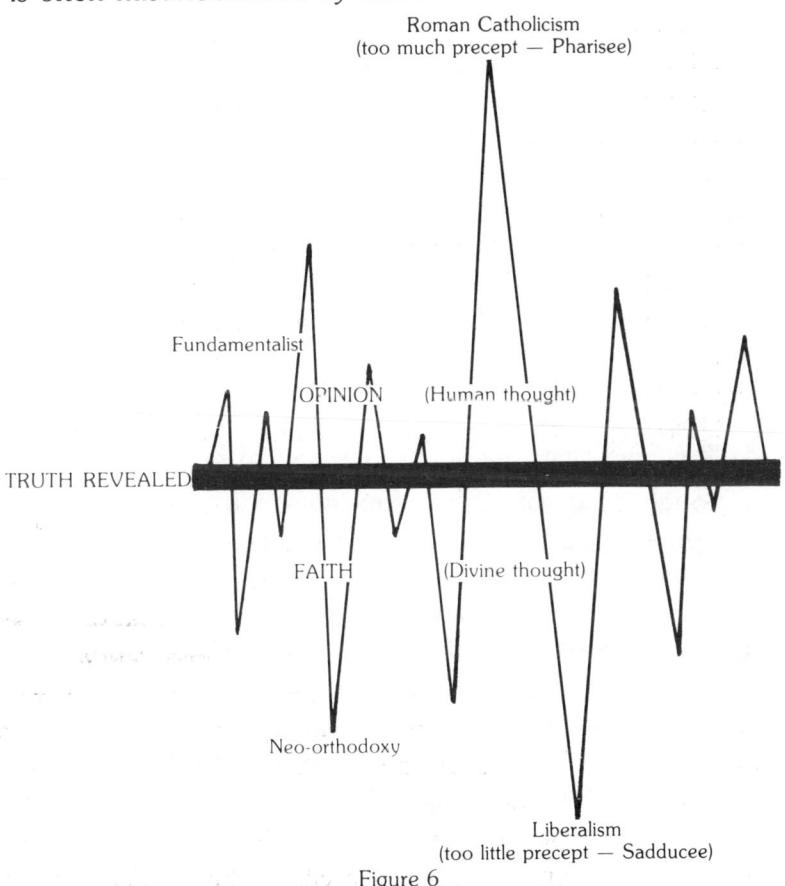

Figure 6

WHAT THE BIBLE SAYS ABOUT FAITH AND OPINION

(1) Falling short of precept! There have been numerous plans advocated to draw the "line" (between faith and opinion) somewhere through the field of precept. For instance, some would claim the distinction of faith vs. opinion is identical with inward attitude (spirit) vs. outward deed (obedience). And that the attitude or motive behind a deed is the issue, whereas the actual outward expression is mere detail or opinion. As J. J. Haley has written:

> The effort to abolish the distinction between the essential and the non-essential, the formal and the spiritual, and the assumption that the outward form is as indispensable as the inward meaning for which it stands is one of the earmarks of a legalistic construction of the Christian religion.[21]

But this is not the distinction Jesus made. In His denunciation of "seven woes" He said,

> "Woe to you, scribes and Pharisees, hypocrites! For you tithe mint and dill and cummin, and have neglected the weightier provisions of the law: justice and mercy and faithfulness; but these are the things you should have done without neglecting the others (Matthew 23:23).

Though Jesus uses the term "weightier" (things which were primary and fundamental) He still says both were to be done.

Again, others will make a distinction in the "letter" and "spirit" of the law—claiming the "letter" is bad, while the "spirit" is good; the "letter" is the legal construction of the wording of law, while the "spirit" is the liberal and general application or motive behind it. This concept is usually conceived in a misinterpretation of the passage, II Corinthians 3.

---

21. J. J. Haley, *Christian Evangelist* (1914), p. 719.

This is not a contrast between the outward and inward sense of Scripture, but the outward and inward power of the Old (legal dispensation of the "letter") and the New (spiritual dispensation of faith in Christ) Covenants. The "letter" and "spirit" in Romans 2:27-29 refers to the law of circumcision —must be inward (spirit) as well as outward (letter). In Romans 7:6 the contrast is that the Christian by his faith ("spirit") is made free from the Law—the Old Covenant ("letter"). Too long people have used these two words to falsely distinguish between a "literal" and a "mystical" meaning of the Word (a practice that dates back to Origen in the third century) — that they are different and that the latter is superior to the former. There are times when the use of these terms in a specific sense is permissible; to use them in dividing the field of precept into essentials and non-essentials is an illegitimate use. For after all, how can any "spirit" of the law ever be obtained except through the medium of the "letter" of the law?

The *Declaration and Address*, written by Thomas Campbell, gives implicit warning against dividing precept into essentials and non-essentials:

> We dare neither assume nor purpose the trite indefinite distinction between essentials and non-essentials, in matters of revealed truth and duty; firmly persuaded, that, whatever may be their comparative importance, simply considered, the high obligation of the Divine Authority revealing, or enjoining them, renders the belief, or performance of them absolutely essential to us, in so far as we know them.[22]

Precept must be kept intact. For an ounce of revelation is worth far more than a pound of speculation. Man must

---

22. Thomas Campbell, *Declaration and Address*, p. 14.

not come short of precept in entering a world of opinion. Bernard Baruch says, "Every man has a right to his opinion, but no man has a right to be wrong in his facts."[23]

(2) Going beyond precept and precedent! Here, the alternate folly is to push the line of demarcation into the field of opinion. And with this practice an opinion, because of antiquity, beauty, simplicity, profundity, gratification, or its authorship will be accepted as a thing essential. Wise is the rule about such matters as coined by Barton W. Stone, ". . . yet that something I find not recorded, and I dare not be wise above what is written."[24] Let all heed the apostolic injunction ". . . that in us you might learn not to exceed what is written" (I Corinthians 4:6).

This is what was meant by the famous Article V of the *Declaration and Address:*

> . . . only such as reduce to practice that simple original form of Christianity, expressly exhibited upon the sacred page; without attempting to inculcate anything of human authority, of private opinion, or inventions of men, as having any place in the constitution, faith, or worship, of the Christian church, or, anything as matter of Christian faith, or duty, for which there cannot be expressly produced a "Thus saith the Lord" either in express terms, or by approved precedent.[25]

(1) Possibly the most common violation of this principle is the current use of *tradition.* The real crime is its misuse. Tradition is common. It is the natural accumulation of human thought which is inevitable. If it is kept in its proper place

---

23. Bernard Baruch, quoted in the *Reader's Digest.*
24. Barton W. Stone as quoted by Robert Richardson, *Memoirs of Alexander Campbell,* II, p. 480.
25. Thomas Campbell, *op. cit.,* pp. 3-4.

OPINION: OPINION DEFINED

and given its proper weight it can do little harm. But tradition is like a dense fog surrounding and enveloping simple Christian facts. The current thought and feeling toward Christmas is a case in which much fancy overshadows little fact.

What is the Christian duty? Destroy all tradition with one sweeping stroke? That is an impossibility. The person who deliberately sets up a policy of being completely "untraditionalized" in any area is constructing a new tradition of his own. Jesus never did this and He came to a "traditionalized" generation. He merely gave tradition its proper weight.

> Then some Pharisees and scribes came to Jesus from Jerusalem, saying, "Why do Your disciples transgress the tradition of the elders? For they do not wash their hands when they eat bread." And He answered and said to them, "And why do you yourselves transgress the commandment of God for the sake of your tradition? For God said, 'Honor your father and mother,' and, 'He who speaks evil of father or mother, let him be put to death.' But you say, 'Whoever shall say to his father or mother, "Anything of mine you might have been helped by has been given to God," he is not to honor his father or his mother.' And thus you invalidated the word of God for the sake of your tradition" (Matthew 15:1-6).

Thus, the Christian duty today is not necessarily the destruction of *all* tradition, but the reducing of it to an expedient minimum, and rendering its influence on precept and precedent harmless. Christians must push through the fog of tradition in order to clearly behold the unclouded will of God. Jesus warned, "But in vain do they worship Me, teaching as doctrines the precepts of men. Neglecting the commandment of God you hold to the tradition of men" (Mark 7:7, 8). Compared to God's doctrine Paul warned,

WHAT THE BIBLE SAYS ABOUT FAITH AND OPINION

> See to it that no one takes you captive through philosophy and empty deception, according to the tradition of men, according to the elementary principles of the world, rather than according to Christ (Colossians 2:8).

The "I think" malady is all too common. In things essential the Lord has already done our thinking for us. All that we need to do is to try to understand it, obey it, and then announce it. Let opinion stay opinion as one acquiesces to the true essentials. This was Thomas Campbell's defense before his synod:

> Nor do I presume to dictate to them or to others as to how they should proceed for the glorious purpose of promoting the unity and purity of the church; but only beg leave, for my own part, to walk upon such sure and peaceable ground that I may have nothing to do with human controversy, about the right or wrong side of any opinion whatsoever, by simply acquiescing in what is written, as quite sufficient for every purpose of faith and duty; and thereby to influence as many as possible to depart from human controversy, to betake themselves to the Scriptures, and in so doing, to the study and practice of faith, holiness and love.[26]

But men will persist in their foolish speculations and divisive disputes to the hurt of the body of Christ (I Timothy 6:4; II Timothy 2:23; Titus 3:9; I Corinthians 1:10-31). Party spirit and evil bickerings in the area of opinion must cease. When this happened in Corinth, Paul brought their attention back to the cross of Christ—the heart, plan, and fact of the gospel, the power of God unto salvation (I Corinthians 1:10-31). It seems as though the nearer one gets to the cross the deeper he gets in the territory of faith, and in turn,

---

26. Thomas Campbell, quoted by Robert Richardson, *Memoirs of Alexander Campbell*, I, p. 227.

OPINION: OPINION DEFINED

the more remote from opinion—the "cleverness of speech" is of none effect except to obscure the meaning of the cross of Christ and often produces wrangling and schism (I Corinthians 1:17). See Figure 7, page 186.

Our non-instrument brethren persist in placing the methods and tools of Christian music in the field of essentials. This one item has caused no little stir in the Restoration Movement. And yet, says C. B. Titus:

> Singing comes among such "non-essentials" as circumcision (Gal. 6:15), i.e. neither singing nor no-singing, (music nor no-music, organ nor no-organ) availeth anything in "getting" and "keeping" saved. And "keeping saved" is "bearing the much fruit" (Jn. 15:8) of "love, joy, peace, longsuffering, gentleness, goodness, faith, meekness, temperance (Gal. 5:22)—"singing" unmentioned. There is no word "singing" in the gospel sayings of Jesus, nor in John's record, nor in James', nor in Peter's, nor in Matthew's, nor in Mark's, nor in Luke's. And why should Paul's two words ("singing") be plucked out of the 181, 253 N.T. words to divide a people who avow they were "called" to get all Christ's followers UNITED?[27]

(2) This leads us to another great factor involved in our principle under discussion. It is the item of "innovation." This word means something new or novel that is introduced as a custom or practice. Are innovations permissible for all noble purposes?—or, at least, in some instances? It has already been pointed out that the entire field of opinion is limited by precept and precedent. This, however, does permit a prescribed area for the proper exercising of innovations. Not *all* innovations are a violation of the authority

---

27. C. B. Titus, *Music in Worship*, p. 10.

WHAT THE BIBLE SAYS ABOUT FAITH AND OPINION

of our Lord. When we say "... where the Scriptures are silent..." we do not mean to omit the practice of an innovation but omit the commanding of it. To forbid any innovation is entirely untenable. But to be consistent and logical innovations must be in harmony with precept and precedent.

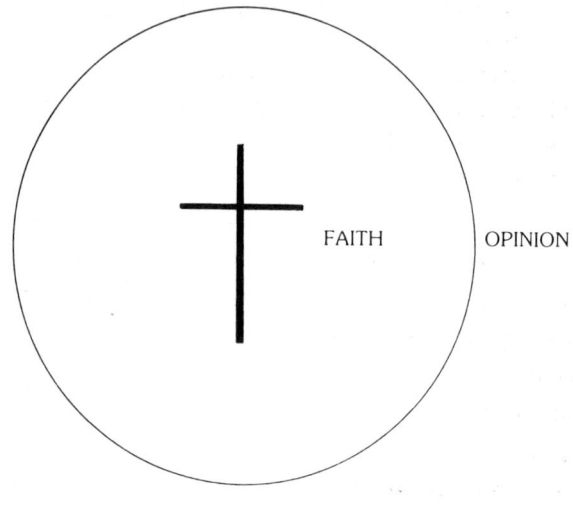

Figure 7

One time Isaac Errett attacked some of the leaders of the "non-instrument brethren" for condemning, without qualification, anything resembling an innovation. Their position had been to pronounce "anathema" on every innovation. Mr. Errett's charge was that of inconsistency:

> Our editorial brethren of the "Times" are, with us, guilty of a great innovation in publishing a weekly religious newspaper; and if they do this as "children of God"—and it would be great injustice to indulge a contrary supposition—

they are doing what they well know has neither a "divine command" nor "an approved precedent" to support it. When they preach, they go into a meeting house, which is an innovation, and take up a hymn-book, which is an innovation, and give out a human hymn, which is an innovation, and this hymn is sung to a tune, which is an innovation, by a choir, which is an innovation, by the aid of tunebook and tuning-fork, which are innovations. They also read from a printed Bible, which is an innovation. Yet who dreams, in all this, of any innovation on the law of God, or the authority of the Lord Jesus Christ? And who would gravely advocate secession in the light of these innovations—insisting that they are without divine command or approved precedent?[28]

Look how many innovations modern times have introduced to the working of Christianity—innovations that help, not destroy or negate the will of God. On this "musical instrument" question Mr. Errett made a fine observation in the following:

But the point to be noted here is that, not only the use of the organ, but *every single quality and characteristic* of our music, both in the singing and the songs that are sung, *is an innovation*, which at some time or other has been earnestly resisted, and resisted because it was thought to be profane and corrupting. Really it is amusing to note with what complacency certain brethren plume themselves upon being apostolic in their worship, simply because they do not use an organ—and yet singing with gusto and a clear conscience Toplady's "Rock of Ages," and Charles Wesley's "Jesus, Lover of My Soul," and hundreds of other pieces far inferior to these, and not only singing them with "melody"—which

---

28. J. S. Lamar, *Memoirs of Isaac Errett*, II (Cincinnati, O.: Standard Publishing, 1893), pp. 43-44.

is a Scriptural word—but with "harmony," which is not—with base, tenor, alto, each of which is an innovation, and, according to *their* principle, morally wrong.[29]

This does *not* license, however, the use of many innovations which hurt, overrule, overshadow, or even destroy the law of God as revealed for our pattern. But, let us apply the "tradition" rule to innovations. All innovations should not be utterly destroyed—only reduced to an expedient minimum, so that their influence over precept and precedent is rendered harmless.

(3) A third matter worthy of our attention is that of *inference*. What is an inference? Citing Webster: Inference—"the act of passing from one judgment to another," "a logical conclusion from given data or premises." Infer—"to derive by reasoning or implication; conclude from facts or premises; to derive as a consequence, conclusion, or probability."[30]

Now, do we have a right to make inferences in Christian thought? from the Scriptures as our premise? Does not our inference (if valid) mean that God implies something? For inference (objective) necessitates implication (subjective). Does God trust the truth with the medium of "implication"? What is the weight of inference?

To begin with there is more than one kind of inference. The first, and most important, is the *necessary* inference. This is a conclusion which, through a deductive or an inductive study of the Bible, is necessitated by the very nature of the facts themselves. Here the student must tread with great care. For the tendency will be most common to catalogue all well thought-out inferences as necessary. This is

---

29. *Ibid.*, p. 32.
30. *Webster's New Collegiate Dictionary* (Springfield, Mass.: G. & C. Merriam Co., 1956), p. 429.

too easy to do. But inferences claiming to be necessary must be examined and re-examined again and again.

Claud F. Witty gives such inferences a good deal of authoritative weight in his statement: "In the realm of faith every issue must be settled by a direct command, by an approved example or by a necessary inference of the New Testament Scriptures."[31] A recent theologian, L. Berkhof writes, "Therefore not only the express statements of Scriptures, but its implications as well, must be regarded as the word of God."[32]

Now this takes the inference out of pure opinion and gives it divine authority. If it is necessary, then it is essential. But essential for what? Thomas Campbell helps clarify this in a passage from his *Declaration and Address:*

> That although inferences and deductions from Scripture premises, when fairly inferred, may be truly called the doctrine of God's holy word, yet are they not formally binding upon the consciences of Christians farther than they perceive the connection, and evidently see that they are so; for their faith must not stand in the wisdom of men, but in the power and veracity of God. Therefore, no such deduction can be made terms of communion, but do properly belong to the after and progressive edification of the Church. Hence, it is evident, that no such deductions or inferential truths ought to have any place in the Church's confession.[33]

A good case to consider is that of the gift of the Holy Spirit today in the measure of miraculous powers. Without going into the problem in detail we simply state the fact that considering the nature, the purpose, the agency, and the methods

---

31. Claud F. Witty, *Christian Unity Quarterly* (July 1943), p. 41.
32. L. Berkhof, *Principles of Biblical Interpretation* (Grand Rapids: Baker Book House, 1950), p. 159.
33. Thomas Campbell, *Declaration and Address*, p. 24.

WHAT THE BIBLE SAYS ABOUT FAITH AND OPINION

or miracles, the duration of the miraculous gift to Christians, is necessarily inferred, i.e., there is no such gift today. Since no miracles are ever recorded as being worked in the New Testament church except by an apostle or one on whom an apostle had bestowed miraculous power by the laying on of his hands, it is a *necessary inference* that miracles ceased when that second generation passed away.

Sometimes an inference made in one passage of Scripture may be sustained, proved, or amplified in another passage, or in a consensus of passages. A good case in point is that of inferring that Cain's offering was not what God had commanded him to give (Genesis 4:3-5). This idea is sustained by other passages of Scripture (Hebrews 11:4; I John 3:12).

Again, the converse, a certain inference may be unwarranted by other Bible teachings (of precept and precedent) which bear directly on the subject considered. One must be most careful to bring to bear all the principles of Bible teaching on every single factor in order to reach the viewpoint the Lord originally intended. And the item of inference has been "thin ice" where all too many continue to drop through to error and false conjectures.

Some inferences are *feasible*, but not necessary. Conclusions which are not necessitated by logic, but are probable by logic, are of this class. They are made because they appear wise and expedient. (More of this will be presented in the next chapter.)

Other inferences are merely *arbitrary*. Such an inference is but one out of a plurality of probable alternatives, any one of which may be held to the personal satisfaction of the student. One inference enjoys as much worth as another.

To show how a single Bible topic is subject to all three varieties of inferences we note the case of Christian baptism.

OPINION: OPINION DEFINED

A *necessary* inference is that an infant can not be a candidate for baptism. By precept and precedent (persons were commanded to have faith, repent, and confess Christ before baptism) we learn that an infant is incapable, through its own inability, to so become a candidate. Next, a *feasible* inference would be to conclude that all of those baptized on the day of Pentecost in the city of Jerusalem were baptized in the pools in the existence in the environs of the city in that day (Acts 2:41). This is not a necessary conclusion, but certainly a wise and intelligent one. And, finally, an *arbitrary* inference would be the answer to the question, what type of body of water should be used today for baptism? Shall it be a pool, a river, a pond, an inside pool, etc.? One inference is as worthy as another.

This discussion now leads us to this conclusion. There are *three* definite classifications of all thoughts and deeds—in dividing essentials from non-essentials. All deeds, institutions, dogmas, fall into one of them.

(1) *Scriptural:* that which has been conceived, designed, commanded, revealed,—and thus blessed, by the Lord through the Scriptures. (2) *Unscriptural:* (prefix "un"—not, negative) that which does not fulfill the above requirements, neither does it violate them. It is merely a negative classification. It may be the result of Scriptural theory, conjecture, or inference. It may be born out of a desire to accomplish some Scriptural purpose or work. Yet, it in itself is not a Scriptural item. (3) *Anti-Scriptural:* (prefix "anti"—opposite, against) that which begins as unscriptural, but reaches out to violate the Scripture. It may be called into existence on the same ground as the unscriptural, however, through its policy, attitude, aim, message, or method it is contrary to Scripture. It may even do some of the work of Scripture, at the same

time violating it. Not all unscriptural items are anti-Scriptural—but certainly all anti-Scriptural items were once unscriptural.

A good case in point is the consideration of organizations. In the New Testament picture there is only one Scriptural organization—it is the church of Christ. By its origin, ownership, purpose, plan, name, guidance—it is divine. Through the years, many unscriptural organizations have arisen, either out of a need by the church (such as a Bible college, seminary, summer camp assembly, publishing house, missionary and benevolent societies, etc.) or because of some failure on the part of the church. Some of these, however, by their violation of the Scripture in principle or practice, have become anti-Scriptural. They have stepped out of place, assumed too much power and authority, risen to unwarranted positions, or actually promoted sinful dogmas.

Alexander Campbell emphasized that all unscriptural agencies are instruments to be used by the church at its own discretion. And never is the instrument bigger nor greater than the hand which wields it. We quote Mr. Richardson:

> He did not regard conventions or societies, composed of messengers of the churches, as independent bodies or as taking out of the hands of the churches the duties to be performed, but considered them as mere instrumentalities employed by the church at large for the accomplishment of important ends demanding mutual assistance, counsel and co-operation.[34]

As J. H. Garrison once wrote:

> Whatever organization other than the local self-governing church may exist, must be purely voluntary, and exercise no

---

34. Robert Richardson, *Memoirs of Alexander Campbell*, II, p. 601.

authority whatever over such local churches. Their recommendations must be only advisory, not compulsory, beyond the compulsion of reason and fraternity.[35]

And let no organization speak with an advisory tongue and act with coercive influence.

Christians must be able to distinguish between these three classifications and properly identify and catalogue every so-called working of Christianity today. The more this is done the purer will be Christianity on earth.

---

35. J. H. Garrison, *The Story of a Century*, p. 217.

Chapter Ten
LAW OF OPINION

Although opinion is the wonderful "free atmosphere" of the exercise of Christian thought, it must never be contaminated by misuse. Man, created in the image of God, will desire to think, to reason, to advance, to invent, to grow, to speculate. But opinion needs oversight lest it become uncontrollable and wreck the whole Christian system. I. B. Grubbs said this of an opinion:

> The right to hold it is absolute; the right to practice it is relative.
>
> A man may so use a correct opinion as to be damned; or he may so use an incorrect opinion as to be saved.[1]

So the Lord has instituted a few simple restraints—checks and balances to keep opinion free but harmless. These are the four guiding compasses which keep the Christian from sailing recklessly and foolishly out to the sea of opinion on to the reefs of error and ruin.

THE LAW OF LIBERTY

Men of any kind of character and aspiration at all have always longed for "the minimum of authority with the maximum of liberty." This has been one of the great themes of history, especially American history. It has been said before that our fathers came to America to "found a state without a king and a church without a pope." What a wonderful word—"liberty." And man must fight for it or it is gone. Said Thomas Jefferson: "Eternal vigilance is the price of freedom." And so it is in Christianity.

---

1. I. B. Grubbs, *Commentary on Paul's Epistle to the Romans*, 6th ed. (Nashville, Tenn.: Gospel Advocate, reprint of 1913 ed.), p. 164.

When liberty has been lost there have arisen champions willing to fight to restore it, then to preserve it. We can see Thomas Campbell, carrying to the people his plea, "Where the Scriptures speak, we speak; where the Scriptures are silent, we are silent." And we can hear the opposition roar at him, for all reformers are unpopular. We can read his *Declaration and Address*, and in many places it sounds like Patrick Henry when he cried out, "Give me liberty or give me death."

Freedom is a word that can not stand alone. It must be related to something. If one is to be free, released from restraint of choice or action, then we ask, "free from whom or what and free to decide what?"

Ann Bridge asks, "What is freedom? It consists of two things: to know each his own limitations and to accept them."[2] When a society of men conform to this concept, regarding all moral and equitable principles, it will provide freedom for its constituents. America, in a large degree, has been so blessed.

Now, in respect to the religion conceived and instituted by the one true God this same principle is evident. When man conforms to the program, principle, pattern of the Father, liberty will naturally and inevitably ensue. This is the liberty God designed for His own children. No authority is good nor wise unless it not only provides the law, and description of obedience to that law, but also provides a generous and considerate amount of freedom — to preserve the moral integrity and self-respect of its subjects. This God has done only as He can do it.

---

2. Ann Bridge, quoted in *Reader's Digest* (June, 1940), p. 5.

WHAT THE BIBLE SAYS ABOUT FAITH AND OPINION

In his great sermon, "Liberty in the Church," Frederick J. Gielow, Jr. traces the pattern of Christian liberty.[3] To begin with there must be a complete integration of human personality into a harmonious unity. This can be attained only by unity with the Creator, His Son whom He sent. This is the plan of redemption, the Christian system. Through this God can still provide, in addition to all His promises for life abundant and life eternal, the complete retention of the individual character and personality—the fullness of the human soul, the integrity of the human conscience, the power of the human reason, as God originally intended it. The liberty of the New Covenant in Christ is rich beyond all measure (II Corinthians 3; Galatians 4, 5; James 1:25; 2:12).

Paul gives instruction and warning concerning the use and misuse of our liberty. "But take care lest this liberty of yours somehow become a stumbling block to the weak" (I Corinthians 8:9). "It was for freedom that Christ set us free; therefore keep standing firm and do not be subject again to a yoke of slavery" (Galatians 5:1). "Am I not free? Am I not an apostle? Have I not seen Jesus our Lord? Are you not my work in the Lord?" (I Corinthians 9:1). "Act as free men, and do not use your freedom as a covering for evil, but use it as bondslaves of God" (I Peter 2:16).

(1) One of the factors of this liberty is the freedom to *hold opinions*. This is the first half of this law. No one dare take that right from the Christian. Liberty in non-essentials is second only to uniformity in essentials.

The rule is simple. Anything which is not commanded and not prohibited in Scripture which is in harmony with the gospel and promotes its objectives is permitted. This is

---

3. Frederick J. Gielow, *Christian Standard* (January 18, 1941), pp. 5-7; (January 25), p. 15.

opinion. This is a vast area. The trouble with some is that they have made the rule read—anything which is not commanded is prohibited. If carried to its logical end, this would exclude all freedom of opinion. For every single factor imaginable would be either commanded or prohibited. Where is there any opinion here?

John B. Cowden says:

> Any detail of Christian work and worship that is in harmony with, or does not do violence to the fundamental truth through Christ is permissible; and Christian unity does not require uniformity as to these details. A failure to recognize this liberty as to minor details has often disturbed and divided the church; whereas a reasonable, sensible application of this principle of liberty would have preserved unity.[4]

The question of the proper attitude toward the silence of the Scriptures came up in the early days of the Protestant Reformation. The great German reformer, Martin Luther, felt that whatever the Bible does not specifically condemn may be allowed, while his Swiss counterpart, Ulrich Zwingli, felt that *anything that the Bible does not authorize is unacceptable.*

There are some "non-instrument" brethren who advocate the "law of exclusion" as a valid hermeneutical rule. They claim "that if pattern authority for a thing is not established (by command, inference, or example), then that thing is excluded."[5] This is a fallacy. For if I must practice everything God says, and cannot practice everything God does not say, then there is no freedom, there is no right of personal opinion. What is not said may be permitted, not necessarily prohibited.

---

4. John B. Cowden, *St. Paul on Christian Unity* (New York: Fleming H. Revell Co., 1923), p. 193.

5. J. D. Thomas, *We Be Brethren* (Abilene, Tx.: Biblical Research Press, 1958), p. 85.

WHAT THE BIBLE SAYS ABOUT FAITH AND OPINION

Clinton Lockhart has given us a sound rule of Bible interpretation when he wrote, "An assertion of truth necessarily excludes that which it is essentially opposed to and no more."[6]

J. D. Thomas considers the "law of exclusion" inadequate, along with other similar approaches.[7] He advocates another argument. He divides "faith and opinion" into "generics, specifics and expedients."[8] His premise is that "generics" are always required, "expedients" are always optional, and a "specific" may be either, depending on whether or not the Scriptures clearly indicate it. So, when he gets to the "musical instrument" question in congregational worship, he points out that making music is the "generic" and singing is the "specific" which must be done to manifest worship. Therefore, he says, using the instrument is another kind of specific and would be sinful—it is a separate and different action—the "required specific (singing) excludes any or all additional or substitute actions on its level (or to its generic!)."[9] This seems to the writer nothing more than a form of the "law of exclusion." This is our artificial arbitration. The question is not whether to sing or play an instrument. It is to sing and leave entirely optional the use of an instrument. And too, there are other factors relative to this matter, e.g., the absence in Scripture of a certain "hour of worship" ("the worship service"), an outline of a worship service, or the questionable exegesis that insists that Ephesians 5:19 and Colossians 3:16 must be confined only to an "official worship service" when the church assembles on Sunday.

He, then, who attempts to force, legislate or pass judgment in this area of opinion has himself violated a precept

---

6. Clinton Lockhart, *Principles of Interpretation* (Delight, Ark.: Gospel Light, reprint of 1901 ed.), p. 32.
7. J. D. Thomas, *op. cit.*, pp. 76ff.
8. *Ibid.*, pp. 19ff.
9. *Ibid.*, p. 26.

of the Lord. It is just as wrong to insist that a matter of opinion is essential as it is to insist that a matter of faith is not essential. Furthermore, it is often the tendency for a person to give "lip service" in claiming a matter to be merely his own opinion and yet by his attitude, actually push it into the area of faith.

The room of opinion is large, and Christians have ample space to exercise this holy prerogative. This is a good and Scriptural brand of "liberalism" and must be preserved. This is the kind of liberalism they accused Thomas Campbell of holding. His reply was:

> If this be Latitudinarianism, it must be a good thing, and, therefore the more we have of it the better; and may be it is —for we are told, "the commandment is exceeding broad," and we intend to go just as far as it will suffer us, but not one hairbreadth further; so at least says our profession.[10]

Listen to the apostle Paul as he defends his own right of opinion, e.g., his right to appeal to civil powers during his ministry to save his own life and protect his own welfare (Acts 22:25-29), his right to circumcise Timothy (Acts 16:1-3) and not Titus (Galatians 2:3-5), his right to marry or not to marry (I Corinthians 7), his right to take a believing wife along with him (I Corinthians 9:5), his right to accept or reject recompense for his ministry in a church (I Corinthians 9:6-27), and his right to eat meat sacrificed to pagan idols (I Corinthians 8:1-8).[11]

(2) The other side of liberty is the realization that *others have the same right to hold opinions.* In nearly every matter which could be considered there is more than one person

---

10. Thomas Campbell, *Declaration and Address* (Lincoln, Il.: Lincoln Christian College, 1971 reprint of 1809 ed.), p. 47.

11. See pages 262-276.

involved. "For not one of us lives for himself, and not one dies for himself" (Romans 14:7). And each man has his own mind, personality, emotion, will, and liberty. And liberty must be guaranteed to all or it is guaranteed to none. Liberty is reciprocal or it vanishes.

Even the infidel Voltaire said, "I do not believe a word you say, but I would fight to the death to defend your right to say it." Thus, the law of liberty in Christian opinion is to be conditioned by this all-important question: how far shall my liberty go without violating the liberty of others? This necessarily causes the Christian to re-examine his own opinions and those of the other parties and the respective attitudes involved.

The problem of human rights *for all* is as old as man. The right of one man will often collide with the right of another. Where is the dividing line? That is one of the great problems in a democracy. One man has the right of free speech while another has the right not to listen to that speech. Here is born a host of inter-personal problems within a government.

This rule is obvious, however; no right of one man should be allowed to destroy the right of another. One man says he has a perfect right to drink liquor and to drive his own car. But this right should be restricted when it endangers the right of a pedestrian to live. Years ago a professor said, "You have a right to swing your arm, but your right ends where the other man's body begins."[12] When the rights of two parties collide, that concilliatory answer which preserves the maximum of liberty for each involved must be the one accepted. Now in regard to Christian life and liberty Paul gives careful instruction. Concerning this matter we make the following observations.

---

12. Quoted in *The Voice of Evangelism* (October 12, 1946), p. 3.

OPINION: LAW OF OPINION

First, one must respect the opinions of others. When one honors this right in others he has tolerance — good tolerance. Tolerance does not mean to agree but to allow. We quote the following in full:

> Now accept the one who is weak in faith, but not for the purpose of passing judgment on his opinions. One man has faith that he may eat all things, but he who is weak eats vegetables only. Let not him who eats regard with contempt him who does not eat, and let not him who does not eat judge him who eats, for God has accepted him. Who are you to judge the servant of another? To his own master he stands or falls; and stand he will, for the Lord is able to make him stand. One man regards one day above another, another regards every day alike. Let each man be fully convinced in his own mind. He who observes the day, observes it for the Lord, and he who eats, does so for the Lord, for he gives thanks to God; and he who eats not, for the Lord he does not eat, and gives thanks to God. For not one of us lives for himself, and not one dies for himself; for if we live, we live for the Lord, or if we die, we die for the Lord; therefore whether we live or die, we are the Lord's. For to this end Christ died and lived again, that He might be Lord both of the dead and of the living. But you, why do you judge your brother? Or you again, why do you regard your brother with contempt? For we shall all stand before the judgment-seat of God. For it is written, "As I live, says the Lord, every knee shall bow to Me, And every tongue shall give praise to God." So then each one of us shall give account of himself to God.
>
> Therefore let us not judge one another any more, but rather determine this — not to put an obstacle or a stumbling block in a brother's way. I know and am convinced in the Lord Jesus that nothing is unclean in itself; but to him who

WHAT THE BIBLE SAYS ABOUT FAITH AND OPINION

thinks anything to be unclean, to him it is unclean. For if because of food your brother is hurt, you are no longer walking according to love. Do not destroy with your food him for whom Christ died. Therefore do not let what is for you a good thing be spoken of as evil; for the kingdom of God is not eating and drinking, but righteousness and peace and joy in the Holy Spirit. For he who in this way serves Christ is acceptable to God and approved by men. So then let us pursue the things which make for peace and the building up of one another. Do not tear down the work of God for the sake of food. All things indeed are clean, but they are evil for the man who eats and gives offense. It is good not to eat meat or to drink wine, or to do anything by which your brother stumbles. The faith which you have, have as your own conviction before God. Happy is he who does not condemn himself in what he approves. But he who doubts is condemned if he eats, because his eating is not from faith; and whatever is not from faith is sin (Romans 14:1-23).

This works both ways. He who holds the narrow opinion must not judge (condemn) the one who does not hold it, and he who does not hold it must tolerate (not look down on) the one who does. Who has the right to condemn one whom God has accepted? This is the beginning of the law. Every man has a right to his own opinion, but, not to fasten it on another. A quick look at everyday life will verify this to be the natural inter-personal relationship situation in matters of opinion.

Man must be fully conscientious in whatever opinion he holds or refuses to hold. God always demands sincerity. Notice carefully that this is the meaning of Romans 14:23 —it is a sin not to believe your opinion is right for you.

Now this law moves along and teaches that one who has the liberty to hold an opinion also has the liberty to forfeit that opinion in the interest of the other party. There may be greater issues at stake — issues that are well worth concession and compromise (these two words may be perfectly at home in the realm of opinion, but not in faith). In this fourteenth chapter of Romans Paul declares a man's conscience is such an issue. This "faith," says Professor Grubbs is not "faith in Christ" but faith in the propriety to hold a certain opinion (eating all things or eating only certain things).[13] This weakness is not one of ignorance, but of doubt in the propriety of a certain opinion. Thus, this discussion is not concerning a weakness of faith or knowledge, but a sensitiveness of *conscience*. This is not a discourse on the subject matter of the opinions held, one being right and one wrong, but of the influence this whole matter brings to bear on one's own conscience. What is the attitude of each side toward the other in respect to the conscience of each? Many are guilty of wounding another's conscience through coercion, bad influence, criticism, unwarranted yielding and not yielding.

At this point we need to make the observation that the terms "liberal" and "conservative" are often used in this sense — those having a broad permissive opinion as opposed to those having a narrow, restrictive opinion. This is quite a relative use of these words.

Of course, a man must always stand by his own conscience first, without violating the conscience of another. This is very difficult for the Christian to practice. At times it seems almost like a great dilemma. But one must honestly ask in every instance, when shall I yield my opinion and when shall I not yield? Sometimes Jesus yielded these matters and sometimes He did not. There is more than one law

---

13. I. B. Grubbs, *op. cit.*, pp. 156-161.

WHAT THE BIBLE SAYS ABOUT FAITH AND OPINION

involved which we shall see. Read Professor Grubbs' summary of this point:

> A man must always approve what he does; if he, by his conduct, approves what his conscience condemns, he is judged; and if he uses his liberty so as to cause another to sin, he sins against Christ (I Cor. 8:12). Happy is the man who always acts in harmony with his own conscience, and does not give offence to the conscience of another.[14]

One has the duty to yield the privilege of using his opinion, when such an act of using an opinion hurts or destroys another's conscience, which in turn hurts the very Kingdom of God (its peace, its joy and its work). An excellent example is that used by Paul:

> Now concerning things sacrificed to idols, we know that we all have knowledge. Knowledge makes arrogant, but love edifies. If any one supposes that he knows anything, he has not yet known as he ought to know; but if any one loves God, he is known by Him. Therefore concerning the eating of things sacrificed to idols, we know that there is no such thing as an idol in the world, and that there is no God but one. For even if there are so-called gods whether in heaven or on earth, as indeed there are many gods and many lords, yet for us there is but one God, the Father, from whom are all things, and we exist for Him; and one Lord, Jesus Christ, through whom are all things, and we exist through Him.
> However not all men have this knowledge; but some, being accustomed to the idol until now, eat food as if it were sacrificed to an idol; and their conscience being weak is defiled. But food will not commend us to God; we are neither the worse if we do not eat, nor the better if we do eat. But

---

14. *Ibid.*, p. 164.

take care lest this liberty of yours somehow become a stumbling block to the weak. For if someone sees you who have knowledge dining in an idol's temple, will not his conscience, if he is weak, be strengthened to eat things sacrificed to idols? For through your knowledge he who is weak is ruined, the brother for whose sake Christ died. And thus, by sinning against the brethren and wounding their conscience when it is weak, you sin against Christ. Therefore, if food causes my brother to stumble, I will never eat meat again, that I might not cause my brother to stumble (I Corinthians 8:1-13).

The first thing the apostle does is show that this issue involved is one of opinion. Next he instructs the one party, not to give up his opinion, but to cease practicing it, lest his liberty become a stumbling block to the weak brother. The aim of the whole affair is to refrain from sinning against a brother's conscience, and thus against Christ. The motive behind it is governed by the law of love. The wisdom of it is governed by the law of expediency (which is treated later).

This one caution: when should one not yield? (See pages 265-267.) When one is demanded to forfeit the practicing, and possibly even the holding of an opinion, one should exercise the liberty. The reason here is twofold. First, it is humanly impossible to meet *every* demand made by men to forfeit one's opinion. One can immediately see that such an attitude would be totally beyond human possibility. It would be entirely inconsistent. It would utterly destroy human personality. Another reason is that liberty is a Christian imperative. One is duty-bound to preserve his own right of opinion (Galatians 2:3-5), just as well as he is obligated to surrender to the right of God to give precept and precedent. It is wrong to recognize and encourage bigotry and opinionism in the unwarranted demands of others. We quote:

But so far as the real question of liberty was concerned, each man's liberty is finally judged by his own conscience and not by that of another. Liberty may be *waived* for the sake of another's conscience, but it is never thus *surrendered*.

. . . The conscience of another man does not make it wrong for me to do that which I am not only permitted to do by my own conscience, but which I even do in a spirit of prayerful thankfulness. Nor does my doing such a thing give him, or any other, a right to speak evil of me, for I do not have to change my conscience to suit the judgment of others. In theory Paul sided with the strong, but in sympathy he was one with the weak; yet he did not permit them to exercise a vexatious tyranny over him because of their scruples.[15]

"Therefore let no one act as your judge in regard to food or drink or in respect to a festival or a new moon or a Sabbath day" (Colossians 2:16).

The Christian must ever be on guard to avoid two extremes. One must *not give in* so long as he does not cause the other brother to violate his own conscience. And, one must *give in* only to that extent which he does not fasten within the other brother a tendency to force his opinion as a standard of right and wrong.

THE LAW OF EXPEDIENCY

A Christian must not only see how many rights he *has* (as a Christian) and *can use* (according to the law of liberty), but now he should proceed to find how his rights can be used *wisely*. Christ owns a Christian's opinion as well as his faith. Man has dedicated all of himself to the Lord. His opinion is not an area of thought and action where he can

---

15. J. W. McGarvey, P. Y. Pendleton, *Thessalonians, Corinthians, Galatians, and Romans*, p. 107.

escape from divine control. In the free exercise of opinion a man is obligated to be wise. God is prudent — filled with understanding — "the practical wisdom in handling affairs"[16] (Ephesians 1:8) and so should we. Man's opinion is a means to an end: in everything he wants to serve the Lord. He must seek to turn every free thought and deed into a consecrated advantage for the Lord. "And whatever you do in word or deed, do all in the name of the Lord Jesus, giving thanks through Him to God the Father" (Colossians 3:17). One can so foolishly use his freedom so as to be a detriment to the cause of Christ.

Things expedient fall entirely out of the realm of faith. They belong in the area of opinion. Said Paul, "All things are lawful for me, but not all things are profitable. All things are lawful for me, but I will not be mastered by anything" (I Corinthians 6:12). "All things are lawful, but not all things are profitable. All things are lawful, but not all things edify" (I Corinthians 10:23). The word "expedient" means "to be an advantage, profitable."[17]

When some one attempted to argue for sprinkling of water as the valid fulfillment of Christian baptism on the grounds of expediency, Z. T. Sweeney charged:

> "We are trying this change in the light of *expediency.*" No, you are not. There is, there can be, no expediency in this matter. Expediency is a choice between two or more courses, *all of which are lawful.* Expediency can not obtain in a choice between a lawful and an unlawful thing. Paul taught expedience *only where "all things are lawful."*[18]

---

16. W. E. Vine, *An Expository Dictionary of New Testament Words* (Westwood, N.J.: Fleming H. Revell Co., 1962), p. 228.
17. *Ibid.*, p. 62.
18. Z. T. Sweeney, *Should Churches of Christ Receive Unimmersed Into Formal Fellowship* (Cincinnati, O.: Standard Publishing, 1942), p. 13.

WHAT THE BIBLE SAYS ABOUT FAITH AND OPINION

What are things expedient? Alexander Campbell says this:

> They are then, in one sentence, those things, or forms of action, which it was impossible or unnecessary to reduce to special precepts; consequently they are not faith, piety, nor morality; because whatever is of the faith, of the worship, or of the morality of Christianity, was both possible and necessary to be promulgated; and is expressly and fully propounded in the sacred scriptures. The law of expediency, then, has no place in determining the articles of faith, acts of worship, nor principles of morality. All these require a *"thus saith the Lord"* in express statements, and the sacred writings have clearly defined and decided them. But in other matters that may be called the circumstantials of the gospel and of the church of Christ, the people of God are left to their own discretion and to the facilities and exigencies of society.[19]

The important thing to remember is that expediency refers to the usage of opinion: whether or not it is advantageous in a given case. It is not a moral decision, but a decision of wisdom.

Hall L. Calhoun places expedient things in a class distinctive of opinion. He says:

> Expedient things are things advantageous. Nothing can belong to the class of expedient things which is either necessary or indifferent. If a thing is necessary, it is more than expedient; and if a thing is indifferent it is less than expedient. All expedient things are right—i.e., scriptural and advantageous; but they are not commanded—i.e., enjoined or prohibited. In Matt. 18:18 Jesus said: "Whatsoever ye shall bind on earth shall be bound in heaven, and whatsoever ye shall loose on earth shall be loosed in heaven." This passage shows that there are some things bound upon us, and it

---

19. Alexander Campbell, *Christian System* (Nashville, Tenn.: Gospel Advocate, 1974 reprint of 1839 ed.), p. 91.

shows just as clearly that some other things are left loose, and the things left loose are just as right—i.e., scriptural—as the things bound. Paul recognized this principle plainly, for in I Cor. 7, speaking in reference to Christians not marrying, he says: "But I speak this by permission and not of commandment." Here was a thing clearly right in and of itself which a man might do or not, just as he thought expedient. This was not a matter of necessity, neither was it a matter of indifference: it was a question of expediency, and the man himself must decide as to its expediency or inexpediency in his own case. In this class of things human judgment must always decide whether any particular thing is expedient or not.[20]

Now what is advantageous? This is entirely a personal decision, each case being examined in its own time and under its own circumstances. Paul did this with the matter of circumcision. The keeping of the Old Testament law became a matter of opinion after the coming of the New Covenant. So in the case of Timothy, Paul had him circumcised. Why? "He took and circumcised him because of the Jews who were in those parts: for they all knew that his father was a Greek" (Acts 16:3). Circumcision was the work or seal of one being a Jew, and being part Jew, he would be ministering among the Jews. A purely expedient issue! However, when it came to Titus, Paul refused to have him circumcised. Here it would have been to a disadvantage, for it would have violated the law of liberty.

But not even Titus who was with me, though he was a Greek, was compelled to be circumcised. But it was because of the false brethren who had sneaked in to spy out our

---

20. Hall L. Calhoun, quoted by John B. Cowden, *St. Paul on Christian Unity*, pp. 196-197.

liberty which we have in Christ Jesus, in order to bring us into bondage. But we did not yield in subjection to them for even an hour, so that the truth of the gospel might remain with you (Galatians 2:3-5).

Paul rebelled at ever making circumcision (or any other law of the Old Covenant) a test of faith. "Behold I, Paul, say to you that if you receive circumcision, Christ will be of no benefit to you" (Galatians 5:2). He refused to give in when demanded. But he freely used such laws and institutions wherever advantageous. At one time Paul stooped to the level of boasting, which was not required of him to say by inspiration (although inspired to write it for us today), in order to silence the charges of his Judaizing enemies in Corinth. Said he, "That which I am speaking, I am not speaking as the Lord would, but as in foolishness, in this confidence of boasting. Since many boast according to the flesh, I will boast also" (II Corinthians 11:17, 18). Thus, he presents an array of testimony of his own labors and trials.

Now, a thing expedient by the very fact that it is a matter of advantage must necessarily vary. One living by the law of God, will find that the "sun" of time and circumstance will cast an ever varying shadow over the area of personal choice. And he will find some of those choices of life to be expedient. See Figure 8, page 211. Again we quote Dr. Calhoun:

> A thing expedient at one time might be inexpedient or even a sin at another time and under different circumstances — e.g., in I Cor. 16:1-7 is an account of the manner in which the churches of Galatia and the church at Corinth were to send their bounty to Jerusalem. This they were to do by the hands of special men approved by them for this purpose. This was doubtless the most expedient way for them at that

time and under their circumstances. But when the people of Galveston, Texas were in need of help a few years ago, if the Christian people of the United States had sent aid to them in the way this aid was sent to Jerusalem, it not only would not have been expedient, it would have been a sin; for some, perhaps many, would have died before the aid could have reached them. To allow our fellow beings to suffer for the want of this world's goods when we could prevent it is a sin. (I John 3:17) And had we left those hungry people to suffer for food till men could go all the way to Galveston and carry personally our bounty we should have been grossly culpable. We sent our aid in a different way because it was expedient to do so. We sent through the United States mail and by express and telegram. This was more quickly and economically done because we have better facilities for sending than they had in Paul's day. It is our duty to use these more expedient means just as truly as it is our duty to be baptized. One is the obligation of necessity, and the other is the obligation of expediency, and both these obligations are scripturally binding upon us. In Gal. 6:10 Paul says: "As we have therefore opportunity let us do good unto all men."[21]

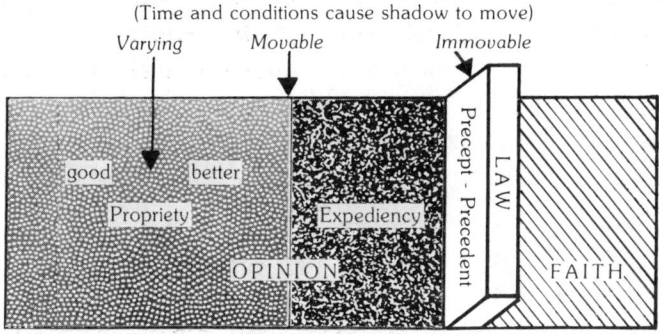

Figure 8

---

21. Calhoun, *op. cit.*, pp. 197-198.

Paul referred to this factor in his discourse on marriage and celibacy in a particular kind of case (I Corinthians 7:25). The precept of God is this, "Let marriage be held in honor among all," (Hebrews 13:4). There is no particular holiness about celibacy. Whether or not a person chooses to marry is purely one of personal choice. However, one must, in his freedom of choice, abide by the law of expediency. In Paul's case, under the troublesome and calamitous times, and in the hazardous conditions under which he had to fulfill his apostleship, he found it expedient not to marry (I Corinthians 7:26). It was not an issue of right and wrong, but one of wisdom (I Corinthians 7:35-40).

So it is with a thousand things which the Christian thinks upon. In the duty of transmitting the word of God one might think of such expediences as translators, printing processes, book-binding processes. In regard to the most essential work of evangelism one might ponder over such expediencies as a house of worship, advertising media, convenient baptistries, modern transportation, scientific implements, (radio, public address systems, television, computers, telephones, office equipment, mailing equipment), co-operative methods, workable plans, revival meetings, and the like. All of these are to be judged by the highest standards of intelligence man is capable of exercising. The Lord requires the best decisions possible, not perfection.

THE LAW OF PROPRIETY

Too many people are so legalistic minded that they classify everything as either being dead right or dead wrong. The fundamentalist is frequently guilty of this "black and white" attitude. But this view is not warranted.

OPINION: LAW OF OPINION

Let us pause long enough to understand this word "legalism." *Webster's Dictionary* says it is "strictness, or the doctrine of strictness, in conforming to law, or, in theology, to a code of deeds and observances as a means of justification."[22] J. D. Thomas has provided this definition. In summary:

Legalism may be defined as:
1. The general attitude that Christianity is simply a plan or set of laws without any special inward coherence, the strict keeping of which earns or achieves salvation. "Good works" are "exchanged" for salvation on a commercial basis. Reverence for the bare externals of lawkeeping predominates; there is no appreciation of the true inner spirit of Christianity or for God's grace. Obedience is motivated only by fear or self interest.
2. Under such extreme reverence and concern for "laws" as such, some have become Legalists by making laws where God has not. They have made traditions or customs (e.g., "three songs and a prayer, and another song," plan of worship), or sometimes perhaps even wishful thoughts, into laws.

The making of "fringe" matters (e.g., "mint, anise and cummin") into central doctrines, as the Pharisees did, is also to be classed as "law-making." . . . They indicate . . . an over concern for strictness—a desire to have a stated law for every minor detail of action. Jesus spoke of "justice and mercy" as being "weightier matters,"—as basic principles—which the Pharisees had overlooked in their meticulous concern for having strict, detailed laws for every little minor matter (Matthew 23:23; Luke 11:42).

---

22. *Webster's New Collegiate Dictionary* (Springfield, Mass.: G. & C. Merriam Co., 1956), p. 480.

In summary, a short definition of "Legalism" is that it is *an overconcern for mere law, as such.* Ways in which such over-concern is often expressed are:
1. Considering Christianity as a mere legal system rather than a grace-faith system.
2. Dependence upon "law-keeping" for salvation, rather than upon Christ.
3. An over-concern to the point that *one makes laws* where God hasn't, because he feels that every detail must be covered by a sharp law, and generic authority only is too vague for a secure feeling.

In the light of the above, BRETHREN should realize that *optional matters,* such as: the number of containers used in partaking of the fruit of the vine; the class method of teaching the Bible; the sponoring-church method of church cooperation; and the use of orphan homes, should not be made into laws! All these are optional expedients; and to make them into law when God has not, is legalism![23]

Let us make this assessment, however, for one to adhere carefully to full trust and obedience in matters of "faith" does not necessarily make one a "legalist." One can have this spirit and practice of fidelity to the Lord without trusting in his own good works or denying the grace of God. Christianity is a "faith" system, not a "merit" system — however, this does not dispense with exacting obedience.

Many issues, which the Christian is called on to decide in his own conscience, are not decisions between right and wrong — but relative decisions — decisions which involve a better or best choice out of a multiple of alternatives. Our Lord acknowledged this in His visit to the home of Mary and

---

23. J. D. Thomas, *We Be Brethren,* pp. 112, 113.

Martha. Both were doing a good work of ministry for Jesus. Even in this good thing, however, Mary had chosen a better thing to do. As Jesus said to Martha, who was quite distracted with the menial tasks of preparation, ". . . for Mary hath chosen the good part, which shall not be taken away from her" (Luke 10:42).

The law of propriety goes a bit further than that of expediency. Things expedient are things wise and advantageous. Whereas things of propriety are that plus some moral factor or consideration. Some things which may be very advantageous may not be quite proper — according to local custom, decorum, or rules of fitness. The nature and variableness of "culture" in everyone's experience must be considered in the holding and practicing of personal "opinions." The area of propriety, then, is similar to that of expediency in that it is variable with the change of time and circumstance. See Figure 8, page 211.

A good case in point was that in which Paul denied himself a salary from the Corinthian church (his perfect right to accept), not only on the basis of expediency, but also propriety (I Corinthians 9:6-27). He did not wish to cast any ill repute on the ministry of this "good news" or on the motives behind his portion in it, so he denied himself a right which was sanctioned by Scripture and the laws of nature. He said, "We did not use this right, but we endure all things, that we may cause no hindrance to the gospel of Christ" (I Corinthians 9:12; cf. Acts. 18:3; II Corinthians 11:7-9; Philippians 4:15, 16). He had to cope with a people who were uninstructed in much of the Christian system and who were apt, at the very outset, to impute evil thoughts of their own to the apostle. Many missionaries have followed this policy today. Frequently, as in this instance, the laws of expediency and propriety are intertwined within a single case.

WHAT THE BIBLE SAYS ABOUT FAITH AND OPINION

Did not Jesus use this law in answering the disciples of John? (Matthew 9:14-17). They had asked why it was that Jesus' disciples did not fast often (according to tradition of Pharisees—realm of opinion, not law). Jesus' answer was on the basis of propriety. J. W. McGarvey says:

> It shows that it would have been absurdly inappropriate to the occasion for his disciples to fast, as much so as to mourn at a wedding, to patch an old garment with unfulled cloth, or to put new wine into old bottles. The arguments not only vindicated his disciples, but taught John's disciples that fasting has value only when it is demanded by a suitable occasion.[24]

So let each Christian weigh in his own heart and mind the propriety of all words and deeds. Whatever the issue is "let each man be fully convinced in his own mind" (Romans 14:5). A man must be conscientious in his every move. For a man may be lost if he follows his conscience, but he is more likely to be if he does not. When one decides on the propriety of some particular opinion it then becomes a moral issue to him. And he then is responsible to his conscience to abide by it, though others may not, nor even be held accountable for their attitude. Said Paul,

> The faith [to hold or not hold a certain opinion as proper] which you have, have as your own conviction before God. Happy is he who does not condemn himself in what he approves. But he who doubts is condemned if he eats, because his eating is not from faith [eats when doesn't believe it is proper to do so]; and whatever is not from faith is sin [to doubt the propriety of holding or using a certain opinion, and yet give in to it, is sinful to that person though permissible to someone else] (Romans 14:22, 23).

---

24. J. W. McGarvey, *New Testament Commentary—Matthew and Mark* (Nashville, Tenn.: Gospel Advocate, reprint of 1875 ed.), p. 84.

OPINION: LAW OF OPINION

THE LAW OF LOVE

The beginning of all Christian growth is faith (Hebrews 11:6, II Peter 1:5) and the fullgrown fruit is love (II Peter 1:7; I Corinthians 13). Love that is rooted in genuine faith in Christ and cultivated according to the will of the great Husbandman is the lovliest and most fragrant flower humanly possible. Christian love is the highest of all Christian attainments. It is the indispensable factor in every Christian activity and that which provides the Spirit of God to make it holy and alive (I Corinthians 13:1-3). It is the supreme moral principle that must saturate and govern every deed. As Alexander Campbell said, *"No code of laws, without it, could make or keep any people pure, peaceable, and happy; and with it, we only want, in most matters, but general laws."*[25]

The law of love is most vital to our opinions. It bears heavily on how we use them, and how we behave toward the opinions of others. W. E. Vine observes:

> Christian love, whether exercised toward the brethren or toward men generally, is not an impulse from the feelings, it does not always run with the natural inclinations, nor does it spend itself only upon those for whom some affinity is discovered. Love seeks the welfare of all, Romans 15:2, and works no ill to any, 13:8-10; love seeks opportunity to do good to 'all men, and especially toward them that are of the household of faith,' Galatians 6:10.[26]

Thus, it is the disciplined, mental commitment of one for another, "to have a preference for, wish well to, regard the welfare of; . . . take pleasure in the thing, prize it above other things, be unwilling to abandon it or do without it; . . . to welcome with desire, long for."[27]

---

25. Alexander Campbell, *Christian System*, p. 94.
26. W. E. Vine, *An Expository Dictionary of New Testament Words*, p. 21.
27. Joseph Henry Thayer, *Thayer's Greek-English Lexicon of the New Testament* (Grand Rapids: MI: Associated Publishers and Authors, 1886), pp. 3, 4.

But it will suffice to say that the Christian needs to imitate the kind of love God has toward the world to send His only begotten Son, and that shown by Jesus in His love for His church (John 3:16; Ephesians 5:25).

(1) Let us first consider its *negative* aspect in the realm of opinion. We phrase it as a question. What shall I do about the opinions of others? Simply allow love to enter into one's attitude — love that knows how to tolerate, overlook, appreciate, or carefully appraise (as the case may be) those varied differences of opinion so common in the other party. The law of love should be vitally in control of attitudes that would otherwise run wild and reckless, and thus hurt the body of Christ — attitudes that may be logical, free, and even wise; but without love, are cold and divisive. The law of love adds Godly peace and warmth to the preceding laws of liberty, expediency, and propriety.

Once, after two old friends had enjoyed a long-delayed reunion the one party departed leaving with the other a slip of paper on which was written the following:

> Oh, the comfort, the inexpressible comfort, of feeling safe with a person, having neither to weigh facts nor measure words, but passing them all right out, chaff and grain together, certain that a faithful hand will take and sift them and with the breath of kindness blow the rest away.[28]

What we need to do is put into practice the virtue of "forbearance." When used in the middle voice the word means "to bear with, endure." Paul writes in his treatment of Christian unity, "with all humility and gentleness, with patience, showing forbearance to one another in love" (Ephesians 4:2).

In that memorable year of 1824 when Alexander Campbell met Barton W. Stone in Kentucky, here were two giants

---

28. W. E. Vine, *op. cit.*, p. 116.

OPINION: LAW OF OPINION

of a common reformation, yet separated by space and from a common influence. Mr. Stone saw few differences of doctrine between them. And for the most part, if not all, these differences were in non-essentials. He then wrote:

> I will not say there are no faults in Brother Campbell; but that there are fewer perhaps, in him, than in any man I know on earth; and over these few my love would throw a veil, and hide them from view forever. I am constrained and willingly constrained, to acknowledge him the greatest promoter of this reformation of any man living. The Lord reward him![29]

Love makes many cases of schism impossible. When men have the essentials in agreement, love can heal the wounds caused by the differences in non-essentials, no matter how many nor how varied. Love is a power.

When a people have learned how to Scripturally weigh essentials and non-essentials, then through the implementation of the law of love the sweet fellowship of unity ought to ensue. To people who are so near this holy ground, it is grave sin to allow this one violation within the realm of opinion to destroy everything accomplished. But this has happened often. Mr. Robert Richardson points out such folly that occured during the work of our "restoration fathers":

> It was impossible to explain satisfactorily, on Christian principles, the necessity of division where there were so many points of agreement, and the unprejudiced were unable to recognize as just reasons those distinctions which appeared so vast as seen through the magnifying glass of

---

29. Barton W. Stone, quoted by J. H. Garrison, *The Story of a Century* (St. Louis, MO: Christian Publishing Company, 1909), p. 144.

sectarian bigotry, but so minute and trivial in the eyes of Christian love.[30]

(2) Now the *positive* side, which is frequently more difficult because of its demand of sacrifice and aggressiveness. What shall the Christian do about his own opinions as he considers the interest of his brother in the working of love? Brotherly love is a Scriptural essential (I John 2:9-11; 3:10-24; 4:20, 21). It is imperative for one to "love the brotherhood" (I Peter 2:17). Therefore, the activity of love in opinion is an indispensible control. In the words of the late Ira M. Boswell, "When we limit our love by our opinions, we show our love for our opinion." Learn how to love your brother with your opinions; they are yours to use to glorify God.

"I have my rights" is a commonly heard apologetic. This is a true claim and does have a legitimate place, but never with the attitude included: "and I don't care about anyone else." This is all too common. For the sake of stubbornness, pride, selfishness, rather than love; such a one holds, and maintains, and uses every right of opinion to his own good pleasure. In so doing he asks, "Why should I give up what is rightfully mine?" Or as Paul worded it, ". . . Why is my freedom judged by another's conscience?" (I Corinthians 10:29).

The answer for the Christian is crystal clear. As stated before, there is a time to waive rights, to forfeit them in the interest of a greater cause than mere personal wish. And the springboard for such selfless retraint is *love*. "Let no one seek his own good, but that of his neighbor" (I Corinthians

---

30. Robert Richardson, *Memoirs of Alexander Campbell*, II (Nashville, Tenn.: Gospel Advocate, 1956 reprint of 1898 ed.), p. 362.

10:24). W. Carl Ketcherside puts it well when he said, "Anyone who loves his opinions more than he does his brethren will defend his opinions and destroy his brethren." The entire Christian message and attitude is one of salvation for all, with no one, not even the least, ever being sacrificed for the sake of any carnal or temporal whim (Romans 14:20). The issue at stake is too great. Man is to be saved. So, love for the lost and the saved is something big to reckon with. Paul named six reasons why he had a right to accept remuneration from the Corinthians, but because he loved the lost (as well as considering its expediency and propriety) he gladly denied himself this right. He still maintained the same opinion but waived it in the name of the Lord's work (I Corinthians 9).

This is the valuable truth Paul taught in that fourteenth chapter of Romans. We quote James Macknight as he paraphrases vs. 15-22:

> *Wherefore, if thy brother*, who thinketh certain meats unclean, *is made to sin through thy* eating such *meat*, whether it be by hating thee as a profane person, or by following thy example contrary to his conscience, or by apostatizing to Judaism, *thou no longer actest according to* the *love* thou owest to thy brother. *Do not* become the occasion of *destroying him with thy meat, for whom Christ died. Let not then the good* liberty *which belongeth to you be evil spoken of*, as an indulgence of appetite to the prejudice of others. Ye need not use your liberty always; *for the religion of Christ does not consist,* either in abstaining from or *in* using *meat and drink, but in a righteous and peaceable behaviour, and in joy in the Holy Ghost. And the brother who, by righteousness, peace, and joy in the Holy Ghost, serves Christ* his Lord, (ver. 9), *is acceptable to God, and* will be *approved of* men. *Well, then, let us pursue the things which promote*

peace, and the things which advance that *mutual edification* which we ought to reap from one another's example. *Do not for the sake of* the pleasure of eating this or that kind of meat, *destroy* your brother's virtue, which is *the work of God. All* kinds of *meats, indeed, are clean* under the gospel; *yet that meat is bad to the man who eateth it,* not from a persuasion of its lawfulness, but *through the influence of example. It is commendable neither to eat flesh* of any kind, *nor to drink wine, nor to do anything,* however innocent, *whereby thy brother is brought into danger of sinning, or is made to sin, or is weakened* in his attachment to the gospel. I wot (know) *thou hast a just persuasion* concerning the lawfulness of all kinds of meat. *Hold that persuasion fast, so far as respects thine own conduct in the presence of God;* but do not use thy liberty, so as to lead others to sin. *Happy is he who doth not subject himself to punishment, by* doing *what he approveth* as lawful. *For he who seeth a difference in meats, is liable to punishment, if* through thy example *he eat* what he thinks unclean; *because he eateth not from a persuasion that it is lawful,* but to please others. This is wrong; *for whatever is done without a conviction of its lawfulness, is really sin,* though it be lawful in itself.[31]

The motive behind this selfless denial is love. And love is a law. Professor Grubbs states the law of love, and the principle on which it is based, in these words:

The law: *The obligation to waive what one deems a mere privilege when the interests of the brethren demand it.*

We can not waive a duty; we can waive what we deem a privilege.

The Principle: *The infinite superiority of God's children to all things external to the kingdom of God.*

---

[31]. James Macknight, *Apostolic Epistles* (Grand Rapids: Baker Book House, 1949 reprint), pp. 128-129.

OPINION: LAW OF OPINION

God's children are worth infinitely more than ten thousand unauthorized expedients. The faithful observance of this Law of Love on the part of all of God's children would preclude any division among them.[32]

Thus, a Christian must realize the weight of law in comparison to that of his opinion, lest by the free misuse of opinion he violate the law of God. Herein opinion which should be free of sin (not being a moral issue at all) becomes sin. Professor Calhoun once wrote:

> Rom. 12:10, "In honour preferring one another." Rom. 15:2, "Let each one of us please his neighbor." It is to these things, mere personal privileges, that the law of love applies, and the violation of this law is a sin as certainly as is the violation of any other law that God has given. I Cor. 8:12, "And thus sinning against the brethren and wounding their conscience when it is weak ye sin against Christ." And in I Cor. 10:33 Paul lays down a rule to govern our conduct in these things, saying, "Even as I please all men in all things, not seeking mine own profit, but the profit of the many." In necessary things Paul would have pleased God even if he had thereby displeased all men, but in indifferent things he always yielded to others.[33]

It is a great task to apply this law of love to actual case histories in life. To know when to exercise freedom and when to waive it in the cause of love is not easy. It takes growth in Christ to slowly, and almost imperceptibly, develop this grace. Once again the fact of two dangerous extremities must be avoided. Too much thought for self, one's own

---

32. Grubbs, *op. cit.*, p. 165.
33. Hall L. Calhoun, as quoted by John B. Cowden, *St. Paul on Christian Unity*, p. 196.

rights and freedoms, is apt to injure the *conscience* of another party and possibly destroy his faith. Too much fastidious and superfluous thought for others is apt to injure the legitimate exercise of one's own rights, to the destruction of the standard of faith and opinion in the mind of the other party.

Now because of the very nature of opinions, over which these laws have control, these said laws will naturally be intertwined and often simultaneous in their operations. Usually more than one law is applicable in a single case of opinion. And care must be taken to be thorough, not preserving one essential at the expense of another. Things must be given their Scriptural priority. It is imperative that Christians limit themselves by law as it pertains to the exercise of free opinion.

Before closing this discussion one more consideration is needful. All applications thus far have been directed toward the individual. However, what about the community of believers, the church? If opinion is personal, how can there be harmony in a fellowship of persons? How shall it decide an opinion (as policy) where a singular choice is imperative to the function of a congregation? For instance, consider the case of such an expedient as a church building. Everyone's opinion can not be honored. It is an impossibility. And there are a thousand church issues which precept and precedent do not answer, but which fall in the realm of free opinion. What means shall a church employ to ascertain an answer necessary to its work as a group? An answer that would preserve the maximum of liberty in the individual?

The Lord has not left the church without instruction. For the church of the New Testament through precedent, has taught us what it did in similar cicumstances under the oversight of inspired men. Though that church was theocratic in faith it was democratic (as much as it was possible) in opinion. Such choices were not episcopal nor papal in nature, but were made by the consenses of opinion rightfully held by the constituents of the church. Alexander Campbell describes this process at work in a matter expedient:

> *Who shall ascertain and who shall interpret this law of expediency?* We all agree that expedients are to be chosen with regard to times, seasons, and other circumstances. Changes in these must always change expedients. . . . Now the law of expediency is the law of adopting the best present means of attaining any given end. But this is a matter which the wisdom and good sense of individuals and communities must decide. This is not, this cannot be, a matter of standing revelation. Now if the church was always unanimous in opinion as in faith—if all its accumulated wisdom gave one uniform decision on all such questions—then the whole church is by one voice to ascertain the law of expediency on any given point. But this is not the case. No class of men, apostles, teachers, privates, ever did agree on questions of expediency. Paul and Barnabas dissented and differed, *without any breach of communion,* on a question of this sort. Hence arises the necessity of the spirit of concession, subordination, bearing, forebearing, submitting to one another. When there are two views or opinions on any question of expediency entertained by two parties, one of them must yield, or there are two different systems of operation, and ultimately two distinct parties. According to the law of expediency, then, the minors in age, experience, or numbers, must give place to the majors in age, experience, or numbers. But as numbers are supposed to represent the ratios of age, wisdom, and knowledge, it is expedient that a clearly-ascertained majority of those whose province it is to decide any matter shall interpret the law of expediency; or, in other words, the minority shall peaceably and cordially

acquiesce in the decisions of the majority. Since the age of social compacts began, till now, no other principle of co-operation, no other law of expediency, can secure the interests, the union, harmony, and strength of any people, but that of the few submitting to the many.[34]

Democracy is the only answer that preserves both the solidarity of the group and the individuality of the constituents to the fullest measure possible. Any other system increases one factor to the hurt of the other. Democracy is the most equitable balance. We quote Isaac Errett:

> In judgments merely inferential, we reach conclusions as nearly unanimous as we can; and where we fail, exercise forbearance, in confidence that God will lead us into final agreement. In matters of expediency, where we are left free to follow our own best judgment, we allow the majority to rule. In matters of opinion — that is, matters touching which the Bible is either silent or so obscure in its revelations as not to admit of definite conclusions — we allow the largest liberty, so long as none judges his brother, or insists on forcing his own opinion on others, or making them an occasion of strife.[35]

God allows man as much autonomy as He, in His infinite wisdom, dares to allow him. Of course, when a congregation employs this means of determining its free issues it must utilize the laws of liberty, expediency, propriety, and love to make democracy workable and sane. Alston H. Chase said:

> At its [democracy] best, it is the noblest of the forms of government because it demands of its citizens the greatest

---

34. Alexander Campbell, *op. cit.*, p. 93.
35. Isaac Errett, *Our Position* (Cincinnati, O.: Standard Publishing, n.d.), p. 8.

nobility and the greatest intelligence. But at its worst, as Plato told men long ago, it is next to the lowest, leading directly to the worst of all, a tyranny. Its members are all likely to sacrifice an ultimate good to an immediate gain.[36]

In its strength there is also weakness. Man may be so gullible for the false, the convenient, the irresponsible, or the indolent means that he sells his democratic soul for a "mess" of controls. This has been the curse of ecclesiasticism.

The other great weakness in democracy is in that choice of man (where he truly wants to exercise the right of democracy) to not govern himself any more than he so desires. A church, by poor and unintelligent decisions, may so choose to be a poor government. A people never govern themselves better than they want to. And God allows the church to reap as she has sown.

Here lies a great problem of the majority and the minority. There is *no* place for a "gloating and moaning" attitude among the household of faith. When one has taken a stand with the majority he must with genuine Christian grace and love be respectful and considerate of those in the minority group. Says Russell J. Clinchy:

> In any association of free men, therefore, whether it be social or religious, the use of the raw power of the majority possesses rights only to the extent that they do not infringe upon the rights of minorities to exist and to express themselves in responsible living.[37]

And if one is of the minority, it is not fitting for one of Christian stature to accept the attitude of the "fighting minority," the "underdog," the oppressed. A loud and troublesome

---

36. Alston H. Chase, *The English Leaflet* (June, 1948).
37. Russell J. Clinchy as quoted by Chester E. Tulga, *Christian Standard* (July 31, 1948), p. 13.

minority has no right to curb the God-given rights of the majority. But one must yield gracefully to decisions which have been fairly reached. This whole matter works both ways: for a democratic people to develop a Scriptural majority and minority takes all the Christ-like character it can build within itself. It is much easier to say "democracy" than it is to live it. One must work it out or it is nothing. If Christians individually learn how to appropriate these four laws of opinion into their attitude and behavior, then the church will begin to take on the peace and unity characteized by the Lord Himself. It is His church, may it grow to be like Him. May it truly learn how to be the "body of Christ" (I Corinthians 12:12-31). If it violates these laws then will appear all the evils of bureaucracy, anarchy, strife, chaos, and weakness, to which democracy is susceptible.[38]

Let the children of God remember the twofold caution (toward others and self) to be heeded in every endeavor declared to be Christian. Said the apostle:

> To the weak I became weak, that I might win the weak; I have become all things to all men, that I may by all means save some. . . . but I buffet my body and make it my slave, lest possibly, after I have preached to others, I myself should be disqualified (I Corinthians 9:22, 27).

And from the Hebrew letter:

> Let us hold fast the confession of our hope without wavering, for He who promised is faithful; and let us consider how to stimulate one another to love and good deeds, not forsaking our own assembling together, as is the habit of some, but encouraging one another; and all the more, as you see the day drawing near" (Hebrews 10:23-25).

---

38. See following pages 271-276.

Chapter Eleven
CHRISTIAN FELLOWSHIP — OPINION

In a previous chapter we defined "Christian fellowship" and indicated the Lord's way of testing it. Here we learned that there were certain issues of percept and precedent which formed a norm or pattern necessary to the consummation of genuine fellowship. These were rightfully delineated as the "tests of fellowship."

Now we are considering the field of opinion. And here we have the principle in converse. Matters of opinion were not (in Scripturally approved cases), can not, and should not (today) be made "tests" of Christian fellowship. It is as much a violation of the Lord's authority to build up arbitrary rules of opinion as tests of fellowship as it is to "let down the bars" of faith in testing fellowship. Both of these extremes are to be avoided. One is too narrow, the other too wide; one is monastic, the other liberal. Above all things in establishing the boundary of God's congregation we must never "exceed what is written" (I Corinthians 4:6). God's word must not be over-stated. On things untaught in Scripture let opinion reign as it ought to in the individual conscience.

It is a precept itself to leave opinion out of testing fellowship. Said Paul, "Now accept the one who is weak in faith, but not for the purpose of passing judgment on his opinions" (Romans 14:1). This passage, which some claim to be mistranslated, must be interpreted in the light of its own context. The subject in point is differences of opinion within the church and the attitudes of one party toward another. Opinions must not destroy the solidarity of a people. For the sake of clarity we quote several versions of this passage: "Him that is weak in the faith receive ye, but not to doubtful disputation" (King James Version). "Welcome a man of weak faith, but not for the purpose of passing judgment on his

WHAT THE BIBLE SAYS ABOUT FAITH AND OPINION

scruples" (James Moffatt). "Treat people who are over-scrupulous in their faith like brothers; do not criticize their views" (Edgar J. Goodspeed). "To speak now about people whose faith is weak, always receive them as friends, but not for the purpose of passing judgment on their scruples" (Twentieth Century New Testament). "As for the man who is weak in faith, welcome him, but not for disputes over opinions" (Revised Standard Version). "Receive him who is weak in the faith, without regard to differences of opinion" (Alexander Campbell, *Living Oracles*). "As for the man who is a weak believer, welcome him (into your fellowship), but not to criticize his opinions or pass judgment on his scruples or perplex him with discussions" (*The Amplified New Testament*). "If a man is weak in his faith you must accept him without attempting to settle doubtful points" (*The New English Bible*). "Welcome the person who is weak in faith, but do not argue with him about his personal opinions" (*Good News Bible*). "Accept him whose faith is weak, without passing judgment on disputable matters" (The New International Version).

This law was one of the cardinal teachings of Mr. Campbell's *Declaration and Address:*

> That with respect to the commands and ordinances of our Lord Jesus Christ, where the Scriptures are silent, as to the express time or manner of performance, if any such there be, no human authority has power to interfere, in order to supply the supposed deficiency, by making laws for the Church; nor can anything more be required of Christians in such cases, but only that they *so* observe these commands and ordinances as will evidently answer the declared and obvious end of their institution. Much less has any human authority power to impose new commands or ordinances upon the church, which our Lord Jesus Christ has not enjoined. Nothing ought to be received into the faith or

OPINION: CHRISTIAN FELLOWSHIP

worship of the church, or be made a term of communion amongst Christians, that is not as old as the New Testament.[1]

Those things which God loosed as opinion, let no man bind on another. That which is not commanded nor prohibited by Scripture must be allowed, in the name of Christian liberty.

Once, as the story goes, there was a king who had an iron bed for all the guests who came to visit him. If a guest was too long for the bed he would have him "cut down" to fit it, and if he was too short, orders were given to have him "stretched" until he filled the bed. So man behaves today using opinion as his "iron bed" toward all others. "No man has a right to judge his brother, except in so far as he manifestly violates the express letter of the law."[2]

But how strong the tendency becomes in Christian growth to bind on others one's own opinions. Lest we ever think our opinions to be unusually right and uniquely standardized let us hear Paul warn, "If anyone supposes that he knows anything, he has not yet known as he ought to know" (I Corinthians 8:2). We often become somewhat like the Scotchman who said that there were only two people sound in the world, he and his brother Sandy—and sometimes he had his "doots aboot Sandy."

Some may not distinctly mark their opinions as tests or claim them as such, but by their attitude they promote them as such. By an attitude of emphasis, prejudice, superiority, or absolute-orthodoxy, one may be guilty of this practice.

Christian fellowship can not be built on opinion. It is not only anti-Scriptural, unwise, but also impossible. Alexander Campbell testified to this:

---

1. Thomas Campbell, *Declaration and Address* (Lincoln, IL: Lincoln Christian College Press, 1971 reprint of 1809 ed.), pp. 23, 24.
2. *Ibid.*, p. 1.

WHAT THE BIBLE SAYS ABOUT FAITH AND OPINION

I have tried the Pharisaic plan and the monastic. I was once so straight that, like the Indian's tree, "I leaned a little the other way." And however much I may be slandered now as seeking "popularity" or a popular course, I have to rejoice that to my own *satisfaction,* as well as to others, I proved that the truth and not popularity was my object; for I was once so strict a separatist that I would neither pray nor sing praises with anyone who was not as perfect as I supposed myself. In this most unpopular course I persisted until I discovered the mistake, and saw that on the principle embraced in my conduct there never could be a congregation or church upon the earth.[3]

When men make communion in religious worship dependent on uniformity of opinion, they make self-love, instead of the love of God, the bond of union, and elevate matters of mere speculation above the one faith, the one Lord and the one immersion.[4]

There are many issues which a church must have the grace to consign to opinion—handled in the manner already prescribed. One such case was that of slavery in the days when it became a highly controversial matter in the nation and naturally in the church. Many Christians failed to properly handle this issue in the days of Isaac Errett.[5] As the issue grew more acute they began more and more to make it a test of Christian fellowship in all parts of the nation. And thus it was keenly felt within single congregations. Mr. Errett had a very definite opinion on the question, and yet he absolutely refused to allow it a position of "testing." For this he was called inconsistent and a compromiser. He held

---

3. Robert Richardson, *Memoirs of Alexander Campbell,* II (Nashville, Tenn.: Gospel Advocate, 1956 reprint of 1898 ed.), p. 137.
4. *Ibid.,* p. 224.
5. Isaac Errett, *Memoirs of Isaac Errett,* I, pp. 85-87.

OPINION: CHRISTIAN FELLOWSHIP

his ground, not only as to his opinion of the evil of slavery, but as to its rightful place in Christian fellowship. The storm finally subsided. Mr. Errett's attitude was proved to be right. The Church at New Lisbon, Ohio, where he ministered, was saved from unwarranted schism.

1. The forcing of opinion in the testing of fellowships is the supreme abuse of this right. There has been hardly any other abuse of opinion that has anywhere caused the amount of grief to the Lord and schism to His body which this has produced in 2000 years.

This problem takes us back to that primary issue, as stated before, of differentiating between matters of faith and opinion. The Scriptures teach us that we must discern between the revelation of God and the wisdom of men (I Corinthians 1:17-31). Alexander Campbell pleaded, "We ask for *faith*, and not for the deductions of reason; for the *testimony of God*, and not the opinions of men."[6] His father said that our goal should be:

> . . . to remove human opinions and the inventions of men out of the way, by carefully separating this chaff, from the pure wheat of primary and authentic revelation; casting out that assumed authority, that enacting and decreeing power by which those things have been imposed and established.[7]

Confusing the issues is like the story told about a man who stole a horse on Saturday night, but was found with the horse early Monday morning at the very scene of his crime. When asked why he had not escaped with his loot he replied, "I have conscientious scruples against traveling on Sunday." Here is opinion placed above precept. And this

---
6. Alexander Campbell, *Campbell on Baptism* (Bethany, Va.: Printed and published by Alexander Campbell, 1853), p. 22.
7. Thomas Campbell, *op. cit.*, p. 17.

same principle has been repeatedly violated by sincere Christians in their testing of fellowship.

There is an amusing, but significant lesson told from the life of Elder John Smith.

> While preaching through the same part of the State, he took occasion to discourse upon the sixth chapter of Ephesians, dwelling at some length on the sharpness and power of the Sword of the Spirit. No one having accepted the invitation of the Gospel, he was about to dismiss the assembly, when a Methodist preacher arose and asked the question:
>
> "If your doctrine be true, Mr. Smith, why has the sword had so little power tonight?"
>
> "Because," promptly replied Smith, "your teachers of human systems have so long hacked it against your traditions and wrapped it about with your creeds and disciplines, and blunted it so against your anxious seats and mourning-benches, that sinners can feel neither edge nor point."
>
> "I'd like to know the difference," said the discomfited preacher, "between your baptism and our mourning-bench."
>
> "Difference?" said Smith, with much emphasis; "one is from Heaven — the other, from the saw-mill."[8]

If only man would carefully weigh the difference of the two and attribute to each its proper weight and usage. Said the *Declaration and Address:*

> Were all these nonpreceptive opinions and practices, which have been maintained and exalted to the destruction of the church's unity, counter-balanced with the breach of the express law of Christ, and the black catalogue of mischiefs which have necessarily ensued, on which side, think you, would be the preponderance? When weighed in the balance

---

8. J. A. Williams, *Life of Elder John Smith* (Cincinnati, O.: Standard Publishing Co., 1904), p. 413.

OPINION: CHRISITAN FELLOWSHIP

with the monstrous complex evil, would they not all appear lighter than vanity? Who then would not relinquish a cent to obtain a kingdom! And here let it be noted, that it is not the renunciation of an opinion or practice as sinful, that is proposed or intended; but merely a cessation from the publishing or preaching of it, so as to give offence; a thing men are in the habit of doing every day for their private comfort or secular emolument, where the advantage is of infinitely less importance.[9]

It is a big enough task for the Christian to confine his attention to an accurate knowledge of and a careful adherence to matters essential—let alone to seek to set up a standard of opinions as necessary to Christian fellowship. Again from the pen of Thomas Campbell:

> Nor do I presume to dictate to them or to others as to how they should proceed for the glorious purpose of promoting the unity and purity of the Church; but only beg leave, for my own part, to walk upon such sure and peaceable ground that I may have nothing to do with human controversy, about the right or wrong side of any opinion whatsoever, by simply acquiescing in what is written, as quite sufficient for every purpose of faith and duty; and thereby to influence as many as possible to depart from human controversy, to betake themselves to the Scriptures, and, in so doing to the study and practice of faith, holiness and love.[10]

Of course, when men confuse faith and opinion they will be like Mr. Rice who charged Mr. Campbell with robbing people of the right to form opinions about precept:

> They allow men to form their own opinions concerning the character and work of Christ, the work of the Spirit, etc.

---

9. *Ibid.*, p. 44.
10. Robert Richardson, *Memoirs of Alexander Campbell*, I, p. 227.

—but on that one subject, immersion, they take the liberty of thinking for us. They will receive no one, unless on that subject he thinks just as they think. He must believe, that baptism is immersion. They say virtually, "you may think for yourself on all other subjects; but let us think for you on this." But I say, if I am to think for myself at all, let me form my own opinion on all subjects. If you are to think for me; why, do all my thinking and save me the trouble![11]

In this regard we have no rights. Precept excludes freedom of opinion: it is a norm. Oftentimes within precept we have the right of opinion to manifest strict obedience in more than one way. Where there is no limiting control there is permission to exercise freedom as long as the substance of precept is not violated. This is the problem of the music question. Said Isaac Errett:

> The New Testament furnishes no standard of music, the melody of the heart being made emphatic. But the requirement to *sing*, implies whatever is necessary to the performance of it. . . . Hence we have hymn books, tune books, tuning forks, choirs, etc., *not because these are commanded*, but because we are commanded to *sing*, and these are necessary to enable us to sing to edification.

He then insisted that the difference between the two parties

> . . . is not a difference of faith, nor is it a difference as to walking in the law of the Lord. *It is a difference of opinion as to the means necessary to obey the precept to sing*. It is, we admit, an important difference, and needs to be adjusted; but, *being a difference of opinion, no man has a right to*

---

11. N. L. Rice, *A Debate Between Rev. A. Campbell and N. L. Rice*, (Nashville, Tenn.: Gospel Advocate, reprint of 1844 ed.), p. 790.

> make it, on either side, a test of fellowship, or an occasion of stumbling.[12]

And yet a sharp contention has harassed much of the brotherhood on this issue for many years. Those who refused this right of opinion found themselves on incompatible grounds with those who did allow it. Said Dean Walker:

> Lard [Moses] headed the opposition, declaring: "Let no one who takes a letter from one church ever unite with another using an organ. *Rather let him live out of a church than go into such a den.* Let all who oppose the organ withdraw from the church if one is brought in." While some were arguing that the organ is an "expedient" in the same class with buildings and hymnals, others argued that it was both inexpedient and illegitimate: inexpedient, for it hinders singing; illegitimate for it is not prescribed in the New Testament.[13]

Thus, the simple truth stated so long ago by the pioneer of restorationism has frequently been violated by those claiming to be emulating his declarations:

> Our inference upon the whole, is, that where a professing Christian brother opposes or refuses nothing either in faith or practice, for which there can be expressly produced a "Thus saith the Lord," that we ought not to reject him because he cannot see with our eyes as to matters of human inference—of private judgment. "Through thy knowledge shall the weak brother perish? How walketh thou not charitably?" Thus we reason, thus we conclude, to make no conclusion of our own, nor of any other fallible fellow creature, a rule of faith or duty to our brother.[14]

---

12. Isaac Errett, *op. cit.*, pp. 39-40.
13. Dean Walker, *Adventuring for Christian Unity*, p. 43.
14. Thomas Campbell, *Declaration and Address*, p. 38-39.

2. Now if the forcing of opinion as a test of fellowship is the gravest abuse of opinion, then *creed-making* is its formal manifestation. Creed-making, the curse of Christianity, dates back to the days of the apostles. John had to mark one of the first such violaters in naming Diotrephes (III John 9, 10). Even Jesus was confronted with John, himself, at an earlier time, when he would have made a test of that early fellowship on the basis of other parties not associated with the apostles in the work and ministry of the Lord.

What is a formal creed? Mr. Campbell defined it:

> A creed or confession of faith is an ecclesiastic document —the mind and will of some synod or council possessing authority—as a term of communion, by which persons and opinions are to be tested, approbated, or reprobated.[15]

The elevation of mere opinion to law—as testing Christian fellowship, is the history of creed-making. Gavin Struther, in one of his essays, points out that in the apostolic day the divine creed of faith in Jesus as the "Christ, the Son of the living God" (Matthew 16:16; Acts 8:37, footnote), was solely recognized as a sufficient test of confession.[16] But with time came every shade of opinion. Rome crystallized some of these opinions into hard and fast laws. The churches of the reformation, in rebelling against the evils developed in these voluminous creeds, rather than return to the original norm, began to make corrections. Thus, were born the great historical creeds of the evangelical churches. The biggest virtue of Protestantism was to correct many of the false

---

15. Alexander Campbell, *A Debate Between Rev. A. Campbell and Rev. N. L. Rice*, p. 762.
16. Gavin Struther, quoted by Robert Richardson, *Memoirs of Alexander Campbell*, I, pp. 409-410.

doctrines as found in the Roman creed, and the biggest error was to write them down into new creeds.

However:

> They did not improve as "helps to the weak"; which was at first their main intention. Covering, as they soon did, the whole ground of "didactic and polemic theology," unlettered men could with difficulty fathom the meaning of their numerous propositions. Like modern acts of Parliament, they became obstruse from their very minuteness of detail, and thus generated endless controversies, and produced many divisions by a labored attempt at shutting out every possible mistake and error.[17]

How does this whole thing happen? Robert Richardson traces it this way:

> Individual assumptions soon become precedents; precedents soon established customs; and customs soon resolved themselves into laws, to which, in the different denominations, there was exacted an obedience more strict than to those of Holy Writ.[18]
>
> It is thus in religions as in civil affairs, that assumed power becomes at length confirmed authority; that the rights of the many are gradually usurped by the few, and that mankind become at length ruled by priests and kings, whose authority it is made heresy or treason to dispute.[19]

This is the process occuring in the course of time, identified as church history. The steps of change and evolution are usually imperceptible, gradually developing over a period of time. Man must be continually on guard that he does not become an instrument in this process today. He must weigh

---

17. Struther, as quoted by Richardson, *Ibid.*
18. Robert Richardson, *Memoirs of Alexander Campbell*, I, p. 389.
19. *Ibid.*, pp. 389-390.

every opinion, and then keep it such. This is a personal issue. Creedalizing, though monumented in great documents, is primarily a personal issue. To avoid this danger every Christian must ask himself: "Am I allowing, promoting, or condoning a matter of opinion to drift into precept or precedent?" Creedalizing does not have to be a published catalogue of articles of faith—it is first an attitude, a spirit, a lack of discerning. Said Alexander Campbell to Mr. Rice:

> Creeds are nuncupative [oral], as well as written. Hence they have made divisions before any of them was formally written out. Their being written is only necessary to give them permanency, and more extended sway. They are, however, as powerful to divide before, as after written. The creed system was just as well developed in the first, and in the last, of that series of ancient schisms, as it was at Nice, or Rome, or Constantinople, under the Christian dispensation.[20]

The great failure of creeds is that they have failed to accomplish what they intended to do. Men with honorable intentions thought they would preserve "the faith," keep the church pure, Scriptural, and united, thus preserving a fellowship with holy solidarity. This was pretty much the defense which Mr. Rice made as he debated Campbell. It is partly evident in this charge:

> The difference between his church and "the sects," is this: The notions and opinions of each individual in his church, form their foundation, and therefore there is no unity of faith; whilst each of "the sects" have a common faith, a common bond of union.[21]

But says George Plattenburg (in regard to creeds):

---

20. Alexander Campbell, *op. cit.*, p. 890.
21. *Ibid.*, p. 770.

OPINION: CHRISTIAN FELLOWSHIP

Through all the centuries of their history, they failed to keep out heresy, to quiet a single contention, to reconcile an enmity or promote the unity and peace of the church of God.[22]

Let us go back to the Fourth Century and listen to Hilary, bishop of Poictiers, in Aquitania. At this early day creeds had utterly failed in their attempts at being a legitimate ground for Christian fellowship:

> It is a thing equally deplorable and dangerous, that there are *as many creeds* as there are opinions among men, as many doctrines as inclinations, and as many sources of blasphemy as there are faults among us; BECAUSE WE MAKE CREEDS ARBITRARILY, AND EXPLAIN THEM AS ARBITRARILY. And as there is but one faith, so there is but one only God, one Lord, and one baptism. We renounce this one faith, when we make so *many different creeds;* and that diversity is the reason why we have *no true faith* among us. We cannot be ignorant, that SINCE THE COUNCIL OF NICE, we have done nothing but make CREEDS. And while we fight against WORDS, litigate about new questions, dispute about equivocal TERMS, complain of authors, that every one may make HIS OWN PARTY triumph, while we cannot AGREE, while we anathematize one another, there is hardly *one* that adheres to JESUS CHRIST.[23]

3. Creeds are powerful things. And the restoration movement has sought to put them in their proper place. As Martin Luther became the "papal emancipator," Alexander Campbell may rightfully be called the "creedal emancipator."

The next thought to be considered is this: What are the *dangers* of creed making?

---

22. George Plattenburg, "The Unity of the Church," *The Old Faith Restated,* ed. by J. H. Garrison (Joplin, Mo.: College Press reprint of 1891 ed.), p. 315.
23. Hilary as quoted by Alexander Campbell, *op. cit.*, pp. 796-797.

WHAT THE BIBLE SAYS ABOUT FAITH AND OPINION

(1) There is no harm in a man searching the Scriptures and his own heart, cataloguing in a logical order the summary of beliefs he holds, and even preaching or publishing them. The whole evil lies in his *misuse* of this "credo," which simply means "I believe."

The severest objection to most established creeds is not their theology. There are all kinds of articles of faith — true and false, wise and foolish, reasonable and unreasonable. As long as they are but personal formations of thought in harmony with the gospel which assist their creators in "working out his own salvation," there is little harm. The true danger is in their being set up as tests of Christian fellowship. And this is the use to which creeds have generally been put.

Going back to the famed Athanasian Creed (Article 44 — the last), here is the power it claims. "This is the Catholic Faith: which except a man believe faithfully (truly and firmly), he can not be saved."[24]

Said Isaac Errett on this:

> We object not to publishing, for information, what we believe and practice, in whole or in part, as circumstances may demand, with the reason therefor. But we stoutly refuse to accept of any such statement as authoritative, or as a test of fellowship, since Jesus Christ alone is Lord of the conscience, and His word alone can rightfully bind us.[25]

When Mr. Campbell challenged Mr. Rice on this issue he made it clear that man was at liberty to formulate his own viewpoints, but not to bind them on others as a creed. To

---

24. Phillip Schaff, *Creeds of Christendom*, II (Grand Rapids: Wm. B. Eerdmans, reprint of 1890 ed.), p. 70.
25. Isaac Errett, *Our Position* (Cincinnati, O.: Standard Publishing, n.d.), p. 7.

make and hold an interpretation, and to "creedalize" it, are two different things. He hit hard with this warning:

> But, mark it well, it is the making of such compends of views, in the ecclesiastic sense, *creeds* (that is, *terms of communion or bonds of union*) — I say again, as ecclesiastic documents, as terms of exclusion and reception of members, we adjure them.[26]

The unavoidable result of this practice is the gradual or sudden pre-eminence of the creed over the Scriptures. This is the old story. George Plattenburg said that creeds

> . . . were held to be offensive because their very existence assumed the inadequacy of the Bible, the imperfection of its legislation, and its insufficiency as a standard of Christian character and fellowship.[27]

Was this not the attitude which Jesus faced and rebuked in the Pharisees who creedalized their traditions and made void the word of God? (Matthew 15:3-9). Jesus did not condemn their traditions, but the *usage* of them, forcing such ideas on others as a test of their faithfulness to God and ultimately of their fellowship of Jews. Professor McGarvey points out the method which Jesus used in uncovering their mischievous way in which they "set aside God's commandments."[28]

(2) From the very nature of the rise of creeds there emerges the next danger — that of *discrimination*. Is fellowship to be tested by the ability and the lack of ability to discern an

---

26. Alexander Campbell, *op. cit.*, p. 784.
27. Plattenburg, *op. cit.*, p. 313.
28. J. W. McGarvey, P. Y. Pendleton, *The Fourfold Gospel* (Cincinnati, O.: Standard Publishing, 1916), p. 395-396.

arbitrarily chosen body of theology? Is doctrinal insight, mental capacity, or keen judgment to be the standard of the test? This certainly is foreign to the single New Testament concept. Said Thomas Campbell:

> That although doctrinal exhibitions of the great system of Divine truths, and defensive testimonies in opposition to prevailing errors, be highly expedient, and the more full and explicit they be for those purposes, the better; yet as these must be in a great measure the effect of human reasoning, and of course must contain many inferential truths, they ought not to be made terms of Christian communion; unless we suppose, what is contrary to fact, that none have a right to the communion of the church, but such as possess a very clear and decisive judgment; or are come to a very high degree of doctrinal information; whereas the church from the beginning did, and ever will, consist of little children and young men, as well as fathers.[29]

Let any one make a study of any of the major denominational creeds and this fact will soon be very apparent. For example in his hand the writer is holding a church membership card. On one side are the words:

REQUIREMENTS FOR MEMBERSHIP

Each candidate for membership in this church shall be expected to give a clear testimony of having been born of the Spirit of God (John 3:5-8), and to having received the Holy Spirit or to be earnestly seeking to be baptized in the Holy Spirit (Acts 2:2-4). It is expected that each applicant will follow the Scriptural command to be baptized in water by immersion in the Name of the Father and of the Son and of the Holy Ghost (Matt. 28:19).

---

29. Thomas Campbell, *op. cit.*, p. 24.

OPINION: CHRISTIAN FELLOWSHIP

A sincere belief in the inspiration of the Holy Scriptures as the Word of God and the final authority in all matters of faith and conduct; separation from worldly amusements such as the theater, movies, cards, dancing, etc.; deliverance from the use of tobacco, intoxicating liquors, etc.; a hope and expectancy of the premillennial coming of the Lord Jesus, are considered to be necessary for membership.

On the other side are the words:

APPLICATION FOR MEMBERSHIP

Having personally experienced the New Birth (John 3:5-8), through faith in the atoning blood of the Lord Jesus Christ; and having considered favorably the doctrines and practices of the Assemblies of God, and being in complete agreement with them; and desiring to be associated with those of like precious faith in Christian fellowship, I hereby apply for church membership.

I agree to be governed by the rules of the church, to attend the means of grace regularly as I have opportunity, and to support its ministries with my tithes and offerings as God shall prosper me.

It is my earnest prayer that God shall keep me true to Him, but if for any reason I shall depart from the faith, or cease to live a godly life, or change my doctrinal beliefs, I shall consider it just to be automatically released from membership in the church.

Notice how certain lines of opinion are mixed with certain matters of faith and error, all of which are made tests of fellowship.

Men may not be tortured nor killed for refusing a creed today, but they may very likely be intimidated, scorned, or discriminated against in some way. They may suffer loss of influence, reputation, opportunities, or freedoms. Creeds are not dead.

WHAT THE BIBLE SAYS ABOUT FAITH AND OPINION

One word of exception must here be noted. There are instances where certain kinds of discrimination are legitimate. All "testing" is not for Christian fellowship. Some "testing" is rightfully executed for other purposes. When the early church of the New Testament presented its norm of testing those for its fellowship by the token of some article of faith it was simply Jesus Christ—He being the creed—who He was, everything He said and did. It was crystallized into that simple pronouncement acknowledging belief in Jesus as the Christ, the Son of God (Matthew 16:16). However, for one who is acknowledged in full fellowship (by his submission to the New Testament standard of admission) there were other tests given. For example, there was that of testing one's qualification for a particular office, such as an evangelist, elder, or deacon. Does not a body of elders have the right to test a candidate for the ministry with certain "credos" to determine whether or not one is Scripturally qualified? This is a "test of leadership" or a "test of Scriptural office"—and not of being a Christian. The two must be distinguished.

Thus, the church, or auxiliaries of the church may set up certain standards to govern co-operation, personnel, methods as long as this practice never becomes a "test of Christian fellowship." This is a precarious issue and must forever be submitted to Christian consideration lest the will of God be violated.

(3) Now by the very nature of a creed, being documented opinion used as a discriminatory tool, it thus must be accepted as *divisive* and *schismatic* in the results it produces. A denominational preacher once said to the writer, "We use our church creed like a fence, to keep our people in." I replied, "That same fence keeps other people out." It may have other aims, but it is bound to have these results. Why is this so? Observe it at work. Mr. Campbell charged:

OPINION: CHRISTIAN FELLOWSHIP

The very attempt to create such a thing immediately divides into parties those who before were one. A affirms his conviction, that the attempt is impious. B argues, that it is expedient to keep out error and secure union amongst those that are now of one opinion. But A responds, we are not required to be, because we cannot be, of one opinion; and so far from the project creating unity of opinion, already it forms two opinions—one concerning this impiety, and the other touching the expediency of the affair. The proposition to create and to adopt is, therefore, essentially heretical and divisive; and, when the proposition is adopted, two parties, before in embryo by the proposition, are now by the resolution actually and formally in existence. The reason of all this is, perhaps, not yet fully developed. It lies, indeed, in the fallibility of human nature.[30]

Members of a little Southern Baptist Church, in reading the two main versions of the Lord's Prayer, observed one to begin "Our Father, which art . . ." and the other "Our Father, who art . . ." Their differences were soon stubbornly fashioned into creeds. Division resulted, not only in thought and spirit, but in organization, so that now the community has two Baptist Churches-the "Which Arts" and the "Who Arts." Said Mr. Campbell: *"No human Creed in Protestant Christendom can be found that has not made a division for every generation of its existence."*[31]

George Plattenburg quotes a Presbyterian who had asked the question as to what creed in history (modern or ancient) could ever form a basis for universal Christian agreement.

---

30. Alexander Campbell, *op. cit.,* p. 764.
31. Alexander Campbell, *Christian System* (Nashville, Tenn.: Gospel Advocate, 1974 reprint of 1839 ed.), p. 109.

Not one! They all have often excluded more Christians than they have included.

> If history teaches us anything plainly, it shows that the attempt to organize churches on the basis of mere dogmatic distinctions will always tend to schism, rather than to unity. They often exclude more Christians than they include, and sooner or later go to pieces in some fresh dissension, and even more difficult would it be to connect together conflicting churches on such a basis. It is certain that none of the leading Protestant Confessions, not the Augsburg, not the Belgic or Heidelburg; not the Westminster, not the Thirty-nine Articles would now be generally accepted by the American churches. It is doubtful if any of the great Catholic creeds, the Athanasian, the Nicene, or even the Apostles' Creed, would afford a platform broad enough to embrace all the denominations calling themselves Christians. And still less could they be marshalled together by any of the new made creeds of our own time and country.[32]

The history of creed-making is the history of denominationalism. Modern sectarianism, with all of its new "unwritten creeds," its standard writings or training courses or its current spokesman is but the extension of the same old practice, only occurring in contemporary times. A creed is a portion of truth (or untruth) crystallized into a "test" and thus founds a peculiar fellowship of adherents. This partial test must result in a partial assembly — thus, a sectarian and denominationalized "Christianity." Quoting Mr. Campbell:

> All creeds and confessions become the constitution of churches. The persons called a church or community are

---

32. Plattenburg, *op. cit.*, p. 325.

said to be builded upon them. They generally, indeed, assume that the creed itself is builded on the Bible, and the church on both. The Bible is, then, the subterraneous basis, or that portion of the foundation buried under ground. The creed is that visible, above ground part of the basis, and on which the church immediately rests, and from which it receives its name. This assumption of a Bible sub-basis, is, however, but a mere illusion. Take, for illustration, the high-church and low-church Episcopal, the Presbyterian, the Methodist and the Baptist, to go no farther. These all are said to be builded on the Bible, but between them and the Bible is interposed the creed from which they receive their name. The Bible, then, is to all the sects in Christendom what the earth is to London, the basis on which the several palaces, castles, and dwellings rest. The earth, however, is the foundation of none of them, in correct language. No one would think of calling the earth the foundation of Westminster Abbey, Windsor Palace, or the old Parliament House. No more can I call the Bible the foundation of the Episcopal, Presbyterian, Methodist, and Baptist Churches, or any one of the scores of communities that pretend to build on it. Contemplated as buildings, creeds are their proper foundations. Contemplated as *bodies*, they are their constitutions.[33]

As many creeds, so many parties; Caesar's maxim fitly illustrates their history. "Money" said he, "will raise soldiers, and soldiers will raise money": Thus creeds will make parties, and parties will make creeds; so the matter has operated from the day of their birth till now.[34]

Oh, the havoc which has been wrought by human creeds! Again, Mr. Plattenburg:

---

33. Alexander Campbell, *A Debate Betweeen Rev. A. Campbell and Rev. N. L. Rice*, p. 762.
34. *Ibid.*, pp. 762-763.

WHAT THE BIBLE SAYS ABOUT FAITH AND OPINION

> Human creeds have made more heretics than Christians; more parties than reformations; more martyrs than saints; more wars than peace; more hatred than love; more death than life; they have killed or driven out all the apostles, prophets, and reformers of the church and world.[35]

It actually was a creed which helped put Jesus on the cross.[36] Pontius Pilate was merely carrying out the decree of the established priesthood and church-court which declared that they had "a law" by which He must die. They could quote the Old Testament on this law, but they had overlooked the teaching of the Old Testament as to what sort of Messiah should come, and they had shut their eyes and ears to Christ's revelation.

The great tragedy to Christianity in every period of its existence has been the ugly fact that it has divided itself in this field of opinion. Where it should have gloried in freedom, it has become "Ichabod" in schism. From the very inception of this sin the story has been the same. Quoting from the *Christian System:*

> Schisms may then exist where there is the most perfect agreement in faith, in doctrine, in all religious tenets. Undue attachment to certain persons, to the disparagement of others, partial regards because of personal preferences, are the true elements of schism or division as it appeared in Corinth, and as the word is used in the New Testament. But few persons, nowadays, can correctly appreciate the force of the word *schism* in the apostolic age, because but a very few experimentally know the intimacies, the oneness of heart and soul, that obtained and prevailed in the Christian profession while all was genuine and uncorrupt. A union formed

---

35. Alexander Campbell, quoted by Plattenburg, *op. cit.*, p. 324.
36. Alexander Campbell, *op. cit.*, pp. 765-766.

on Christian principles—a union with Christ and with His people, on views, sentiments, feelings, aims, and pursuits —a real copartnery for eternity—almost annihilated individuality itself, and inseparably cemented into one spirit all the genuine members of Christ's body. Kindred drops do not more readily mingle into one mass, than flowed the souls of primitive Christians together in all their aspirations, loves, delights, and interests. Hence arose that jealousy in the Apostle Paul when first he learned that particular persons in Corinth began to attract to themselves notice and attachment for mere personal, individual, and fleshly considerations, as leaders or chiefs in the Christian family. In these indications he already saw the dissolution of the church. Although yet but one visible community, having one Lord, one faith, one baptism, one table, one ostensible supreme and all-controlling interest; still, in these attachments to particular persons he not only saw a real division or breach in the hearts of the people, but foresaw that it would issue in positive, actual, and visible disunion or heresy.[37]

Thus we observe that he that loves Wesley for any sectarian attribute hates Calvin just in the ratio of his attachment to his leader; as he who loves Calvin for his humanisms hates Wesley for opposing them. While he that loves only what is Christian in the two in no sense hates either; but grieves for the errors and delinquencies of both.[38]

No wonder Paul had to write to the Corinthians, ". . . that perhaps there may be strife [I Corinthians 6:7], jealousy [11:19, 22], angry tempers, disputes [1:11], slanders, gossip, arrogance [8:1, 2], disturbances" (I Corinthians 12:20).

Therefore, sectarianism becomes an *attitude* as well as a practice and a belief. It is a sinful attitude whether the issue

---

37. Alexander Campbell, *Christian System*, p. 95.
38. *Ibid.*, p. 99.

is right or wrong. It is a blanket violation of the fields of faith and of opinion, with their attendant rules of regulation and usage. It is possible for one seeking to hold to the truly valid name of "Christian" to become sectarian in his attitude and use of it.

So the mere writing of an essay, the preaching of a sermon, the editing of a journal, the publishing of a book, the composing of a hymn, or the creating of a church tract is not necessarily a creed. Only the usage of these expediencies determines this issue, and the attitude involved. Said Isaac Errett:

> The right of a religious body to inform the public of its peculiarities, simply to meet the demand for information, may be freely conceded, without impairing in the least this protest against human creeds *as terms of religious fellowship.* The former is simply the exercise of a right and privilege growing out of the relations which a religious community sustains to the public; but the latter is the exercise of fearful power, *unauthorized by any relation existing between the party which asserts it and the party on whom it is exercised.* "One is your Master, even Christ; and all ye are brethren."[39]

So cautioned Thomas Campbell as he began to state the proposition of his famous *Declaration and Address:*

> Let none imagine that the subjoined propositions are at all intended as an overture towards a new creed, or standard, for the church, or, as in any wise designed to be made a term of communion;—nothing can be further from our intention. They are merely designed for opening up the way, that we may come fairly and firmly to original grounds upon

---

39. J. S. Lamar, *Memoirs of Isaac Errett,* I (Cincinnati, O.: Standard Publishing, 1893), pp. 295-296.

clear and certain premises: and take up things just as the Apostles left them.[40]

Now, one must be reminded that the danger warned against in this chapter is not a blanket condemnation of every creed. There is the divine creed (by revelation) and human creeds (by conjecture) which must be identified, analyzed, and catalogued in a legitimate manner. On this score those who claim to be a part of the "restoration movement" have been unduly misunderstood and censored. They have only sought to avoid two calamitous extremes. From the pen of Isaac Errett:

> The advocates of human creeds have sought to place us in the same category with Unitarians, Universalists and various other heterodox societies. They have argued, with some degree of plausibility, that the mischievous errors and semi-infidel vagaries which some of the creedless parties have advocated, are legitimate offshoots of the no-creed doctrine, and that there is no safeguard against the wildest latitudinarianism except in a distinct avowal of the fundamental teachings of the Scriptures in the form of a creed. We, however, object to a classification which assigns us a place with these creedless specimens of heterodoxy, and also to the conclusion in favor of human creeds, attempted to be drawn from the errors and extravagancies of the parties referred to. We occupy a ground as distinct and as distant from that of the no-creed advocates, as from that of the advocates of human creeds. We admit, with the latter, the absolute necessity of a creed, both for a positive affirmation of essential truth, and for a safeguard against false and pernicious doctrines. We affirm, with the former, the unauthorized and tyrannical dogmatism of human creeds and

---

40. Thomas Campbell, *op. cit.*, pp. 26-27.

their schismatical tendencies. But we deny, what the latter asserts—the necessity of a *human* creed; and we affirm, what the former denies—the necessity for a *divine* creed. We call attention to this peculiar position, as the only safe resort from the extremes and mischiefs alike of the orthodox and heterodox parties.[41]

With the change of times and men the problems of the "restoration ideal" change. Consider the divine creed, confirmed by our Lord: "Thou art the Christ, the Son of the living God" (Matthew 16:16). Sometimes this is an *understatement to* men. They go too far, adding to it a human catalogue of articles claimed to be absolutely essential. They violate the area of opinion. This was the major problem of the early restoration days. Our pioneers frequently quoted the goal: "Where the Scriptures speak, we speak; where the Scriptures are silent we are silent." Said Mr. Richardson:

> It was this last point particularily, viz.: that the silence of the Scriptures is to be respected equally with its teachings, that was almost peculiar to the reformation urged by Mr. Campbell, and continued to be one of its most important and characteristic traits.[42]

Here was the working of human creeds. And how they unnecessarily divided a Christian world. Mr. Campbell fought hard on this point: "The creation of false tests and standards of faith and fellowship, and, so, the consequent exclusion of many true believers from 'the household of faith.' "[43]

Now, in this generation, the picture has changed, other factors entering in. The problem of the divine creed becoming an *overstatement* is more acute. There is more of

---
41. Isaac Errett, *op. cit.*, pp. 294-295.
42. Robert Richardson, *Memoirs of Alexander Campbell*, I, p. 352.
43. Quoted by Plattenburg, *op. cit.*, p. 317.

an attitude of under-belief rather than over-belief. Out of this current approach has issued the all too common plea, "after all, it does not make any difference what you believe." When men were bitterly contending for their historic creeds a century ago they never would have said that. So, whereas the Campbells had to confine the majority of efforts to the latter part of their slogan, we today, must be alert to emphasize the first half of it. That is the major issue now.

When the Constitution of the World Council of Churches states that it is to be "a fellowship of Churches which accept our Lord Jesus Christ as God and Saviour." Is He the Christ of Strauss, Renan, Kierkegaard, Bultmann, tradition, "inner consciousness," a cultic writer or what? Have not the trends of liberalism, through its characteristic methods, diluted the one holy creed to the point where we need to extol repeatedly the warning "Where the Scriptures speak, we speak . . ."? Each extreme is foolish and sinful. To avoid them both is the task of this study.

NOT MAN'S OPINION BUT GOD'S WORD

Not my opinions may I speak,
If so, my witness will be weak;
Not what in human books I find,
Or the conclusions of men's minds:
But what my God has deigned to give —
The teaching whereby we may live:
The Book of Heaven — the Sacred Page —
The Rock of Faith in every age!
That only must my message be,
If I shall bless humanity.
I am not left, to seek, forsooth,
In learning's page to find the Truth:
But here it is, beneath my hand
The Word, which shall forever stand;
Unalterable, enduring, sure,
Flows the Divine Fount, fresh and pure.
— *William Olney*

Chapter Twelve
SOURCES AND ATTITUDES

Christianity absorbs into itself all kinds of people. Christianity is big and wide. Its universal appeal reaches out to people regardless of mortal differences. Its discriminatory power is aimed at the basic moral response in the human soul, and not at the manifold variations in human flesh which are natural to mortality. Matters of faith look to the man-immortal; matters of opinion to the man-mortal.

The fact that we are made for this world, means that we possess human frailties and tendencies. When a man becomes a Christian it does not "dehumanize" him. Though a "babe in Christ" he must still cope with the same frailties and tendencies in that they might all be completely subjected by the spirit. During this mortal struggle and growth man is never freed from the flesh till death.

Thus, men of every fleshly kind are in the church. This is one price we pay for a glorious universal gospel. A Christian must acknowledge this as true within himself, and in his relationships with other Christians. Out of this heterogeneous condition is born the vast field of "differences of opinion." It is natural, it is to be expected — because it is human. We now list six basic factors which play an influential part in determining the nature of, and the use of personal opinion.

1. *Primary training* we list first. No intelligent being will deny the power of those first influences in his or her early formative years of life. We absorb many permanent ideas and the "raw material" for opinions long before we become a Christian. First impressions are great, and many of us retain certain Christian opinions primarily because we were taught such and shown such in the early days of growth. And as we grew up we were never able to competely unshackle ourselves from those primary influences, whether good or bad. How difficult it was for the apostle Peter to

"unlearn" things which he was always taught as a Jew (Acts 10). This same principle works all through the field of Christian opinion.

2. *Environment* and *Circumstances* in which a person finds himself, will naturally bear on his formulating opinion. The degree to which man is influenced by environment has always been debated. Nevertheless, in some degree, the influencing factor is present and must be reckoned with. A Christian must live in the world, and try to keep himself "unspotted" from its evil influences as much as possible. Still he can not isolate himself so thoroughly that he will be untouched by the civilization of which he, himself, is a part. Everyone is a part of some culture. So, to some degree, he will be affected.

We quote from two men who noted that this environmental influence helped give birth to the difference of opinion which arose in the brotherhood over the use of instrumental aids in church music. Dean Walker states:

> From both Baptist and Presbyterian connections the Disciples had inherited Calvin's antipathy to the organ. During the eighteenth century the Congregationalists in New England had a violent controversy over the use of the bass viol in worship. When the Restoration Movement began the people among whom they moved were unused to the instrumental accompaniment in either religious or other meetings, except the fiddle at the dance. It was this Protestant background, and this unsavoury association of the fiddle, that aroused opposition to the use of an instrument as an aid to worship. But as the amenities of life increased, organs were purchased for the American "parlour"; and "Music Halls" or "Opera Houses" were built in which concerts were held, and organs were installed to assist. They proved very popular. America had discovered music.

WHAT THE BIBLE SAYS ABOUT FAITH AND OPINION

Led by Isaac Errett, a great body of Disciples seized this new interest in music as a means of enriching the aesthetic side of worship.[1]

Concerning this era of Mr. Errett, J. S. Lamar observed the following:

> It should be known that originally the chief successes of the Disciples had been achieved among rural populations — a people in a country comparatively new, noted for simple tastes, sterling integrity, staid habits, industrious, frugal, honest — earnest in their religious life, and devoted to truth and goodness, but with little learning or culture, and hardly any polite accomplishments. It was a good, productive soil in which to cast the primal truth; and much of the rich harvest which has since been garnered from that truth is due to the singelness of eye and simplicity of heart of those who first embraced it.
>
> Their Sunday meetings were a feast to them, affording a blessed change from the monotonous drudgery and dullness of their daily lives, and to some extent cultivating the social along with the worshiping elements of their natures. The sermons were doubtless often crude and ill-digested, but they furnished food for thought and points for discussion, and thus gave exercise to the discriminating and logical faculties, and as for the rest — the worship, properly so called — they gave themselves no trouble about it. Whether the singing, for example, was good or bad, it was all they wanted; it was up to the standard of the times; and their neighbors had no better. When all alike were uncultivated, there were no sensibilities to be offended, and no fine, aesthetic tastes to be shocked and harrowed. If "Amazing Grace" was set too high, or "Come, ye Sinners" too low; if "Jesus, my All,

---

1. Dean Walker, *Adventuring for Christian Unity* (Cincinnati, O.: Standard Publishing, 1935), p. 43.

to Heaven is Gone," was sung with many unprecedented turns and many surprising twists, what of it? Nobody was hurt. No head hung down in shame and mortification. It was rather a joke upon the leader than a grief to the worshiper.

It is needless to inquire whether, after all, and in the long run, it would not have been well for this state of childlike simplicity and blissful ignorance to continue—needless, because in such a country as this, with its vast resources, its wide-awake enterprise, its growing network of railroads, its multiplied schools and colleges, its widely disseminated literature, and its constantly increasing culture, it could not continue. Boys and girls came to be educated. They went away from home and saw the world. Many of them took music lessons; many more of them became accustomed to the charms of harmony, and their ears and tastes were attuned to appreciate and enjoy it. Can we blame them if they no longer took pleasure in the cracked, piping and timeless dissonance which, by courtesy, was called "singing," and, *par excellence*, "singing the praises of God"? And then pianos and organs began to be introduced into parlors, and to the accompaniment of these, pious young gentlemen and ladies would sing the songs of Zion, and make melody in their hearts to the Lord. They *felt*, they were *conscious*, they *knew*, that such accompaniments were helpful and not hurtful to them; and if helpful in the parlor, why not in the Sunday-school? and why not in the church? Even among the older people, many began to favor this; some were neutral; some where opposed. But here and there, where the public sentiment decidedly predominated in its favor, a melodeon or organ was introduced tentatively into the Sunday-school, to see how it would work; and when it became manifest that good rather than evil resulted—that the singing was improved, that the young were held in the church, and that the instrument, instead of being a substitute for the worship, was simply an aid to the worshiper; first one church and then another began to use it in the worship. Thus, naturally, and as a matter of course, the practice began to be common, coming on, not as the result of pride or vanity or worldliness—as many really supposed—but as the inevitable consequence of growth and culture.

Meanwhile a storm of opposition had been brewing. In some instances the opponents were evidently deeply earnest and sincere; in others, it was just as evident that the opposition was grounded in partisan feeling, and the lust of ruling or crushing. Necessarily, however, both these elements concerned and co-operated—those who *would* have yielded if they conscientiously could, and those who really had no conscience in the matter, but who talked loudest about it, and who felt that they could advance their own interests by pandering to the prejudices of the uninstructed and zealous. Such a combination was formidable and dangerous. Those who were in it for the sake of personal power, were prepared to go to any length rather than suffer defeat; those who were in it for the sake of individual conscience, and the maintenance of apostolic purity in the worship, felt that in no possible contingency could they be brought to yield a sacred principle.[2]

3. *Personal knowledge* and *wisdom* play a great part in formulating opinions. No one is completely immune from the natural frailties and incapacities of the mind, e.g., ignorance, preconceived notions, prejudices, wishful thinking, unwarranted assumptions, ambiguity, hasty generalizations.

Therefore, the weaknesses and powers of human knowledge and wisdom—both in regard to divine revelation and

---

[2]. J. S. Lamar, *Memoirs of Isaac Errett*, II (Cincinnati, O.: Standard Publishing, 1893), pp. 23-26.

OPINION: SOURCES AND ATTITUDES

human wisdom, will greatly affect the set of opinions which one adopts. Even a little matter like "common sense" must be acknowledged as a powerful force.

Out of this may spring the powerful motive of conviction. Many opinions are the result of an honest and careful study of the Scripture; plus a profound faith in every word of that testimony; plus a sincere effort to make fair deductions, conclusions, and inferences from said material—and to adhere to these findings. Many opinions are honest and noble convictions.

4. Next, is the *emotion* factor. This deserves a consideration all of its own. For many of man's behavior habits and thought forms are regulated by the balance, or imbalance, between mind and emotions. Emotion is a power in the soul. It can, and does, color many of our opinions.

Allowed to run wild and uncontrolled, emotion will so affect opinion as to become harmful by actually invading the fields of precept and precedent. Such would be the case of "love"; if undisciplined by genuine Christian faith and Godly wisdom, it will move out of its proper place and actually become evil (II Peter 1:5-8). Misguided emotions are a dangerous threat to constructive and intelligent opinions.

5. The *moral* factor is next. How often will one undisciplined moral condition project itself into a thousand opinions. Sin has many ramifications in the field of opinion. One who is selfish, too easily hurt by others, void of Christian courage, envious, proud, or at enmity with another, etc., will soon find that his opinions are to some degree inconsistent and inferior. This is another result of sin.

6. The last factor, though overplayed in some circles, can not be entirely overlooked. It is that of the *psychological* influences on one's opinions. Many opinion problems are

more psychological than theological. They are nothing but "human nature" matters.

There are such forces as fixations (not growing up), regressions (turning backward), frustrations, obsessions, wishful thinking, phobias, inhibitions and hysterias, introversion and extroversion, microparanoia (egotism), and microdepressivity (moods). These are technical terms; however, one who is in any degree intelligent can not deny their existence, though he may not call them by scientific names. Though some may seriously debate whether they are inherited or acquired conditions, nevertheless, in human nature they are there.

In closing this discussion, it is well to note that there is often an inter-playing and an over-lapping of these six factors on a single opinion. This is to be expected. Human nature is complex. So it would require a master to trace an opinion back to its origin in all points. We can but scratch the surface when we ask of a person, "Why does he hold such an opinion?"

Now for that all-important matter—the *attitude* toward opinion, what shall it be? Attitudes in life are indicative of character. And when the complexities of human nature coincide and clash then this is a grave consideration in the field of Christian behavior. As J. S. Lamar noted in the days of Mr. Errett, certain leaders and factions had arisen to contest some of these "opinion" issues. They claimed that:

> A church must not employ a regular preacher, must not use an organ as an aid in singing, must not take up a collection for the Missionary Society, must not accept contributions to its treasury from any who were not members—and all because somebody objected, and put his objections upon the ground of conscience. It mattered not that the rest of the

church conscientiously *favored* these things, for manifestly they had no *right* to favor them; they were introducing *innovations*, they had grown tired of Bible; they were departing from the good old way; where was the line of Scripture, the the chapter and the verse that authorized these things? The New Testament says never a word about a missionary society, nor any society; it is equally silent respecting organs and salaried pastors, and Sunday-schools and notebooks, and even hymn books such things are necessarily wrong, because unsupported by apostolic precept or primitive example.[3]

Such was the case when man made his own conscience an ever-present and insuperable statuatory law for himself and for others. How foolish, unscriptural, yea, anti-Scriptural! Has not man learned by this time that for every opinion he holds there is somewhere a counter-opinion? And who should settle the difference? Said Alexander Campbell:

> If *Christ* had appointed an infallible judge upon earth, or men were to be determined by an implicit faith in their superiors, there would be an end of such differences; but all the engines of human policy that have been set at work to obtain it have hitherto failed of success.[4]

The answer, then, is that there is no such judgment accounted legitimate in the eyes of God. Therefore, it must be settled on the "attitude" basis which has been authoritatively answered in the Word. The Lord has definitely taught Christians how to use opinion by the method of precept and precedent. So the misuse of opinion is an outright sin against the authority of Christ.

---

3. J. S. Lamar, *op. cit.*, I, p. 228.
4. Alexander Campbell, *A Debate Between Rev. A. Campbell and Rev. N. L. Rice* (Nashville, Tenn.: Gospel Advocate reprint of 1844 ed.), p. 769.

WHAT THE BIBLE SAYS ABOUT FAITH AND OPINION

Isaac Errett once laid down a general threefold outline on what issues must be considered in answering this problem. He used "instrumental music in worship" as his example in the following words:

> That the question of using instruments is not a question of the purity of the integrity of the worship, but simply a question of expediency as to a proposed means of aiding the singing of the church; a question, therefore, on which there may be variety of opinions without affecting the Christian integrity of those who differ.
>
> That it is altogether in opposition to the teaching of the New Testament to attempt to erect such a question into a test of fellowships, or to make it a reason for division in the churches. To us such a course is essentially factious, and should, wherever it reveals itself, be reprobated.
>
> That the law of Christ requires the advocates of instrumental music to yield their preferences, on account of the conscientious scruples of their brethren.[5]

Carrying these thoughts a step further we might combine two of these points and add one more. Thus, every difference of opinion must be settled by answering: 1. Is it definitely opinion? 2. What is the duty of him who holds it? 3. And what is the duty of him who does not hold it?

This issue always works two ways, both of which are tempting to human nature (Romans 14:3). The freedom of opinion may be violated by the taking of offence at another's opinion, as well as the giving of offence by our own opinion. Quoting again from the *Declaration and Address:*

> We shall get rid of two great evils, which, we fear, are at this day grievously provoking the Lord to plead a controversy with the Churches: we mean the taking, and giving of

---

5. J. S. Lamar, *Memoirs of Isaac Errett,* II, p. 40.

unjust offences; judging and rejecting each other in matters wherein the Lord hath not judged, in a flat contradiction to his expressly revealed will. But, according to the principle adopted, we can neither take offence at our brother for his private opinions, if he be content to hold them as such, nor yet offend him with ours, if he do not usurp the place of the lawgiver; and even suppose he should, in this case we judge him, not for his *opinions*, but for his *presumption*.[6]

Now, the first two points have been answered in a previous chapter. We are now seeking a solution to the third issue: what shall be one's attitude toward the opinions of others? It is well to keep in mind, however, that often this attitude is to be determined by the nature of that opinion, and the manner (or spirit) in which it is held by the other party. Such teaching has been given us on several occasions in the teaching and practice of our Lord, and in the admonitions given in the Christian epistles. We list the various attitudes as commonly held.

1. *Contempt*—Is it ever permissible to show contempt for the opinions of others? Would the presence of such conditions as capriciousness, superstition, credulity, triviality, extreme importunity, ever merit contempt in the second party? Even if such conditions were motivated in a cantankerous, or rebellious, or authoritative, or unrelenting spirit?

Look at Jesus. Did He not choose contempt on some select occasions? When the Pharisees spied out His liberty (Matthew 9:10-13), broke the precepts of God with their opinions (Matthew 15:2-6; Mark 7:3-9), authoritatively demanded Him to respect their traditions (Luke 6:1-11).

---

6. Thomas Campbell, *Declaration and Address* (Lincoln, Il.: Lincoln Christian College Press, 1971 reprint of 1809 ed.), p. 41.

WHAT THE BIBLE SAYS ABOUT FAITH AND OPINION

Jesus showed contempt. Naturally we do not possess the powers our Lord had. Nevertheless, we can follow Him insofar as we are able, and as He taught us by the word of the apostles (Colossians 2:8).

One reservation must be necessarily made in this regard. Never, in dealing with the opinions of others, are we to violate the law of love (pp. 217-228) in order to maintain the law of liberty. Neither need be sacrificed at the expense of the other.

2. *Ridicule* — Is it ever permissible to ridicule opinions which might fall in the class mentioned above? Opinions that obviously are so trivial and ridiculous that any other attitude would be out of place? Here we are more narrowly limited than in the case of "contempt," with the law of love curtailing such feelings far more severely. How can ridicule ever emanate from anything but hate, selfishness, or pride except under the most exceptional conditions? The circumstances, motives, and results must be taken into account when irony is used to convince some one of the error of his way.

3. *Withstanding* or *intolerance* — The delicate question now arises: how far should one go in giving up his own opinions which conflict with those of others before he finally ceases to give in, and instead, withstands and refuses to waive his right of opinion? Where is that point?

Chapter fourteen of the Roman letter teaches us that one Christian may not despise or judge the opinions of another. They are private property, when held in good conscience before God. Now the converse of this principle is that all have this inalienable right to private opinion, which, if it were not so, would then abolish all such right. For it would be utterly impossible for any one of human nature to succumb to the conscientious scruples of all others. This extreme is

OPINION: SOURCES AND ATTITUDES

humanly an untenable position. Therefore, there must be times when one will not tolerate the surrendering of his right to an opinion. And that time comes when the second party becomes so demanding that to yield to that person would be building up in him a false conception that he can in turn build up a moral standard (of precept from opinion) for the first party. That is the point of resistance, and it must be arrived at with all wisdom and love.

Jesus tolerated many opinions of the Jews—and they were almost innumerable. And yet when the Pharisees became demanding toward Jesus and His apostles (as in the case of their eating wheat grain on the Sabbath (Matthew 12:1-8), then Jesus withstood them and refused to give up his right to so eat—and no doubt ate all the more. If He had not withstood them at this particular point, to what extreme would they have gone?

The twofold principle in regard to the treatment of another who holds a different opinion is as follows: One may give in to the opinions of another to that extent where he does not foster a tendency in the second party to force his opinion as a standard on the first party (Galatians 2:3-5). And, let one not give in to the opinions of another to that extent where he will not cause the second party to violate his own conscience in regard to his opinion. And let it all be motivated by the law of love. (See pages 217ff. and pages 204-206.)

4. *Tolerance*—Tolerance is a noble virtue when properly directed. When not genuine, according to the divine standard, then it often dwindles into spineless compromise with Satan. Jesus did not tolerate sin. It was clear that He could not stand the outright profaning of the temple of God; however, in view of Jewish tradition prevalent in that day, think

of the numerous traditions of the Talmud our Lord refused to rebuke or bring into the open.

In the name of unity of the body of Christ, many opinions need to be tolerated. "We have the right to differ but not to divide" in this matter; we are "not to antagonize but to harmonize."[7] The bond of peace in the church is worth the price of tolerating opinions, no matter how great may seem the sacrifice (Ephesians 4; I Timothy 1:6, 7; II Timothy 2:14-18; Titus 3:9), so long as the fundamental principles of the gospel are not violated.

5. *Forbearance* — This is something different from tolerance. To forbear requires sacrifice and personal injury, whereas tolerance finds its objective more indifferent. Said Alexander Campbell:

> But on the subject of forbearance, I have to remark that there is not a greater misapplication of a word in our language than of this one. In strict propriety, it does not apply at all to the subject in relation to which it is commonly used. No man can be said to forbear with another except in such cases as he has done him an injury. Now when Christians differ in opinion on any subject, unless it can be made to appear that the opinion of B is injurious to A, the latter can not forbear with the former. There is no room or occasion for forbearance, for A is not injured by the opinion of B. To say that Christians must exercise forbearance with one another because of difference of opinion, is admitting that they have a right to consider themselves injured, or that one Christian has a right to consider himself injured, because of another man's difference in opinion.[8]

---

7. John B. Cowden, *St. Paul on Christian Unity* (New York: Fleming H. Revell, 1923), p. 41.

8. Robert Richardson, *Memoirs of Alexander Campbell*, II (Nashville, Tenn.: Gospel Advocate, 1956 reprint of 1898 ed.), p. 133.

OPINION: SOURCES AND ATTITUDES

Rare is the occasion for the exercise of forbearance, for usually in differences of opinion any kind of personal injury is altogether absent. Tolerance is common, forbearance the exception.

Nevertheless, when occasion does arise for this attitude, the growing Christian should meet the test. God forbears with us. As His children, why can not we forbear with one another? In the *Declaration and Address* Thomas Campbell wrote:

> Upon the whole, we see one thing is evident; the Lord will bear with the weaknesses, the involuntary ignorances, and mistakes of His people; though not with their presumption. Ought they not, therefore, to bear with each other—"to preserve the unity of the spirit in the bond of peace; forbearing one with another in love."[9]

Thus, when Christians refuse to exercise tolerance, and forbearance if need be, then unwarranted schism will necessarily result. So was the plea of Mr. Campbell fruitless as he made his defense before the Presbytery of his day:

> Surely, brethren, from my steadfast adherence to the Divine standard—my absolute and entire rejection of human authority in matters of religion—my professed and sincere willingness to walk in all good understanding, communion, and fellowship with sincere and humble Christian brethren, who may not see with me in these things—and, permit me to add, my sincere desire to unite with you in carrying forward that blessed work in which you have set out, and from which you take your name—you will do me the justice to believe, that if I did not sincerely desire a union with you, I would not have once and again made application for that

---

9. Thomas Campbell, *op. cit.*, p. 43.

purpose. A union not merely nominal, but hearty and confidential, founded upon certain and established principles; and this, if I mistake not, is firmly laid on both sides. Your standard informs me of your views of truth and duty, and my declarations give you precisely the same advantage. You are willing to be tried in all matters by your standard, according to your printed declaration; *I* am willing to be tried on all matters by *my* standard, according to my written declaration. You can labor under no difficulty about my teaching and practicing whatever is expressly taught and enjoined in the Divine standard, as generally defined in my "Declaration," and although I have not the same clearness about everything contained in your standard, yet when I cannot see, believing you to be sincere and conscientious servants of the same great and gracious Master who freely pardons His willing and obedient servants their ten thousand talents of shortcomings, I am, therefore, through His grace, ready to forbear with you; at the same time, hoping that you possess the same gracious spirit, and therefore will not reject me for the lack of those fifty forms which might probably bring me up to your measure, and to which, if necessary, I also, through grace, may yet attain, for I have not set myself down as perfect.[10]

6. *Respect*—Within the great area of opinion there should be developed the fine Christian grace of respect for the opinions of others. The great majority of opinions rightly deserves this attitude, which is all too often absent or false. The spirit of Paul, in firmly holding to precept, while graciously respecting the opinions of other Christians, needs to be initiated today within the church (Acts 21:17-26). Quoting W. R. Walker, we read:

---

10. Robert Richardson, *Memoirs of Alexander Campbell*, I, p. 228.

If Christ has left me the authority in a certain sense or degree, to decide what my own conduct as a Christian should be, that liberty or authority of mine is entitled to respect from others.

In turn, I must respect the authority of others to regulate their conduct likewise, in those "areas of silence." If I refuse to grant them that right, I am invading an area of authority shared by them and Christ, but where I have no right to enter.

I can respect the authority of Christ only by respecting that which He has conferred on others as sacred to them.[11]

Remember, the right of private opinion is completely reciprocal. There can be no double standard like the communist who said, "What's mine is mine; what's yours is negotiable."

7. *Ignoring*—The final attitude to be mentioned needs to be emphasized for the power which it is able to yield in keeping the peace and unity in the body of Christ. It is the difficult practice of ignoring the opinions of others, which so merit it. Where opinions, the nature of which are so insignificant or inconsequential; and where differences of opinions are negligible, an ignoring of the situation is wise and peaceful. Alexander Campbell made the claim:

Nine times in ten, mere opinion, when let alone, will die a natural death, or lead an inoffensive life. But if you want an opinion to live, gain power, make a party, and descend to after times, call a council, get up a debate, assemble the orators, and keep it for a few years before the public mind, and then you secure a party. I say, call no council, make no decrees, excite not human passions.[12]

---

11. W. R. Walker, *Christian Unity Quarterly* (April, 1943), p. 9.
12. Alexander Campbell, *A Debate Between Rev. A. Campbell and Rev. N. L. Rice*, p. 809.

WHAT THE BIBLE SAYS ABOUT FAITH AND OPINION

> It is not the object of our efforts to make men think alike on a thousand themes. Let them think as they like on any matters of human opinion and upon "doctrines of religion," provided only they hold the Head Christ and keep His commandments. I have learned not only the theory, but the fact, that if you want opinionism to cease or subside, you must not call up and debate everything that men think or say. *You may debate anything into consequence, or may by a dignified silence, waste it into oblivion.*[13]

It can easily be seen, where, in the exercising of these attitudes, that the important problem of unity and peace within a congregation is ever impending. One man's freedom can not quench another's. To have harmony and peace there must be a maximum of consideration for the greatest number. This idea has led men to become democratic in their working and living together. There must be power in the majority. So that any individual may hold any opinion, just so it doesn't prohibit the exercising of the opinions of the majority. So we have the Preamble of the Constitution of the United States.

> We the People of the United States, in order to form a more perfect union, establish justice, insure domestic tranquility, provide for the common defence, promote the general welfare and secure the blessings of liberty to ourselves and our posterity, do ordain and establish this Constitution for the United States of America.

The weakness of this system is found in the weakness in the majority; however, its strength lies in the greatest amount of freedom possible for all.

---

13. *Ibid.*, p. 797.

God foresaw this problem in the church, and knew it was imperative to settle. So, in this vast field of opinion, the church should aim to be as purely democratic as possible. It is the burden of every congregation to "work out its own salvation." This field of opinion, says W. R. Walker:

> . . . gives each local church authority to administer the gospel to its own constituency in that manner, or by that procedure, which in the consecrated judgment of its membership may be most conducive to spiritual growth and culture.[14]

This quotation from John B. Cowden:

> What shall we do with these differences? Well, if neither Christ nor His inspired Apostles said anything about these things, or did anything about them; nor no light can be had from His character on these things, then these things are non-essentials; and our differences over such are immaterial, and should be treated as such. We therefore must say nothing about these things, nor do nothing about them that will disturb the unity of the church. For instance, differences over such things as missionary and benevolent societies, Bible schools, church papers, church buildings, organs, choirs, song books, tuning forks, orders of worship, etc., are of this class. They belong to the class of things spoken of by Paul in his letters such as "eating meat," "keeping days," etc., the faith we have about such things, Paul says, "Have thou to thyself before God"; and it must be exercised in such a way as to "cause no one to stumble or fall"; and when such comes up for congregational action, the will of the majority should be accepted; yet the will of the minority must be respected "for the sake of the conscience of the weak brother,"

---

14. W. R. Walker, *op. cit.*, p. 9.

WHAT THE BIBLE SAYS ABOUT FAITH AND OPINION

if there be any that make it a matter of conscientous faith. In such cases Christian love is to determine the wise thing to do.[15]

And out of the *Millennial Harbinger* of 1835, as quoted by W. L. Hayden, we note this statement by Alexander Campbell:

> A question arises of some consequence — nay, of great consequence: On what occasions and for what purposes are Christians authorized to decide matters?
>
> They are not to pass on questions of faith, piety or morality. Truth is not to be settled by a vote, nor is any divine institution respecting the worship or morality of the Christian church to be decided by a majority. These are matters of revelation, of divine authority, and to be regulated by a "thus saith the Lord," and not by a *thus saith the majority.* But in all matters not of faith, piety or morality, in all matters of expediency, there is no other way of deciding but by a vote of the brotherhood.
>
> There is no revelation that A, B or C shall be chosen elders or deacons, that D, E or F shall be sent on any special message; that the church shall meet in any given place at any given hour; or that this or that measure is to be adopted in reference to any particular duty arising out of the internal or external relations of the church.
>
> . . . .
>
> A matter of greater importance occurs. Must the church be always unanimous before it acts upon any question of fact or expediency? While it is possible to be of one faith and of one hope, however desirable it may be, it is not to be expected that a congregation will always be of one mind in all

---

15. John B. Cowden, *St. Paul on Christian Unity,* p. 72.

questions of expediency which may occur in our earthly pilgrimage.

It is sometimes inexpedient for the majority to carry all in its power. There may be occasions when it is better for the majority to waive its privileges than to carry its point.

The only question, then, is, whether it is most expedient and comely that the minority submit to the majority, or the majority to the minority; for one of them must yield. Unanimity very generally gives to the smallest minority the absolute control of the whole congregation. There can be no debate. The minority will, in the spirit of love and in the spirit of Christian modesty, agree to submit to a clear and decided majority.[16]

In every difference of opinion there will be a majority and a minority group. This is natural. When it happens between Christians, then those "majority" Christians should properly conduct their attitudes toward the minority group in the spirit of Christ and His teaching. Likewise the "minority" Christians toward the majority group. This requires genuine Christian maturity, the lack of which brings schism, heartache, and weakness to the body of Christ. Let each one always manifest love for his brother (Romans 14:15), desire to keep his brother (I Corinthians 8:9-13; Romans 14:7, 21), a desire to edify his brother (I Corinthians 10:23; Romans 14:19), and a realization that each child of God is individually judged by the Lord (Romans 14:10-12), when he thinks of the opposing side.

But if that day comes, when the minority member is absolutely unable to tolerate or forbear that opinion of the majority; if he cannot endure his own conscience in view of

---

16. From the *Millennial Harbinger* (1835), pp. 511-513 as quoted by W. L. Hayden, *Church Polity* (Kansas City, Mo.: Old Paths Book Club, reprint of 1894 ed.), pp. 134-135.

this difference, let him withdraw himself peaceably and seek out a faithful community of believers where he can have peace of mind. This is always the last resort, but may be done within the law of the Lord. (See pages 223-227.)

As a final consideration in regard to attitudes we should stress the spiritual nature of the Christian. When a person truly is "born again," converted by faith and obedience to the Lord Jesus Christ, that person is given the Holy Spirit (Acts 2:38; 5:32). The means by which this is done is simply allowing the Word of God, the "sword of the Spirit" (Ephesians 6:17) to lead him wheresoever it chooses. Such a person is thus to be filled with the Spirit (Ephesians 5:18; Acts 13:52). The spiritual person is one who is fully committed to Jesus Christ as Lord (Romans 13:14) and will take on His nature (Galatians 2:20; Philippians 2:5; 4:2; II Corinthians 3:18) and be a real spiritual person as contrasted from a natural person (I Corinthians 2:10—3:3). The end result will be that of "walking by the Spirit" and manifesting the fruit of the Spirit, "love, joy, peace, patience, kindness, goodness, faithfulness, gentleness, self-control" (Galatians 5:22, 23).

We can see what bearing this has on every phase of this subject of faith and opinion. We definitely need the ministry of the Holy Spirit in our lives in learning and living the truth. "Retain the standard of sound words which you have heard from me, in the faith and love which are in Christ Jesus. Guard through the Holy Spirit who dwells in us, the treasure which has been entrusted to you" (II Timothy 1:13, 14).

Chapter Thirteen
OPPORTUNITIES AND DANGERS

There is a splendid dignity about man which is the grand heritage of creation. Being made "in the image" of God, and yet a created being has provided man with a unique station in life (Genesis 1:26-28; 2:7). He is less than God but more than animal. He is not a mere automaton, a piece of worldly machinery created to serve a higher creation. He is "God-breathed" and "God-imaged." Thus, when a person becomes a Christian this blessed status should be enhanced and developed with Jesus Christ (God in the flesh) as the ideal pattern and motivating force.

In the area of opinion God has endowed man with certain "inalienable rights" which, under normal conditions (chapter 10), ought never to be surrendered. They are opportunities that rightfully belong to the human soul. And Christians, above all people, ought to recognize and honor them. Progressively stated, these opportunities are listed as follows:

1. The *individuality of the human soul* is first. Diversity of thought and action is a God-given right which must be zealously guarded. Where God has allowed man to be a complete self-governing entity (field of opinion—not precept and precedent), let him never surrender one element of this precious heritage. The Christian, though he decides to be completely subservient to the Lord, finds that great area of human opinion completely at his own disposal. Said W. R. Walker:

> That in all those details of procedure in the exercise of my "liberty in Christ" both as an individual Christian and as one of a group organized into a local congregation of believers, Christ has laid upon me the necessity of deciding in the light of His expressed will, what will be advantageous or disadvantageous, what will aid or hinder, what will promote or retard, the accomplishment of His will through me. To

be very specific here, I am persuaded that Christ, by His silence, in every situation concerning which He has left no direct teaching, has bestowed on me the authority to act for myself. I am assuming that my conduct will be governed by a genuine desire to please Him. But my point is that He has given me individual authority to decide on what is, and what is not, well pleasing unto Him, in all matters where opinion, and not revelation, controls.[1]

Opinion must be kept as private property, lest we surrender our individuality. How often and fervently Alexander Campbell pleaded that:

> It is not the object of our efforts to make men think alike on a thousand themes. Let men think as they please on any matters of human opinion, and upon "doctrines of religion" provided only they hold THE HEAD Christ and keep his commandments.[2]

Individuality that is noble, aspiring, and genuine is one of the rare opportunities of the soul. Let man treasure it. When it is properly cultivated in Christianity it should lead to a further opportunity.

2. *Unity without uniformity.* These two terms must not be confused. One must carefully discriminate between unity of faith and on the one hand, and uniformity of opinion on the other. Such uniformity is not required, not often expedient and wise, and certainly not desirable. Ignorance of the nature and purpose of the community of saints (the church) has often led to a desire for uniformity at the expense of unity. The classic example of this contorted idea is the Roman Catholic Church. Quoting George Plattenburg:

---

1. W. R. Walker, *Christian Unity Quarterly* (April, 1943), p. 8.
2. Alexander Campbell, *A Debate Between Rev. A. Campbell and Rev. N. L. Rice* (Nashville, Tenn.: Gospel Advocate, reprint of 1844 ed.), p. 797.

OPINION: OPPORTUNITIES AND DANGERS

Such is papal unity, a corporation founded on Papal Supremacy and not on Christ, on tradition and not on the Bible, which is a closed book to its blind votaries. Papal domination means the abolition of thought and the total extinction of liberty. Its unity means death—and Rome is *semper idem*.[3]

The "seamless coat of Christ" is a favorite metaphor with ecclesiastical writers for the unity of the church. Perhaps it may not be impertinent to remark that the metaphor appears to be neither Scriptural nor appropriate. The *Body* rather than the Coat of Christ—the body not a bone of which was broken—designates, in St. Paul, the unity of the church. The seamless coat, however, better answers to the doctrine of so-called "Catholic" unity—or rather uniformity.[4]

So, that uniformity of the Roman Church, which has been so often mistaken for genuine unity, is one of the methods, tradition, systems, orders, and ecclesiasticism—not one of genuine Christian unity. This latter factor is lacking, and always has been so, says J. M. Trible:

There was schism before the reformation. The monastic orders, as the Augustinians and Dominicans, were literally often, and figuratively always, at daggers' points. The German and the Italian sections of the church hated each other with perfect hatred. Bishops were often in arms one against another. The Reformation did heal somewhat these schisms within the Roman church, or at any rate, taught the schismatics the policy of keeping their strifes secret. But if any think that the Roman church is even now a united and peaceful household he is grievously deceived. Whatever its name and its claim for unity, it abounds in jealousy and

---

3. George Plattenburg, "The Unity of the Church," *The Old Faith Restated*, J. H. Garrison, ed. (Joplin, Mo.: College Press reprint of 1891 ed.), p. 322.
4. Author unknown, *Inspirational Prose Quotations*, ed. by J. W. Horine (Nashville, Tenn.: Cokesbury Press, 1932), p. 282.

strife; its union is one of policy rather than of faith, hope and love.[5]

S. S. Lappin pin-points the issue in what ought to be the strength of the New Testament Church today, when he said, "Our safety is in diversity, not uniformity; in differentiation, not in regimentation; in dispersion, not in centralization."[6]

When will growing Christians learn these two lessons just mentioned? How difficult it is to develop a genuine Christian individuality, while at the same time avoiding the curse of unwarranted uniformity by not allowing opinion to remain strictly private. This is what Alexander Campbell pled for in his insistence on unity as opposed to uniformity:

> We do not ask them to give up their opinions—we ask them only not to impose them upon others. Let them hold their opinion, but let them hold them as private property. The faith is public property; opinions are, and always have been, private property.[7]

W. N. Briney points out that this historic problem of making private opinion an issue of public contention has always been with us:

> Grieved by the dispute between Alexander, bishop of Alexandria, and Arius, one of his presbyters, the Emperor Constantine sent a letter to the disputants, urging them to be reconciled, and rebuking them for disturbing the peace of the church on account of petty and idle disputes about words. "Questions of this nature," he wrote, "may, indeed, be permitted as an exercise of the intellectual faculties. We ought, however, to confine them within our own bosoms,

---

5. J. M. Trible, "Reformation in the Church," *The Old Faith Restated*, J. H. Garrison, ed., p. 302.
6. S. S. Lappin, *Christian Standard* (September 2, 1944), p. 16.
7. Alexander Campbell, quoted by W. N. Briney, *The Watchword of the Restoration Vindicated* (Cincinnati, O.: Standard Publishing, n.d.), p. 28.

not readily bringing them forward at public meetings, nor rashly confiding them to the ears of every one. . . . Your subtle disputes and inquiries respecting these most trifling matters, if you can not agree in sentiment, should remain in your own thoughts, and be laid up in the secret depths of the mind.[8]

Does it seem incredible to ask for individuality and unity to exist together within a body of Christian believers? Are they contradictory or incompatible? Mr. Garrison made this analogy years ago:

> The variety in nature is often referred to as illustrating the truth that God likes variety better than sameness. True again, but entirely without force as an objection to Christian union. Indeed, it is an argument in favor of such unity, for if the unity of nature is not disturbed, but manifested by its variety, why should it be thought incredible that the church can be one with variety of opinions and methods among its members.[9]

3. Out of these two factors is issued that glorious opportunity of *Christian liberty*. Liberty is a blessing resulting from certain conditions existing within a community of Christians in their worship and service activities together—conditions of the heart, mind, and behavior of the individuals. John B. Cowden, in defining liberty, claimed:

> He [Christ] made it clear that liberty is not license but freedom within law. It does not mean the throwing off and disregard of all law, but rather a state of freedom that is the result of conformity to law. "If ye abide in my word (by obeying the same), then are ye truly my disciples; and ye

---

8. W. N. Briney, *Ibid.*, p. 29.
9. J. H. Garrison, *The Story of a Century* (St. Louis: Christian Publishing Co., 1909), p. 215.

shall know the truth, and the truth shall make you free." David expressed the same truth thus, "I will walk at liberty, for I will seek thy precepts"; and James speaks of the gospel as "the law of liberty," because by obedience to the same one is made free. Liberty through the knowledge and obedience to truth is therefore Christian liberty. In fact, all true liberty is a state of freedom that results from the knowledge of and obedience to the laws of being that form and regulate life. This is true in every realm and department of life,— in the material, social, intellectual, and religious. Anyone, therefore, that would be free in God's world must conform to the laws of the same; otherwise he is under condemnation and slavery that comes to all lawbreakers.[10]

The only perfect example of a "free" man was Christ himself.

He lived a life of absolute freedom in the midst of a people that were politically, socially, intellectually and religiously enslaved; and in the end He died that all might be likewise free.[11]

We belong to Christ, not to any man, and therefore, all Christ offers us is certainly ours (I Corinthians 3:21-23; John 8:36; Galatians 5:1).

But are unity and liberty incompatible? J. H. Garrison asks the question:

How can we stand fast in the liberty wherewith Christ has made us free, while standing fast also in the unity wherewith Christ hath made us one? Roman Catholicism secured union of a kind, but it sacrificed liberty. Protestantism secured liberty, but at the sacrifice of union. Are these two principles,

---

10. John B. Cowden, *St. Paul on Christian Unity* (New York: Fleming H. Revell Co., 1923), pp. 189-190.
11. *Ibid.*, p. 190.

OPINION: OPPORTUNITIES AND DANGERS

then, essentially antagonistic, the one to the other? Are they mutually exclusive terms, so that they who enjoy the one must do so at the sacrifice of the other? This can not be, for Christ not only taught both union and liberty as principles of his kingdom, but he enjoined them upon his followers. How can they be reconciled? . . . Liberty in Christ and union through loyalty to Christ—that is the harmonization of these two principles of the gospel. Loyalty to all that Christ has commanded—that gives us unity. Loyalty to Christ only, and the rejection of all human authority in religion—that gives us liberty.[12]

Here is the answer. Let every sincere Christian delineate between unity (which pertains to precept and precedent) and liberty (which pertains to opinion)—unity in essentials but liberty in non-essentials. Quoting John Cowden again:

> Paul in this letter [Ephesians] sets forth the essentials of unity, with respect to which there is no liberty. Liberty has to do with the non-essentials, which constitute the realm of Christian liberty, which is fully treated by Paul in his letters to the Corinthians and Galatians. In these letters Paul endeavors to define the scope and application of Christian liberty so as to insure unity; and the connecting link between the two is loyalty. *Liberty, loyalty* and *unity* constitute the Scriptural trinity of the New Testament Church.
>
> . . . .
>
> The Catholic church has unity without liberty; and the Protestant church has liberty without unity; but the Apostolic church had unity with liberty, which was realized and maintained through loyalty. However, when these three become separated, and it is necessary to choose between the three, loyalty must be placed before liberty and unity.[13]

---

12. J. H. Garrison, *op. cit.*, p. 100.
13. John B. Cowden, *op. cit.*, pp. 187-188.

WHAT THE BIBLE SAYS ABOUT FAITH AND OPINION

Loyalty is always supreme — with liberty and unity as fruits or results. They, in their pure form, issue forth from a community of loyal subjects. And let that loyalty be properly motivated and inclined or else freedom will not be genuine:

> Freedom does not come through mere obedience to law; there must also be the proper spirit manifested in this obedience. The spirit of Christ's obedience was that of deep humility and willing submission to all the laws of His being; and, where this spirit is, there is liberty.[14]

Let no one ever believe the lie that Roman Catholic "unity" is the only kind obtainable in this day. But consider gravely the cost of such a theory:

> The Roman Catholic Church proposes a return to the mother church where, they claim, there was unity until Luther and other reformers broke it up. This plan would undoubtedly secure unity, but it would do so at the price of two things in the world that are worth more than unity; namely, loyalty and liberty, without which it would not be Christian unity; and besides, such a unity would not satisfy the requirements of Scriptural faith, and could not, therefore, be Scriptural unity.[15]

Our aim should be to have the maximum of loyalty and liberty abiding side by side in the body of Christ. And still further, combining the three elements together, let Christians work individually, and as a group, to grasp the opportunity of welding individuality, unity, and liberty into one body. This is a difficult task, yet it is noble, and also very possible. H. W. Everest once wrote:

---

14. *Ibid.*, p. 191.
15. *Ibid.*, pp. 63-64.

OPINION: OPPORTUNITIES AND DANGERS

The one body forbids formulas of doctrine made to serve as foundations of new organizations; forbids the leadership of men in religious matters; forbids the segregation of the friends of Jesus into parties and denominations; and forbids those party names which must needs be, if parties are to be. It requires that all those differences which may co-exist with Christian worthiness shall be tolerated in the same body. It allows individual liberty where this divine basis of doctrinal unity does not bind us; and the liberty wherewith Christ has made us free is quite as necessary as the unity. Nor is this toleration impossible, for we often find greater difference between members of the same church than between the different churches, only these individual differences have not yet been builded into party walls.[16]

At this point we should pause long enough to carefully weigh the power of opinion. Do we truly assess all the effects and ramifications of simply "holding an opinion"? We know its place but do we know its power. Let me create a hypothetical case:

I have a definite opinion. I have carefully thought it out and feel justified that it is rational. It is not something that has come from the Word of God, but from my own experience and thinking of the past. It is this. I hold that anyone younger than 50 years of age has altogether a different concept and attitude about money than one who is older. Ideas about thrift, value, financial independence, spending and indebtedness vary considerably. He did not experience the depression of the "thirties." He did not encounter the struggle of securing bare necessities, of losing hard-earned possessions and of going without normally accepted things of

---

16. H. W. Everest, *Missouri Christian Lectures* (St. Louis, Mo.: Christian Publishing Co., 1892), pp. 18-19.

WHAT THE BIBLE SAYS ABOUT FAITH AND OPINION

today. He has never had to live without many of the economic securities and guarantees which modern life takes for granted. His life is more saturated with a socialistic culture. Thus, I hold the opinion that such a person has a different attitude and philosophy about wealth and labor than he who is older — a poorer concept of the meaning of thrift and worth.

Now what have I done? I have manufactured a division (of more or less intensity). I have caused some to differ with me and some to agree. I may have caused some to react and possibly even rebel. I may have created a partisan spirit or influenced someone that this is a good opinion. Though it was not my intention, I may even have caused someone, who being influenced by my leadership as a minister, to hold this view so firmly that it becomes to him a "matter of faith." Of course, other factors enter the picture, such as my attitude, my insistence, my repetition, etc.

I do not believe many of us are able or willing to see the power exerted by our holding of opinions. It reminds me of the story of the airline passenger who was proudly relating his experience on board an ill-fated flight. He was telling how he looked out the window while the plane was flying and saw that engine #3 was on fire. "Well," he said, "I remained perfectly calm, walked up to the front cabin, entered it, gently tapped the pilot on the shoulder and warned him of the problem." After the plane safely landed he was repeating his story to some of the crowd that had gathered when two men carried the pilot off on a stretcher — he had a broken shoulder.

The antithesis of opportunities would be dangers. Facing each opportunity in the field of opinion we find a certain set of dangers which always pose a menace. This is natural

OPINION: OPPORTUNITIES AND DANGERS

in any phase of life, Christian conduct not excepted. These dangerous tendencies, lying in the shadow of the blessings of opinion, forever threaten their bright hopes. They must be acknowledged, marked, defined, and exposed so as never to totally quench the high aspirations and potential blessings of sincere Christians. Here we list some of those dangers that are common and devastating.

1. Because of the genesis and nature of opinion, *inconsistency* is one of the most prevalent stumbling blocks. No one is thoroughly immune to it. Since man is mortal, of this earth, opinion is his field. Therefore, his weaknesses of the mind, emotion, environment, etc., will all affect his set of opinions. His temptations and powers will decide many of his choices. The constraining forces of natural likes and dislikes can not be entirely shunned. So, the educated man, the good man, the sincere man, the sane and logical man, will find at times (but not always willing to admit) that inconsistency in judgments of opinion will rear its ugly head. The reason has been stated. Man is imperfect, thus his field of mental operation (opinion) will never reach complete consistency — an exclusive mark of divine powers. Nevertheless, let the Christian seek to be as consistent as possible in all his personal judgments, and these in turn with all the judgments of God, and the laws of common sense. Jesus easily and readily exposed the inconsistency of Pharisaical traditions when the occasion arose (Luke 13:10-17; 14:1-6).

2. The apostle Peter's instruction to Christians provides us with the next danger, when he said, "For such is the will of God that by doing right you may silence the ignorance of foolish men. Act as free men, and do not use your freedom as a covering for evil, but use it as bondslaves of God" (I Peter 2:15, 16).

WHAT THE BIBLE SAYS ABOUT FAITH AND OPINION

It is not easy to be a free person in Christ. Freedom requires a certain degree of alertness, unselfishness, self-restraint. Liberty is never to be marred by evil motives nor by unbecoming conduct of Christian toward Christian. Said Alexander Campbell, "Liberty without licentiousness, and government without tyranny, is the true genius of the Christian institution."[17]

Whereas some seek to use ignorance as a cover for their sins (John 15:22), others hide behind their "right to do as they please" in opinion. This right is misused and, rather than become a blessing, it becomes a spring board for the curse of sin. Such was the case of the Gentile Galatian Christians (as contrasted with the Jew under the law) mentioned by Paul and instructed as such: "For you were called to freedom, brethren; only do not turn your freedom into an opportunity for the flesh, but through love serve one another" (Galatians 5:13).

3. Can it not be said that man is instinctively and automatically *traditional*? Here is a twofold danger. Some have a natural or acquired love for that which is traditional and receive it with great reverence and subservient respect.

Or others have a tendency to traditionalize their own opinions and make them precedential for the future, for self as well as others. Tradition must be defined and properly catalogued lest it gets out of hand. (See pages 165ff.)

In this regard J. W. McGarvey once wrote:

> All Protestants agree that it [Bible] is the only infallible rule, but many hold that we are at liberty to frame creeds and rules of discipline based on our own fallible judgement.

---

17. Alexander Campbell, *Christian System* (Nashville, Tenn.: Gospel Advocate, 1974 reprint of 1839 ed.), p. 82.

OPINION: OPPORTUNITIES AND DANGERS

This question has been decided for us by Jesus in deciding for the Jews one which involved the same principle. Their wise men, in the course of ages, had concluded that in addition to the law which God had given them, some other rules were important, if not indispensable; and they adopted such rules, one by one, until they accumulated a large body of them, which they styled the tradition of the elders. These they enforced on the consciences of the people, and Jesus was himself adjudged a sinner when he neglected to observe them. He dealt with these rules in a most summary manner. He first pointed out the fact that at least one of them made void a Commandment of God; and, adopting the language of one of their prophets, he indignantly repudiated the whole body of their tradition, and laid down a law to govern all such matters, in these words: "In vain do they worship me, teaching as their doctrines the precepts of men." This rule preemptorily excludes from the realm of observance and faith in the Church of God every precept of men; and it limits our worship and our teaching to that which God has appointed and taught.[18]

4. There are always those who seek to *"spy out" the liberty* of others, who explore the rights and opinions of others in view of depriving them of such private property. This even becomes an obsession with some.

Jesus found this attitude most repugnant in the practice of the Pharisees (Matthew 9:10-13). And in the days of the primitive church the Judaizers were possibly the greatest offenders in this sin. This caused Paul to say to the Galatians, "But it was because of the false brethren who had sneaked in to spy out our liberty which we have in Christ Jesus, in order to bring us into bondage" (Galatians 2:4).

---

18. J. W. McGarvey, "Grounds on Which We Receive the Bible as the Word of God," *The Old Faith Restated*, J. H. Garrison, ed., pp. 45-46.

WHAT THE BIBLE SAYS ABOUT FAITH AND OPINION

This tendency was the initial step which involved Thomas Campbell in his defense before his Presbytery when it charged him with being unfaithful to his church standards. It was a Mr. Wilson who "spied out his liberty" in regard to his serving the Lord's Supper to all who wished it as he ministered in the Allegheny Valley above Pittsburgh.[19]

There will always be men who wish to gain some kind of an advantage over another man. Such a motive is evil. What we shall do with our feelings is just as important as what we shall do with our differences. This hunger "to get others" is not easily suppressed. It grows. It hurts.

5. The fifth danger we mention is that of *idle conjecture* and *debate* in the area of opinion. Such surmisings, theorizings, and banterings, when promoted in the heat of ambition and sustained in the spirit of pride, only lead to strife and fruitless speculation (II Timothy 2:23; I Timothy 6:3-4; Titus 3:9).

Certainly the Christian has the right of free thought and discussion in this field. But never shall such a thirst for conjecture be insatiable to the hurt of the human soul and the disruption of peace within the body of Christ. Alexander Campbell said:

> Liberty of speech and of the press, is not with me licentious extravagance nor disregard for the opinions of others; nor is the proper use of our rights the sustaining of every restless demogogical spirit who will be conspicious for something — for anything. On all Bible facts, precepts, promises and declarations, on all its various documents, ordinances and statutes, we go for full and free discussion; but we say it is abhorrent to the Reformation for which we plead to propagate mere opinions and speculations; and that it is entirely

---

19. Robert Richardson, *Memoirs of Alexander Campbell*, I (Nashville, Tenn.: Gospel Advocate, 1956 reprint of 1897 ed.), p. 225.

off the ground we occupy to favor those who devote their tongue or their pens to build up any theory, ancient or modern, original or borrowed.[20]

Such a practice is vain. It robs precept and precedent of their true value, and gives unwarranted attention to human opinion. So wrote Robert Richardson:

> Thus has it ever been that while the *false value* attached to the inferences and deductions of human reason has originated and perpetuated religious strife and division, a sincere submission to the plain teachings of the word of God has promoted the cause of truth, unity and peace.[21]

There always has been ample strife over essentials in the historical record of Christianity without continually igniting the fires of discord with these non-essentials. This led Thomas Campbell to point out that:

> Our desire, therefore, for ourselves and our brethren would be, that rejecting human opinions and the inventions of men, as of any authority, or as having any place in the church of God, we might forever cease from farther contentions about such things; returning to, and holding fast by the original standard; taking the divine word alone for our rule; the Holy Spirit for our teacher and guide, to lead us into all truth; and Christ alone as exhibited in the word, for our salvation, that by so doing, we may be at peace among ourselves, follow peace with all men, and holiness, without which no man shall see the Lord.[22]

6. Next we consider the ever imminent danger of *creedalizing* one's own opinion. This practice follows so easily in

---

20. Robert Richardson, *Memoirs of Alexander Campbell*, II, pp. 445-446.
21. Robert Richardson, *Ibid.*, p. 248.
22. Thomas Campbell, *Declaration and Address* (Lincoln, Il.: Lincoln Christian College Press, 1971 reprint of 1809 ed.), p. 2.

the wake of the preceding danger. It refers to the manner of holding opinions in relationship to fellow-Christians. One must fully be aware of the "privacy" of opinions, and that they are highly susceptible to error and misjudgment. So that a person *may* be wrong in his opinion, but when he seeks to force that opinion or another he definitely *is* wrong, regardless of what the opinion is. A bitter and uncompromising attitude in view of extending personal opinion into the conscience of another is evil. This is creedalizing.

In the famous *Declaration and Address*, Mr. Campbell stated three progress steps in this sinful act. (a) The first thing done wrong is "to determine expressly, in the name of the Lord, when the Lord has not expressly determined...."[23] This is speaking, with divine authority, when there is no authority. F. D. Power points out that this is the age-old practice as recorded in church history:

> The old Arian and Athanasian controversy found its way in some form in religious teaching from the third century. The attempt to define the indefinable, to formulate all doctrine, even that which could not be formulated, led to endless differences and difficulties and divisions.[24]

(b) When this is done in a spirit of dogmatism, then the next act is that of looking upon a brother who has violated our judgment and "judging him to be a transgressor of the law in so doing."[25] This general practice has been evidenced in the various denominational crusades in such particular instances as the following, quoting Charles E. Titus:

> The old Order Mennonite Church opposed the introduction of the English language in the church services. The

---

23. (Deuteronomy 18:20; I Corinthians 7:25, 40) *Ibid.*, p. 50.
24. F. D. Power, *Missouri Christian Lectures* (St. Louis: Christian Publishing Co., 1892), p. 58.
25. Thomas Campbell, *Declaration and Address*, p. 50.

River Dunkers opposed baptisteries, and another denomination the individual communion cups. The Amish Church refused to fellowship those who wore buttons instead of hooks and eyes, and the 7th Day Adventists those who would not worship on Saturday. Certain ministers and churches of Christ refused to fellowship those who used organs and pianos in church singing.[26]

(c) And then "by rejecting him, or casting him out of the church, as unworthy of a place in her communion; — and thus, as far as in our power, cutting him off from the kingdom of heaven,"[27] we commit the final act of this sin. And man, when so corrupted, will use any means at his disposal (and yet it even may be in keeping with his own conscience) to force the issue. Either the other party's opinion must go, or he, himself, must go. This is why any ecclesiastical power can be so dangerously wrong. From H. E. Luccock, quoted by Chester E. Tulga, we note:

> Whenever men have power over their fellows, their fellows are treated as a means to their own aggrandizement, their own prestige, their own increase of power. The surroundings differ; the costumes change. The instruments and agencies vary. The essential fact is the same — exploitation.
>
> Even when power takes the form of benevolence, of philanthrophy, or religion, there is an essential immorality about it in that the possession of unrenounced power and privilege puts one into the place of patronage.[28]

Methods change, principles never do. The various implementations of creedalizing vary from one generation to

---

26. Charles B. Titus, *Music in Worship* (Cherokee, Okla.: published by author, n.d.), p. 4.
27. Thomas Campbell, *op. cit.*, p. 51.
28. H. E. Luccock as quoted by Chester E. Tulga, *Christian Standard* (July 31, 1948), p. 13.

another, however, the principle remains the same. Our "restoration fathers" had to rebel against the practice of those who creedalized tradition and denominatinal concepts. Today the same sin wears new masks in the form of ecclesiastical authority of the "new" liberalism, "new" cultism, "new" orthodoxy, "new" fundamentalism. Says Mr. Tulga:

> The modernist flees logic in theology but embraces logic in ecclesiasticism. He renounces authority in religion and establishes and supports ecclesiastical authority. He renounces any and all theological tenets as tests of fellowship, while creating a new test of fellowship and preferment—loyalty to an ecclesiastical organization. He fears the authority of a creedal statement, lest it be used to discipline him, but creates a steadily increasing ecclesiastical authority which history has revealed to be the consistent foe of free spirits. He sees the perils of creedal authority over the human mind, but is blind to the menace of ecclesiastical authority over the human spirit. The growth of theological liberalism in the democratic religious organizations in America has been accompanied by the steady centralization and strengthening of centralized ecclesiastical authority. The growth of modernism among Baptists has been co-incidental with the steady undermining of the independence of the local church, Baptist bulwark against the tyranny of ecclesiasticism. The pseudo-liberalism of our time has won control of the major denominations, while at the same time it has so strengthened ecclesiasticism that it has greater weapons to use against the free spirit than ever before. Modernistic liberalism has destroyed the authority of creeds and at the same time constructed an ecclesiastical gallows, forgetting the warning that sooner or later every organization strangles the truth which gave it birth.[29]

---

29. Chester E. Tulga, *Christian Standard* (July 31, 1948), p. 13.

OPINION: OPPORTUNITIES AND DANGERS

7. How noble it would be if man were to put into spirit and practice the principle invoked by the elder Campbell:

> We declare ourselves ready to relinquish whatever we have hitherto received as matter of faith or practice, not expressly taught and enjoined in the word of God, so that we and our brethren might by this mutual condescension, return together to the original concension, return together to the original constitutional unity of the Christian church, and dwell together in peace and charity. By this proposed relinquishment, we are to be understood, in the first instance, of our manner of holding those things, and not simply of the things themselves; for no man can relinquish his opinions or practices till once convinced that they are wrong; and this he may not be immediately, even supposing they were so. One thing however, he may do, when not bound by an express command, he need not impose them upon others, by any wise requiring their approbation; and when this is done, the things, to them, are as good as dead; yea, as good as buried too; being thus removed out of the way.[30]

This would, to a large degree, overcome the final danger of *unwarranted schism* among Christians — the climactic and culminating end to all the foregoing threats. It is the last stage. And how often it arises over the fumbling of mere opinion. And how conscientious Christians will push on toward division at any price. Although not accepting many of the conclusions of Amos Wells on the subject of "unity," we do quote his excellent statement on this issue of fighting to the end for one's conscientious opinion:

> If ever the history of conscience is written (intricate and ungracious task!), many such transformations will be recorded. Some of them alas! Will be recorded of the Christian sects.

---

30. Thomas Campbell, *op. cit.*, pp. 42, 43.

> For an opinion at variance with our brothers; if it is true and vital, may require us to fight for it and perhaps to die for it. Then we are heroes of conscience. But if, after the battle is won, or the truth ceases to be vital, it serves us as an excuse for continued variance, we are idolaters of conscience and its heroes no longer.
>
> Our courage is transformed into pugnacity, our determination into obstinacy, our self-sacrifice into the spirit of persecution, and our self-forgetfulness into vainglory.
>
> At first we contend for principles; but now, for place and power. At first we were content that truth should prevail, but now we seek self-aggrandizement. At first we desired the reform of others, but now we wish their adhesion to ourselves.[31]

So, sectarianism is a spirit, an attitude, as well as a practice. It is frequently found in the "littlest" things of opinion. But its devastating effect on unity is great. If man is sectarian at heart, and not teachable nor penitent, he will find something, somewhere (no matter how insignificant) to satisfy his divisive spirit.

The efforts at restoring New Testament Christianity have been plagued with a division that resulted in overplaying an inconsequential difference of opinion—shall music in Christian worship utilize an instrumental accompaniment? Over this some became divisive, and division ensued. Isaac Errett said of certain of these opposing champions:

> Preachers pledged themselves never to preach for such churches, and advised brethren holding letters not to take membership in such churches. Such sentiments were declared worthy to be printed in letters of gold. The result of this

---

31. Amos R. Wells, *That They All May Be One* (New York: Funk and Wagnalls Co., 1905), p. 45.

OPINION: OPPORTUNITY AND DANGERS

style of treatment has been twofold. (1) It has encouraged brethren opposed to instrumental music to make *a test of fellowship* out of their opinions, or prejudices, and has encouraged them to secede from churches in which they could not carry their point. (2) It has exasperated those friendly to the use of instruments, and led them to a persistence in accomplishing their desires, from which a gentler spirit might have saved them.[32]

However I believe the current situation in this regard has improved immeasurably. It appears to the writer that the past 10 years or so has lessened the intensity of this division. More and more individuals are making this "instrument" issue more of a matter of personal preference and less a matter of strict defense. The problem is still present today but not to the same degree.

In closing may I offer the following 12 guidelines as a brief summary on "how to hold an opinion."

1. Make sure you identify your opinion as an opinion.
2. Beware of the tendency to hold too many opinions. Many sincere people feel obligated to hold some definite, clear-cut opinion about everything. Why? To withhold a judgment, to delay a decision pending more knowledge or dismiss a nonessential matter with no comment is not necessarily a sign of weakness in Bible knowledge or Christian maturity. Too many well-meaning people have too many opinions — and they feel they are obligated and privileged to clearly and boldly express every one of them. And, that's my opinion! (Titus 3:9, 10).
3. Beware of the next attitude that often follows — to claim a thing an opinion "in word," but make it a matter of

---

[32]. Isaac Errett, *Christian Standard* (April 30, 1870).

faith "by attitude." Attitudes are important. The opinion "hit-and-run," the "bully," the "prima donna," the "pouter," the opinion "snob" and the "arguer" are all repulsive. In God's plan of unity and harmony for His people it is just as vital an ingredient to possess the right spirit as it is to believe the right things. Ephesians 4:1-3 is not less divine requisite of a pattern for unity and harmony than 4:4-6 (II Timothy 2:23, 24).

The person, holding a narrow opinion, is often manifesting a system of insecurity or having an inferiority complex. This spirit thus becomes a great "ego builder" and gives the opinionated person a false sense of "spiritual" security. On the other hand another opinionated person may fall into the trap of succumbing to the "law of reaction" and strongly take the opposite view just to assert himself and bolster his own ego. This practice goes "round and round."

4. Then beware of the driving temptation to want to know everyone's opinion — to insist on it, especially how it agrees or disagrees with your own. Opinions are basically private property, except where they materially affect others or the whole church. Often other Christians demur at such insistence, because it doesn't really mean that much to them, or they aren't that firm in regard to a particular opinion, or they resist such a demand on the part of the questioner. Such an abnormal curiosity is a mark of being opinionated. We use the term "opinionated" as simply referring to any person who simply attaches more importance to his own opinion than God has granted.

5. And now for this warning. Another sympton of being opinionated naturally follows. A strongly opinionated

OPINION: OPPORTUNITY AND DANGERS

person usually dislikes another opinionated person. They often are suspicious of each other and will even avoid each other. However, when such a person champions the same opinion, then the other party emotionally and enthusiastically comes to life—and they often become "bosom friends." They even translate their common rapport in opinion in terms of tests of loyalty and revel in such teaching and preaching. To hold certain opinions in common seems more unifying than to hold matters of faith in common.

6. Remember how you formed your opinion—or, as the case may be, how this opinion was formed in you. There are many factors and influences of life that give birth to opinions—the results of many differences in human life. They are formed psychologically, geographically, biologically, influentially, environmentally, circumstantially, culturally, educationally and emotionally.

7. Also, remember that "to grow in grace and knowledge" as a Christian is not synonymous with becoming narrower and narrower in opinion. To "cut out" some practice or idea is not a guarantee that one has grown spiritually. Sometimes in maturing as a Christian we "narrow" our opinions and sometimes we "broaden" them.

8. Now, if you have a "narrow" opinion, don't judge a person who does not have it, and if you have a "broad" opinion, don't look down on a person who doesn't have it (Romans 14:1-4). Neither make it a test of faith nor a test of fellowship.

9. Make it imperative in your personal life to adhere to the four laws of opinion—freedom, expediency, propriety and love as you exercise the privilege of holding this opinion.

WHAT THE BIBLE SAYS ABOUT FAITH AND OPINION

10. Now, your attitude toward others is imperative. The spirit of respect, tolerance and forbearance must be carefully and lovingly manifested.
11. Though your right to hold your opinion is absolute, your right to practice it is relative. Be willing to forfeit the practice of your opinion for the salvation of another, and resist the surrendering of your opinion should the other person demand you give up your freedom. In your church life learn how to be in the "majority" and in the "minority."
12. Finally, love peace, harmony and unity of God's people with a passion. Manage your privately owned and controlled property (opinion), all to the greater glory of God's Kingdom and its great witness as a united church. Love the Lord and His church with your opinion.

Chapter Fourteen
CONCLUSION

The two thousand year record of Christianity, laden with failures and division, is distressing in some respects. And yet, that is the frank story in so many instances. Even as we approach the "enlightened era" of our time, this has been so evident.

What awful and distressing effects have those sad divisions produced! what aversions, what reproaches, what backbitings, what evil surmisings, what angry contentions, what enmities, what ex-communications, and even persecutions!!! . . . Have we not seen congregations broken to pieces, neighborhoods of professing Christians first thrown into confusion by party contentions, and, in the end, entirely deprived of gospel ordinances; while in the meantime, large settlements, and tracts of country, remain to this day entirely destitute of a Gospel ministry, many of them in little better than a state of heathenism, the churches being either so weakened with divisions, that they can not send them ministers, or the people so divided among themselves that they will not receive them.[1]

The devil, since time began, has flaunted *division* in the face of God and His creation, as being his great "Har-Magedon" in the struggle for the allegiance of man. How Satan must gloat over this one prize. By enticing the flesh to become faithless and immoral he has wrought much schism in the world. And yet, how much of it has been due to the failure on the part of Christians to grasp the one great lesson of this book. Again from the pen of Mr. Campbell:

That (in some instances,) a partial neglect of the expressly revealed will of God; and (in others,) an assumed authority for making the approbation of human opinions and human

---

1. Thomas Campbell, *Declaration and Address* (Lincoln, Il.: Lincoln Christian College Press, 1971 reprint of 1809 ed.), p. 6.

inventions a term of communion by introducing them into the constitution, faith, or worship, of the Church, are, and have been, the immediate, obvious, and universally acknowledged causes, of all the corruptions and divisions that ever have taken place in the Church of God.[2]

The issue of faith and opinion must not "take a back seat" in this problem of unity; it reaches the very heart of it. For Christian unity is a New Testament concept. And it must be achieved by New Testament methods, measure up to New Testament standards, and be rewarded by New Testament blessings. We must not allow ourselves to make unity mean any more or any less than New Testament unity. That is our norm. A false basis of unity has been all too prevalent. Says John B. Cowden:

> In the first place, the failure of the above plans has taught us that Christian unity can not be an ecclesiasticism, where one man or a number of men constitute the head of the church; that has always been religious tyranny and spiritual despotism. Not a union of denominations, where one denomination swallows up all the others; that would be a denominational monster, or monstrosity. Not a federation of sects, where each sect is fitted into its allotted niche and place, and agrees to occupy as little space as possible; that would be stagnation and death. Not an aggregation of unreconciled sects, where each has signed an armistice; that has always resulted in renewed hostilities. Not a peace by compromise, where all agree to maintain a respectful silence such as the tombs of a graveyard; that would be a living death. Not a bargain, where one thing is given up by one, and another thing is given up in return by another; that would be selling out. Not a forced union, where all speak

---

2. *Ibid.*, p. 26.

CONCLUSION

the same thing through slavish fear; that would be a new edition of "The Book of Martyrs." Not a uniformity of opinions, where each one sneezes when the other takes snuff; that would be religious hypocrisy. Not a union of all the theories and philosophies of the religious thinkers and dreamers of the past; that would be a religious museum. Not a union of all the modern cults and isms; that would be fanaticism, of which the world is full already.[3]

And from the writing of H. W. Everest, these words:

> It (Christian unity) must not be a show, a sham, a mere outward seeming. It must not be an unwilling union compelled by outward pressure, nor a compromise by the sacrifice of truth and conscience, nor a temporary truce between contending factions; but a real, organic, vital union resulting from a spiritual union with Christ and one another.[4]

Many of the historic cases of "unity" attempts by the Christian world have been no more genuine than that of the two churches of Fayetteville, New York. The local Baptist church had a preacher but no coal in the cellar while the Presbyterian church had plenty of coal but no preacher. So they "united." A quotation from Dr. Armitage is as follows:

> It is a popular idea that kneeling on the same floor, sitting on the same bench, singing the same hymn, uniting in the same prayer (when we have never been divided at all as to the floor, the bench, the hymn or the prayer), and being as different in all other respects as possible, constitutes Christian union. Men of every hue of faith and opinion, and every variety of practice, too, happen to meet in one board, or on one platform, or under one roof, and because they are

---

3. John B. Cowden, *St. Paul on Christian Unity* (New York: Fleming H. Revell Co., 1923), p. 65.
4. H. W. Everest, *Missouri Christian Lectures* (St. Louis: Christian Publishing Co., 1892), p. 9.

not bitter, and feel kindly toward each other, they consider that they are making great attainments in the mysteries of Christian union. Yet not a point of difference is yielded in any respect; and this is looked upon very generally as good, fair Bible union.[5]

Differences, which are at the root of division, must be considered to answer Christian unity. Said Mr. Cowden:

> What shall we do with our differences? is a baffling question; yet it can not be ignored in any practical plan for unity. To say nothing about differences in a discussion of Christian unity is like the city man that hired to a farmer, and, on being ordered to grease the wagon, greased it all over except on the axles, the only places that needed greasing. Just so with our differences, the points of friction are the places to oil; and, if the unity wagon ever rolls, it must be greased at the places of our differences.[6]

Where is the common denominator of Christian faith? Is it in methods, opinions, organizations, the concensus of sectarian theology, or in "nothingness"? Is it not in a oneness of precept and precedent, and a diversity of opinion? As H. W. Everest once wrote, "an apostolic deliverance determines the maximum and the minimum limits of doctrinal oneness."[7] Quoting W. R. Walker:

> The Scriptural basis of Christian unity is identical with the terms of membership in the New Testament church. This, in turn is identical with the law of induction into Christ. . . .
> The Scriptural basis for the practice or maintenance of Christian unity will be found in the practices or customs of

---

5. Dr. Armitage, quoted by John B. Cowden, *op. cit.*, pp. 69-70.
6. *Ibid.*, p. 69.
7. H. W. Everest, *op. cit.*, p. 18.

CONCLUSION

the New Testament church, which were authorized by express command or approved precedent of the apostles.[8]

And adding to this the conclusive remarks of J. H. Garrison:

> This, it would seem, is Christianity reduced to its least common denominator. In other words, it is the "irreducible minimum" without which you can not have a church, or Christianity in any visible or practicable form. On this foundation of faith in Christ, and of loyal obedience to him; has been built the church of the Lord Jesus, and on that foundation it rests today. There are a thousand things which may enter into the enrichment of Christian life when we have once built upon this foundation, but these things are not to be added to the foundation and made a part of the conditions of entrance upon the Christian life.[9]

The unity then of the New Testament order is one of faith—first a unity of man with Christ (John 17), because of a unity of belief in one doctrine (I Corinthians 1; Ephesians 4), resulting in a natural unity of Christian with Christians. There is no "short cut" nor temporary basis by which genuine unity may be expedited. So wrote Professor Charles L. Loos in the *Millennial Harbinger* years ago:

> In the enthusiasm for union, men will hasten to reach their object by ignoring and throwing aside, as obstacles to the realizing of their wishes, often what is essential and positive in the doctrine of Christ, and what can never be yielded up without offending God, without destroying the integrity, and therefore the divine power, of the religion of Christ.[10]

---

8. W. R. Walker, *Christian Standard* (March 25, 1944), p. 5.

9. J. H. Garrison, *The Story of a Century* (St. Louis: Christian Publishing Co., 1909), p. 214.

10. Charles L. Loos, *Millennial Harbinger* (1869).

WHAT THE BIBLE SAYS ABOUT FAITH AND OPINION

The singular ground of true unity is Jesus Christ, and His recorded plan. None other will suffice, said Alexander Campbell:

> *Faith in Jesus as the true Messiah, and obedience to Him as our Lawgiver and King, the only test of Christian character and the* ONLY BOND *of Christian union, communion, and co-operation; irrespective of all creeds, opinions, commandments and traditions of men.*[11]

Now a valid union between Christians should follow this, but let us remember, it should follow. Quoting Robert Richardson:

> By Christian UNITY, we understand *a spiritual oneness with Christ;* by Christian UNION, *an avowed agreement and co-operation of Christians with each other.* There can be no true *Christian union,* unless there be first *Christian unity;* for, since oneness with Christ, is the very substance of Christianity, we must first have true Christians, before these can be united with each other.[12]

And adding to this the words of Isaac Errett:

> This is Christian union on a Christian basis. It involves the sacrifice of nothing that is stamped with the name and image of Jesus; *it involves the sacrifice of everything else.* Party names and creeds and tests it throws overboard. Private opinions it requires every man to keep to himself. The faith in a Divine Savior, which all these parties accept; the repentance towards God, which they unanimously enjoin; the immersion of believers—the only description of baptism which they all acknowledge; the observance of the Lord's

---

11. Alexander Campbell, quoted by George Plattenburg, "The Unity of the Church," *The Old Faith Restated,* J. H. Garrison, ed. (Joplin, Mo.: College Press reprint of 1891 ed.), p. 338.
12. Robert Richardson, *Millennial Harbinger* (1859), p. 64.

CONCLUSION

day, which they all delight in; the life of righteousness and holiness, which they all urge, and the administration of discipline according to the New Testament, which they all consent to; these are the essentials of Christian union — to attain which no sacrifice is necessary save the sacrifice of opinionism and sectarianism. "There is one body and one Spirit, even as ye are called in one hope of your calling; one Lord, one Faith, one Baptism, one God and Father of all, who is above all, and through all, and in all."[13]

Where does this lead? It leads to the foremost fact that Christian unity is primarily a personal matter. Though unity involves cooperation, it must first be personal. No one can implement unity on behalf of another. It is strictly a personal issue. When individuals are properly united to Christ and His Word they have established a basis of unity among themselves. Let each Christian confess "unity must begin with me." Hear the words of S. S. Lappin:

> The unity of God's people is not to be found in a federation of several great parties each with its own overhead system, not in compromises of the creeds and ecclesiasticisms of so-called "Christendom"; not in any plan or proposal of man. It is in the unity of believing men and women with Jesus Christ, the head of His body the church. This unity that included all believers in the beginning can do so again, and it will. But it will not come by joining something, by getting into something; rather it will be by getting out of everything but Jesus Christ. In Him alone is to be found freedom from schism and full joy in Christian service.[14]

So Christian unity will come only to the degree to which individuals will work for it as well as pray for it. This means

---

13. J. S. Lamar, *Memoirs of Isaac Errett*, I (Cincinnati, O.: Standard Publishing Co., 1893), p. 236.
14. S. S. Lappin, *Christian Standard* (April 22, 1944), p. 5.

that the individual must work at his faith and knowledge, and in turn couple them with true obedience to the divine plan. Thus, unity is a result rather than a goal in itself (Ephesians 4:12, 13). Unity is a natural result of two or more persons having a like faith and obedience in the essentials—precept and precedent. And when these two or more, share together their Christian duties they have fellowships in Christian unity. Wherever this happens there we will find unity, and the prayer of our Lord fulfilled—even if it be between but two individuals (John 17). This led Thomas Campbell to make his famous statement:

> That the church of Christ upon earth is essentially, intentionally, and constitutionally one; consisting of all those in every place that profess their faith in Christ and obedience to Him in all things according to the Scriptures, and that manifest the same by their tempers and conduct, and of none else as none else can be truly and properly called Christians.[15]

When two parties are properly united to Christ, unity will naturally ensue. When men properly weigh precept (Part I), precedent (Part II), and opinion (Part III) in testing fellowship—then Christian unity will inevitably follow. You can not help but have unity. So it was with the movement led by Barton W. Stone and the movement led by the Campbells. Years ago when they were providentially led into a mutual contact, they found that they had unity. It led Mr. Stone to defend the ensuing action by asking:

> But what else could we do, the Bible being our directory? Should we command them to leave their foundation on which we stood—the Bible alone—when they had come

---

15. Thomas Campbell, *op. cit.*, p. 27.

CONCLUSION

upon the same? By what authority should we command? Or should we have left this foundation to them, and have built another? Or should we have remained and fought with them for the sole possession? They held the name *Christian* as sacred as we did, — they were equally averse from making opinions the test of fellowship—and equally solicitous for the salvation of souls. This union, irrespective of reproach, I view as the noblest act of my life.[16]

But, until faith and opinion are carefully distinguished and respected this kind of unity can not be had. How well Alexander Campbell knew this and defended it.

We long since learned the lesson that to draw a well-defined boundary between faith and opinion, and while we earnestly contend for the faith, to allow perfect freedom of opinion and of the expression of opinion, is the true philosophy of church and union and the sovereign antidote against heresy. Hence in our communion at this moment we have as strong Calvinists and as strong Arminians as any, I presume, in this house—certainly many that have been such. Yet we go hand in hand in one faith, one hope, and in all Christian union and cooperation in the great cause of personal sanctification and human redemption. It is a pleasure to see such persons holding in abeyance their former opinions—conclusions and opinions the results of an early education and the effects of youthful associations— sacrificing all their predilections and partialities for the sake of the pure and holy principles of a religion that was fully and perfectly taught, before the age of Luther, or Calvin or of any of the Reformers of popery or any other superstition, living or dead. They see not those specks while Heaven's bright sun of righteousness and truth shines into their souls in all its glorious effulgence.[17]

---

16. Barton W. Stone, quoted by J. H. Garrison, *op. cit.*, p. 142.
17. Alexander Campbell, *A Debate Between Rev. A. Campbell and Rev. N. L. Rice* (Nashville, Tenn.: Gospel Advocate, reprint of 1844 ed.), p. 797.

And, in part, he learned this principle from his father, who placed at the heart of his *Declaration and Address* this claim:

> But this we do sincerely declare, that there is nothing we have hitherto received as matter of faith or practice, which is not expressly taught and enjoined in the word of God, either in express terms, or approved precedent, that we would not heartily relinquish, that so we might return to the original constitutional unity of the Christian church; and in this happy unity enjoy full communion with all our brethren, in peace and charity.[18]

This is the genius of the "Restoration Movement." When individuals restore primitive Christianity to themselves by the pattern of the New Testament (for "restorationism" teaches that man can understand the pattern as well as accept it) then they can do it in the community of believers. This is the act of restoring the primitive church, as marked by the norm in the New Testament (See pages 89-94.) in this present day in which we live.

> Is it not as evident as the shining light, that the Scriptures exhibit but one and the selfsame subject matter of profession and practice, at all times and in all places and that, therefore, to say as it declares, and to do as it prescribes, in all its holy precepts, its approved and imitable examples, would unite the Christian Church in a holy sameness of profession and practice throughout the whole world?[19]

This is the only perfect pattern, even though human frailties often prohibit our perfectly following it. This is the only alternative for us today. Quoting Ira M. Boswell:

> If the Bible is not the inspired Word of God, there is nothing else upon which to be united than opinions, and all talk

---

18. Thomas Campbell, *Declaration and Address*, p. 13.
19. *Ibid.*, p. 56.

CONCLUSION

about loyalty to the aims of the "Restoration Movement" and all professions of attempts to carry them out on the part of those who accept the "modern interpretation of the New Testament," are nothing more than soap bubbles, fascinating to those who chase rainbows. And, moreover, if "the New Testament present no uniform pattern of the church either in regard to organization, worship or doctrine"; and, if "the one bond between the churches was loyalty to Jesus Christ"; and, if this loyalty did not rest on a doctrinal basis, but was a matter of "attitude and of personal devotion," to restore the New Testament church would be to restore "confusion worse confounded," for it would be a restoration upon the unstable and shifting foundation of human opinions and expediences. It could not be the restoration of New Testament Christianity, but the introduction of a progressive Christianity built upon the ever changing opinions of men, scientific or otherwise, and would ultimately result in a Christianity less the Christ. Such a union would be the result of ecumenical compromises enforced through denominational machinery, and would mean the death of freedom of thought and action and the subservience of the will of the majority to the thinking and dictation of a hierarchy of a self-opinionated minority. Opinion would wear the tiara, and would eventually have to make alliances with secular powers in order to enforce its mandates upon its servants.[20]

Thus, it led one of our "restoration pioneers," Robert Richardson to confess:

We have found the edifice of modern Christianity to rest largely on human opinions; and, despairing of success in any effort to repair its separated and tottering walls, we have sought to build anew upon the *rock*—the true and

---

20. Ira M. Boswell, *Christian Standard* (October 28, 1944), p. 1.

firm foundation originally laid in Zion. We have found denominational union, without Christian unity; and Christian unity, without the possibility of Christian union; and we have sought to break down the partition walls which bigotry has erected, and to restore the Christian liberty and fraternity of the first and purest period of the church.[21]

As George Plattenburg said of this movement:

The thing sought was not an alliance, not a unanimity in opinion, not a plea for the union of sects on the ground of compromise and concessions, thus forming a new sectarianism, but a restoration and reunion of the people of God on the primitive ground as an all sufficient foundation.[22]

And the power of this whole "restoration idea" is that it is based upon the Word of God. It always has worked, and it always will. For when a people will restore the plan of the New Testament they will reap the blessings of the New Testament, Christian unity being one of them. It is possible for any group, in these times, to refuse to become a "party," a denomination, a federated sect, and to be only a church of the New Testament norm, and in turn it will find a natural and rich unity with other groups who have a "like precious faith." This was the Stone-Campbell story in Kentucky, and it can be repeated at any time, in any place. Said Claud Witty of this historic incident:

This union of the Christians and the Disciples was not a surrender of the one party to the other; it was an agreement of such as already recognized and loved each other as brethren, to work and to worship together.

It was a union of those who held alike the necessity of

---

21. Robert Richardson, *Millennial Harbinger* (1859), p. 65.
22. George Plattenburg, *op. cit.*, p. 337.

CONCLUSION

implicit faith and of unreserved obedience; who accepted the facts, commands, and promises as set forth in the Bible; who conceded the right of private judgment to all; who taught that opinions were no part of the faith delivered to the saints; and who were now pledged that no speculative matters should ever be debated to the disturbance of the peace and harmony of the church, but that when compelled to speak on controverted subjects, they would adopt the style and language of the Holy Spirit.[23]

Unity is more than a word, a theological tenet; it is a holy blessing, a gift of God, a mark of the divine. What a privilege! What a sweet and heavenly relationship!

All that are enabled, through grace, to make such a profession, and to manifest the reality of it in their tempers and conduct, should consider each other as the precious saints of God, should love each other as brethren, children of the same family and father, temples of the same Spirit, members of the same body, subjects of the same grace, objects of the same Divine love, bought with the same price, and joint heirs of the same inheritance. Whom God hath thus joined together no man should dare to put asunder.[24]

How soon will men learn that the New Testament way to achieve this unity is the only way. In his *Harbinger*, Mr. Campbell gave two principles, followed by a grand conclusion:

That the union of Christians is essential to the conversion of the world.

That the word or testimony of the apostles is of itself all sufficient and alone sufficient for the union of all Christians.

Let the BIBLE *be substituted for all human creeds;* FACTS *for definitions;* THINGS *for words;* FAITH, *for speculation;* UNITY OF FAITH, *for unity of opinion;* THE POSITIVE

---

23. Claud Witty, *Christian Unity Quarterly* (July, 1943), p. 30.
24. Thomas Campbell, *op. cit.*, p. 25.

WHAT THE BIBLE SAYS ABOUT FAITH AND OPINION

COMMANDMENTS OF GOD, *for human legislation and tradition;* PIETY, *for ceremony;* MORALITY, *for partisan zeal;* THE PRACTICE OF RELIGION *for the mere profession of it,* and the work is done.[25]

God wants man to have unity. It is for his own good.

That it is the grand design and native tendency of our holy religion to reconcile and unite man to God, and to each other, in truth and love, to the glory of God, and their own present and eternal good, will not, we presume, be denied, by any of the genuine subjects of Christianity. . . . In so far, then, as his holy unity and unanimity in faith and love is attained, just in the same degree is the glory of God and the happiness of man promoted and secured.[26]

"Christian unity means economy, efficiency and victory; division means waste, weakness, and failure." It also means a happy and glorious heritage from heaven to earth. Unity is a "must"—the church must unite to save herself as well as the world. When the proper concept of this "faith versus opinion" problem is obtained and maintained, unity will result. A world that is divided, schismatic, sinful—yea, lost—demands all Bible loving people to solve this problem. IF NOT, THE CHURCH WILL NOT BE *ONE* IN CHRIST, NOR WILL THE WORLD BE *WON* TO CHRIST (John 17).

---

25. Alexander Campbell, quoted in *Christian System* (Nashville, Tenn.: Gospel Advocate, 1974 reprint of 1839 ed.), pp. 107-110.
26. Thomas Campbell, *op. cit.*, pp. 5, 6.

TOPICAL INDEX TO WHAT THE BIBLE SAYS ABOUT FAITH AND OPINION

As arranged in *Monser's Topical Index and Digest of the Bible* edited by Harold E. Monser with A. T. Robertson, D. R. Dungan and Others.

ACCEPT. Acts 24:3; II Cor. 8:12 (A.V.) David accepted—I Sam. 8:5 (A.V.) *Accepts Abigail's offering*—I Sam. 25:35. Deliverance—Heb. 11:35. Esau may accept—Gen. 32:20. Exhortation—II Cor. 8:17. God accepts—Gen. 19:21. Offering—Lev. 1:4; 7:18; 10:19 (A.V.); 22:21; 23:11; I Sam. 26:19; Ps. 20:3; 119:108; Is. 56:7; 60:3; Jer. 14:12; Hos. 8:13; Amos 5:22; Mal. 1:10,13. Persons—Gen. 4:7; 11:3; Amos 24:23; Job 13:8, 10 (A.V.); 32:21 (A.V.); 34:19 (A.V.); 42:8, 9; Ps. 82:2 (A.V.); Jer. 14:10, 12; Ez. 20:40, 41; 43:27; Hos. 8:13; Mal. 1:8, 9; Acts 10:35 (A.V.); II Cor. 5:9 (A.V.); Gal. 2:6; Eph. 1:6 (A.V.) Work—Deut. 33:11; Eccl. 9:7. See Lu. 20:21. Mordecai—Esth. 10:3. Petition—Jer. 37:20 (A.V.); 42:2 (A.V.). Punishment—Lev. 26:41, 43. Saints—Rom. 15:31 (A.V.). Saying—I Tim. 1:15; 4:9. Time—II Cor. 6:2 (A.V.). Words—Deut. 33:11; Eccl. 9:7.

ACCEPTABLE. Pr. 10:32; II Cor. 8:12; I Pet. 2:19. Brethren, To—Deut. 33:24. Counsel—Dan. 33:24. Day—Is. 58:5. God, To—I Tim. 2:3; 5:4; Heb. 12:28; I Pet. 2:20. Righteousness—Pr. 21:3; Acts 10:35; I Tim. 5:4. Words of Mouth—Pr. 19:14.

ACCORD. One.—Josh. 9:2; Jer. 5:5; Acts 1:14; 2:1 (A.V.); 2:46; 4:24; 5:12; 7:57; 8:6; 2:20; 15:25; 8:12; 19:29; Rom. 15:6; Phil. 2:2. **Own.** —Acts 12:10; II Cor. 8:17.

ACKNOWLEDGE. Gen. 38:26; Is. 61:9; 63:16; I Cor. 14:37 (A.V.); Col. 2:2; Philemon 6. Brethren—Deut. 33:9; I Cor. 16:18; II Cor. 1:13, 14. God—Pr. 3:6; Is. 33:13; Dan. 11:39. Sin—Ps. 32:5; 51:3 (A.V); Jer. 3:13; 14:20. Truth—II Tim. 2:25 (A.V.); Tit. 1:1 (A.V.).

AGREE. Lu. 5:30; Rev. 17:17 (A.V.). Adversary, with thine—Mt. 5:25. Ananias and Sapphira—Acts 5:9. Gamaliel, with—Acts 5:40. Householder—Mt. 20:2, 13. Jews—John 9:22. One, In—I John 5:8. Two—Amos 3:3; Mt. 18:19. Witnesses—Mk. 14:56, 59. Words of the prophets—Acts 15:15.

AGREEMENT. Dan. 11:6. Sheol, With—Is. 28:15, 18. Temple of God—II Cor. 6:16.

ALLOW. Rom. 7:15 (A.V.); 14:22 (A.V.).

APPROVE. I Cor. 16:3. Disciples—Rom. 5:4; 14:18; 16:10; I Cor. 11.19; II Cor. 6:4 (A.V.); 7:11; 10:18; 13:7; Jas. 1:12. Excellent, Things that are—Rom. 2:18; Phil. 1:10. See Rom. 14:22. God, Of—Acts 2:22; I Thess. 2:4; II Tim. 2:15. Sayings—Ps. 49:13. Subvert a man in his cause, God does not—Lam. 3:36.

ASSURANCE.—Heb. *Aman*, "To go to the right hand," hence "Assurance"; Gr. *Plerophoria*, "Entire confidence," "To completely assure."

Of God's care.—Job. 13:15; Ps. 23:4; 46:1-3; 73:26; 118:5-6; Jer. 32:41; II Cor. 5:1; Eph. 3:12, 13; II Tim. 4:18.

Of acceptance with God.—Gen. 19:21; Is. 12:2; Acts 10:35; Rom. 5:1-2; I Thess. 1:4-5; II Pet. 1:10, 11; I John 3:19-22.

315

WHAT THE BIBLE SAYS ABOUT FAITH AND OPINION

Of knowledge.—I Sam. 28:1; I Ki. 1: 13, 17, 30; Job 19:25; Acts 2:36; II Cor. 5:1; Phil. 4:12; Col. 2:2; II Tim. 1:12; 3:14, 15; I John 4:13.
Of life.—Ex. 20:12; Deut. 28:66; Job 24:22; Jer. 38:17; Mt. 10:39; Mk. 10:17-21; John 5:24; 6:47, 51, 54; 10:10; II Cor. 12:8-10; Eph. 6:2, 3.
Of redemption.—Rom. 8:22, 23; I Cor. 6:14; 15:54-57; Eph. 1:7, 13, 14; 4:30; Rev. 5:9, 10; 14:1-5.
Of faith.—Rom. 5:1, 2; Eph. 3:12; Heb. 10:22 (margin); 11:1.
Of hope.—Job 14:14, 15; Ps. 42:11; Rom. 8:24, 25; II Cor. 4:8; Heb. 6:11, 19; I Pet. 1:3, 4.
Of love.—John 13:35; 15:13; Rom. 8:38, 39; Eph. 3:19, I John 3:18, 19; 4:7-13.
The effect of righteousness.—Lev. 27:16-18; Is. 32:17, 18; John 13: 17; Rev. 22:14.
Of righteous judgment.—Acts 17:30, 31; Rev. 22:10-12.
False assurance.—Ju. 9:15; 17:13 with 18:14-20; I Sam. 17:41, 42-44; II Ki. 8:12, 13; Pr. 25:19; Jer. 6:14; 8:11; 14:13-15; John 13:37, 38.
Assurance of punishment.—Ps. 9: 17; Is. 57:20, 21; Jer. 8:12, 13; 49:12, 13; Ez. 7:25-27; Mt. 13:49, 50; 25:41-46; II Pet. 3:3-7; Rev. 20:14, 15.
AUTHORITY. Ju. 18:7. Mt. 20:25; Mk. 10:42; 13:34; Lu. 19:17; 22: 25; I Pet. 3:22; Rev. 2:26. All—I Cor. 15:24; I Tim. 2:2 (A.V.); Titus 3:1. Apostles—Mt. 10:1; Lu. 9:1. Beast—Rev. 13:2. Centurion—Mt. 8:9; Lu. 7:8. Esther—Esth. 9:29. Eunuch—Acts 8:27. Governor—Lu. 20:20. Righteousness—Pr. 29:2 (A.V.). Saul, king of Israel—I Sam. 9:17. Saul of Tarsus—Acts 9:14; 26:10, 12; II Cor. 10:8; I Thess. 2:6. Titus—Titus 2:15. Woman—I Cor. 11:10; I Tim. 2:12 (A.V.).
Jesus' teaching.—Mt. 9:6, 8; 10:1; 16:18, 19; 18:18, 19; 21:23-27; Lu. 19:17, 19, 22-27; John 5:25-27. See Mt. 7:28, 29; Mk. 1:21, 22; Lu. 4:6, 31-32, 36.
All authority given to Jesus—Mt. 11: 27; 28:18; John 17:2.
AVOID. II Cor. 8:20. David avoids Saul—I Sam. 18:11. Factions—Rom. 16:17 (A.V.). Fornication—I Cor. 7:2 (A.V.). Path of the wicked—Pr. 4:15. Profane babblings—I Tim. 6:20 (A.V.) Questionings—II Tim. 2:23; Titus 3:9 (A.V.).
BELIEF, BELIEVE. Mk. 9:23; 11:24; John 1:7.
God, In.—Gen. 15:6; Num. 14:11; II Ki. 17:14; Ps. 27:13; Acts 16:34; Rom. 4:3, 11, 18; Gal. 3:6; Jas. 2:23:
Jesus, On.—Mt. 8:13; 9:28; 27:42; Mk. 5:36; 16:16; Lu. 24:25; John 3:16, 36; 7:5; 11:25-27; 12:36, 44; 17:21; 20:25; Acts 16:31; Rom. 10:9-11.
Message, Our.—Is. 53:1.
Moses and the prophets.—John 5: 45-47; Acts 26:27. See Lu. 24:44-47; Acts 28:23, 24.
Scriptures, The—John 2:22; 5:45-47.
BELIEVER. I Cor. 9:5; I Pet. 1:21.
BRETHREN. Neighbor better than brother far off—Pr. 27:10. Prophet of thy brethren—Deut. 18:15; Acts 7:37. Rule over, Ye shall not—Lev. 25:46; Deut. 24:14. Teach no more every man—Jer. 31:34; Heb. 8:11.
Disciples of Christ called brethren.—Establish—Lu. 22:31. Firstborn among—Rom. 8:29; I Cor. 15:20;

TOPICAL INDEX

Col. 1:18. Friend sticks closer than —Pr. 17:17; 18:24. Hating and loving—I John 1:9-11; 3:10-12, 14, 15, 16. Heart lifted above—Deut. 17:18-20. Law with, Going to with —I Cor. 6:5-8. Least of, Inasmuch as—Rev. 22:9. Mother and—Mt. 12:49-50; Mk. 3:33. Reconciled with—Mt. 5:23, 24. Sinning—I John 5:16. Strife with, No—Gen. 13:8; Ps. 133:1; Pr. 6:19; Acts 7: 26; I Cor. 6:5-8; Jas. 4:11. Those who do will of God are my—Mt. 12:49-50; Mk. 3:33. Ye are my—Mt. 23:8-10.

Jesus' teaching—Lu. 12:13-15; John 11:21-23. Anger toward—Mt. 5:22. Brother against brother—Mt. 10:21; Mk. 13:12, 13. Mote in brother's eye—Mt. 7:3-5; Lu. 6:41, 42. We must be reconciled to—Mt. 5:23, 24; 18:15-17. Forgive, we must—Mt. 18:21, 22; Lu. 17:3, 4. *Prodigal son*—Lu. 15:11-32. Those who do His will are His brethren—Mt. 12: 46-50; Mk. 3:31-35; Lu. 8:19-21. Disciples of Christ called brethren—Mt. 23:8-10; 25:40; Lu. 22:31.

CHRISTIAN GRACES. Faith.—Rom. 4:20; I Thess. 1:3; II Pet. 1:1; Jude 20, 21. Examples—Heb. Ch. 11.

Virtue.—Pr. 31:29; Phil. 4:8; II Pet. 1:3, 5.

Knowledge.—Rom. 15:14; I Cor. 1: 5; II Cor. 4:6; Eph. 3:19; II Tim. 3:3; 4:13; Phil. 1:9; 3:8; Col. 1:9; 3:10.

Self-control.—Pr. 23:1, 2; Acts 24: 25; I Cor. 9:25; Gal. 5:23; Eph. 5:18; Tit. 1:8; 2:2; II Pet. 1:6.

Patience.—Lu. 8:15; Rom. 2:7; II Cor. 6:4; I Thess. 1:3; II Thess. 1:4; I Tim. 6:11; Tit. 2:2; Heb. 12:1; Jas. 1:4; 5:11; I Pet. 2:19-21; II Pet. 1:6; Rev. 2:2; 3:10. Examples—*Job*—Job 1:21. *Simeon*—Lu. 2:25. *Paul*—II Tim. 3:10. *Abraham*—Heb. 6:15. *John*—Rev. 1:9.

Godliness.—I Tim. 2:2; 4:8; 6:6, 11; II Tim. 3:5; Tit. 1:1; II Pet. 1:3; 3:11.

Brotherly kindness.—I Sam. 15:6; II Sam. 9:3; Job 6:14; Pr. 3:3; 19: 22; 31:26; Dan. 1:9; II Cor. 6:6; Gal. 5:22; Col. 3:12; II Pet. 1:7. Instances—Gen. 24:18-20; Ex. 2: 17; Josh. 2:12; Ruth 2:8-16; I Sam. 20:8-16; II Sam. 9:1-7; Esth. 2:9; Acts 28:2; I Tim. 6:17-19; Heb. 13: 16; Jas. 2:14-17; 3:13.

Love.—John 13:34; 15:12; Rom. 12:9, 10; I Cor. 13:1-13; Gal. 5: 22; Col. 1:8; I Thess. 1:3; I John 4:7-12, 16-21.

Benevolence.—Rom. 12:13; 15:27; I Cor. 13:5-7; II Cor. 9:6-15; Gal. 2:10; Eph. 4:28; Phil. 4:14-16; Col. 3:12, 13; I Tim. 6:18, 19; Heb. 13: 16.

Mercy.—Mt. 5:7; 9:13; 18:21-35; Lu. 6:36; 7:40-43; Rom. 11:30, 31; 12:8; Phil. 2:1, 2; Col. 3:12-14.

Gentleness.—II Sam. 22:36; Ps. 18: 35; II Tim. 2:24-26; Tit. 3:2; Jas. 3:17, 18.

Humility.—II Chr. 34:27; Pr. 16:19; 29:23; Is. 57:15; Mt. 18:3, 4; 23: 12; Eph. 4:1, 2; Col. 3:12; Jas. 4: 10; I Pet. 5:5, 6.

Meekness.—Num. 12:3; Ps. 22:26; 25:9; 37:11; 147:6; 149:4; Pr. 15: 1; Is. 11:4; 29:19; 61:1; Mt. 5:5; 11:29; Gal. 5:23; Eph. 4:2; II Tim. 2:25; Tit. 3:2; Jas. 1:21; 3:13; I Pet. 3:4, 15.

Toleration.—Lu. 9:49, 50; 9:52-55; Rom. 14:1-21; I Cor. 6:1-8; 8:1-9; 10:23-33.

Peacefulness.—Job 22:21; Ps. 34: 14; 122:6; Is. 32:17, 18; 48:22;

55:12; Jer. 6:14; 8:14, 15; Mt. 5:9; 10:13; Lu. 2:14; John 14:27; Acts 10:36; Rom. 5:1; 8:6; 12:18; 14: 17-19; Gal. 5:22; Eph. 2:14, 15; 4:3; 6:15; Phil. 4:7; Col. 3:15; I Thess. 5:13; II Thess. 3:16; II Tim. 2:22; Jas. 3:17, 18.
Unselfishness.—Mt. 10:39; 16:25; 20:26-28; Mk. 8:35; 10:44, 45; Lu. 9:23; 12:15, 16-21; 16:19-26; Rom. 14:8; Gal. 5:13-15; Heb. 13:16; Jas. 2:14-17; 3:13.
Hospitality.—Mk. 9:41; Acts 16:15; Rom. 12:13; II Cor. 8:8-24; Phil. 4:9-18; II Tim. 1:16-18; I Pet. 4:9, 10; I John 3:17; III John 5-10.
Fellowship.—Acts 2:42; 4:32; Rom. 15:1-7; I Cor. 1:10; 10:16, 17; 12: 13; Gal. 2:9; 6:2; Eph. 2:14-22; Phil. 1:3-5, 27; 2:1, 2; Heb. 10:24; I Pet. 3:8, 9; I John 1:3, 7.
COMMANDMENTS. Jesus' teaching—Of Moses—Mt. 19:7-9; Mk. 10: 3-12. *Ten commandments*—Mt. 5:21-37; 15:4-6; 19:17-19; 23:16-22; Mk. 1:44; 7:8-13; 10:19, 20; 12:29, 30; Lu. 10:27; 18:20, 21. Making void through traditions of men—Mt. 15:1-6; Mk. 7:8-13. Jesus came to fulfil—Matthew 5:17-19. Commandments summed up by Christ—Mt. 5:43-48; 7:12; 22:35-40; Mk. 12:28-34; Lu. 6:31-38; 10:25-37. He commanded—Mt. 11:1; 14:19; 15:35; Mk. 6:39; Lu. 9:21; John 15:14, 17. A new commandment—John 13:34; 15:12, 17. Keeping commandments—Mt. 5:19; John 14:15, 21, 23; 15:10-14.
CONDEMN. Mt. 12:41, 42; Lu. 6: 37; 31:32; John 8:11. Disbeliever—Mk. 16:16. Innocent—Ps. 94: 21; Mt. 12:7; John 8:10. Jehovah, By—Job 10:2; Is. 54:17; I Cor. 11:32; Heb. 11:7. Jesus—Mt. 20: 18; 27:3; Mk. 10:33; 14:64; Lu. 24:20; Acts 13:27, 34. Job—Job 32:3. Jesus, By—Rom. 8:34. Self—Job 9:20; 15:6; I John 3:20, 21; Rom. 2:1; Tit. 3:11. Sin—Rom. 8:3. Sodom and Gomorrah—II Pet. 2:6. Wicked—Ex. 22:9; Deut. 25:1; I Ki. 8:32; Pr. 12:2; Mt. 12:37.
CONSCIENCE. Gr. *suneidesis*, "Co-perception or moral consciousness." Term occurs thirty times in New Testament.
Sphere of.—Rom. 9:1, 2; 13:5; I Tim. 3:9; II Tim. 1:3; Heb. 10:22; I Pet. 3:21.
Heart the organ *(fig.)*.—Mt. 10:37-39; Lu. 14:33-35; John 15:10-14; Acts 26:9.
Prophecy.—Is. 55:6-9; Jer. 23:16, 17; Amos 3:6-8; II Pet. 3:11-14.
Approving.—Job 27:6; Acts 23:1; Rom. 2:15; 9:1; II Cor. 1:12; I Tim. 1:5; Heb. 13:18; I Pet. 3:16.
Disapproving.—Rom. 2:15.
Active.—Gen. 31:36-42; 39:7-9; Job 31:16-22; Dan. 1:8; Acts 4:19; 23: 1; 24:16; Rom. 2:15; I Pet. 2:19.
Conciliatory.—Rom. Ch. 13; 15:1, 2; I Cor. Ch. 8; 10:25-31; II Cor. 4:2.
Weak.—Lu. 14:33-35; I Cor. 8:7, 10, 12.
Accusing.—Ps. 32:3-5; 38:1-8; 51:3; Mt. 26:75; 27:3-5; Mk. 6:16-20; John 8:9; I Tim. 1:19.
Considerate.—I Cor. 10:25-29.
Seared.—Pr. 30:20; Jer. 6:15; Rom. 1:21-25; I Tim. 4:2.
Defiled.—I Cor. 8:7; Tit. 1:15; Heb. 10:22.
Conceit of.—Pr. 21:2; John 8:33; Acts 26:9.
Conscience acts according to the light possessed.—Rom. 2:10-16.
Consciences in conflict with each other.—I Cor. 10:28f.
Witness of the conscience.—Rom. 9:1f. *Cf.* I John 5:10.

TOPICAL INDEX

CONTENTION, CONTENTIOUS. Pr. 22:10. Bars of a castle, Are like—Pr. 18:19. Cease, Cause to—Pr. 18:8. Fool's lips enter into—Pr. 18:6. Man of—Jer. 15:10. Man, So is a—Pr. 26:21. Pride, by, cometh—Pr. 13:10. Sharp—Acts 15:39. Who hath contention? — Pr. 23:29. Woman, With a—Pr. 21:19.
CONTROVERSY. Deut. 21:5. II Chr. 19:8. Gates, Within thy—Deut. 17:8. Inhabitants, With—Ez. 44:24. Judah, With—Mic. 6:2. Men, Between—Deut. 19:17; 25:1. Nations, With the—Jer. 25:31. Without—I Tim. 3:16.
CORRECT. Acts 24:2; II Tim. 2:25; 3:16. Child—Pr. 22:15; 23:13; 29:17. God, By—Job 5:17; 37:13; Ps. 39:11; 94:10; Pr. 3:1; Jer. 2:30; 5:3; 10:24; 30:11; 46:28; Hab. 1:12. Wickedness—Jer. 2:19.
CUSTOM. Abominable—Lev. 18:30. Against—Acts 28:17. All—Acts 26:3. As his custom was—Lu. 4:16. Change—Acts 6:14. Feast, Of—Lu. 2:42. Have a—John 18:39. Impose—Ezra 7:24. Israel, In—Ju. 11:39. No such—I Cor. 11:16. Law, Of—Lu. 2:27. Pay—Ezra 4:13. Priests, Of—I Sam. 2:13. Lu. 1:9. Render—Rom. 13:7. Sealed according to—Jer. 32:11. Vanity—Jer. 10:3 (A.V.). Walk after—Acts 21:21.
DECEPTION. Deceit is falsehood—Ps. 119:118; Pr. 14:25. Comes from the heart—Mk. 7:22; Jer. 18:9. A continual habit with some—Ps. 38:12. Hard to give up—Jer. 8:5. Unbecoming a saint—Job 27:4. God abhors—Ps. 5:6. Warned against deceitful testimony—Pr. 24:28. Devise against peaceful people—Ps. 35:20. Such persons grow away from good—Ps. 36:3. Cheat in wages—Pr. 11:18. Uncertain counsel—Pr. 12:5. Jeremiah has a bad opinion of—Jer. 9:4-6. Deceived by pride of heart—Ob. 3. Wax worse and worse—II Tim. 3:13. Not to deceive ourselves—I Cor. 3:18. Nor handle word of God deceitfully—II Cor. 4:2. Nor mock God—Gal. 6:7. Nor deny our sin—I John 1:8. Must not blame sin on the wrong person—Jas. 1:13-16. False estimates—II Cor. 6:8. Deceivers who are antichrist—II John 7.
Christ free from.—Is. 53:9; I Pet. 2:22. Saints free from—Job 31:5; Ps. 24:4; 111:7; 120:2-3; Eph. 4:14; 5:6; Col. 2:8; I Pet. 2:1; Rev. 14:5.
Satan a deceiver.—Gen. 3:4-5; I Ki. 22:22; Lu. 22:3; John 8:44; 13:27; Acts 5:3; Rev. 12:9.
Exemplified.—Serpent and Eve—Gen. 3:1-5. Abraham and wife—Gen. 12:18; 20:2. Isaac and wife—Gen. 26:7. Rebekah and Jacob deceive Isaac—Gen. 27:6-23. Laban substitutes Leah for Rachel—Gen. 29:23-25. Jacob's sons in entrapping the Shechemites—Gen. 34:13-29. Joseph's brethren deceive Jacob concerning Joseph—Gen. 37:31-35. Joseph in dealing with his brethren in Egypt—Gen. 42:7-17. Gibeonites, in misrepresenting place of residence—Josh. 9:3-15. Ehud deceives Eglon—Ju. 3:15-22. Jael and Sisera—Ju. 4:20. Delilah deceives Samson—Ju. 16:4-20. David feigns madness —I Sam. 21:13. Amnon deceives Tamar—II Sam. 13:6-11. The old prophet—I Ki. 13:18. Gehazi and Naaman—II Ki. 5:20-24. Herod concerning young child—Mt. 2:8. Pharisees seeking to entrap Jesus—Mt. 22:15-22. Also chief priests—Mk. 14:1. Ananias and Sapphira—Acts Ch. 5.

319

WHAT THE BIBLE SAYS ABOUT FAITH AND OPINION

DISCERN. Gen. 27:23; 31:32; 38: 25; Ruth 3:14; Ezra 3:13; Neh. 6:12; Job 4:16; 6:30; 38:20; Ps. 19:12; Pr. 1:2; 2:3; 7:7; 10:13; Dan. 9: 13, 25; Jonah 4:11; Mal. 3:18; Mt. 16:3; I Cor. 1:19; 11:29, 31; 14: 29; Phil. 1:9; Heb. 4:12. Good and evil—II Sam. 14:17; 19:35; I Ki. 3:9; Eccl. 8:5; Heb. 5:14. Justice—I Ki. 3:11; Job 6:30. Spirits—I Cor. 12: 10. Unclean—Ez. 22:26; 44:23.

DISOBEDIENCE, DISOBEDIENT. Lu. 1:17; Tit. 1:16; 3:3; Neh. 9: 26; I Pet. 2:8. Avenge—II Cor. 10: 6. Heavenly vision, Unto—Acts 26: 19. Jehovah, Unto—I Ki. 13:21, 26. Man's—Rom. 5:19. Parents, To— Rom. 1:30; II Tim. 3:2. People, Unto—Rom. 10:21. Recompense, Received—Heb. 2:2. Sons of—Eph. 2:2; 5:6; Col. 3:6 (A.V.). Spirits— I Pet. 3:20.

DISPUTATION. Mk. 9:34; Heb. 6: 16; 7:7; II Tim. 2:8. Body of Moses, About—Jude 9. Jew, Against—Acts 9:29. Man, With—Acts 24:12. Stephen, With—Acts 6:9. Synagogue, In—Acts 17:17. Words—I Tim. 6:4. World, Of—I Cor. 1:20.

DOCTRINE. In the gospels "teaching" is the word used to express what Jesus taught, not yet formulated into specific doctrines. The apostles had the living word and the following generation the inspired utterances of apostles and spirit-filled men. Doctrine in its usual sense occurs only in the later pastoral epistles—I Tim. 1:3; 1:10; 4:6, 13; 6:3; II Tim. 3:6; Tit. 1:9; 2:7, 10. Used in a disparaging sense—Mt. 15:9; Mk. 7:7; Eph. 4:14; Col. 2:22. Meaning instruction—Deut. 32:2; Job 11:4; Prov. 4:2; Is. 29:24. First principles of—Heb. 6:1. False doctrine, called heresy—II Pet. 2:1.

False doctrine, to be avoided.—I Tim. 1:4; II Tim. 4:3; Rev. 2:14. Teachers of, described—Acts 20:29, II Cor. 11:13; I Tim. 6:3, 4; II Tim. 3:8; Tit. 1:11; II Pet. 2:3; Jude, 4, 8.

EDIFICATION. An essential to Christian life.—Rom. 15:2; II Cor. 12: 19.

Love edifies.—I Cor. 8:1.

Edification the perfection of saints. —Rom. 14:19; 15:2; I Cor. 14:26; Eph. 4:12-16, 29; I Thess. 5:11.

Instruments of.—Acts 20:32. Paul's teaching as—I Cor. 13:10.

Edification of the church.—Acts 9:31; I Cor. 14:3-5, 12, 26; II Cor. 10:8; 13:10.

All things do not edify.—Rom. 16: 17, 18; I Cor. 10:23; 14:17.

ENSAMPLE. II Pet. 2:6. Apostles, Of —Phil. 3:17; II Thess. 3:9; I Tim. 1:16. Christian, Of—I Thess. 1:7; I Tim. 4:12; Tit. 2:7. Elders, Of— I Pet. 5:3.

ERR, ERRED. Lev. 5:18; Num. 15: 22; I Sam. 26:21; Job 6:24; 19:4; Ps. 119:118; Pr. 10:17; 14:22; Ez. 45:20; Mt. 22:29; Mk. 12:24, 27; I Tim. 6:21. Heart, In—Ps. 95:10; Heb. 3:10. Instruction causes—Pr. 19:27. Lies caused to—Amos 2:4. People—Is. 9:16; Jer. 23:32; Mic. 3:5. Spirit, In—Is. 29:24. Truth, From—II Tim. 2:18; Jas. 5:19. Vision, In—Is. 28:7. Wayfaring men shall not—Is. 35:8. Wine, Through —Is. 28:7.

ERROR. Job 19:4; Eccl. 5:6; 10:5; Dan. 6:4. Baalam, Of—Jude 11. Converteth a sinner from—Jas. 5: 20. Last shall be worse—Mt. 27:64. Live in—II Pet. 2:18. People, Of— Heb. 9:7. Recompence of—Rom. 1:27. Smote for—II Sam. 6:7. Spirit of—I John 4:6. Utter—Is. 32:6.

Way, Of his—Jas. 5:20. Wicked, Of—II Pet. 3:17.

EXAMINE. Himself—II Cor. 11:28. Jesus—Lu. 23:14. Keepers—Acts 12:19. Matter, The—Ezra 10:16. We—Ps. 26:2. Paul—Acts 22:29; 24:8; 28:18; I Cor. 9:3. Peter and John—Acts 4:9. Scriptures daily—Acts 17:11. Yourselves—II Cor. 13:5.

EXAMPLE. Christ an example.—John 13:15; Acts 20:35; I Pet. 2:21, 22; I John 2:6; 3:3.

Christians admonished to be.—Mt. 5:48; II Cor. 4:10; Eph. 3:19; Phil. 2:5; 3:17; I Thess. 1:6, 7; II Thess. 3:9; Heb. 7:26; 12:3-5; I Pet. 1:15, 16; I John 2:6; 3:3. To youth—I Tim. 4:12. Paul as an example as far as he imitated Christ—I Cor. 11:1; I Tim. 1:16.

Like prophets.—Jas. 5:10.

Elders.—I Pet. 5:3.

Examples of disobedience.—I Cor. 10:6, 11; Heb. 4:11; II Pet. 2:6; Jude 7.

Miscellaneous.—Example to Moses—Heb. 8:5. Many may not be public example—Mt. 1:19.

EXPEDIENT. I Cor. 6:12; 10:23; II Cor. 8:10; 12:1. Jesus, Crucifixion of—John 11:50; 16:7; 18:14.

FAITH. *Pisteuo*, to believe. A union of assurance and conviction—Heb. 11:1. See Hab. 2:4; Mt. 6:25-34; Lu. 12:22-31; 18:8; Heb. 13:7.

Given by God.—Lu. 17:5, 6; Rom. 12:3; I Cor. 2:4, 5; 12:8, 9.

Comes by hearing the Word of God.—Acts 15:7; Rom. 10:13-17; I Cor. 1:21; Gal. 3:1, 2; I Thess. 2:13.

Distinction between Old Testament and New Testament faith. In Old Testament: In God.—II Chr. 20:20; Ps. 3:3-6; 4:3, 8; 7:1, 10; 9:9, 10; 13:5; 23:1-6; 32:10; 33:18-22; 36:7-9; 40:3, 4; 55:22; 56:3, 4; 62:8; 84:5, 12; 91:2; 115:9-18; 116:10; 118:8, 9; 125:1; 143:8; Pr. 3:5, 6, 24-26; 16:20; 29:25; Eccl. 11:1; 12:2; Is. 26:3, 4; 41:10-14; 43:1-5; 49:15; 50:10; 51:12, 13; Jer. 17:7, 8.

In the New Testament: Faith is usually in Christ.—John 1:12; 3:14-18, 36; 6:29, 40; 7:38; 8:12, 21-32; 9:35-38; 10:25-28; 12:36, 46; 14:1; 20:31; Acts 2:36-41; 8:37 *marg.*; 10:43; 13:38, 39; 14:22; 15:11; 16:29-34; 18:8; 19:4, 5; 20:21; 26:18; Rom. 1:16, 17; 3:21-26; 5:1, 2; 10:1-10; I Cor. 1:21-24; 3:10, 11; Gal. 2:20; 3:22; Eph. 1:12-14; 2:19-22; 3:11, 12; Phil. 1:27-29; 3:9-11; Col. 2:12; I Tim. 1:13, 14; II Tim. 1:12; Philemon 5; I John 5:1, 10, 13; Heb. 12:1, 2; Jas. 2:1.

In God.—Lu. 1:38-55; Acts 27:25; Heb. 6:1; I Pet. 1:21; 4:19; I John 3:21.

Facts produce feeling.—Mt. 23:37-38, 27:3-5, 54; Lu. 15:4-10, 16-20; John 11:8, 16, 32-33; 21:15-17; Acts 2:22-24, 37; 5:27-28; 7:51-54; II Cor. 5:14-15.

Testimony produces faith.—John 1:7; 3:11-12; Acts 2:40-42; 8:4-8; 10:39-43; 26:16-18; Rom. 10:13-17; I John 1:1-3; 5:8-10.

The assurance of faith.—John 1:12; 3:16; 5:24; 6:35, 47; 11:26; Rom. 8:1; Eph. 1:13; 2:6-8; Phil. 1:6; II Tim. 1:12; Heb. 6:12; I Pet. 1:8; I John 2:23-25; 5:5, 10.

Great faith.—Mt. 8:10, 13; 9:2, 22, 29; 15:28; Mk. 2:5; 5:34; 10:53; Lu. 5:20; 7:9, 50; 8:48; 17:19; 18:42; II Cor. 8:7.

Apostolic faith weak.—Mt. 6:26-34; 8:24-27; 14:23-33; 16:5-12, 21-

WHAT THE BIBLE SAYS ABOUT FAITH AND OPINION

23; 17:7; 19:23-29; Mk. 6:47-52; 8:14-21; Lu. 5:9-11; 12:22-34; 24:19-27; John 6:16-21; 14:7-13.
Faith an active principle.—Leads to utterance—II Cor. 4:13. Grows exceedingly—II Thess. 1:3. Obtains a fulness—Heb. 10:22. The work of God—John 6:9. Works through love—Gal. 5:6. Purifies the heart—Acts 15:9. Brings salvation—Acts 16:31. Assures life—John 3:14-16, 36; 5:24; 6:47; 11:25, 26; Rom. 1:17; Gal. 3:11; Heb. 10:38, 39. Enables us to stand—Rom. 11:20; I Cor. 16:13; II Cor. 1:24; Col. 1:23. Enables us to walk—II Cor. 5:7. To fight—II Cor. 4:7, 8; I Tim. 6:11-17. Helps to overcome—I John 2:14; 5:4. Is the means of justification—Rom. 3:25-28. Awards the sonship to us—Gal. 3:26. Makes us heirs and joint heirs—Rom. 8:17. Gives us access to God—Rom. 5:2; Eph. 3:12. Secures peace with God—Rom. 5:1. Enables us to please God—Heb. 11:6. Leads to sanctification—John 17:17; Acts 26:18; Col. 1:23, 24.
Objects of faith.—God—Num. 20:12; Deut. 1:32; 9:23; II Ki. 17:14; I Chr. 5:20; II Chr. 20:20; Ps. 78:22, 32; 118:8, 9; Is. 26:3; 43:10, 12; Dan. 3:17, 18; 6:23; Mt. 6:25-34. The prophets—II Chr. 20:20; Lu. 24:44-45; Acts 26:27. The word of God—Deut. 32:1-3; Ps. 119:15, 16, 24, 35, 40, 97, 98, 99, 105, 111. The Gospel—Mt. 13:18-23; Mk. 4:14; 16:15-16; Lu. 8:11-15; John 8:31-32; 20:31; Rom. 1:16-17; II Thess. 2:12; II Tim. 3:15; Heb. 4:2; I Pet. 1:22-23.
The power of faith.—Mt. 21:21; Mk. 9:23; 11:23; Lu. 17:5, 6; John 14:12. Curing the blind—Mt. 9:27-30.

Child possessed with evil spirit—Mk. 9:17-29.
Unity of faith.—John 17:17-21; I Cor. 1:10-13; 12:13-20; Eph. 2:19-21; 4:1-6, 15, 16, 25.
Faith as a grain of mustard seed.—Mt. 17:19, 20; Lu. 17:5, 6. Faith of Abraham—Rom. 4:18-22. In quenching fiery darts—Eph. 6:16. The prayer of faith—Jas. 5:15. (See also Heb. Ch. 11.)
The aim of faith.—To grow in the knowledge of the truth—Ps. 119:97-105, 129-131; John 8:31-32; II Tim. 2:15; Heb. 6:4-6; I John 2:5, 14. To grow into the favor of God—Acts 2:46-47; Rom. 4:4-5; 5:2; I Cor. 15:10; Eph. 4:15; Heb. 4:16. To attain unto a perfect manhood—Eph. 2:20-22; 4:1-3, 11-13, 15-16. To be transformed into the image of Christ—Rom. 8:29; I Cor. 15:49; II Cor. 3:18; 4:3-6. To be kept in constant security—Rom. 6:12-14; 11:20; I Cor. 9:27; 15:1-2; Phil. 4:7; II Thess. 3:3; II Tim. 4:7-8; I Pet. 1:3-5; I John 1:9. To be joyful on earth—Rom. 5:2-5, 11; 15:13; Phil. 1:18-19; 2:17-18.
The obedience of faith.—Mt. 28:19-20; Acts 6:7; Rom. 6:8-14; 8:1-11; Phil. 2:1-16; 3:8-16. Not works of law—Rom. 3:27-28; 4:1-8. The work tells—Mt. 3:8; John 6:29; Rom. 6:16-18; 16:19; II Cor. 10:5-6; II Thess. 1:8; I Tim. 1:5; Heb. 5:8-9; Jas. 2:14-18, 26; 3:13; I Pet. 3:1-2.
Works of faith.—Gal. 5:6; I Thess. 1:3; 2:13; II Thess. 1:11; Jas. 1:3.
Righteousness of faith.—Rom. 1:17; 3:21-30; 4:3, 11; 9:31-33; 10:4-11; Gal. 2:16; Phil. 3:9; Heb. 11:7.
The testing of faith.—I Pet. 1:5-9, 21; 4:19; Abraham's offering—Gen.

TOPICAL INDEX

22:15-18. Caleb's courage—Num. 13:30. Joshua's renunciation—Josh. 24:14-15. Job's patience—Job 19:25-27. Daniel's refusal—Dan. 1:8. Shadrach, etc.—Dan. 3:16-18. Martha's trustfulness—John 11:21-22. Jesus in Gethsemane—Mt. 26:36-46; Mk. 14:32-42; Lu. 22:40-46. Peter and John—Acts 4:19-20. Stephen—Acts Ch. 7. Paul's afflictions—Rom. 8:28, 35-39; II Cor. 4:8-18; 6:3-10; 11:23-29; Phil. 1:21; I Tim. 1:15-17. Trials in life—Jas. 1:3; I Pet. 1:7.

The fruits of faith.—Remission of sins—Lu. 24:47; John 20:22-23; Acts 2:38-39; 3:19; 10:43. The indwelling of Christ—Eph. 3:17-19. The sealing of the spirit—Gal. 3:14. The father's love—John 16:27; Rom. 8:35-39. Heavenly mansions—John 14:2. The crown of life—Rev. 2:10. Eternal life—John 10:28; I Tim. 4:10; I Pet. 1:9.

Failing faith is fatal.—Mt. 14:30-31; Lu. 22:31-32; John 20:25-29; I Cor. 15:12-19; I Tim. 6:10-11; II Tim. 4:3-4; Heb. 3:14-19; I Pet. 5:8-9; II Pet. 1:5-9.

What faith is proof of: Unworthiness—Mt. 8:8; Lu. 15:18-19. Teachableness—Mt. 13:23; Lu. 8:15; Jas. 1:21-25. Adoption—John 1:12-13; Rom. 8:14-16; Gal. 3:26-27. Entrance into rest—Heb. 4:1-3.

Prayer without faith is vain.—Pr. 28:9; Mt. 21:22; Acts 10:31-33; Eph. 6:16-18; Heb. 10:21, 22; 11:6; Jas. 1:5-7; 5:15-18.

The denial of faith.—Josh. 24:27; Pr. 30:8-9; Mt. 10:33; 26:34; Mk. 14:30; 16:16; Lu. 12:9; I Cor. 15:12-14; I Tim. 5:8; II Tim. 3:5; II Pet. 2:1; I John 2:22-23; Jude 3; Rev. 2:13; 3:8.

Whatsoever is not of faith is sin.—Rom. 14:22, 23.
Unfeigned faith.—II Tim. 1:5.
Through the spirit by faith wait for the hope of righteousness.—Gal. 5:5-7.
Breastplate of faith.—I Thess. 5:8.
Shield of faith.—Eph. 6:16.
Examples in the Old Testament.—Abel—Heb. 11:4. Abraham—Gen. 12:1-7; 15:4-18; 22:1-10; 24:7, 40; John 8:56; Rom. 4:18-21; Heb. 11:8-19. Caleb—Num. 13:30; Josh. 14:6, 12. Daniel—Dan. 6:4-23. David—I Sam. 17:45-49; 30:6; I Chr. 27:23; Acts 2:25-31; Heb. 11:32. Elijah—I Ki. 17:13-16; 18:21-39. Enoch—Heb. 11:5. Gideon Ju. 6:14-18, 36-40; Heb. 11:32, 33, 39. Habakkuk—Hab. 2:4; 3:17-19. Hagar—Gen. 16:13. Hezekiah—II Ki. 18:5, 19. Isaac—Heb. 11:20. Isaiah—II Ki. 19:6, 7; 20:8-11. Jacob—Gen. 48:8-21; 49:1-27; Heb. 11:21. Jahaziel—II Chr. 20:15-17. Jehoshaphat—II Chr. 20:20. Job—Job 1:21, 22; 2:9, 10; 5:6-27; 13:15, 16; 14:14, 15; 16:19; 19:25-27; 23:6. Jonah—Jonah 2:2; 3:1-4. Joseph—Gen. 50:20, 24; Heb. 11:22. Joshua—Num. 14:6-9; Josh. 1:11-15; 10:25. Manoah, Wife of; Mother of Samson—Ju. 13:23. Micah—Mic. 7:7-9, 18-20. Moses—Ex. 14:13-31; 15:1-19; 17:15; Num. 16:28, 29; Deut. 1:20, 21, 29-31; 3:2, 22; 7:1-24; 8:2; 20:1; 31:8, 23; Heb. 11:24-29. *Lack of faith*—Ex. 3:11, 12; 4:10-16. Nehemiah—Neh. 4:20; 8:22. Ninevites—Jonah 3:5. Noah—Gen. 6:14-22; 7:1-24; Heb. 11:7. Rahab—Josh. 2:9-21; Heb. 11:31. Shadrach, Meshach and Abednego—Dan. 3:8-30. Widow of Zarephath with cruise of oil and a handful of meal—I Ki. 17:18-24.

WHAT THE BIBLE SAYS ABOUT FAITH AND OPINION

In the New Testament: Anna the prophetess—Lu. 2:36-38. Antioch, People of—Acts 11:21-24. Barnabas—Acts 11:24. Blind men—Mt. 9:27-31; 20:30-33; Mk. 10:46-52; Lu. 18:35-42; John 9:1-38. Canaanitish woman—Mt. 15:21-28; Mk. 7:24-30. Colossians—Col. 1:2-4. Cripple at Lystra—Acts 14:8-10. Crispus and Corinthians—Acts 18:8; I Cor. 1:14; 15:11. Disciples—John 2:11, 22; 16:30, 31; 17:7, 8, 20. Elisabeth—Lu. 1:25. Ephesians—Eph. 1:15. Ethiopian eunuch—Acts 8:26-39. Eunice, Lois and Timothy—Acts 16:1; II Tim. 1:5. Father of epileptic boy—Mt. 17:14-19; Mk. 9:17-24; Lu. 9:38-42. Five thousand—Acts 4:4. Gentiles—Acts 11:19-21; 13:48; 15:7. Jailer, Philippian—Acts 16:25-34. Jews at Jerusalem—John 2:23; 8:30; 11:45; 12:11. Jews at Rome—Acts 28:24. John—John 20:8. Joppa, People of—Acts 9:42. Joseph, Husband of Mary—Mt. 1:18-25; 2:13, 14. Lepers, Ten—Lu. 17:11-19. Lydda and Sharon, People of—Acts 9:35. Lydia—Acts 16:14. Martha—John 11:27. Mary (Martha's sister)—Lu. 10:39, 42; John 11:32. Mary, Mother of Jesus—Lu. 1:38-55. Multitudes—Acts 5:14. Nathaniel—John 1:49. Nobleman—John 4:50-53. Paralytic, Friends of—Mk. 2:4, 5. Paul—Acts 9:29; 27:23-25; II Tim. 4:7. Peter—Mt. 16:15-20; Lu. 5:8; Acts 3:16. Philemon—Philemon 1, 5. Philip—John 1:45, 46. Priests—Acts 6:7. Ruler—Mt. 9:18, 19, 23-25; Mk. 5:22-24, 35:42; Lu. 8:41, 42, 49-56. Samaritans—John 4: 39-42; Acts 8:12. Sergius Paulus—Acts 13:12. Sick of Gennesaret—Mt. 14:34-36; Mk. 6:54-56. Simeon—Lu. 2:23-25. Simon the sorcerer—Acts 8:13. Stephen—Acts 6:8. Thessalonians—I Thess. 1:6; 3:6-8; II Thess. 1:3, 4. Thomas—John 20:28. Three thousand at Pentecost—Acts 2:41. Timothy—I Tim. 6:12. Unclean spirit, Man with—Mk. 1:24; Lu. 4:34. Woman with issue of blood—Mt. 9:20-22; Mk. 5:25-34; Lu. 8:43-48.

Jesus' teaching.—Mt. 6:25, 32, 33; 10:29-31; 23:23; Mk. 4:40; 9:23; 11:22, 23; Lu. 8:25; 12:6, 7, 32; 18:8; John 6:29, 45. As a mustard seed—Mt. 17:19, 20; Lu. 17:5, 6. Great faith—Mt. 8:10, 13; 9:2, 22, 29; 15:28; Mk. 2:5; 5:34; 10:52; Lu. 5:20; 7:9, 50; 8:48; 17:19; 18:42. Man must believe—Lu. 8:12, 13. He that disbelieveth is condemned—Mk. 16:16. He that believeth hath eternal life—Mk. 16:16; John 5:24; 6:47; 11:25, 26. On, or in Jesus—John 3:14-18, 36; 6:29, 40.

FAITHFULNESS. Consistency with expressed or known character.
God's faithfulness.—Deut. 7:9; Ps. 143:1; 119:86, 138; Is. 49:7; Jer. 42:5; I Cor. 1:9; 10:13; I Pet. 4:19; Heb. 10:23. Extent of—Ps. 36:5; 40:10; 88:11; 119:75, 90. Exalted—Ps. 89:1, 2, 5, 8, 24, 33, 92:2; Is. 25:1; Lam. 3:23.
God's promise to the faithful.—I Sam. 2:35; Ps. 31:23; 101:6; Pr. 28:20.
Of Christ.—Is. 11:5; I Thess. 5:24; II Thess. 3:3; II Tim. 2:13; Heb. 2:17; 3:2; 10:23; I John 1:9; Rev. 1:5; 19:11.

TOPICAL INDEX

Of followers of Christ.—Eph. 1:1; Col. 1:2, 7; Rev. 17:14. Required—I Cor. 4:2; Rev. 2:10. **Of words.**—I Tim. 4:9; II Tim. 2:11; Tit. 1:9; 3:8; Rev. 21:5; 22:6. **Of men.**—Neh. 13:13; II Tim. 2:2. Special mention of: Moses—Num. 12:7; Heb. 3:5. Abraham—Neh. 9:8; Gal. 3:9. Hanani—Neh. 7:2. Hananiah—Neh. 7:2. Daniel—Dan. 6:4. Tychicus—Eph. 6:21; Col. 4:7. Onesimus—Col. 4:9. Paul—I Tim. 1:12. Silvanus—I Pet. 5:12. Timothy—I Cor. 4:17. **Lack of faithfulness in enemies.**—Ps. 5:9. **Of women.**—II Sam. 20:19. Admonished—I Tim. 3:11. Examples of: Sarah—Heb. 11:11. Lydia—Acts 16:15. **Of people in service to God.**—II Ki. 12:15; 22:7; II Chr. 19:9; 31:12; 34:12; Hos. 11:12; III John 5. Witnesses—Ps. 89:37; Pr. 14:5; Is. 8:2. **Proverbs concerning.**—Pr. 11:31; 13:17; 14:5; 20:6; 25:13; 27:6. **Figurative.**—Hos. 2:20. City—Is. 1:21, 26. **FALSEHOOD. Father of.**—Ps. 7:14; John 8:44. **Falsehood begets falsehood.**—II Ki. 5:21-27; Mk. 14:70-71. **Falsehood.**—For gain—Acts 5:1-9. For concealment—Mt. 28:12-15. For conquest—I Ki. 22:20-22. For worship—Jer. 10:14; 51:17. **Dealing falsely.**—Gen. 21:23; Ps. 119:118; 144:8, 11; Is. 28:15; 57:4; 59:13; Jer. 13:25. **False witness.**—Ex. 20:16; 23:1; Deut. 5:20; 19:16-18; II Ki. 9:12; Ps. 27:12; 35:11; Pr. 6:19; 12:17; 14:5; 17:4; 19:5, 9; 21:28; 25:18; Mt. 15:19; 19:18; 26:59, 60; Mk. 10:19; 14:56-57; Lu. 18:20.

False persons and things.—Accusations—II Ki. 9:12; Jer. 40:16; Lu. 19:8; II Tim. 3:3; Tit. 2:3; I Pet. 3:16. Answers—Job 21:34. Apostles—II Cor. 11:13. Balances—Pr. 11:1; 20:23; Amos 8:5; Hos 12:7. Brethren—II Cor. 11:26; Gal. 2:4. Christs—Mt. 24:24; Mk. 13:22. Anti-christs—I John 2:18, 22; 4:3; II John 7. Divinations—Ez. 21:23; Jer. 14:14. Dreams—Jer. 23:32; Zech. 10:2. Gifts—Pr. 25:14. Lips—Job 27:4; Pr. 17:4. Oaths—Zech. 8:17. Prophets—I Ki. 13:17-18; Is. 30:10; Jer. 5:31; 29:9; Acts 13:6; II Pet. 2:1; I John 4:1; Mt. 7:15; 24:11, 24; Mk. 13:22; Lu. 6:26; Rev. 16:13. Reports—Ex. 23:1; Jer. 37:14. Swearers—Lev. 6:3, 5; 19:12; Jer. 5:2; 7:9; Hos. 10:4; Zech. 5:4; Mal. 3:5. Teachers—II Pet. 2:1. Tongues—Job 27:4; Ps. 120:3; Rom. 3:13; Jas. 1:26; 3:5-9. Visions—Jer. 14:14; Lam. 2:14. **False teachers, Jesus' teaching.**—Mt. 5:19; 7:15, 22, 23; 15:9, 13, 14; 23:3, 4, 13; 24:4, 5, 24; Mk. 13:22; Lu. 11:35, 52; John 5:43; 10:1-12. **FELLOWSHIP: With Christ** (I Cor. 1:9; I John 1:3).—Life—John 14:19; II Tim. 2:11. In sufferings—Rom. 8:17; Phil. 3:10; Col. 1:24. Death—Rom. 6:3f., 10, 11; Col. 2:12; II Tim. 2:11. Resurrection—Rom. 6:5f.; Col. 2:12; Eph. 2:6. Sonship—I John 3:2. Heirship—Rom. 8:17. Fruitfulness—John 15:1-5. Power—John 14:12; Phil. 4:13. Authority—I Cor. 6:2, 3; II Tim. 2:12; Rev. 2:26, 27. Possession—John 16:15; I Cor. 3:21-23. Baptism—Rom. 6:1, 3-10; Col. 2:12. **Fellowship of Jesus with us.**—II Cor. 8:9; Heb. 2:10-18.

WHAT THE BIBLE SAYS ABOUT FAITH AND OPINION

With the saints.—Standing and responsibility—Rom. 11:17-21; I Cor. 14:20; Eph. 2:19-22; 4:17-24; Tit. 3:1, 2. Unity—Ps. 133:1-3; Eph. 4:1-6, 11-16; I John 1:7; Rev. 2: 13. Cooperation—Neh. 4:6, 15; Acts 2:44, 45; 4:32-35; Rom. 12: 4-8; I Cor. 3:8, 9; 12:4-11; II Cor. 8:4; Phil. 1:5; Heb. 10:24, 25. Duties —Ex. 17:12, 13; Num. 32:6, 7; II Sam. 10:11, 12; I Ki. 22:4; Ezra 1: 3, 4; Rom. 12:1; I Cor. 12:14-27; Gal. 6:2. Worship—Mt. 18:19, 20; Acts 1:14; 2:1, 42; Eph. 5:19, 20; Heb. 10:25. Sympathy—Acts 11: 29; Rom. 12:15, 16; Gal. 2:9; 6:2; Eph. 4:31, 32; Phil. 2:1, 2. Study of Scriptures—Deut. 4:9, 10; Neh. 8:1, 2; John 5:39; Acts 17:11; I Cor. 10:11, 12. Liberality—II Cor. 8:1-4, 11-15. Love—John 13:34, 35; Eph. 5:1, 2; I John 4:7-13. Joy— I John 1:3, 4.

With friends.—Ruth 1:16, 17; I Sam. 20:16, 17; Lu. 15:6, 9; III John 14.

Dangerous fellowship.—Gen. 11:5, 6; Num. 14:4-10; Ezra 4:1, 2; Pr. 19:4; Acts 8:19-21; I Cor. 5:11; Eph. 5:11; I John 1:6.

Fellowship with God.—Ps. 94:20; Acts 8:19-21; 10:20; II Cor. 6:14-18.

Fellowship.—(Its nature)—As respects word of life—I John 1:3. Sinfulness—I John 1:5-10. Advocacy with Father—I John 2:1-2. Obedience—I John 2:3-11. Its fruit— Holiness—I John 3:1-10. Love of brethren—I John 3:11-24. Its law —Truth—I John 4:1-6. Its life— Love—I John 4:7-21. Its root—Faith —I John 5:1-21.

Results of Fellowship.—Partakers of: Flesh and blood—Heb. 2:14. Divine nature—II Pet. 1:4. Holy Spirit—I Cor. 12:13; Heb. 6:4. Christ—Heb. 3:14. Holiness—Heb. 12:10. Promise—Eph. 3:6. Heavenly calling— Heb. 3:1. Sufferings—II Cor. 1:7; I Pet. 4:13. Chastisement—Heb. 12:8. Comfort—II Cor. 1:7. Unity —John 17:20, 21. Future inheritance—Rom. 8:38, 39; Col. 1:12; Heb. 12:22, 23. Future glory— Rom. 8:18; I Pet. 5:1.

FOLLOW. Gen. 24:8; Deut. 11:6; Hos. 6:3; Mk. 5:37; 9:38; I Tim. 4:6; Lu. 17:23. Angel—Rev. 14: 8, 9. Baal—I Ki. 18:18, 21. See II Ki. 13:2, 11. Balaam, Way of—II Pet. 2:15. See Num. Chs. 22-24. Baal-peor—Deut. 4:3. See Num. 25:1-9. Fables, Cunningly devised —II Pet. 1:16. Good, After—I Thess. 5:15. Good work, Every—I Tim. 5:10. Glories that should—I Pet. 1: 11. Hades—Rev. 6:8. Hard after— Ju. 20:42, 45; Ps. 63:8. Heart, After own—Num. 15:39. Jehovah—I Ki. 18:21. Jews—John 11:31. Lamb —Rev. 14:4. Lascivious doings— II Pet. 2:2. Love, After—I Cor. 14: 1. Paul—Acts 13:43; 16:17; II Thess. 3:7, 9. Peace, After—Rom. 14:19; Heb. 12:4. Peter, Afar off—Mt. 26: 58; Mk. 14:54; Lu. 22:54. Rewards —Is. 1:23. Righteousness, After— Pr. 15:9; 21:21; Is. 51:1; Rom. 9: 30, 31; II Tim. 2:22. Signs that— Mk. 16:17, 20. Sins—I Tim. 5:24. Soul followeth—Ps. 63:8. Spiritual rock—I Cor. 10:4. Steps of—I Pet. 2:21. Stranger, Will not follow— John 10:5. Vain persons—Pr. 28: 29. Wickedness—Ps. 119:150. Works follow—Rev. 14:13. John 1:37. Andrew—John 1:40. Blind men— Mt. 9:27.

Jesus.—Acts 21:36. Cross, Take up

TOPICAL INDEX

and follow—Mt. 10:38; 16:24; Mk. 8:34; Lu. 9:23. Disciples—Mt. 8:23; Mk. 6:1; Lu. 22:39. Left all and—Mt. 19:27; 10:28; Lu. 5:11, 28. Left nets and—Mt. 4:20; Mk. 1:18. Loved, Disciple—John 21:20. Me—Mt. 8:22; 9:9; 19:21; Mk. 2:14; 10:21; Lu. 5:27; 9:59, 61; John 1:43; 12:26; 21:22. Multitutdes—Mt. 4:25; 8:1; 19:2; 20:29; Mk. 3:7; John 6:2. Received sight and—Mt. 20:34; Mk. 10:52; Lu. 18:43. Sheep—John 10:4, 27. Ship, Left and—Mt. 4:22. Simon—John 18:15; 20:6. Whithersoever thou goest—Mt. 8:19; Lu. 9:57. Women, many—Mt. 27:55. Young man—Mk. 14:51.

FORBEAR. Ex. 23:5; II Chr. 35:21; Job 16:6; Pr. 25:15; Jer. 40:4; 41:8; Zech. 11:12; II Cor. 12:6; I Thess. 3:1, 5. Children of Israel—Ez. 2:5, 7; 3:11, 27. Fight, To—I Sam. 23:13; I Ki. 22:6, 15; II Chr. 18:5, 14. One another—Eph. 4:2; 6:9; Col. 3:13. Prophet—II Chr. 25:16. Vow, To—Deut. 23:22. Weary, Of—Jer. 20:9. Working—I Cor. 9:6.

FORBEARANCE. Mt. 18:33; Eph. 4:2; 6:9; Phil. 4:5; Col. 3:13; II Tim. 2:24. God, Of—Ps. 50:21; Is. 30:18; Rom. 3:25; I Pet. 3:20; II Pet. 3:9.

GRACE. Gr. *Charis*, "Graciousness," "Good-will," "Favor," "Joy-bringing." **Winsomeness of person or character.** —Ps. 45:2; Pr. 1:9; 3:22; 4:9; 22:11; 31:30. **Kindness sought.**—Gen. 32:5; 33:8; 34:11; 47:25; 50:4; Ex. 34:9; Num. 32:5; Ju. 6:17; Ruth 2:2; I Sam. 1:18; 27:5; II Sam. 16:4; Acts 25:3. **Kindness bestowed.**—Gen. 6:8; 19:19; 39:4; Ex. 33:12, 13, 16, 17; I Sam. 20:3; II Sam. 14:22; Jer. 31:2.

Good-will.—Lu. 1:30; 2:52; Acts 2:47; 7:10; Rom. 1:73; 16:20; I Cor. 1:3; 16:23; II Cor. 1:2; Gal. 1:3; Eph. 1:2; 6:24; Phil. 1:2; 4:23. (All saluations.) **God's spiritual force working through truth.**—John 1:16; Acts 11:23; Rom. 5:2; I Cor. 15:9, 10; II Cor. 6:1; 8:1; 9:14; 12:9; Eph. 2:4, 5; I Tim. 1:14; II Tim. 2:1; II Pet. 3:18. **Free gift to God's love in contrast to bondage of law.**—John 1:16; Rom. 5:2; Gal. 1:3; Eph. 2:8-10. **Salvation by grace.**—Acts 11:19-23; 18:27; 20:24-32; Rom. 3:24, 25; 4:4; 5:1, 2; 6:1, 14; 11:5-8; I Cor. 10:30; 15:10; II Cor. 1:12; 6:1; Eph. 2:5, 7; Heb. 12:15; Tit. 2:11-14; I Pet. 4:10. **God shows His grace in his kindness toward man through Christ.**—John 1:17; Acts 15:11; Rom. 1:4-7; 3:24; 5:1, 2, 15-21; II Cor. 4:14, 15; 8:9; 9:8; Gal. 2:21; Eph. 1:4-11; 2:4-7; II Tim. 1:9, 10; Tit. 2:11-14; 3:4-7; Heb. 2:9, 10; 10:29. **We have access by faith into this grace.**—Rom. 3:25; 4:16; 5:2; II Cor. 6:1; Eph. 2:8; I Pet. 1:7-11.

HEAR. Advice—Mt. 18:15-17. Deaf—Mt. 11:5; Mk. 7:37; Lu. 7:22. Father's instruction of—Pr. 1:5, 8; 4:1; 8:33; 19:20, 27; 22:17; 23:19. Hearing they hear not—Mt. 13:13, 14; Mk. 8:18; Lu. 8:8. Jesus—Mt. 17:5; Mk. 7:14; Lu. 5:1, 15; 6:17; 10:24; 15:1; 19:48. Moses and the prophets—Lu. 16:29, 31. Preacher, Without—Rom. 10:14. Who hath ears let him—Mt. 11:15; 13:9, 43; Mk. 4:9, 23; 7:16; Lu. 14:35; Rom. 11:8; Rev. 2:7, 29; 3:6, 13, 22; 13:9. Ye him—Mt. 17:5.

WHAT THE BIBLE SAYS ABOUT FAITH AND OPINION

IGNORANCE: Concerning God.—Job 18:21; John 7:28; 8:19; 8:55; 15:21; Acts 17:23; II Thess. 1:8.
Concerning the things of God.—Ps. 92:5, 6; Eccl. 11:2-6; Is. 1:2, 3; Jer. 33:3; Mk. 4:27; John 15:15; Rom. 10:3; 11:25; I Cor. 2:4-14; 8:2; 10:1-4.
Respecting the Christ.—Mt. 16:13, 14; Mk. 6:14-16; Lu. 9:7-9; John 1:26; 4:32; 8:19; 9:29; 11:49-52; 13:7; 14:5.
Spirit.—Mt. 12:24-28; Lu. 9:25 (margin); John 14:17; I Cor. 12:1-3; I John 4:1-3.
Coming of the Lord.—Mt. 24:42; 25:13; Mk. 13:32; Rev. 3:3.
Scriptures.—Mt. 22:29; Mk. 12:24; I Tim. 6:3-5.
Sinning.—Lev. 4:2, 13, 22, 27; 5:15, 18; Num. 15:24-29; Lu. 12:48; 23:34; Acts 3:17; 17:30, 31; Eph. 4:18; I Tim. 1:13; I Pet. 1:14.
Idolatry.—John 4:22; I Cor. 8:1-13.
Revelation.—I Cor. 13:9-12; 14:36-40.
Ignorance of the way.—John 12:35; 14:5-7; Heb. 11:8; I John 2:11.
Of the future.—Eccl. 8:6-8; 9:1, 12; I Thess. 4:13, 14.
Wilful ignorance.—John 8:19, 42, 43; 9:15-24; II Pet. 3:5.
Pretended ignorance.—Mt. 26:70-74; Mk. 14:68; Lu. 22:57-60; Tit. 1:16.
Ignorant asking.—Mt. 20:22; Mk. 10:38; Rom. 8:26.
Respecting riches.—Ps. 39:6; Pr. 23:4, 5; I Tim. 6:9, 17.
Respecting Satan.—Mt. 13:19; Mk. 4:15; Lu. 8:12; II Cor. 2:10, 11; Rev. 2:24.
Punishment of ignorance is more ignorance.—I Cor. 14:38.

IMAGINATION, IMAGINE. II Cor. 10:5. Evil—Gen. 6:5; 8:21; Deut. 31:21. Jehovah understands—I Chr. 28:9. Proud, Of—Lu. 1:51. Rich, Of—Pr. 18:11. Righteous—I Chr. 29:18. Vain things—Acts 4:25.
INSTRUCTION, or, TEACHING, and TEACHERS: Importance.—Valued as one's life—Pr. 4:13; 6:23. Die without—Job 4:21; 36:12; Pr. 5:23. Gives freedom—John 8:32. Better than gold—Pr. 8:10; I Cor. 14:6. Wisdom is knowledge of God and the way of life—Ps. 34:11-14; Pr. 1:7; 8:32-35; 23:15-18; John 7:17; 17:3; 20:31.
Who instruct?—God—Deut. 4:36; Job 35:11; 36:22; Ps. 71:17; 90:12; 94:10, 12. He taught Moses—Ex. 4:12, 15. Ordinances—Ps. 119:108. Statutes—Ps. 119:93, 102, 171. The good way—I Ki. 8:36; II Chr. 6:27; Ps. 25:8, 12; 27:11; 32:8; 86:11; Is. 2:3; 8:11; 48:17; Mic. 4:2. War—II Sam. 22:35; Ps. 18:34; 144:1. How to live—Tit. 2:12.
The Holy Spirit.—Neh. 9:20; Is. 44:3, 4; Joel 2:28, 29; Zech. 12:10; Mt. 10:19, 20; Lu. 12:12; John 14:26; 16:13; Acts 2:4, 11, 17, 18, 33, 36; 4:8; 6:10; 10:19, 20; I John 2:27.
Jesus called teacher.—Mt. 8:19; 9:11; 10:24, 25; 12:38; 17:24; 19:16; 22:16, 24, 36; 26:18; Mk. 4:38; 5:35; 9:17, 38; 10:17, 20, 35; 12:14, 19, 32; 13:1; 14:14; Lu. 3:12; 6:40; 7:40; 8:49; 9:38; 10:25; 11:45; 12:13; 18:18; 19:39; 20:21, 28, 39; 21:7; 22:11; John 1:38; 3:2; 8:4; 11:28; 13:13, 14; 20:16. He taught with authority—Mt. 7:29; Mk. 1:38, 39; Lu. 4:32. Sitting down—Mt. 5:1; Lu. 5:3; John 4:6. Claims to teach God's words only

328

TOPICAL INDEX

—John 3:11-13; 5:19; 8:28. By apostles—Acts 4:2, 18; 5:21, 25, 28, 42; Eph. 4:20, 21; II John 9, 10. Still teaching—Acts 1:1.

Parents. —Abraham — Gen. 18:19. Jonadab—Jer. 35:6, 8, 18. The law—Ex. 12:26, 27; 13:8, 14, 15; Deut. 4:9, 10; 6:7, 20-25; 11:19; Pr. 1:8; 4:1-4, 11; 6:20; 13:1; 30:17; 31:1; Song of Sol. 8:2; Joel 1:3; II Tim. 3:14; Tit. 2:3.

Doctors called rabbis.—Mt. 23:7, 8; Lu. 2:46; 5:17; John 1:38, 49; 3:2, 26; 6:25.

Moses.—Ex. 18:20; 24:12; Deut. 4:1, 5, 14; 5:31.

Priests.—Lev. 10:11; Deut. 24:8; 33:10; II Chr. 35:3; Ezra 7:10, 25.

Princes.—II Chr. 17:7, 9.

Judges.—Deut. 17:10, 11; I Sam. 12:23.

Sages.—Job 4:3; Dan. 11:33.

Scribes.—Ezra 7:6, 10; Neh. 8:1-3; Mt. 7:29; 13:52; 23:22; Mk. 1:22; 9:11; 12:35.

Apostles.—Their commission.—Mt. 28:20. Their practice—Acts 2:42; 4:2; 5:21, 28, 42; 11:26; 15:35; 18:11; 20:20; I Cor. 4:17; Col. 1:28; 3:16.

Pharisees.—Jews—Mt. 16:6, 11, 12; 23:2, 3; Mk. 8:15-21; Lu. 12:1.

Christians.—Acts 15:1, 5.

Evangelists.—I Tim. 4:11; 6:2; II Tim. 4:2.

Figurative.—Beasts—Job 12:7. Old age—Job 32:7. Former age—Job 8:8. Thy right hand—Ps. 45:4. Heart—Pr. 16:23. Earth—Job 12:8. Idols cannot teach—Jer. 10:8; Hab. 2:19.

False teaching.—Prophets—I Ki. 13:11-18; 22:5, 6, 10-12, 19-23; Jer. 14:13-16; 23:31, 32; 28:8, 9, 21--23; Zech. 10:2. Idolaters taught abomination—Deut. 20:18. Teachers—I Tim. 1:7; II Tim. 2:7, 8; 4:3, 4; Tit. 1:9, 10. For money—Mic. 3:11; Tit. 1:11. Judaizes—II Cor. 11:13-15; Gal. 1:6-9.

What was taught.—Arts—Gen. 4:21, 22; Ez. 17:17; Deut. 31:19, 22; II Sam. 1:18; I Chr. 25:7, 8; Dan. 1:4. Jehovah is the one God and is to be loved—Deut. 6:4-7; Ps. 25:4, 5, 9; 34:11. The law—Deut. 6:1; 31:9-13; Josh. 8:32-35; II Ki. 23:2; Ezra 7:10; Neh. 8:1-3, 8, 9; Ps. 119:12, 26, 64, 68, 124, 135; I Tim. 1:7. Jesus Christ or the gospel—Acts 4:2; 5:20, 21, 28, 40-42; 14:21; 15:35; 18:11; 20:24; 28:23; I Cor. 4:17; I Tim. 1:10; 2:7; II Tim. 1:11; Tit. 1:9; 2:7, 12; Heb. 5:12; 8:11; I John 2:27; II John 9:10.

Who were taught?—All Israel—Ex. 4:12; Lev. 10:11; Deut. 17:11; 24:8; 33:10; I Ki. 8:36; II Chr. 6:27; Jer. 6:8; Ez. 44:23. Children—Ex. 12:26, 27; 13:8, 14; Deut. 4:10; Rom. 2:20. All nations—Is. 2:3, 4; 42:4; 60:3; Mic. 4:2; Zech. 2:10, 11; Mt. 28:19, 20. Christians—Lu. 1:3, 4; Acts 2:42; 18:25, 26; I Cor. 14:26; Col. 1:28; 2:7; 3:16.

Methods of instruction.—**Miracle.** Precept—Neh. 9:14; Ps. 119:4, 15, 27, 40, 45, 56, 63, 69, 78, 87, 93, 94, 100, 104, 110, 128, 134, 141, 159, 168, 173; Is. 28:10, 13; 29:13; Jer. 35:18; Dan. 9:5; Mk. 10:5; Heb. 9:19. Revelation—Deut. 29:29; I Sam. 3:7, 19-21; Is. 22:14; Dan. 2:19, 22, 28, 29, 30, 47; Mt. 11:25, 27; 16:17; Lu. 10:21, 22; I Cor. 2:10; 14:6, 26, 30; II Cor. 12:1, 7; Gal. 1:12; 2:2; 3:23; Eph. 1:17; 3:3, 5; I Pet. 1:12; Rev. 1:1.

JUDGMENT: The Judge, God.—Gen. 16:5; Ju. 11:27; I Sam. 2:10; 24:

WHAT THE BIBLE SAYS ABOUT FAITH AND OPINION

12, 15; I Chr. 16:33; Job 21:22; Ps. 16:1, 2; 35:24; 50:4, 6; 58:11; 75:7; 76:8, 9; 82:8; 96:13; 135:14; Pr. 29:26; Eccl. 3:17; 11:9; 12:14; Is. 2:4; 3:13; 28:17; 30:18; 33:22; Dan. 7:10; Mal. 3:5; Acts 17:31; I Cor. 5:13; Heb. 10:30; 12:23; Rev. 11:17, 18; 16:5; 18:8.
Christ.—Mt. 16:27; 25:31-46; John 5:22, 23, 27, 30; Acts 10:42; Rom. 2:16; I Cor. 4:5; II Cor. 5:10; II Tim. 4:1, 8; Rev. 22:12.
The saints.—Mt. 19:28; I Cor. 6:2.
Sentence rendered according to righteousness.—Gen. 4:7; 18:25; I Sam. 26:23; Job 34:11, 12; Ps. 62:12; Acts 10:34, 25; Mt. 16:23; 23:13; Mk. 10:21; John 1:47; 6:70; Acts 10:34, 35.
According to one's deeds.—Pr. 12:14; 24:12; Is. 3:10, 11; 59:18; Jer. 17:10; 32:19; Ez. 7:3; 18:4, 9, 19-32; 33:8-20; Hos. 4:9; 12:2; Zech. 1:6; Lu. 12:47, 48; 19:12-24; John 3:20, 21.
Final judgment.—Mt. 13:30; 25:31-46; Acts 17:31; Heb. 9:27; II Pet. 3:7, 10, 12; Rev. 20:11-13.
Judgment as criticism.—Mt. 7:3-5; Lu. 6:41, 42; Rom. 2:1; I Cor. 5:12.
Unfair judgment forbidden.—Mt. 7:1; Rom. 14:10, 13; Jas. 4:11.
Must not judge by appearances.—John 7:24; 8:15.
Must not usurp judgment.—Rom. 14:10; I Cor. 4:5.
JUSTIFICATION. Gr. *Dikaiosis.* **I. As respects redemption.**—The act of God—Is. 45:25; 50:8; Rom. 3:26; 8:33.
God cannot justify the wicked.—Ex. 23:7; Pr. 17:15; Is. 5:23.
Not by law.—Law requires perfect obedience—Rom. 10:5; Gal. 3:11, 12; Jas. 2:8-10.
Man cannot attain to it.—A trial permitted—Lev. 18:5. Must do as well as hear or teach—Rom. 2:13, 17-23. Task too great—Rom. 3:9-12, 19, 20, 23.
Not by works of law.—Rom. 3:20, 28; 4:1-5; Gal. 2:16.
Fate of those who return to law.—Gal. 4:21-23, 30; Gal. 5:1-4.
Is obtained only through Christ.—Acts 13:38, 39; Rom. 3:21-26; 5:1, 2, 16-18; I Cor. 6:11; II Cor. 1:19-22; Gal. 2:16, 17; Col. 1:12-14.
Freely by grace.—Rom. 3:24. By faith—Rom. 3:26; 5:1; Gal. 2:16; 3:24; 5:4f.
Christians manifest it by their works.—Mt. 5:16; Rom. Chs. 6-8; Eph. 2:10; Phil. 2:12, 13; Jas. 2:14-26.
II. Other aspects of justification.—God's decisions justifiable—Gen. 18:25; Ps. 51:4; Rom. 3:4; 8:30-34.
Wrong to justify oneself.—Job 9:20; 11:2, 3; 32:2; Lu. 10:29; 16:15.
Wrong conceptions of.—Job 11:2; 33:32, 33; Rom. 3:27-30.
One justified rather than the other.—Deut. 25:1; I Ki. 8:32; II Chr. 6:23; Job 32:2; Jer. 3:11-13; Ez. 16:51, 52; Lu. 18:14.
Consciousness of right.—Job 13:18; 27:5; I Cor. 4:4.
Words and works justify one.—Mt. 12:37; Lu. 7:31-35; Jas. 2:25.
III. Word studies.—Five aspects of. (1) Spring of—Grace—Rom. 3:24. (2) Principle of—Faith—Rom. 5:1: Gal. 3:24-26. (3) Ground of—Blood—Rom. 5:9. (4) Acknowledgment of—Resurrection of Jesus—Rom. 4:25; I Pet. 1:3, 5. (5) Assurance of—Works—Mt. 11:19; Jas. 2:21, 24; Rom. Ch. 6-8.
Involved in four questions.—Who? Believer in Jesus—Acts 13:39; Rom.

TOPICAL INDEX

3:26. Why? Because God loves us—John 3:16, 17; Rom. 5:8. Where? In the death of Jesus—Rom. 5:8, 9. What? On believing in Christ as personal saviour—Rom. 4:3f.; 6:17f.; 10:3-10.
KNOWLEDGE, Divine: Practical application. — To prophesy — Deut. 29:29; 30:1-3; Dan. 2:19, 20, 27, 28, 45, 47. To prayer: Daily needs—Mt. 6:8. Special—II Ki. 11:14-20; Is. 37:14-23. Forgiveness—Ps. 44:21; 69:5; Mt. 18:35. God's knowledge of man's needs—Ps. 94:11; 103:14; 139:1-6.
Human.—The Bible reveals God and duty, the highest and wisest subjects of thought; hence, human ignorance of nature is described—Job Chs. 38 and 39.
One subject at issue between God and man in each age. Adamic.—The sovereignty of God—Gen. 3:5, 9; 11:5; 18:20, 21; Heb. Ch. 11.
Mosaic.—Is Jehovah the God?—Ex. 7:16, 17; 16:12; 31:13; Deut. 6:4.
Gospel.—Is Jesus the Christ, God's Son?—Mt. 16:16, 17, 20; Mk. 14:61-64; Lu. 2:11; John 1:1-3, 14; 11:27; 20:30; Acts 2:36; 4:12. Christ alone can reveal God—Mt. 11:27; Lu. 10:22. Lack of this knowledge is darkness and death—Hos. 4:6; Mt. 4:16. This knowledge is eternal life — John 1:4; 17:3. Not to be merely intellectual, but with the heart —Deut. 6:5, 6; Mt. 22:37; Mk. 12:30; Lu. 10:27; Rom. 10:9, 10; I Cor. 8:1-3; 13:1-3; Eph. 6:24. With the life—Deut. 8:6; 11:26-28; 30:15-20; Mt. 7:24, 25; Lu. 6:47, 48; John 7:17; 8:31, 32; 15:1, 2; Rom. 1:21; 2:19-21; Heb. 6:4-6; 10:38, 39; Rev. 22:14.
Gift of God.—I Ki. 3:12; Dan. 1:17-20; 2:21; 9:22; Jer. 11:18; I Cor. 12:8; Eph. 12:8.
Fear of God the beginning of knowledge.—Ps. 111:10; Pr. 1:7; 9:10; 15:33; Is. 11:2.
Sin destroys man's knowledge of God. —I Sam. 2:12; Jer. 2:8; 9:3-6; 11:10; John 3:19, 20; Rom. 1:25, 28; Eph. 2:1, 11, 12.
It is power.—Neh. 10:28, 29; Pr. 24:5; Rom. 15:14; Eph. 3:18, 19.
Who possess it?—The wise—Pr. 5:2; 10:14; 14:6; 15:2; 18:15; 21:11; Eccl. 12:9. The prudent—Pr. 13:16; 18:15.
Knowledge of the truth.—Lu. 1:77; John 8:32; I Tim. 2:4; II Tim. 3:7; Heb. 10:26; II Cor. 4:6; Phil. 3:8; Col. 1:9.
Value of.—Ps. 119:98-100; Pr. 8:10; Mal. 2:7; II Pet. 2:20. Is transient—I Cor. 13:8, 9. To increase—Is. 11:9; Dan. 12:4.
Knowledge of good and evil.—Tree of—Gen. 2:9, 17; 3:5. Discerning between—I Ki. 3:9. Children void of —Deut. 1:39.
Knowledge of sin.—John 9:41; 15:22, 24; Rom. 3:20; 7:7-12.
Holding to the form of.—Rom. 2:20-24; 6:17; II Tim. 1:13.
Wicked have no desire for.—Job 21:14; Pr. 1:22, 29; Hos. 4:6; Rom. 1:28.
What false knowledge does.—Puffs up—I Cor. 8:1; I Tim. 6:3-5. Destroys—I Cor. 8:11.
Desire for truth.—Ps. 119:66; Pr. 2:10; 15:14. Prayer for—I Ki. 3:9; II Chr. 1:10-12; John 17:3, 8, 23.
Fruitless knowledge.—Job 15:2-3; 35:16; 38:2; 42:3; Is. 44:25; Rom. 10:2; I Cor. 1:19-21; 2:6; 3:19, 20.
Hindrance of.—Lu. 11:52; Rom. 1:18.

Responsibility for.—Deut. 17:12; I Sam. 2:3; Mal. 2:7; Lu. 12:47; John 9:41; Rom. 1:19-21; 2:17-21; Jas. 4:17.
LAW: Adamic.—Broad permission with but one prohibition—Gen. 2:16, 17; 3:2, 3.
The law given to Noah.—To abstain from eating blood, from murder, to multiply and replenish the earth—Gen. 9:4-7.
The Law of Moses.—Was added because of transgression—Rom. 5:20, 21; Gal. 3:19; I Tim. 1:8-10. Given by Jehovah, through Moses, at Sinai—Ex. 19:11, 20; 20:1-17; Deut. 5:1-5, 27, 28; John 1:17; 7:19.
The law of ordinances given.—Ex. Chs. 21-23.
Given through the ministration of angels.—Acts 7:53; Gal. 3:19; Heb. 2:2.
Called.—Law of Moses—Ezra 7:6; Neh. 8:1; Heb. 10:28. Fiery law—Deut. 33:2. Letter—Rom. 2:29; II Cor. 3:6. Word spoken by angels—Heb. 2:2. Ministration of death—II Cor. 3:7. Ministration of condemnation—II Cor. 3:9; Gal. 3:10-13. See Deut. 27:26; 29:21; Heb. 12:18-21; Jas. 2:10-13. Living oracles—Acts 7:38; Rom. 3:2. Royal law—Jas. 2:8. Book of the law—Deut. 29:21; 30:10; 31:26; Josh. 1:8; 8:34; II Ki. 22:8; II Chr. 34:14, 15. Book of Moses—II Chr. 25:4; 35:12. Book of the covenant—Ex. 24:7; II Chr. 34:30.
The law given to the children of Israel.—Lev. 26:46; 27:34; Deut. 4:5; 29:1.
Gentiles did not have the decalogue.—Rom. 2:11-16; 9:1-5; I Cor. 9:21; Gal. 3:2-14, 19.
References to the law.—Moses cites the law—Deut. 5:1-21. He relates the circumstances connected with the giving of the law—Deut. 10:1-5; 33:1-4. Moses wrote the law in the book of the covenant and delivered it to the priests—Deut. 31:9-13, 24-29. He orders that it be put by the side of the ark—Deut. 31:26-29. Tables of the law put into the ark—Ex. 25:16, 21, 22; Deut. 10:5; I Ki. 8:9, 21; II Chr. 5:10; 6:11; Heb. 9:1-4. Written on stones—Deut. 27:2, 3. Upon gates and doorposts—Deut. 6:9; 11:20. Carried in frontlets between the eyes and bound on the hands—Ex. 13:9; Deut. 6:8. Read every seven years—Deut. 31:9-10. By Joshua—Josh. 8:34.

Children of Israel required.—To know the law—Ex. 18:16. To keep the law—Deut. 4:5-9. Not to add to or diminish—Deut. 4:2. To teach it to their children—Deut. 4:9-10; 6:6; 11:18-19. Lay it up in their hearts—Deut. 6:6; 11:18. To obey it—Deut. 4:40; 5:32-33; 6:17; 7:11; 10:12-13; 27:1; 30:10-14; Josh. 1:7; I Ki. 2:3-4.

The law rightly used.—Is a royal law—Lev. 19:18; Jas. 2:8. Is a revealer of sin—Rom. 3:20; 4:15; 7:7-8. It is holy and good—Rom. 7:12, 16. Is magnified and made honorable—Is. 42:21. Is a tutor to bring us to Christ—Gal. 3:24. A shadow of good things to come—Col. 2:14, 17; Heb. 8:5; 9:23; 10:1-9.

The law violated.—Is a fiery law—Deut. 33:2; Heb. 12:18-20. Is a ministration of condemnation and death—II Cor. 3:7-9; Gal. 3:10-13. See Deut. 27:26; 29:21; Heb. 12:18-21; Jas. 2:10-13. Is an administration of guilt and judgment—John 5:45; Rom. 2:12; 3:19, 20.

TOPICAL INDEX

The law interpreted by.—Priests and Levites—Lev. 10:11; Deut. 33:10; II Chr. 35:2-3; Neh. 8:7; Mal. 2:7. Scribes—Ezra 7:10; Mt. 7:29; 13:52; Ch. 23. Apostles—Acts 13:15-16; 17:1-3; 18:4. Jesus—Mt. 5:17-48; 22:35-40; Mk. 12:28-34; Lu. 10:25-37.
Facts concerning.—Read responsively at Ebal and Gerizim—Deut. 27:12-26; Josh. 8:33-35. Discovered by Hilkiah in the temple—II Ki. 22:8; 23:2. Read before Josiah the king with effect—II Ki. 22:10-20. Reformation instituted—II Ki. Ch. 23. Read by Ezra on the return from Babylon—Neh. Ch. 8. Read in the synagogues every sabbath—Acts 13:14-15; 15:21; II Cor. 3:14. Following after the law the Jews rejected Christ—Rom. 9:31-33. Christ accused of breaking it—John 19:7 (Lev. 24:16).
Inherent defects of the law as respects salvation.—Could not make perfect—Heb. 7:11, 18, 19; 9:9, 10; 10:1, 2. Could not justify—Acts 13:38, 39; Rom. 3:20, 27, 28; Gal. 2:16; 3:10-12; 5:4. Could not give peace of conscience—Heb. 9:9; 10:1, 2. Righteousness could not come by the law—Rom. 3:21; 4:15; 5:13; 7:7; 9:30-32; Gal. 2:21; 3:21; Phil. 3:6. Has no grace for man—John 1:17. Could not give life—Rom. 4:15; 7:9-13; II Cor. 3:6-13; Gal. 2:19; 3:21.
Christ fulfils.—Mt. 5:17; Mk. 1:15; Lu. 24:44-47; Acts 17:3; Rom. 10:4; Gal. 4:4-6; Eph. 1:9, 10.
Christ sums up.—Mt. 22:35-40; Mk. 12:28-34; Lu. 10:25-37. See Lev. 19:18; Deut. 6:5; 10:12; 30:6, 16, 20; Mt. 5:43, 44; 7:12; 19:19; Lu. 6:31-35; Rom. 12:14, 20; 13:8, 10; 15:1; Gal. 5:14, 15; 6:2; Jas. 2:8.
Temporary character of.—Rom. 7:1-6; II Cor. 3:7-14; Col. 2:14; Gal. 3:23-25; 4:1-5.
References.—Ps. 19:7; 119:70, 97, 109; Is. 8:20; Lu. 16:16, 17; John 7:51; I Cor. 6:1; I Tim. 1:7.
LEARN. Doctrines—Is. 29:24; Rom. 16:13; I Cor. 4:6. Industrious, To be—I Tim. 5:13. Jesus, Of—Mt. 9:13; 11:29; John 6:45; Eph. 4:20. Obedience—Heb. 5:8. Parable—Mt. 24:32; Mk. 13:28. Prudence—Pr. 19:25. Righteousness—Ps. 119:7; Is. 1:17; 26:9, 10; Jer. 12:16; Tit. 3:14. Statutes—Ps. 119:71, 73. War—Is. 2:4; Mic. 4:3. Wisdom—Pr. 30:3.
LIBERTY. Of the gospel.—II Cor. 3:17; Gal. 5:1. Law of liberty—Gal. 6:2; Jas. 1:25; 2:12. False teachers of—Gal. 2:4; II Pet. 2:19; Jude 4; Rev. 2:2. Not to be abused—I Cor. 8:9; Gal. 5:13; I Pet. 2:16; II Pet. 2:19.
LOVE. Song of Sol. 8:6, 7; Lu. 7:42, 47; I Cor. 8:1; 13:1-13; 16:14; Eph. 5:2; Phil. 1:9; Col. 3:12-14; I Thess. 5:8; I Tim. 1:5.
Source is in God.—I John 4:16.
Love of God.—For men—Ex. 20:6; Deut. 5:10; 7:9; 10:18; II Sam. 12:24; Job 7:17; Ps. 91:14; 103:13, 14, Pr. 8:17; Mt. 5:43-45; 10:29-31; 18:1-14; Lu. 6:35; 12:6, 7; John 14:21, 23; 16:27; 17:23, 26; II Cor. 9:7; 13:19; II Thess. 2:16; I Tim. 2:3, 4; II Pet. 3:9, 15; I John 3:1; Jude 21.
He manifests His love for man—Ps. 31:19, 21; 90:1; Pr. 3:12; Is. 38:17; 56:6, 7; Jer. 32:18; Mal. 3:16-18; Mt. 5:45; I Cor. 2:9; Heb. 11:16; 12:6.

WHAT THE BIBLE SAYS ABOUT FAITH AND OPINION

By sending His Son—John 3:16; 14: 21, 23; 15:13; 17:26; Rom. 5:6-8; 8:31, 32, 38, 39; II Cor. 5:14-19; Gal. 2:20; Eph. 1:3-14; 2:4-7; 3: 1-6; Col. 1:19, 20; Tit. 3:4-6; I John 4:7-19. For Israel—Ex. 6:7, 8; Deut. 4:37; 7:7, 8, 12, 13; 13:17; 23:5; Is. 43:3, 4; 63:9; Zeph. 3:17; Mal. 1:1-5; Rom. 11:28, 29.

His love manifested—Ex. 6:7, 8; 19: 4; Lev. 25:42; 26:12; Deut. 28:9; 32:9-14; Is. 5:1-4; 49:14-23; 54: 5-17; Jer. 31:1-14; Hos. 11:4.

For Christ—Mt. 3:17; 12:18; 17:5; Mk. 9:7; Lu. 9:35; John 3:35; 5: 20; 15:9; 17:23, 24, 26.

Love for God.—Deut. 7:9; 10:12; 11:1, 22; 19:9; 30:6, 16, 20; Josh. 23:11; Ju. 5:31; Ps. 5:11; 18:1; 31:23; 37:4; 63:5, 6; 69:36; 73: 25, 26; 97:10; Pr. 23:26; Lu. 11: 42; 8:28; I Cor. 8:3; II Thess. 3:5; I John 5:2-5.

With all the heart—Deut. 6:5; 11:13; 13:3; 30:6; Josh. 22:5; Mt. 22:37; Mk. 12:30; Lu. 10:27.

Love of Christ.—Passeth knowledge —Eph. 3:17-19. Constraining—II Cor. 5:14. To the Father—John 14:31. For the lost—Is. 40:11; Mt. 23:37; Mk. 3:5; 10:21; Lu. 19:10. For His church—Eph. 5:2, 25, 29. For John the apostle—John 13:23; 19:26; 20:2; 21:7, 20. For Peter— Lu. 22:31-32.

For His disciples—John 14:21; 15:9-15; Rom. 8:35-39; Gal. 2:20; II Thess. 2:13; I John 4:19; Rev. 1:5; 3:9, 10. For Lazarus, Mary, and Martha—John 11:5, 33-36.

Love for Christ.—Mt. 10:37-39; 26: 35; Mk. 16:10; Lu. 7:37-50; 23: 27, 55, 56; 24:1-10; John 8:42; 10:17; 11:16; 13:37; 14:21-24; 19:38-42; 20:1-18; 21:15-17; II Cor. 8:8, 9; Jas. 1:12; I Pet. 1:8.

For brethren.—Ps. 33:1-3; Mal. 2: 10; John 13:14, 15, 34, 35; 15:12, 13, 17; Acts 21:13; 28:15; Rom. 12:14-16; 13:8; 14:19, 21; 15:1-7; I Cor. 10:24; 16:22; Gal. 5:13-15; 6:1, 2, 10; Eph. 4:2, 32; Phil. 2:2; I Thess. 3:12; 4:9, 10, 18; Col. 2:2; Philemon 6; Heb. 13:1; I Pet. 1:22; 2:17; 3:8; 4:8; 3:10-19, 23; 4:7-11, 20, 21; 5:2.

For neighbors.—Ex. 20:17; Job 31: 16-22; 42:11; Pr. 17:9; Mt. 7:12.

As thyself—Lev. 19:18; Mt. 19:19; 22:39, 40; Mk. 12:31, 33; Lu. 10: 25-37; Rom. 13:8-10; Gal. 5:14, 15; Jas. 2:8.

For friends.—Ex. 32:31, 32; I Sam. 16:21; 18:1, 16; 20:16, 17; II Sam. 1:26; I Ki. 5:1; 18:4; Neh. 5:17-19; Pr. 17:17; 18:24; 27:10, 17; Lu. 7:2-10; John 11:11; 15:13-15.

Love for enemies.—Ex. 23:4, 5; Pr. 24:17; Mt. 5:43, 44, 46; Lu. 6:27, 32, 35; Acts 7:60; 26:29; Rom. 12:20, I Cor. 13:5.

For sojourners.—Ex. 22:21; Lev. 19: 34; 25:35; Deut. 10:18, 19; II Ki. 6:21-23; Jer. 2:25.

Love for children.—Gen. 22:2; 30:1; 44:20; II Sam. 1:23; 18:33; Ps. 127: 3-5; Is. 2:17-18; Mk. 10:13-16; Lu. 18:15-17; Tit. 2:4.

Man's love for his fellow-man.—Ps. 133:1-3; Mt. 25:34-40; Mk. 9:41; Lu. 6:31-35; I Cor. 10:24; Gal. 6:1, 2, 10; Eph. 4:2, 32; Phil. 2:2; I Thess. 5:8, 13, 14; Jas. 1:12.

Love of man and woman.—Gen. 24: 67; 29:18-20, 30, 32; 34:3, 12; Ju. 16:4; Ruth Chs. 2-4; I Sam. 1:5; II Sam. 13:1; I Ki. 11:1; II Chr. 11: 21; Esth. 2:17; Song of Sol. 1:4, 7; 2:4-8; 3:2; 4:1, 7-10; 5:1, 9, 16; Hos. 3:1; John 11:5, 36; Eph.

TOPICAL INDEX

5:25, 28-31; Col. 3:19; Tit. 2:4.
Love for God cannot exist with: Love of the world—I John 2:15; Jas. 4:4. Love of mammon—Mt. 6:24; Lu. 16:13. Love of self—Mt. 10:39; 16:25-26; Mk. 8:35-36; Lu. 9:24-25; John 12:25-26. Love of Satan—Ps. 97:10; Mt. 4:10; Lu. 4:8; John 12:31; 14:30. Sinful fear—II Tim. 1:7; I John 4:18. Hatred of a brother—Mt. 5:22; I John 3:10-16; 4:20-21. Love's antagonism with sin—Gen. 18:23-33; Ex. 20:5; Deut. 7:10-11; 10:17-18; Ps. 27:5; 97:10; Is. 63:1-4; Hos. 3:1; Mt. 23:37-39; 26:48-50; 27:3-5; Lu. 15:11-32; John 13:21-27; I Cor. 4:21; Heb. 12:6; Rev. 2:2-6; 2:9-10; 2:13-16; 2:19-28; 3:1-5; 3:8-12; 3:15-21.
Love as an active principle.—John 14:15; Gal. 2:19-20; Heb. 13:1-2; Jude 21; I John 2:5; 3:17; 4:8; II John 6.
An evidence of the new life.—John 13:35; 14:23-24; Gal. 2:19-20; Col. 1:4-8; I Thess. 1:3; II Tim. 1:7; I John 3:14-17; 4:12-13.
Love is the fulfilling of the law.—Mt. 22:40; Mk. 12:23; Lu. 10:28; Rom. 13:10; I Cor. 13:1-7; I Tim. 1:5.
Love is the fruit of the Spirit.—Mt. 7:16-20; Rom. 5:3-5; 6:21-22; I Cor. 13:4-7; Gal. 5:22; Eph. 5:8-11; Col. 3:12-14.
True love is without hypocrisy.—Mt. 7:3-5; 22:16-22; Rom. 12:9; Eph. 6:24; I Pet. 1:22; II Pet. 2:15.
The measure of love.—Mk. 12:33; John 3:16; 13:34; 15:13; Rom. 8:35-39; I Cor. 2:2; II Tim. 4:8; I John 4:10-11.
Love constrains to unselfish service.—I Cor. 4:9-13; 9:16-23; II Cor. 4:8-12; 5:14; Gal. 4:15; Phil. 4:12-13; Heb. 10:24; I Pet. 3:10.

Love at its topmost height.—Mt. 26:6-13; John 13:34-35; 15:12; I Cor. 16:14; Gal. 2:20; 6:14; Phil. 2:12-18; II Tim. 4:6-8.
The characteristics of love.—Precious—Pr. 15:17. Unquenchable—Pr. 17:17; Song of Sol. 8:7. Covereth sins—Pr. 10:12; I Pet. 4:8. Strong as death—Song of Sol. 8:6. Worketh no ill—Rom. 13:10. Casteth out fear—I John 4:18.
Is without hypocrisy.—Rom. 12:9. Is tenderly affectionate—Rom. 12:10.
In honor prefers another.—Rom. 2:10. Accords with others—Phil. 2:2.
The Christian "in love," in twelve particulars: Before God in love—Eph. 1:4. Rooted and grounded in love—Eph. 3:17. Forbears one another in love—Eph. 4:2. Speaks the truth in love—Eph. 4:15. Edifies body in love—Eph. 4:16. Walks in love—Eph. 5:2. Knit together in love—Col. 2:2. Does all his acts in love—I Cor. 16:14. Is unfeigned in love—II Cor. 6:6. Is truthful in love—I John 3:18. Keeps himself in love with God—Jude 21. Increases in love—I Thess. 3:12.
Forsaken love.—Mt. 26:14-16; John 5:42; 5:66-67; Gal. 3:1-3; II Tim. 4:10; Rev. 2:4; 3:1-2.
Loving chief seats.—Mt. 23:6; Lu. 11:43; 20:46.
Loving darkness rather than light.—John 3:19.
Love to stand praying.—Mt. 6:5.
MESSAGE. Believed—Is. 53:1.—Have a—Ju. 3:20. Proclaimed—II Tim. 4:17. Sent—Gen. 50:16. This is the—I John 1:5; 3:11. Understand—Is. 28:9, 19. Word of—I Thess. 2:13.

335

OBEDIENCE. A fundamental law. —Deut. 13:1-4; Rom. 5:19; 6:16; Phil. 2:12.

Life depends on obedience. —God's instructions to Adam—Gen. 2:16-17. To Israel through Moses—Lev. 18:5; Deut. 8:1-3. Through Joshua —Josh. 5:6; Rom. 5:18-19.

Faith is assured by obedience. —Acts 6:7; 5:31-32; Rom. 1:5; 5:19; 6:17-18; II Cor. 7:15; Heb. 5:8-9; 11:7-8; I Pet. 1:22.

Christ an example of. —Mt. 3:14-15; John 15:10; Phil. 2:5-11; Heb. 5:8.

Can obey but one God. —Deut. 4:1-4; I Ki. 18:21; Lu. 16:13; Acts 5:29; Gal. 1:6-9.

Knowing depends on obedience. —John 7:17; 13:34-35; II Cor. 9:12-13; II Thess. 1:8; I John 1:3-6; 3:23-24; 5:2-3.

Fulfilment of promises depends on obedience. —Old Testament—Deut. 11:8-9, 26-28; 32:46-47; 28:1-14; Jer. 38:20; Zech. 3:7. New Testament—Mt. 19:17; Lu. 11:28; John 10:27-28; 14:15-16, 23; Acts 2:38 -39; 3:19-20; Jas. 1:25; Rev. 22:14.

Obedience must be from the heart. —Deut. 11:13; Mk. 12:33; Rom. 10:8-10; 6:17.

Obedience better than sacrifice. —I Sam. 15:22; Ps. 50:8-15; 69:31; Pr. 15:8; 28:9; Is. 1:12-17; Jer. 6:20; Hos. 6:6; Amos 5:22; Mt. 9:13; 21:19; Mk. 12:33.

Obedience must be rendered to masters. —Eph. 6:5; Col. 3:22; Tit. 2:9.

By children to parents. —Eph. 6:1; Col. 3:20. By Disciples—Tit. 3:1-2.

General fruits of obedience. —Gen. 18:19; Lev. 26:3-13; Num. 14:24; Deut. 7:9, 12-15; 15:4; 28:1-15; Josh. 1:8; 14:6-14; I Ki. 2:3-4; II Ki. 21:8; I Chr. 22:13; 28:7-8; II Chr. 26:5; 27:6; Job 36:11; Is. 1:19; Jer. 7:3-7; 11:1-5; 22:16; Mal. 3:10-12. New Testament—Mt. 5:19; 7:24; 12:50; 25:20-23; Mk. 3:35; Lu. 6:46-48; 8:21; 11:28; 12:37-38; John 12:26; 13:17; 14:23; 15:10, 14; Jas. 1:25; I John 2:17; 3:24; Rev. 22:7.

Examples of obedience: Noah—Gen. 6:22. Abram—Gen. 12:1-4; 22:3, 12; Heb. 11:8. Jacob—Gen. 35:1-4. Moses and Aaron—Ex. 7:6; 40:16-33. Israelites—Ex. 12:28; 24:7; 39:42-43; Num. 9:20-23. Caleb and Joshua—Num. 14:24; 32:12; Josh. 10:40; 11:15. Elijah—I Ki. 17:5. David—I Ki. 11:34. Hezekiah —II Ki. 18:6-7. Josiah—II Ki. 22:2. Jehoshaphat—II Chr. 17:3-6. The three Hebrews—Dan. Ch. 3. Cornelius—Acts 10:33. Paul—Acts 26:16-20. Disciples—Rom. 6:17.

OBSERVE. Coming—Jer. 8:7. Customs—Acts 16:21. Days—Ex. 12:14; Deut. 28:13; Gal. 4:10. From my youth up—Mk. 10:20. Idols—Acts 17:23. Jehovah does—Ps. 66:7. Roman laws—Acts 16:21. Leprosy—Deut. 24:8. Night of deliverance—Ex. 12:42. Precepts—Ps. 105:63, 134. Sabbath day—Ex. 31:16; Deut. 12:5. These things —Ps. 107:43; Mt. 19:20; 28:20; Mk. 10:20; I Tim. 5:21. Words of Jehovah—Ps. 119:57, 88, 101, 146.

ORDINANCES (authoritative and established rites).

Ordinances of Israel. —Ex. 15:25; Num. 15:15, 16; Ps. 122:4. The passover—Ex. 12:14, 24, 43; 13:8-10; Num. 9:14; II Chr. 35:13. Trumpet blowing—Lev. 23:24. Num. 10:1-10; Ps. 81:3-5. Concerning building a house for Jehovah

—II Chr. 2:4. Ordinance of mourning—II Chr. 35:25. Putting away false gods—Josh. 24:23-25. Jehovah's ordinances are compulsory—Lev. 18:4-5; II Chr. 33:8.
The first covenant had ordinances. —Num. 9:3, 14; Lev. 18:4-5; Heb. 9:1-5.
These ordinances imposed for a time. Jer. 31:31-34; Heb. 9:10.
Ordinances blotted out.—Eph. 2:14-16; Col. 2:14-15. Unduly depended upon—Is. 1:10-14; Mic. 6:6-8.
Folly of turning back to Jewish ordinances.—Gal. 5:1-14; 6:12-15; Eph. 2:14-22; Col. 2:20-23; 3:1-4; Heb. 7:11-19.
Ordinances of David.—Concerning the courses of priests and Levites—II Chr. 8:14. Concerning going to battle—I Sam. 30:22-25.
Teaching on ordinances.—Ps. 19:9; 119:13, 30, 39, 43, 62, 91, 102, 106, 149, 156, 160, 164, 175.
Ordinances of the Jews.—Concerning the altar—Ez. 43:18; 46:14. Failure to keep ordinances—Ez. 11:9-12; Mal. 3:13-15.
Walketh faithfully in the ordinances. —Neh. 12:28-33; Is. 58:2; Lu. 1:6.
Christian ordinances.—Baptism—Mt. 3:15; 28:19-20; Mk. 16:16; Acts 2:38-39; Rom. 6:3-6. The Lord's Supper—Mt. 26:26-29; Mk. 14:22-25; Lu. 22:14-20; I Cor. 11:23-26.
Civil ordinances.—Must submit—Rom. 13:2; I Pet. 2:13.
Ordinances of the heavens.—Job 38:33; Ps. 8:3-4; 19:1-4; Jer. 31:35-36; 33:25.
PATTERN. David gave—I Chr. 28:11. Hold the—II Tim. 1:13. Jehovah had showed Moses—Num. 8:4. Like to the true in—Heb. 9:24.

Measure—Ez. 43:10. Tabernacle, Of—Ex. 25:9, 40; Heb. 8:5.
PEACE: God the author of.—Job 25:2; Ps. 147:14; Is. 45:7; Rom. 15:33; 16:20; I Cor. 14:33; II Cor. 13:11; Phil. 4:9.
Jesus the peacemaker.—John 16:33; Eph. 2:14; Col. 1:20; II Thess. 3:16. By way of the sword—Mt. 10:34; Lu. 12:51.
Peacemakers.—Pr. 12:20; Is. 27:5; Mt. 5:9; Jas. 3:18.
A gift.—John 14:27; Ps. 29:11; 72:7; Is. 57:19.
A command.—Mk. 1:25; 4:39; 10:48; Rom. 12:18; II Cor. 13:11.
Necessary for enjoyments.—Ps. 34:12-14; Phil. 4:7; I Pet. 3:10, 11.
Offering for.—Deut. 27:7; Ju. 20:26; I Sam. 5:12; 6:4; 10:8; 11:15; II Chr. 30:22.
Covenant of.—Gen. 9:14, 15; Num. 25:12; Josh. 9:15; I Sam. 20:42; I Ki. 5:12; Is. 54:10; Ez. 34:25; 37:26; Mal. 2:5.
Conditional.—Ps. 85:8; Pr. 3:2; 16:7; Is. 26:3; 48:18, 22; 57:21; Ez. 7:25; Mt. 10:13; Lu. 14:32; Rom. 5:1; 8:6.
Uncertain.—I Ki. 22:27, 28; II Ki. 9:17-22; Jer. 6:14; 8:11, 15; Ez. 13:10; Mt. 10:34.
Enforced.—Deut. 20:10-12; Job 13:5, 13; Mk. 1:25; 4:39; Lu. 4:35; 19:38-40.
Worth the struggle.—Ps. 34:14; Pr. 17:1, 28; Eccl. 4:6; Lu. 19:42; Rom. 12:18; 14:19; II Cor. 13:11; Heb. 12:14.
Disposition for.—Gen. 13:8, 9; Esth. 10:3; II Sam. 2:26, 27; Lu. 14:31, 32; Acts 12:20.
National.—I Ki. 4:25; 5:4, 5; II Ki. 15:19; I Chr. 4:40; II Chr. 14:1, 2; Ps. 147:14. Universal—Is. 2:4; 9:7.

WHAT THE BIBLE SAYS ABOUT FAITH AND OPINION

Preached to the world.—Is. 52:7; 62:6; Acts 10:36; 18:9; Rom. 10:15; Eph. 2:17.
Salutations.—John 20:26; I Cor. 1:3; II Cor. 1:2; Gal. 1:3; Eph. 1:2; Phil. 1:2; Col. 1:2; I Thess. 1:1; II Thess. 1:2; I Tim. 1:2; II Tim. 1:2; Tit. 1:4; Philemon 3; I Pet. 1:2; II Pet. 1:2; II John 3; Rev. 1:4.
Benedictions.—Ps. 125:5; Lu. 24:36; John 14:27; 20:19, 21, 26; Rom. 15:13; III John 14.
Bond of Unity.—Ju. 4:17; Is. 32:16-18; Zech. 8:19-23; Mk. 9:50; Eph. 2:15-17; 4:3; I Thess. 5:13.
Prayer for.—Ps. 122:6-9; Jer. 29:7; I Tim. 2:2.
Under chastisement.—Job 5:17-24; Is. 53:5; Heb. 12:11.
Happy ending of.—Gen. 15:15; Ex. 18:23; Ps. 37:37; Is. 55:12; Lu. 2:29; Rom. 8:6; 14:17; II Pet. 3:14.
Haters of.—Ps. 120:6, 7; 28:3; 35:20.
Opposers of peace.—Josh. 10:1-5; 11:19; Is. 59:8. False visions—Ez. 13:16.
Peace despised.—II Ki. 9:17, 18; Rom. 3:16, 17.
PRECEPT. Col. 2:22. Jehovah, Of—Ps. 19:8; 103:18; 119:4-173; Jer. 35:18; Dan. 9:5. Precept upon precept—Is. 28:10, 13.
REASON, *n.* II Pet. 3:12. Affliction, Of—Ps. 88:9. Bondage, Of—Ex. 2:23. Concerning hope within you—I Pet. 3:15. Darkness, Of—Job 37:19. Disquietness, Of—Ps. 38:8. Glory, Of—II Cor. 3:10. Ice, Of—Job 6:16. Render a—Pr. 26:16. Shame, Of—Ps. 40:15. Smoke, Of—Rev. 9:2. Strength, Of—Ps. 99:10. Things, Of—Eccl. 7:25. Voice, Of—Ps. 102:5. Wine, Of—Ps. 78:65. Wind, Of—John 6:18. Without—II Pet. 2:12.

REASON, *v.* Acts 19:8. Among themselves—Mt. 16:7, 9. Cause—Jer. 12:1. God, With—Job 13:3. Hearts, In—Lu. 3:15. In the synagogue—Acts 17:17. Let us—Is. 1:18. Righteousness, Of—Acts 24:25. With him—Job 23:7. Within himself—Lu. 12:17.
RECEIVE. Abundance—Rom. 5:17. Adoption of sons—Gal. 4:5. Almighty, From—Job 27:13. Blessing—Ps. 24:5; Heb. 6:7. Brother's blood—Gen. 4:11. Burnt-offerings—I Ki. 8:64; II Chr. 7:7. Commandments—Pr. 10:8. Correction—Jer. 5:3. Corruptible crown—I Cor. 9:25. Crown of glory—I Pet. 5:4. Crown of life—Jas. 1:12. Edifying—I Cor. 14:5. Good, Evil—Job 2:10. Grace—Rom. 1:5. Holy Spirit—Acts 2:38; 8:17, 19. Inheritance—Num. 34:14; Josh. 13:8; 18:7. Instruction—Pr. 1:3; 8:10. Interest—Ez. 18:17. Law—Job 22:22; Acts 7:53. Me to glory—Ps. 73:21. Money—II Ki. 5:26. More blessed to give than—Acts 20:35. Plagues, Of—Rev. 18:4. Pledge—Gen. 38:20. Power—Acts 1:8. Prayer, My—Ps. 6:9. Prize—I Cor. 9:24. Present—Gen. 33:10. Promise—Gal. 3:14; Heb. 11:17. Recompence—Rom. 1:27; Col. 3:24. Remission of sins—Acts 26:18. Reward—II John 8; I Cor. 3:8. Sayings—Pr. 4:10. Shame—Hos. 10:6. Stripes—I Cor. 11:24. Testimony—Acts 2:18. Tithes—Heb. 7:8. Words, My—Pr. 2:1. Ye one another—Rom. 15:7.
REGARD. Jas. 2:3. Captives—Jer. 24:5. Christ, Of—Eph. 5:32. Folly, Not—Job 24:12. Gourd, For—Jonah 4:10. Grace, Of—II Cor. 8:4. Have—Dan. 11:30. Iniquity, Not

TOPICAL INDEX

—Job 36:21. Life—Pr. 12:10. Lightly, Not—Heb. 12:5. Lying words—Ex. 5:9. Man—Lu. 18:4. Oath, Of—Eccl. 8:2. Prayer—Ps. 102:17. Reproof—Pr. 15:5. Rich—Job 34:19. Vanities—Ps. 31:6; Jonah 2:8. Word of Jehovah, Not—Ex. 9:21. Works—Ps. 28:5.
REJECT. Builders—Ps. 118:22; Mt. 21:42; Lu. 20:17. Cast off and—Ps. 89:38. Commandment—Mk. 7:9. Despised and—Is. 53:3. Elders, Of—Lu. 9:22. God hath—Ps. 53:5. I should be—I Cor. 9:27. Jehovah—Num. 11:20. Judah, Jer. 14:19. Law—Amos 2:4. Man—I Thess. 4:8. Me—Jer. 15:6; Lu. 10:16. Ordinances—Ez. 5:6. Seed of Israel—II Ki. 17:20. Statutes—II Ki. 17:15. Stone—I Pet. 2:4, 7. This generation, Of—Lu. 17:25. Those in whom thou trustest. Us—Lam. 5:22.
REVELATION: The disclosure of heavenly knowledge.—Ps. 119:19, 130; Eph. 1:17-20. Revelation is the self-manifestation of God as the God of a gracious purpose—Eph. 1:9, 10. Inspiration is that divine influence which imparts this manifestation to the human mind—John 16:13. Revelation has to do with the content—II Tim. 3:11-17. Inspiration with the mode of delivery—II Pet. 1:21.
Revelation of God in Christ.—Is. 7:14; Mt. 1:23; John 1:14; 3:16; 14:9, 10; I Cor. 1:24, 30; Eph. 1:9, 10; Rev. 1:1.
Revelation of Christ's glory.—John 17:4, 5; Rom. 8:18; I Pet. 4:13, 14; 5:1.
Revelation of the Lord Jesus.—II Cor. 12:1-4; II Thess. 1:7. Of the Son of Man—Lu. 17:30.
How revelation came.—Through the prophets—Is. 9:6, 7; Rom. 16:25, 26; I Pet. 1:12. Through the Holy Spirit—Lu. 12:12; John 14:26; 15:26; 16:13; I Cor. 2:10; Eph. 3:5. Through Jesus Christ—John 8:26; 17:8; Rom. 10:17; I Cor. 1:7, 24; 15:1-4; Gal. 3:22-26. Through the apostles—Mt. 28:19, 20; Mk. 16:15, 16; Lu. 12:11, 12; 24:45-49; John 15:27; I Cor. 2:6-16; 14:6; II Cor. 5:19, 20. Through the gospel—Rom. 1:16, 17.
What revelation does.—Brings to nought human wisdom—I Cor. 1:20-29. Pierces the sinful heart—Acts 2:37. Giveth light—Ps. 119:130. Giveth knowledge of duty—Gal. 2:2. Reveals inheritance of God in Christ—Eph. 1:11-20. Brings truth to babes—Lu. 10:21; I Cor. 1:26-29.
Other revelations.—Of secrets—Deut. 29:29; Pr. 11:13; 20:19; Dan. 2:22, 28, 29, 47; Amos 3:7.
Of judgment.—John 3:18, 19; 8:21-24; 16:7-11; Rom. 2:5. Of wrath—Rom. 1:18; II Thess. 1:7-10.
Man of sin.—II Thess. 2:3 10.
RIGHTLY. Song of Sol. 1:4. Dividing the word—II Pet. 2:15 (A.V.) Judged—Lu. 7:43. Named—Gen. 27:36. Teachest—Lu. 20:21.
SALVATION.—IN THE OLD TESTAMENT:
NATIONAL SALVATION FROM ENEMIES.—Deut. 21:8; 32:15; 33:29; I Sam. 2:1; 10:19; II Sam. 3:18; 7:23; 22:28, 36; II Ki. 14:27; I Chr. 16:23, 35; Neh. 1:10; 9:19-31; Ps. 14:7; 17:7; 18:27; 20:5-9; 33:2; 44:7; 60:5; 67:2; 68:19, 20; 69:35; 70:4; 72:4; 74:12; 77:15; 78:22; 80:3; 98:1-3; 106:4; 107:2, 13; 136:24; Is. 12:2, 3; 17:10; 25:9; 43:1, 9-12; 44:24; 45:8, 17, 20, 22; 46:13; 49:25; 59:1, 11; 62:

WHAT THE BIBLE SAYS ABOUT FAITH AND OPINION

11, 12; Jer. 3:23; Hos. 7:13; 13: 4, 10; Mic. 6:4; Lu. 1:71.

Deliverance from captivity.—Ps. 106: 42-47; Jer. 8:20; 15:20; 23:1-4; 29:12-14; 30:10, 11; 31:4-12; 42: 11, 12; 46:27, 28; Ez. 36:21-38; 39:23-29; Hos. 1:7; Mic. 4:10; Zeph. 3:17-20; Zech. 8:7, 8, 13-15.

Deliverance from bondage in Egypt.—Ex. 6:6-8; 14:13, 30; 15:4-19; Deut. 7:8; 9:26; 13:5; 15:15; 24: 18; I Sam. 10:18; II Sam. 7:23; I Chr. 17:21; Ps. 80:8-19; 106:7-11, 21, 22; Neh. 9:9-15; Mic. 6:4; Jude 5.

Salvation in time of war.—Num. 10:9; Deut. 20:4; II Ki. 19:32-34; Neh. 9:24, 27-31; Ps. 44:7; Is. 37: 35. Instances of—Gideon—Ju. 6: 12-24, 36-40; 7:1-25; By Samuel —From the Philistines—I Sam. 7: 4-11; 9:16; From the Ammonites —I Sam. 11:13; Jonathan's victory over the Philistines at Michmash— I Sam. 14:6-23, 39, 45, 46; David and Goliath—I Sam. 17:32, 53; 19: 5; David at Pasdammim—I Chr. 11: 14; By Jehoshaphat from Moab and Ammon—II Chr. 20:17-23.

PERSONAL SALVATION FROM ENEMIES.—Ps. 37:39, 40; 40: 16; 71:1-5, 15, 23; 72:13, 14; 91: 16; 109:31; 119:81, 123; 121:1-8; Pr. 20:22; Jer. 17:14; Mic. 7:7. For David—II Sam. 4:9; 22:3, 4, 36, 46-49; I Ki. 1:29; Ps. 3:8; 7: 10; 9:14; 13:5; 18:2, 3:35, 46; 21: 5; 25:5; 27:1, 9; 28:8; 34:6; 35: 3, 9; 38:22; 62:1, 2, 7; 69:13, 18, 29; 86:13, 16; 103:4; 109:26; 138: 7; 140:7; 144:10.

EQUIVQALENT TO PERSONAL RIGHTEOUSNESS.—II Chr. 6: 41; Ps. 132:9, 16; 149:4; Is. 61:10.

Salvation conditional.—Ex. 15:26; Lev. 26:3-8, 14-20; Deut. 7:12-26; 11:13-15; 28:1-68; I Ki. 3:14; 15: 1-6; Ps. 106:7-47; 145:20; Is. 59: 115; Jer. 3:23-25; Ez. 3:17-21; 18: 19-32; 33:1-19; 39:23, 24.

God the Author.—I Sam. 2:9. II Sam. 14:14; I Chr. 16:35; Ps. 3:7, 8; 28: 8, 9; 31:5, 16, 23; 33:18-22; 37: 1-40; 41:1-4; 68:18-20; 71:23, 24; 74:12; 76:8, 9; 85:9-12; 97:10; 107:2-7; 118:14; 121:7, 8; 145: 20; 149:4; Pr. 2:8; Jer. 29:14; 31: 4-12; Ez. 39:23-29; Jonah 2:9; Hab. 3:8.

Delivers from Egypt—Ex. 3:7-17; 6: 2-8; 15:2-19; Is. 19:20.

God called a Redeemer—II Sam. 4: 9; I Ki. 1:29; Job 19:25; Ps. 19:14; 78:35; Pr. 23:11; Is. 41:14; 44:6, 24; 47:4; 54:5, 8; 60:16; Jer. 50: 34.

God called a Savior—II Sam. 22:3; Ps. 106:21; Is. 43:3-21; 45:15, 21, 22; 60:16; 63:8, 9; Jer. 14:8; Hos. 13:4.

SALVATION FROM SIN: OR, THE CONSEQUENCES OF SIN: Under the Jewish dispensation—Gen. 49: 18; Job 13:16; Ps. 24:5; 34:18; 50:23; 51:12, 14; 65:5; 85:4, 7, 9; 86:2; 91:16; 95:1; 96:2; 107: 9; 116:13; 118:14, 15, 20-25; 119: 41, 155, 166, 174; 145:19; Is. 1: 18; 26:1; 35:4; 50:2; 52:7-10; 59: 16, 17; 63:1-5, 8, 9; 64:1-8; Lam. 3:22; Mic. 7:7.

Prophecies concerning salvation through Christ—Is. 35:8; 45:17; 47:12, 13; 49:6-11; 51:5, 6; 52:7-10, 13-15; 55:1-7; 59:16, 17; 60:18; 62:1, 2, 11, 12; 63:4, 8, 9; Zech. 9:9; Mal. 4:2.

In the New Testament prior to the death of Jesus—Mt. 1:21; 9:12, 13; 18:

11-14; Mk. 2:17; Lu. 1:69, 77; 2: 30-32, 38; 3:6; 5:30-32; 7:36-48; 8:12; 15:1-10; 19:9, 10; John 3: 16, 17; 4:22; 5:34; 12:47.

After the death of Jesus—Acts 2:47; 4:10-12; 5:31; 10:43; 13:23, 26, 38, 39, 47; 16:17; Rom. 5:8; 10:9, 10; 11:11-26; I Cor. 3:15; II Cor. 2:15; Eph. 1:13; I Tim. 1:15; Heb. 5:9; I Pet. 1:8-12; 3:5; 4:14; Jude 3; Rev. 5:9; 7:10; 14:3, 4; 19:1.

Salvation for all men.—Lam. 3:31-38; Ez. 18:1-32; 33:10-20; Joel 2: 32; Mt. 18:12-14; Lu. 2:10, 31; John 1:7, 9; 3:16, 17; 4:14; 7:37; 10:16; 12:47; Acts 10:34, 35; Rom. 5:15-20; 10:11-15; II Cor. 5:14, 15; Eph. 3:9; I Tim. 2:3, 4; 4:9, 10; Tit. 2:11; II Pet. 3:9; I John 2:2; Rev. 22:17.

Blessing to all men through seed of Abraham—Gen. 12:3; 18:18; 22: 18; 26:4; Rom. 4:16-25; 9:6-33. Blessing through Christ—Ps. 72: 17; Acts 3:25, 26; Gal. 3:8, 14, 27-29.

Prophecies concerning a world-wide gospel—Ps. 2:8; 22:27; 98:2, 3; Is. 52:10. Jesus a light to the Gentiles—Is. 42:6; 49:6; 60:1-3. See Lu. 2:32; Acts 13:47.

The gospel to be preached to all men —Mt. 28:19, 20; Mk. 16:15, 16; Lu. 24:47; Acts 1:8; Col. 1:5, 6, 23.

To the Jew first.—Mt. 10:5, 6; 15: 24; John 4:22; Acts 3:25, 26; 10: 34-37; 13:26, 32, 33; Rom. 1:16; 2:9-11; 3:1, 2; 9:3-33; 15:8, 9. Beginning at Jerusalem—Is. 2:3; Mic. 4:2; Mt. 23:37; Lu. 13:34; 24:47; Acts 1:8.

Salvation through Jesus rejected by the Jews.—Mt. 11:20-24; 13:57, 58; 23:37; Mk. 6:3-6; Lu. 13:34; 19:14; John 1:11; 5:15, 16, 36-47; 8:37-59; Acts 7:51-54; 13:26-29, 46; 18:5, 6; 28:24-28; Rom. 11: 11; I Thess. 2:14, 16.

Jesus a stone of stumbling to those who reject Him—Is. 8:14; Lu. 2:34, 35; 20:17, 18; Rom. 9:31-33; I Cor. 1:22, 23; I Pet. 2:6-8.

Parables concerning the rejection of Jesus by the Jews: The Vineyard—Mt. 21:33-46; Mk. 12:1-10; Lu. 20:9-19. The Marriage Supper—Mt. 22:1-10; Lu. 14:16-24. The Prodigal Son—Lu. 15:11-32. The Rich Man and Lazarus—Lu. 16:19-31.

The Gospel sent to the Gentiles.—John 10:16; Acts 28:28; Rom. 2:9-11; 3:29, 30; 10:12; 11:17-25; 15: 6-29; I Cor. 1:22-24; Eph. 2:11-17; I Thess. 2:16.

Gentiles are Abraham's seed—Rom. 4:16-25; 9:6-9, 30-33; Gal. 3:1, 8, 14, 27-29.

Gospel sent to the Samaritans—Acts 8:1-25. To the Ethiopian eunuch —Acts 8:26-40. To Cornelius—10: 1-48; 11:1-18.

Paul an apostle to the Gentiles—Acts 9:15; 13:42, 46-49; 14:27; 18:5, 6; 22:17-21; 26:16-18, 20, 23; Rom. 1:13-16; Gal. 1:15, 16, 22-24; Eph. 3:6-8; Col. 1:21-27; I Thess. 2:14-16; I Tim. 2:4-7; II Tim. 4:17.

Conferences in Jerusalem—Acts 11:1-18; 15:1-31; 21:17-26; Gal. 2:1-16.

Prophecies concerning—Is. 9:1, 2 (Mt. 4:14-16); Is. 11:1, 10 (Rom. 15: 12); Ps. 118:22; Is. 28:16 (Mt. 21: 41-44); Is. 42:1-7 (Mt. 12:14-21); Is. 49:6, 22 (Lu. 2:30-32); Is. 54: 3; 55:8 (John 10:16); Is. 61:9; 62: 2; 65:1; Hos. 1:10; 2:23 (9:24-26); Amos 9:11, 12. See Acts 15:16,

WHAT THE BIBLE SAYS ABOUT FAITH AND OPINION

17; Rom. 10:20; I Pet. 2:10.

Salvation conditional: In the Old Testament.—Ps. 34:14-19; 50:23; 85:9; 86:2; 145:19; Lam. 3:25; Joel 2:32.

For the righteous only—Ps. 118:15; 119:155; Is. 55:6, 7; 64:5-7; Jer. 3:19-25; Ez. 18:1-32; 33:10-20.

In the New Testament: Before the death of Jesus.—Mt. 7:13, 14; 18:3; 23:37; 25:31-46; John 5:40; 7:34; 8:12; 10:9.

Man must hear, believe, repent, and obey—Deut. 18:19; Mt. 10:32-39; 13:15; Lu. 6:46-49; 8:12; John 1:12; 3:3-9; 5:24; 6:28, 29, 40, 44, 45, 47; 20:30, 31.

Must practice self-denial, be unselfish, bear the cross—Mt. 19:23-30; 25:31-46; Mk. 10:23-31; Lu. 9:23-26; 14:26, 27; 16:10-17; 18:24-30.

The rich young ruler—Mt. 19:16-22; Mk. 10:17-25; Lu. 18:17-24.

Instances of conditional salvation.—The Paralytic—Mt. 9:1-7; Mk. 2:1-12; The sinful woman in the Pharisee's house—Lu. 7:36-50; Zaccheus the Publican—Lu. 19:1-10; The Women taken in adultery—John 8:1-11.

Parables concerning conditional salvaltion.—The Sower—Mt. 13:1-23; Mk. 4:1-20; Lu. 8:4-15; The Tares—Mt. 13:24-30, 36-43; The Net—Mt. 13:47-50; The Laborers in the Vineyard—Mt. 20:1-16; The Two Sons—Mt. 21:28-32; The Wedding Supper—Mt. 22:1-14; The Lost Sheep, the Lost Coin, and the Lost Boy—Lu. 15:1-31; The Rich Man and Lazarus—Lu. 16:19-31; The Pharisee and the Publican—Lu. 18:9-14; The Pounds—Lu. 19:12-27; Ten Virgins—Mt. 25:1-13; The Talents—Mt. 25:14-30.

After the death of Jesus.—Acts 2:37, 38; 3:19; 9:6; 10:33, 48; 11:14; 16:30-33; 22:10, 16; Rom. 10:9, 10; Heb. 2:2, 3; 12:24, 25; 13:4; I Pet. 3:21.

The wicked shall not inherit the kingdom of heaven—I Cor. 6:9, 10; Eph. 5:3-6; Col. 3:5-10; Jas. 5:1-6; I Pet. 4:1-16.

The judgment—Mt. 8:11, 12; 10:11-15; 12:36, 37; 16:24-27; 25:31-46; Mk. 6:10, 11; 8:34-38; Lu. 10:10-12, 16; John 5:24-30; 12:47-50; Rom. 2:6-16; I Cor. 3:8; II Cor. 5:10; Heb. 10:28-31; Rev. 2:23; 22:10-15.

God the Author.—Ps. 3:8; 34:16-22; 37:1-40; 76:8, 9; 103:2-4; 111:9; 118:14; 132:16; 145:20; Pr. 2:6-20; Is. 46:13; 52:10; Jer. 3:23; Mt. 10:28; Lu. 1:68; 3:6; John 6:44, 45, 63-65; Jas. 4:12; Rev. 7:10; 19:1; Called Saviour—Is. 45:15, 21, 22; Lu. 1:47; I Tim. 1:1; 2:3; 4:10; Titus 1:3; 2:10; 3:4; Jude 25; Sends His Son to redeem men—Lu. 2:30-32; John 3:27-36; 17:4; Acts 4:26; II Cor. 5:18-21; Gal. 4:1-7; II Tim. 1:8-10; Heb. 6:17-20; To do His will—Mt. 26:39, 42; John 4:34; 5:30; 6:38, 40; Heb. 5:5-10; To die for mankind—Mt. 26:39, 42; John 3:14-17; 10:18; 14:28-31; 18:11; Rom. 3:24, 25; 8:3; Phil. 2:5-11; I John 4:9-11.

God loves men.—Pr. 3:12; Jer. 32:18; Mt. 5:43-45; Lu. 6:35; 12:6, 7; Rom. 8:38, 39; 11:28, 29; II Cor. 13:11; Eph. 2:4-7; I Tim. 2:3, 4; Tit. 3:4-7; Heb. 12:6; II Pet. 3:9, 15.

God's love for Israel—Deut. 4:37; 7:8, 12, 13; 10:15; 23:5; Is. 63:7-9; Jer. 31:3; Mal. 1:1-5.

God so loved the world that He gave

342

TOPICAL INDEX

His only begotten Son—John 3:16, 17; Rom. 5:8; I John 3:1, 16; 4:7-16.
God is merciful.—Deut. 4:31; Ps. 69: 13; 98:3; 107:1; 111:4; 116:5; 130:7, 8; 136:4, 8, 26; 145:8, 9; Is. 63:9; Lam. 3:22, 23; Dan. 9:4, 9; Lu. 1:50, 54, 68-72; Rom. 2:4; 15:9; I Cor. 7:25; II Cor. 4:1; Tit. 3:5; Jas. 5:11; I Pet. 1:3-5; 2:10; II Pet. 3:15.
God's mercy conditional—Ex. 20:6; 34:6, 7; Num. 14:18, 19; Deut. 5: 10; 7:9-11; II Chr. 30:9; Ps. 62:12; 106:17, 18; Is. 55:7; Joel 2:12, 13.
God's mercy in spite of transgressions—Neh. 9:17-31; Ps. 78:38; 86:5, 15; 103:7-16; 106:6-46; Jer. 3:12; Lu. 6:35-37; Rom. 11:30-32; I Tim. 1:13, 16; Heb. 8:12. *Parables concerning*—The Good Samaritan—Lu. 10:25-37; The Two Debtors—Lu. 7:36-47.
God plans man's salvation.—I Cor. 2:7-9; Gal. 4:1-5.
The wicked husbandmen—Mt. 21: 33-42.
Sends His Son to save—John 3:14-34; 4:34; 5:36; 6:38; 10:18; 17: 4; 19:30; Acts 2:23; I John 4:7-14.
Prepares a place for His children—Mt. 20:23; Mk. 10:40; Heb. 11:16.
Plans before the foundation of the world—Mt. 25:34; Rom. 16:25; Eph. 1:3-14; 3:1-11; II Thess. 2: 13, 14; II Tim. 1:9, 10; Tit. 1:2, 3; II Pet. 1:10-12, 18-20; Rev. 13:6.
Foretells through His prophets—Is. 35: 1-10; 45:21; 46:10; 49:8 (II Cor. 6:2); 53:1-12; Dan. 9:20-27; Mt. 5:18; Lu. 24:25-27, 44-47; Acts 3:18, 21-26; 17:2, 3; 18:28; 26: 6, 22, 23; Rom. 3:21; 16:25, 26. *That the seed of David should sit on his throne*—II Sam. 7:12, 13; Is. 9:6, 7 (Acts 2:25-30, 34, 35; 13: 23; Rom. 1:1-3). *"Thou art my Son, this day have I begotten Thee"*—Ps. 2:7 (Acts 13:32, 33). *The stone that the builders rejected*—Ps. 118: 21-23; Is. 28:16 (Mt. 21:42; Mk. 12:10, 11; Lu. 20:17-19; Acts 4:11; Rom. 9:32, 33; Eph. 2:20; I Pet. 2:6-8). *A light to lighten the Gentiles*—Is. 9:1, 2; 42:6-9; 49:5-11 (Mt. 4:15, 16; Lu. 2:30-32; Acts 13:47; 26:16-18, 23). *The coming of John the Baptist*—Is. 40:3-5; Mal. 3:1-3 (Mt. 3:3; 11:10; Mk. 1:2, 3; Lu. 3: 4-6; 7:27; John 1:23). *The coming of Elias*—Mal. 4:5 (Mt. 11:14; Mk. 9:11-13; Lu. 1:16, 17).
Man is saved through Jesus Christ.—Mt. 1:21; Lu. 4:16-21; 24:44-47; John 3:14-17; 5:34-40; 12:47; Acts 3:26; 4:10-12; 10:43; 13:38, 39; 15:11; Rom. 5:15-21; 8:1-3, 10; 11:26, 27; I Cor. 6:11; Gal. 1: 4; 2:20; 3:26-29; Eph. 5:2; I Thess. 1:10; 5:9; I Tim. 1:15; 3:16; II Tim. 2:10; 3:15; Heb. 2:1-3; 5:9, 10; II Pet. 2:20; I John 3:5; 4:9, 10; 5: 11, 12.
Christ came to save sinners—Mt. 9: 13; Mk. 2:17; Lu. 5:30-32; 19:10.
Jesus is called: The Author of salvation—Heb. 2:10. The Bread—John 6:33-56. The Door or Way—John 19:9; 14:6; Heb. 10:20. Our High Priest—Zech. 6:13; Heb. 2:17; 4: 14-16; 7:1-28; 8:1-4; 10:21, 22. *Anointed and called of God*—Heb. 3:1, 2; 5:4, 5. *After the order of Melchizedek*—Ps. 110:4; Heb. 5: 6, 10; 6:20; 7:15-17. *Offers Himself as a sacrifice*—Heb. 7:27; 9:11-14, 23-28. *Typified by Melchizedek*—Gen. 14:18-20. *By Aaron*—Ex. 40:12-15. The Lamb—John 1:29, 36; I Pet. 1:19; Rev. 7:10, 17; 12:

WHAT THE BIBLE SAYS ABOUT FAITH AND OPINION

10, 11; 14:4; 21:23, 27. The Life —John 11:25, 26; 14:6; Col. 3:4. The Light—Mt. 4:12-16; John 1:4-12; 8:12; 9:5; 12:35, 36, 46; Acts 13:47. The Mediator—Gal. 3:19, 20; I Tim. 2:5, 6; Heb. 8:6; 9:15, 24; 12:24. The Passover—I Cor. 5:7. The Redeemer—See Rom. 8:34; Eph. 2:13; 3:11, 12; Heb. 7:24-27; 9:24. The Resurrection—John 11:25. The Saviour—Lu. 2:11;John 4:42; Acts 5:31; 13:23; Eph. 5:23; Phil. 3:20, 21; I Tim. 2:3-6; Tit. 1:4; 2:13; 3:3-7; II Pet. 1:1, 11; 2:20; 3:2, 18; I John 4:14. *Prophecies concerning Jesus as a Saviour*—Is. 9:2; 42:6, 7; 49:6-12; 53:4-6, 8-11; 59:20; 61:1-3, 10, 11; Dan. 9:26; Zech. 9:9. The Truth—John 14:6.

Reconciles man to God—Rom. 5:6-11; II Cor. 5:17-21; Eph. 2:13-18; Col. 1:20-22; Heb. 2:9-18.

Man saved by the life of Jesus.—John 14:19; Rom. 5:10; 8:17; II Cor. 1:7; 4:10, 11; Phil. 3:10; Heb. 7:25-28; I Pet. 5:1. By His Example—Mt. 11:29, 30; John 8:46; 13:15; Rom. 15:1-5; Phil. 2:5-8; I Pet. 2:21; 4:13; I John 2:6.

Man saved by the death of Jesus.—Dan. 9:26; John 3:14-17; 10:15, 17, 18; 12:31-34; Rom. 5:6-15; 8:34; 14:8, 9; I Cor. 1:17, 18, 23, 24; 2:2; II Cor. 4:10, 11; 5:14, 15; 13:4; Gal. 1:4; 2:20; 3:1; 6:14; Eph. 2:13-18; Phil. 2:5-11; 3:10; II Tim. 2:11, 12.

IN FULFILMENT OF THE SCRIPTURES—Lu. 24:25-27; Acts 3:18; 17:2, 3; 26:22, 23. Christ died to redeem Man—Is. 53:4-12; I Cor. 5:7; 6:20; 7:23; Gal. 4:4, 5; I Thess. 1:10; I Pet. 1:18-21; II Pet. 2:1; I John 2:2; 3:16; 4:10; Rev. 5:9; 13:8.

The life of Christ a ransom—Mt. 20:28; Mk. 10:45; I Tim. 2:6.

Christ gave his life for mankind—John 6:51; 10:11, 15; 11:49-53; 15:13; Rom. 4:25; 5:6-9; 8:3, 32; 14:15; II Cor. 5:14-21; Gal. 3:1, 8, 13, 14; Eph. 5:2, 25; I Thess. 5:9, 10; Tit. 2:13, 14; Heb. 2:9-18; 7:24-27; 9:11-17, 25-26; I Pet. 2:21-24; 3:18.

Christ's death for the remission of sins—Dan. 9:24; Lu. 24:44-47; Acts 5:30, 31; Rom. 4:25; 5:6-8; 6:3-11; I Cor. 15:1-3; Gal. 1:4; Heb. 1:3; 7:27; 9:14, 26-28; 10:12; I Pet. 2:24; 3:18.

Man reconciled to God through the death of Jesus—Dan. 9:24; Rom. 5:10, 11; Eph. 2:13-23; Col. 1:20-22; 2:14.

Man saved by the blood of Jesus.—Christ's blood shed for the remission of sins—Mt. 26:28; Mk. 14:24; Rom. Rom. 3:25; Eph. 1:7; Col. 1:14; Heb. 9:11-14; 13:12; I John 1:7; Rev. 1:5; 7:14, 15.

Redemption through His blood—Rom. 3:24, 25; Eph. 1:7; Heb. 9:12-15; I Pet. 1:18-20.

Christ purchased with His blood—Acts 20:28; I Cor. 6:20; 7:23; II Pet. 2:21; Rev. 5:9.

Man reconciled through Christ's blood—Rom. 5:9, 10; Eph. 2:13; Col. 1:20-22; Heb. 10:19-22.

Man saved by the resurrection of Christ.—Acts 3:26; Rom. 4:25; 10:9; 14:8, 9; I Cor. 15:12-19; I Thess. 4:14; I Pet. 1:21.

Salvation by the gospel.—Mk. 13:10, 11; 16:15, 16; John 5:34; 6:33-45; 20:31; Acts 2:22-42; 8:5, 12-14, 30-38; 9:15; 14:21-27; 16:14-17; 19:1-5; 26:15-23, 31; Rom. 1:15-17; 2:16; 15-16, 19-21; I Cor. 1:17-24; 15:1-4; Gal. 1:6-16; 3:8;

TOPICAL INDEX

Eph. 2:13-17; 3:6-8; Phil. 1:27-29; I Thess. 2:2-16; II Thess. 2:10-15; I Tim. 2:4; II Tim. 1:10; 2:25; I Pet. 1:12, 25; II John 9.

Called Good Tidings—Is. 40:9-11; 52:7; 61:1; Nah. 1:15; Mt. 11:5; Lu. 4:18-19, 43; 8:1; Rom. 10:15; Heb. 4:2.

Words or sayings—Mt. 4:4; Mk. 8:31; Lu. 9:26; 24:44-48; John 8:31, 32, 37, 51; 12:48-50; 15:3; 17:6-8, 14, 17, 20; 20:31; Acts 4:4, 29-37; 6:4, 7; 8:4, 14, 25; 10:22, 36-44; 11:1, 14, 19; 12:24; 13:5-12, 15-49; 14:3, 4; 15:7; 16:6-14, 29-34; 17:11; 19:10, 18-20; 20:24, 32; Rom. 18:8-10, 14-17; I Cor. 2:4, 5, 13; II Cor. 4:1-5; 5:19; Eph. 1:13; 5:25, 26; Phil. 2:15, 16; Col. 1:5, 6, 23; I Thess. 1:5-8; II Thess. 3:1; Heb. 2:2-4; 6:4-6; I John 2:5, 7, 14; Rev. 1:2, 9; 6:9; 20:4. A sword —Eph. 6:17; Heb. 4:12. Words of Life—John 6:63, 68; 12:48-50; Acts 5:20; Phil. 2:16. *Shall not pass away*—Mk. 13:31; Lu. 21:33.

Parable of the Sower—Mt. 13:3-9, 18-23; Mk. 4:3-9, 14-20; Lu. 8:5-15.

Begotten of the gospel—I Cor. 4:15; I Thess. 2:11; Philemon 10; Jas. 1:18, 21; I Pet. 1:3, 33. See Lu. 8:11; John 3:3-8.

The gospel revealed to the apostles. —Mt. 11:25; 13:11; 16:17; 19:11; Gal. 1:11, 12, 15, 16. By the Holy Spirit—Mt. 10:19, 20; Mk. 13:11; Lu. 12:12; 21:15; 24:49; John 14:26; 16:13; Acts 2:2-4; 15:28; I Cor. 2:4, 5, 10-16; 14:6; Eph. 1:16, 17; 3:1-6; I Tim. 4:1; I Pet. 1:12; II Pet. 1:20, 21; I John 2:20, 27.

The Holy Spirit directs the movements of the apostles in the preaching of the gospel.—Acts 8:29, 39; 10:19; 11:12; 13:2-4; 16:6-10.

The Holy Spirit confirms the preaching of the gospel with signs and wonders.—Acts 2:38, 43; I Cor. 12:4-11; Eph. 4:7, 8; Heb. 2:4.

The power of the Spirit promised—Mk. 16:17, 18; Lu. 24:49; Acts 1:8; 2:16-20.

Instances of: *The Lame Man*—Acts 3:2-10. *In Solomon's porch*—Acts 4:30-36; 5:12-16. *By Stephen*—Acts 6:8. *By Philip*—Acts 8:6. *By Paul*—Acts 19:11; Rom. 15:18, 19; I Cor. 2:4; II Cor. 12:12; I Thess. 1:5. *By Paul and Barnabas*—Acts 14:3; 15:12.

Man must believe.—Lu. 8:12, 13; John 1:7; Acts 13:38, 39; 15:7-9; 11:20; I Cor. 1:21; Gal. 3:8; Eph. 2:8; II Thess. 2:12, 13; I Tim. 4:10; Heb. 10:39; 11:6; I Pet. 1:9; I John 3:23.

He that disbelieveth is condemned— Mk. 16:16; John 8:24.

He that believeth hath eternal life— John 5:24; 6:47; 11:25, 26; *On, or in, Jesus*—John 3:14-18, 36; 6:29, 40; Acts 10:43, 16:31; 19:4; Rom. 10:10-17; Gal. 2:16-20; 3:22; Eph. 1:13; 3:11, 12; Phil. 1:27-29; 3:9-11; I Tim. 1:13, 14; I John 5:10, 13; *In the name of Jesus* —John 1:12; I John 3:23; 5:13; *That Jesus is the Christ*—John 20:31. *That God hath raised Him from the dead*—Rom. 10:9; I Cor. 15:12-17.

The commandments of the gospel must be obeyed.—Acts 5:29-32; 6:7; Rom. 1:5; 2:8; 6:16-18; 16:19, 26; II Cor. 9:13; 10:5, 6; Gal. 5:7; II Thess. 1:7-10; Heb. 5:8, 9; Jas. 1:22-25; I Pet. 1:14, 22; 4:17; I John 2:5. The words of Jesus or the will of God—Mt. 7:21-27; 12:50; Lu. 6:46-49; 8:21; John 8:51;

WHAT THE BIBLE SAYS ABOUT FAITH AND OPINION

14:23, 24; 15:10, 14; Rev. 1:2, 9; 3:8. The gospel commandments — Mt. 28:19, 20; Mk. 16:15, 16; Lu. 24:26, 47; Acts 2:37-42; 8:12, 13, 36-38; 9:6, 18; 10:33-35, 47, 48; 16:14, 15, 30-33; 19:1-5; 22:10, 16.

Obedience the test of love and faith — Mt. 7:16-27; Gal. 5:6; Heb. 11:1-40; Jas. 2:14-26.

Salvation by faith in Christ without the works of the Mosaic law. — Acts 13:38, 39; Rom. 3:20, 21, 27-30; 4:1-25; 9:30-33; Gal. 2:16-21; 3:10-14, 19-29; Eph. 2:8-10; Phil. 3:8-10. Circumcision not necessary — Acts 15:1-21, 28; Rom. 2:25-29; 3:29, 30; 4:9-13; I Cor. 7:18, 19; Gal. 2:1-16; 5:1-6, 11-15; 6:12-16; Phil. 3:2-7; Col. 3:11.

Calling on the name of the Lord. — Joel 2:32; Acts 2:21; Rom. 10:13.

Confession of faith in Christ as the Son of God necessary. — Lu. 9:26; Rom. 10:9, 10; II Cor. 9:13; Phil. 2:11; I Tim. 6:12; Heb. 3:1; 4:14; 10:23; I John 2:22, 23; 4:2, 3, 15; II John 7. See John 9:22; 12:42.

Christ will confess those who confess Him — Mt. 10:32, 33; Mk. 8:38; Lu. 12:8, 9; II Tim. 2:12.

Instances of: *Christ's confession* — Mt. 26:63, 64; 27:43; Mk. 14:61, 62; Lu. 22:67-70; I Tim. 6:13. *Confession of the angels* — Lu. 1:32-35; 2:11. *By John the Baptist* — John 1:29-34. *By the man with the unclean spirit* — Mk. 1:24; Lu. 4:34. *By the unclean spirits* — Mk. 3:11. *By the Gadarene demoniacs* — Mt. 8:29; Lu. 8:28. *By disciples in the boat* — Mt. 14:33. *By Nathaniel* — John 1:49. *By Peter* — Mt. 16:16; Lu. 5:8; 9:20; John 6:68-69. *By Martha* — John 11:27. *By the blind man* — John 9:35-37. *By Thomas* — John 20:28. *By the eunuch* — Acts 8:37 marginal. *By Paul* — Acts 9:20.

Repentance essential to salvation. — Taught by John the Baptist — Mt. 3:2, 3, 7-11; Mk. 1:4, 5; Lu. 3:3-14; Acts 13:24; 19:4.

By Jesus — Mt. 4:17; Mk. 1:15; Lu. 13:3-5; 16:30; 24:47.

Jesus calls sinners to repentance — Mt. 11:20-24; 12:41, 42; Lu. 10:11-15; 11:32. *Jesus compares ancient cities with the cities of His day, and condemns those of His time* — Mt. 21:28-32; Lu. 5:30-32; 15:3-32.

By the apostles — Mk. 6:12; Acts 2:38; 3:19; 5:31; 8:22; 11:18; 17:30; 20:21; 26:20; Rom. 2:4; II Cor. 7:9-11; 12:21; II Tim. 2:25; Heb. 6:1; II Pet. 3:9; Rev. 9:20, 21; 16:9-11.

Repentance for, or unto, remission of sins. — Mk. 1:4, 5; Lu. 3:3; 24:47; Acts 2:38; 3:19.

Baptism required. Taught by John the Baptist — Mk. 1:18; 11:30-33; Lu. 7:29, 30; 20:4-8; John 1:26-28, 31, 33; Acts 3:23; 10:40; Acts 1:5, 22; 10:37; 11:16; 18:25; 19:3, 4.

The baptism of Jesus — Mt. 3:13-17; Mk. 1:9-11; Lu. 3:21.

Unto repentance for the remission of sins — Mt. 3:6-11; Lu. 3:3, 7, 10-14.

By Jesus — Mt. 28:19; Mk. 16:16; John 3:22, 26; 4:1, 2.

By the disciples of Jesus after His death — Acts 2:38, 41; 8:12, 13, 36-38; 9:18; 16:14, 15, 33; 18:8; 19:3-5; Rom. 6:3-17; I Cor. 1:13-17; Eph. 4:5; Col. 2:12; Heb. 10:22; I Pet. 3:21.

Into the name of Jesus — Acts 2:38; 8:12; 19:3-5.

346

In water—Mt. 3:11; Mk. 1:5, 8, 9; John 1:26, 31, 33; Acts 8:36-38; 10:47; 19:5.

SALVATION OF SAINTS. Acts 15: 11; Rom. 13:11; II Cor. 1:6; 6:2, 3; 7:10; Gal. 1:4; Eph. 4:30; 6:17; Phil. 1:19; 2:12; 3:8-14; I Thess. 5:9; II Thess. 2:13; II Tim. 3:15; Heb. 2:10; 5:9; 6:9; 9:28; Jas. 1:21; I Pet. 1:3-11; II Pet. 3:15; Jude 3; Rev. 7:10; 12:10.

Called eternal life—Mt. 25:46; Mk. 10: 17; John 5:24-30; 6:40, 44, 47, 51, 58, 68; 10:28, 29; 11:26; 17:2, 3; 20:30, 31; Rom. 5:21; 6:22, 23; II Tim. 1:10; Tit. 1:2; 3:7; I John 2:25; 3:14; 5:11, 13, 20.

Called an inheritance—Mt. 25:34; Mk. 10:17; Acts 20:32; 26:18; Rom. 8:17; Gal. 3:29; 4:7; Eph. 1:11, 14, 18; 5:5; Phil. 3:11, 12; Col. 1: 12; 3:24; I Thess. 2:12; II Tim. 2: 12; Tit. 3:7; Heb. 1:14; 6:12; 9: 15; I Pet. 1:4; Rev. 21:7.

Salvation conditional.—Mt. 7:13, 14, 21-27; 12:36, 37; 25:31 46; Lu. 6:46-49; 13:23-30; John 3:16-19, 36; 8:21, 24, 51; 11:25, 26; 20:30, 31; Rom. 2:6-16; 14:10-12; I Cor. 3:8, 15; 10:12; II Cor. 5:10, 19-24; 7:10; Gal. 5:4, 7; 6:7, 8; Phil. 2:12-16; 3:11-14; I Thess. 5: 1-11; Heb. 2:2, 3; 4:1-10; 5:9; 6: 9; 9:28; 10:25-29; I Pet. 1:17-23; 4:18; II Pet. 1:2-11; I John 1:7; 5: 10-12; Rev. 2:23; 20:12; 21:27; 22:12-15.

Disciples must bear fruit—Mt. 7:16, 20; 12:31-35; Lu. 6:44; John 15: 5-8.

Must endure—Mt. 10:22; 24:13; Mk. 13:13; Rom. 11:22; I Cor. 9:24-27; 10:13; 15:2; Col. 1:23; II Tim. 2:12; Heb. 3:6, 14; 4:14; 10:35-39; Jas. 5:7-11.

Must pracice self-denial—Mt. 5:29, 30; 10:39; 16:24-27; Mk. 8:34-38; 10:29, 30; Lu. 6:22, 23; 14:26, 33; 16:25; 18:18-30; 22:28-30; John 12:25; I Cor. 9:24-27; Gal. 5:24; Col. 3:5-7; II Tim. 2:12, 13; Tit. 2: 12.

Must suffer tribulation—John 15:18, 20; 16:33; Acts 9:16; 14:22; Rom. 5:3; 8:17; Phil. 1:28, 29; I Thess. 3:3; II Tim. 2:11; 3:12; I Pet. 1:6-9; 2:21; Rev. 2:9-11; 7:14.

Must bear the cross—Mt. 10:38, 39; 16:24-27; Mk. 8:34-37; Lu. 9:23-26; 14:27-33.

Must not be conformed to this world—John 17:15, 16; Rom. 12:2; Eph. 4:7; Col. 3:2; I Pet. 4:3-6; I John 2:15-17; 4:5.

Parables concerning conditional salvation: *The Sower*—Mt. 13:18-23; Mk. 4:13-20; Lu. 8:11-15; *The Pounds*—Lu. 19:12-27; *The Ten Virgins*—Mt. 25:1-10; *The Talents*—Mt. 25:14-30; *The Rich Man and Lazarus*—Lu. 16:19-31.

These shall not have a part in this inheritance:

The Covetous—Mt. 6:19-24; 19:16-30; Mk. 10:17-27; Lu. 6:24-26; 16: 13-31; 18:18-30; 19:12-27; Eph. 5:5; Col. 3:5; I Tim. 6:9-11; Jas. 5:1-5; II Pet. 2:3.

The Drunkard—Lu. 21:34-36; Rom. 13:13; I Cor. 6:9, 10; I Pet. 4:1-5.

The Lascivious—I Cor. 6:9, 10; Eph. 5:5; Col. 3:5-10; Heb. 13:4.

The Apostate—Lu. 9:61, 62; 11:24-26; Gal. 5:1-4; Eph. 4:14, 15; Col. 1:22, 23; I Tim. 1:19; Heb. 3:12, 13; 4:11-16; 6:4-6; 10:26-29; II Pet. 2:1-22; 3:13-17; I John 5:10-12.

Salvation illustrated by: A rock—Deut. 32:4, 15, 18, 30; Ps. 95:1; A horn

WHAT THE BIBLE SAYS ABOUT FAITH AND OPINION

—Ps. 18:2; Lu. 1:69; A helmet—Is. 59:17; Eph. 6:17; A shield—II Sam. 22:36; A lamp—Is. 62:1; Clothing—II Chr. 6:41; Ps. 132:16; 149:4; Is. 61:10; Wells—Is. 12:3; Walls and bulwarks—Is. 26:1; 60: 18; Chariots—Heb. 3:8; Victory—I Cor. 15:57; A crown—I Cor. 9: 25; Rev. 2:10; 3:11.

SCRIPTURES. Searching of, commended—Deut. 17:19; Josh. 1:8; John 5:39. Cannot be broken—John 10:35. Given by inspiration from God—Acts 1:18; II Tim. 3:16; Heb. 1:1; 3:7; 10:15; II Pet. 1:20, 21. Given through prophets—Lu. 16: 31; Rom. 3:2; Heb. 1:1. Fulfilled in Christ—Mt. 5:17; Lu. 24:27; John 19:24; Acts 13:29. Expounded by Christ—Mt. 4:4; 26:54; Lu. 4:19-21; 24:26, 27, 32; John 7:42. By Peter—Acts 2:16-36; 3:17-24. By Stephen—Acts 7:51-53. By Philip—Acts 8:25-35.

STUMBLE. Pr. 3:23; 4:12, 19; Is. 5: 27; 8:15; 59:10. Brother—Rom. 14:21; I Cor. 8:13. Cause—Mt. 5: 29; 13:41; 18:7; John 6:61. Guard from—Jude 24. Judgment, In—Is. 28:7. Law, At—Mal. 2:8. Mountain, Upon—Jer. 13:16. Oxen—I Chr. 13:9. Persecutors shall—Jer. 20: 11. Proud shall—Jer. 50:32. Ways, In—Ju. 18:15. Word, At—I Pet. 2:8.

STUMBLING-BLOCK: Laws concerning.—Lev. 19:14.

Before Israel.—Ez. 44:12; Rev. 2:14.

Used in prophecy.—Is. 57:14; Ez. 3: 20; 7:19; 14:3, 4, 7; Jer. 5:21; 18: 15; Zeph. 1:3; Mal. 2:8.

In teachings of Paul.—Rom. 11:9; 14:13; I Cor. 1:23. Warning—I Cor. 8:9. Self-denial for others—Rom. 14:21. Stumbling-block of the cross

—Gal. 5:11. Stone of offence—Rom. 9:32.

THINK. Pr. 23:7; Jonah 1:6; Mt. 26: 36; Lu. 8:18; 10:36; 12:51; John 5:39; 11:56. Above all that we ask or—Eph. 3:20. Affliction, To raise up—Phil. 1:17. Christ, Of—Mt. 22: 42. Eternal life, Ye have—John 5: 39. Evil, No—I Cor. 13:5. Heart, In his—Pr. 23:7. Highly, Not of himself more—Rom. 12:3. Himself—Prophet, To be a—I Cor. 14:37. Kill, To—Ex. 2:14. Not—Mt. 24: 41. Rom. 12:3. Prophet, Himself to be a—I Cor. 14:37. Religious, To be—Jas. 1:26. Reprove—Job 6:26. Soberly—Rom. 12:3. Something, To be—Gal. 6:3. Spirit, I have —I Cor. 7:40. Standeth, That he —I Cor. 10:12. These things, On —Phil. 4:8. Wise, That he is—I Cor. 3:18.

TRADITION. II Thess. 3:6. Elders, Of the—Mt. 15:2-6; Mk. 7:3-13. Fathers, Of—Gal. 1:14. Hold fast —I Cor. 11:2; II Thess. 2:15. Men, Of—Col. 2:8.

TRUST. Job 39:11. Brother, In any —Jer. 9:4. Jehovah, In—Ps. 4:5; 22:9; Jer. 17:7; Mt. 27:43; I Tim. 4:10; 5:5; Heb. 3:13; I Pet. 3:5. Jesus, In—Mt. 12:21; Rom. 15:12; Phil. 2:19. Lying words—Jer. 7:4. Moses, In—John 5:45. Name, In His—Mt. 12:21. Princes, In—Ps. 146:3. Riches—Mt. 10:24; Mk. 10: 24; I Tim. 6:17. Tent, In—Job 18: 14. Themselves, In—Lu. 18:9. True riches—Lu. 16:11. Wife, In—Pr. 31:11.

TRUTH. In Old Testament usually means faithfulness, permanence, fidelity, sincerity, trustworthiness, honesty, justice, and reality.

TOPICAL INDEX

God's faithfulness to covenant promises. — His stability and sincerity — Gen. 24:27; 32:10; Ex. 34:6; II Sam. 2:6; Ps. 25:2, 10; 30:9; 31:5; 40: 10, 11; 43:3; 57:3, 10; 69:13; 71: 22; 86:11, 15; 89:14; 91:4; 96:13; 108:4; 111:7, 8; 115:1; 117:2; 132: 11; 138:2; 146:6; Is. 25:1; 38:19; 61:8; 65:16; Dan. 4:37. See. Rev. 15:3.

Trustworthiness in man. — I Ki. 17: 24; Pr. 8:7; I Cor. 13:6; Eph. 4:14, 15; III John 3. Honesty — Gen. 42: 16; Pr. 12:17; Eph. 4:15, 25; John 8:44; I Tim. 2:7; II John 3. Justice — Ex. 18:21; Pr. 20:28; Rom. 2:2; Rev. 16:7. See Rev. 15:3. Justice of Messianic king — Ps. 45:4; Is. 16: 5; 42:3.

God requires truth in character. — Ps. 51:6; Jer. 4:2; Zech. 8:16, 19; Eph. 4:15, 25; 6:14; I John 3:18.

Collective system of statements which conform to reality. — Law is truth — Ps. 119:142, 151, 160; Dan. 9: 13; Mal. 2:6-8; Rom. 2:20. Words of truth — Pr. 22:19;21. Word of truth — Ps. 119:43; Eph. 1:13; Col. 1:5; II Tim. 2:15; Jas. 1:18.

Gospel such a collective system. — John 8:31, 32; Rom. 1:18; II Cor. 13:6; Gal. 2:5; I Tim. 2:7; II Tim. 4:4; Tit. 11:14; Jas. 3:14; II Pet. 1:12; 2:2; I John 3:19; II John 2; III John 3, 4, 8, 12. Knowledge of the truth — Col. 1:5; I Tim. 2:4; 4: 3; II Tim. 2:15, 25; 3:7; Tit. 1:1; I John 2:21. Heard — Col. 1:5, 6. Believed — II Thess. 2:10, 12, 13; I Tim. 4:3. Obeyed — Gal. 5:7; I Pet. 1:22.

Truth disregarded. — Is. 59:4, 14, 15; Jer. 7:28; 9:3, 5; I Tim. 6:5.

Man must serve God in truth (= Sincerity). — Josh. 24:14; I Sam. 12: 24; I Ki. 2:4; 3:6; II Ki. 20:3; Ps. 15:2; 26:3; 86:11; 145:18; Is. 38: 3; John 4:23; II John 4.

Exhortation to truth. — Pr. 3:3; 22: 21; 23:23; I Cor. 5:8; 13:6; I John 3:18.

Reality. — Deut. 13:14; Ju. 9:15; Pr. 12:17; Is. 43:9; Dan. 7:16; Mk. 5: 33; John 8:40, 45, 46; 16:7; Acts 26:25; Rom. 9:1; Gal. 4:16; Eph. 4:15, 25; Phil. 4:8; I Thess. 2:13; I Tim. 2:7; I John 2:21, 27; 3:18, 19; II John 1, 3.

Welfare. — State of society in which justice and honesty prevail — II Ki. 20:19; Esth. 9:30; Ps. 85:10; Zech. 8:16, 19.

Jesus the expression of the divine life. The highest expression of truth. — John 1:14; 8:31-36; 14:6; 18:37, 38; Eph. 4:15, 21.

Spirit of truth. — John 14:17; 15:26; I John 4:16.

Witness unto the truth. — John 5:33; 18:37; III John 12.

Church a pillar and ground of truth. — I Tim. 3:15.

Of a truth. — I Sam. 21:5; II Ki. 19: 17; Job 9:2; Is. 37:18; Jer. 26:15; Dan. 2:47; Mt. 14:33; Lu. 4:25; 9:27; 12:44; 21:3; 22:59; John 7: 40; Acts 4:27; 10:34.

UNBELIEF. Because of their — Mt. 13:58; Mk. 6:6; Heb. 3:19. Heart of — Heb. 3:12. Help thou mine — Mk. 9:24. I did it ignorantly in — I Tim. 1:13. Upbraided them with their — Mk. 16:14. Wavered not through — Rom. 4:20.

UNBELIEVER. Before — I Cor. 6:6. Believer with — II Cor. 6:15. Worse than an — I Tim. 5:8. Yoked with — II Cor. 6:14.

UNBELIEVING. I Cor. 14:22; Tit. 1: 15. Fearful and — Rev. 21:8. Husband — I Cor. 7:14. Unlearned or

349

WHAT THE BIBLE SAYS ABOUT FAITH AND OPINION

—I Cor. 14:23. Wife—I Cor. 7:12.
UNDERSTAND. Deut. 32:29; Jer. 23:20. Aged that—Job 32:9. Concerning the loaves, Not—Mk. 6:52. Hear and—Mt. 13:14; 15:10. Hereafter—John 13:7. Know and—John 10:38. Let him that readeth—Mt. 24:15. None that—Rom. 13:11. Not these things—John 3:10. Readest, What thou—Acts 8:30, 31. Sought to—Dan. 8:15. Speech, My—John 8:43. That I am he—Jer. 43:10. Worlds have been framed, That—Heb. 11:3.
UNDERSTANDING. I Ki. 7:14; Job 12:3, 12; 26:12; Pr. 7:4; Is. 10:13; Jer. 10:12; Mt. 11:25; Col. 1:9; Jas. 3:13; I John 5:20. Almighty giveth—Job 32:8. Amazed at—Lu. 2:47. Apply heart to—Pr. 2:2. Bribe destroyeth—Eccl. 7:7. Darkened in—Eph. 4:18. Faileth—Eccl. 10:3. Full assurance of—Col. 2:2. Give me—Ps. 119:34. Given, to the mind—Job 38:36. Hath no—Pr. 17:16; 27:9. Hid heart from—Job 17:4. Infinite—Ps. 147:5. Lean not upon thine own—Pr. 3-5. Lord shall give—II Tim. 2:7. Made heavens, By—Ps. 136:5. Manifold in—Job 11:6. No delight in—Pr. 18:2. Passeth all—Phil. 4:7. People of no—Is. 27:11. Perceive my—Eph. 3:4. Place of—Job 28:12. Returned—Dan. 4:36. Searching of—Is. 40:28. Sing praises with—Ps. 47:7. Strength of—Job 36:5. Take away—Hos. 4:11. Times, Of the—I Chr. 12:32. Unfruitful—I Cor. 14:14. Void of—Job 11:12; Rom. 10:19. Wellspring, Is a—Pr. 16:22. Without—Jer. 5:21; II Cor. 10:12.
UNITY. Gr. *Henotes.* Oneness.
God.—Deut. 4:35, 39; 6:4, 5; Is. 43:10-13; 44:6-8; Rev. 1:8; 15:3, 4.

Christ with God.—Mt. 22:41-45; Lu. 24:37-40; John 1:1, 2, 14; 20:25-28; Heb. 12:2; Rev. 22:13.
Of the spirit.—I Cor. 12:4-13; Eph. 4:3.
Christ, the center of.—(Unity in Christ)—Gal. 3:28; Eph. 1:9, 10; 2:6, 7, 10, 13, 20: 3:6, 11; Col. 2:6. Desire for—John 17:20, 21.
Man.—Gen. 1:26, 27; 5:1, 2; Acts 17:26; Gal. 3:26-28; Phil. 3:20; I Thess. 5:23; Heb. 2:11-14.
The Saints (Church—Local and general).—Ps. 133:1-3; John 15:5; 17:22-26; Acts 2:42-47; Rom. 12:4, 5; I Cor. 1:10-13; 10:16, 17; 12:12; II Cor. 13:11; Eph. 2:19-22; 4:13; 5:25-27; I Pet. 2:4-6; 3:8.
In diversity.—Rom. 12:4-8; I Cor. 12:14-23.
Action.—Ezra 1:3, 4; Neh. 4:6; Acts 2:1-4, 44, 45; 11:29, 30; I Cor. 3:12, 13; 12:21.
The faith.—Acts 11:23; Eph. 4:4, 5, 13; Phil. 1:27; Jude 3.
Sufferings.—Rom. 8:17, 35-39; I Cor. 12:26; Phil. 3:10; II Tim. 2:12.
Burden-bearing.—Num. 11:11-16; Ex. 17:11, 12; Josh. 1:12-15; Mt. 20:12; Rom. 15:1-3; Gal. 6:2.
WISDOM. God fills with the spirit of—Ex. 28:3; 31:3; 35:31-35. God shows the secrets of—Job 11:6; Ps. 51:6; Pr. 2:3-7; Eph. 1:7-10; Jas. 3:17. Its value hard to estimate—Job 28:12-19; Pr. 3:13-18; 16:16. Fear of the Lord is—Deut. 4:5, 6; Job 28:28; Ps. 111:10; Pr. 1:7. Conceit defeats—Shall die with you—Job 12:2. Rages against it—Pr. 18:1-2. Cease from thine own—Pr. 23:4; 28:11; Rom. 11:25. Too high for the fool—Pr. 24:7.

TOPICAL INDEX

Wisdom of this world: Foolishness. —Is. 29:14; I Cor. 1:20; 3:19.

The wisdom of Solomon. —I Ki. 4: 29-34; 5:12; 10:4-8, 23, 24; 11: 41; II Chr. 1:10, 12; 9:1-8, 22, 23. Came from far to hear Solomon— Mt. 12:42; Lu. 11:31.

Vanity of worldly. —Eccl. 1:16-18; 2:21; 9:15, 16.

Wisdom as related to Jesus. —Filled with—Lu. 2:40. Increased in—Lu. 2:52. Whence hath this man this— Mt. 13:54. Christ the wisdom of God —I Cor. 1:24.

Wisdom to be sought and used. —Ps. 90:12; Rom. 16:19; Eph. 5:15; Col. 1:9; 3:16; 4:5; Rev. 13:18; 17:9-14.

Special references. —No wisdom in the grave—Eccl. 9:10. Youths skilful in—Dan. 1:4; 2:20-24. Give you a mouth and—Lu. 21:15. Look out seven men full of—Acts 6:3, 10. God gave Joseph—Acts 7:10, 22. Greeks seek after—I Cor. 1:22. Not with words of man's—I Cor. 2:4, 5, 6, 7. If any lack, let him ask of God—Jas. 1:5. According to wisdom given me—II Pet. 3:15.

A LIST OF OTHER TOPICS RELATING TO WHAT THE BIBLE SAYS ABOUT FAITH AND OPINION

Use an exhaustive concordance to find what the Bible says about these topics:

abstain	counsel	forbid
add	counsellor	forbidding
appoint	covenant	foreordained
author	damnation	forgive
baptism	damned	form
baptize	disannul	free
beseech	disobedience	fulfil
beware	divided	good
bind	dividing	grant
blaspheme	division	harden
blinded	do	hearer
blindness	doubteth	hearing
bondage	doubtful	heart
bound	duty	heed
brotherhood	edify	heresies
brotherly	election	highminded
charity	enjoin	immutability
church	establish	implacable
command	exhort	impossible
commanded	expressly	inexcusable
commandment	faithless	iniquities
communion	fidelity	inordinate
constrain	finishes	interpretation
contrary	followers	intreat

OTHER TOPICS

itching	meaning	proclaim
judge	meant	proclamation
judged	meek	promise
judgest	meekness	prophesy
judgeth	mercy	proverb
keep	message	purpose
know	mind	read
lack	must	reasonable
language	nay	rebel
lawfully	necessary	record
lawless	necessity	refrain
laws	needeth	refuse
learned	no	remember
letter	obey	remembrance
liar	offence	repliest
license	oracle	reprobate
lie	oracles	reprove
loosed	ordain	resist
Lord	ordained	restore
lying	order	reveal
maintain	ordered	rule
make	ought	saith
manifest	perfect	schism
mark	perform	selfwilled
master	permission	separate
matters	pervert	shew
may	preach	should
mean	predestinate	silence

WHAT THE BIBLE SAYS ABOUT FAITH AND OPINION

sin	teach	unwise
sound	teaching	void
speak	temperance	walk
spoken	temperate	warn
stablish	testify	weightier
stand	testimony	well-doing
standard	think	wellpleasing
statute	thought	will-worship
stiffnecked	transgress	wisdom
study	transgression	wise
subject	trespass	withdraw
subjection	true	word
submit	unlawful	works
subvert	unlearned	write
surety	unsearchable	written
taught		

Selected Bibliography

Campbell, Alexander, and N. L. Rice. *A Debate Between Rev. A. Campbell and Rev. N. L. Rice.* Nashville, Tenn. Gospel Advocate, reprint of 1844 ed.

Campbell, Alexander. *Campbell on Baptism.* Bethany, Va.: Printed and published by Alexander Campbell, 1853.

_____. *Christianity Restored.* Rosemead, Ca.: Old Paths Book Club, 1959 reprint of 1835 ed.

_____. *Popular Lectures and Addresses.* Cincinnati, O.: Standard Publishing, 1861.

_____. *The Christian System.* Nashville, Tenn.: Gospel Advocate Co., 1974 reprint of 1839 ed.

Campbell, Thomas. *Declaration and Address.* Lincoln, Il.: Lincoln Christian College Press, 1971 reprint of 1809 ed.

Cowden, John B. *Christian Worship.* Cincinnati, O.: Standard Publishing, 1920.

_____. *Saint Paul on Christian Unity.* New York: Fleming H. Revell Co., 1923.

Dungan, D. R. *Hermeneutics.* Cincinnati, O.: Standard Publishing, n.d.

Errett, Isaac. *Our Position.* Cincinnati, O.: Standard Publishing, n.d.

Everest, H. W., B. C. Deweese, and J. J. Haley. *Missouri Christian Lectures.* St. Louis, Mo.: Christian Publishing Co., 1892.

Garrison, J. H. *The Story of a Century.* St. Louis, Mo.: Christian Publishing Co., 1909.

_____, ed. *The Old Faith Restated.* Joplin, Mo.: College Press, reprint of 1892 ed.

Grubbs, I. B. *Commentary on Paul's Epistle to the Romans,* 6th ed., edited by George Klingman. Nashville, Tenn.: Gospel Advocate, reprint of 1913 ed.

Hayden, W. L. *Church Polity.* Chicago: S. J. Clarke, 1894.
Kershner, Fredrick D. *The Restoration Handbook,* vols. I-IV. Joplin, Mo.: College Press reprint.
Lamar, J. S. *Memoirs of Isaac Errett,* vols. I & II. Cincinnati, O.: Standard Publishing, 1893.
Lockhart, Clinton. *Principles of Interpretation,* 2nd ed. Delight, Ark.: Gospel Light, reprint of 1913 ed.
Macknight, James. *Apostolical Epistles.* Grand Rapids, Mi.: Baker Book House reprint.
McGarvey, J. W. *New Commentary on Acts of the Apostles.* Cincinnati, O.: Standard Publishing, 1892.
_____. *The New Testament Commentary,* vol. I, *Matthew and Mark.* Nashville, Tenn.: Gospel Advocate, reprint of 1875 ed.
_____, and Philip Y. Pendleton. *Thessalonians, Corinthians, Galatians, and Romans.* Cincinnati, O.: Standard Publishing, 1916.
_____, and Philip Y. Pendleton. *The Fourfold Gospel.* Cincinnati, O.: Standard Publishing, 1914.
Richardson, Robert. *Memoirs of Alexander Campbell,* vols. I & II. Nashville, Tenn.: Gospel Advocate, 1956 reprint of 1897, 1898 eds.
Schaff, Phillip. *Creeds of Christendom,* vols. II & III. Grand Rapids, Mi.: Wm. B. Eerdmans Publishing Co., reprint of 1890 ed.
Sweeney, Z. T., compiler. *New Testament Christianity,* vols. I-III. Columbus, Ind.: New Testament Christianity Book Fund, Inc., 1926 & 1930.
_____. *Should Churches of Christ Receive Unimmersed Into Formal Fellowship?* Cincinnati, O.: Standard Publishing, 1942.
Thomas, J. D. *We Be Brethren.* Abilene, Tx.: Biblical Research Press, 1958.

Walker, Dean. *Adventuring for Christian Unity.* Cincinnati, O.: Standard Publishing, 1935.

Walker, W. R. *A Ministering Ministry.* Cincinnati, O.: Standard Publishing, 1938.

Welshimer, P. H. *Concerning the Disciples.* Cincinnati, O.: Standard Publishing, 1935.

_____. *The Open Membership Quesiton.* Cincinnati, O.: Standard Publishing, n.d. (from *Christian Standard* of May 31, 1919).

Williams, John Augustus. *Life of Elder John Smith.* Cincinnati, O.: Standard Publishing, 1904.